ACTING (RE)CONSIDERED

Theories and practices

Edited by Phillip B. Zarrilli

London and New York

First published 1995
by Routledge
11 New Fetter Lane, London EC4P 4EE

Simultaneously published in the USA and Canada
by Routledge
29 West 35th Street, New York, NY 10001

Reprinted 1996

Typeset in Times by Solidus (Bristol) Limited
Printed and bound in Great Britain by
Redwood Books, Trowbridge, Wiltshire

Text design: Mark Bedford, Simon Josebury

British Library Cataloguing in Publication Data
A catalogue record for this book is available from the British Library

Library of Congress Cataloguing in Publication Data
Acting (Re)Considered. Theories and Practices/edited by Phillip B.
  Zarrilli.
    p.   cm. - - (Worlds of performance)
    1. Acting.   I. Series.
  PN2061.A3 1994
  792' 028—dc20 93-48186

ISBN 0-415-09858-0 (hbk)
ISBN 0-415-09859-9 (pbk)

For my own Krishna …
the absent one.
Let us dance,
and dance …

Your Radha

Also,
for Haris Pašović
and all the artists and people
of Sarajevo
and Bosnia/Herzegovina …

CONTENTS

Pis - Quote

ILLUSTRATIONS

CONTRIBUTORS

Philip Auslander is Associate Professor in the School of Literature, Communication and Culture of the Georgia Institute of Technology. He has contributed articles on the theory of performance to the *Drama Review*, *Theatre Journal*, *Performing Arts Journal*, *Essays in Theatre* and other publications. He is the author of *The New York School Poets as Playwrights* (1989) and *Presence and Resistance: Postmodernism and Cultural Politics in Contemporary American Performance* (1992).

Augusto Boal is a Brazilian theatre director, writer, and theorist. He directs Le CEDITADE (Centre d'Etude et de Diffusion des Techniques Actives d'Expression – Méthode Boal) in addition to travelling and lecturing extensively in other countries. He is the author of *Theatre of the Oppressed* (1985) and *Games for Actors and Non-Actors* (1992; [trans. Adrian Jackson]).

Susana Bloch was trained as a psychologist at the Universidad de Chile in Santiago. She did post-doctoral studies and research at Harvard and at Boston University in experimental psychology and psychophysiology. Currently based as a senior scientist in Paris at the University of Pierre et Marie Curie, she has continued her research on human emotions and further developed the technique presented in this chapter (now called *Alba Emoting*). She has done many residencies with theatres in Europe, North America, and South America.

Sears Eldredge is Chair of Dramatic Arts and Dance Department at Macalester College in St Paul, MN. His forthcoming text on mask improvisation, entitled *The Compelling Image: Mask Improvisation for Actor Training and Performance*, presents a complete training program in the Neutral and various Characters Masks.

Kathy Foley is Provost of Porter College and an Associate Professor of Theatre Arts at University of California, Santa Cruz. She performs as a *dalang* (puppetmaster) in the tradition of the Sundanese of West Java, having trained under Dalang Abah Sunarya and Dalang Otong Rasta. She wrote Southeast Asian selections in the *Cambridge Guide to World Theatre*, is Southeast Asian editor for *Asian Theatre Journal* and was a member of the American advisory committee for the 1990–1 festival of Indonesia.

Mel Gordon is Professor of Theatre at the University of California–Berkeley. He is author of numerous essays and books including *Lazzi: the Comic Routines of the Commedia dell'arte* and *The Stanislavsky Technique: Russia*. He was formerly the Associate Editor of *TDR*.

Hollis W. Huston is a professional actor. He holds a doctorate in theatre and film and has taught at Washington University and the University of Delaware. He is author of *The Actor's Instrument: Body, Theory, Stage* (1992).

Adrian Jackson is currently Associate Director at the London Bubble Theatre. He translated and wrote the introduction to Augusto Boal's *Games for Actors and Non-Actors*.

Ron Jenkins researched the comic technique of Dario Fo and served as onstage simultaneous translator for Fo's first American tour. He has subsequently translated Fo's plays for the American Repertory Theater, the Yale Repertory Theater, and off-off Broadway. Currently a professor of Performing Arts at Emerson College in Boston, Jenkins is the author of *Acrobats of the Soul: Comedy and Virtuosity in Contemporary American Theater* (1988) and is writing a book about comic performance to appear in 1994.

Michael Kirby acted for five years with the Wooster Group in *LSD*, played leading roles in Raul Ruiz' film *The Golden Boat* and Tom Kalin's *Swoon* and appeared as the psychotic killer in Woody Allen's *Shadows and Fog*. He has written and directed many plays, performances and Happenings in the USA, Europe and Israel and is the author of *Happenings*, *The Art of Time*, *Futurist Performance* and *A Formalist Theatre*. From 1971 to 1985, Kirby edited the *Drama Review*. He is now a Professor Emeritus in the Performance Studies Department at New York University's Tisch School of the Arts.

Duane Krause received his Master of Fine Arts in Acting from University of Wisconsin in 1991. He currently resides in Chicago.

Eelka Lampe is a New York-based writer who has researched perform-ance processes as well as collaborated as dramaturg and director in Germany, France, the USA and Canada. Her writing on performance art and avant-garde theatre has been published in the *Drama Review* and *Women in Performance*. Her most recent project is a book on the directing of Anne Bogart.

Laurie Lassiter is a writer and performer living in New York City.

I Wayan Lendra is a Ph.D. candidate in the Department of Theatre and Dance at the University of Hawaii under a grant from the East–West Center. He has spent 25 years as an actor-dancer, working both in keybar and topeng dance-theatre. He was one of Jerzy Grotowski's technical specialists in the Objective Drama Project at the University of California–Irvine.

Lauren Love received her M.F.A. degree from the University of Wisconsin, and is currently working as a secretary in a Chicago law firm. She has appeared with various degrees of resistance in several productions at small Chicago theatres. Since turning down the role of Goody Putnam in Miller's *The Crucible*, for which she would have been required to shriek such lines as: 'She's a witch. I saw her flying over the barn', Ms Love has helped to form Theatre Praxis, a feminist theatre company.

Pedro Orthous (deceased 1974) was Professor of Acting and Directing at the Theatre School (Universidad de Chile). He was one of the finest directors in Latin America, and a pioneer in experimenting with new acting techniques.

John Rouse is Associate Professor of Theatre and Dance and Director of the Program in Literary Theory at Tulane University. He is the author of *Brecht and the Contradictory Actor* (UMI, 1989) and various articles on Brecht, contemporary German theatre, Robert Wilson, and performance theory. He is currently at work on a book about the playwright Heiner Muller.

Guy Santibañez-H is a psychologist, having done post-doctoral research in the USA and Europe in the general field of Neuropsychology. He held the position of Professor of Physiology at the Medical School and of Epistemology at the Department of Psychology, Universidad de Chile in Santiago. Currently, he is Professor of Behavioral Physiology at the Humboldt University School of Medicine in Berlin.

Deidre Sklar has investigated movement as a theatre director, corporeal mime, dance ethnologist (M.A. UCLA 1983), and performance scholar (Ph.D. NYU 1991). Her most recent work is a "movement ethnography," *Dancing with Virgin: Enacting Religious Belief in Tortugas, New Mexico*, to be published by the University of California Press. She teaches part-time at Empire State College in New York City.

Bert O. States is Professor of Dramatic Arts at the University of California at Santa Barbara. His most recent books are *HAMLET and the Concept of Character* and *Dreaming and Storytelling*.

Tadashi Suzuki is the founder and director of the Suzuki Company of Toga (SCOT), Chairman of the Japan Performing Arts Center (which sanctions the Toga International Arts Festival), Artistic Director of the Mitsui Festival (a biennial international theater festival, held in Tokyo, sponsored by the Mitsui group), and Artistic Director of the Acting Company Mito Theater. He is also creator of the Suzuki Method of Actor Training which has been taught in schools and theatres throughout the world, including the Juliard

School from 1981–3, and the University of Wisconsin at Milwaukee from 1980–4.

Ian Watson teaches in the Theatre Program at the University of Pennsylvania and is on the Editorial Committee of *New Theatre Quarterly.* He is especially interested in performance theory and the acting process. His book on Eugenio Barba and the Odin Teatret, *Towards a Third Theatre*, was published by Routledge in 1993.

Phillip B. Zarrilli is Professor of Theatre and Drama, South Asian Studies and Folklore at the University of Wisconsin–Madison where he directs the Asian/Experimental Theatre Program. His books include *The Kathakali Complex: Actor, Performance, Structure* (1984), (editor) *Asian Martial Arts in Actor Training* (1993), and the soon to be completed ethnography of a South Indian martial art, *Paradigms, Practices, and Discourses of Power.* He has also taught at UCLA, Northwestern, and NYU.

PREFACE

As a performance theorist who teaches actors as well as graduate courses in critical theories and methodologies of performance, this book was prompted by a growing recognition of the need for a collection of essays which could speak to students of acting *and* students of theory. In their practical work with me students are immersed in daily training intended to discipline the bodymind through the Asian martial arts and related acting exercises as a psychophysiological basis for acting (Chapter 14). For the majority of my students this is their first exposure to a rigorous psychophysiologically based approach to acting which often causes them to (re)consider not only how acting is embodied but also how they think and talk about acting, that is, their preconceptions about acting are questioned. This often leads to a desire to explore paradigms and techniques of acting which can either complement or provide alternatives to psychological realism. This book is intended to fill some of the gaps between practice and thought.

In spite of the particular concerns of American students which prompted this collection of essays, it is hoped that the issues which are addressed throughout will speak to others as well.

Phillip B. Zarrilli

ACKNOWLEDGEMENTS

The ideas which inform my organization of this book, and my own writing within it, owe much to many. I have been fortunate to have been at the University of Wisconsin–Madison in an environment that has allowed me to explore the relationship between theory and practice. Especially since 1986, I have been involved in a number of production projects, classes, and graduate seminars that have helped me to theorize practice and to practice theory. I want to thank the students with whom I have been so favored to work, especially Dora Lanier, John Jaraczewski, Soogi Kim, Darcey Engen, Krista Bourquein, David Richards, Duane Krause, Denise Myers, Michelle Mountain, Lauren Love, George Czarnicki, Stacy Wolf, Michael Peterson, "Jimbo", and Sharon Grady.

And thanks also to Indonesian playwright/director Putu Wijaya, kathakaḷi performer M.P. Sankaran Namboodiri and percussionist Kalamandalam Balaraman. An interdisciplinary group from all over the Madison campus has been supportive and offered both production input and critical post-production commentary. Among this group, I want to single out Jack Kugelmass (anthropology and folklore), Judy Miller (French and Italian), Laurie Beth Clark (fine arts), Kirin Narayan (South Asian studies and anthropology), and Joyce Flueckiger (South Asian studies). Among my theatre department colleagues, I thank Mary Karen Dahl, Patricia Boyette, Karen Ryker, John Staniunas, Andre Both, and most especially Jill Dolan for her breadth of thought and co-direction of our cross-gender *A Midsummer Night's Dream*.

Finally, a word of thanks to editorial assistants Patty Gallagher and E.J. Westlake for their organizational skills and editorial eyes. And to Worlds of Performance Series Editor Richard Schechner as well as to Talia Rodgers of Routledge for their support of and work on this project from its inception.

Portions of Chapter 2, "Introduction to Part I," by Phillip B. Zarrilli were previously published as "Thinking and Talking About Acting" in the *Journal of Dramatic Theory and Criticism* (1989, Vol. 3, No. 2) and are reprinted by permission of the *Journal of Dramatic Theory and Criticism*.

Chapter 3, "The Actor's Presence: Three Phenomenal Modes" (*Theatre Journal*, 35, 3: 359–75, 1983), by Bert O. States is reprinted by permission of Johns Hopkins University Press and the author.

Chapter 5, "'Just Be Your Self': Logocentrism and Difference in Performance Theory" (*Art & Cinema*, 1986: 1: 10–12), by Philip Auslander is reprinted by permission of the author.

The following essays were previously published in *TDR* and are reprinted by permission of MIT Press and/or the authors:

Chapter 4, "On Acting and Not-Acting" by Michael Kirby (16, 1: 3–15, 1972).

Chapter 7, "Meyerhold's Biomechanics" by Mel Gordon (18, 3: 73–88, 1974).

Chapter 8, "Etienne Decroux's Promethean Mime" by Deidre Sklar (29, 4: 64–75, 1985).

Chapter 9, "Actor Training in the Neutral Mask" by Sears A. Eldredge and Hollis W. Huston (24, 4: 19–28, 1978).

Chapter 11, "Bali and Grotowski: Some Parallels in the Training Process" by I Wayan Lendra (35, 1: 113–139, 1991).

Chapter 13, "My Bodies: The Performer in West Java" by Kathy Foley (34, 2: 62–80, 1990).

Chapter 18, "Dario Fo: The Roar of the Clown" by Ron Jenkins (30, 1: 191–179, 1986).

Chapter 22, "Rachel Rosenthal Creating Her Selves" by Eelka Lampe (32, 1: 170–190, 1988).

Chapter 23, "Task and Vision: Willem Dafoe in LSD" by Philip Auslander (29, 2: 94–98, 1985).

Chapter 24, "David Warrilow: Creating Symbol and Cypher" by Laurie Lassiter (29, 4: 3–12, 1985).

Chapter 10, "Eastern and Western Influences on Performer Training at Eugenio Barba's Odin Teatret" (*Asian Theatre Journal*, 5, 1: 49–62, 1988), by Ian Watson is reprinted by permission of the author and the University of Hawaii Press.

Chapter 12, "Culture is the Body," by Tadashi Suzuki, compiled and translated by Kazuko Matsuoka, was published in *Interculturalism and Performance: Writings from PAJ, 1991*, edited by Bonnie Marranca and Gautam Dasgupta, and is reprinted by permission of Johns Hopkins University Press and the Japan Performing Arts Center, Tokyo.

Chapter 15, "Effector Patterns of Basic Emotions: a psychophysiological method for training actors" (*Journal of Social and Biological Structures*, 10: 1–19, 1987), by Susana Bloch, Pedro Orthous and Guy Santibañez-H is published by permission of Jai Press Inc. and the authors.

Chapter 17, "Brecht and the Contradictory Actor" (*Theatre Journal*, 36, 1: 25–41, 1984), by John Rouse is reprinted by permission of Johns Hopkins University Press and the author.

Chapter 19, "Forum Theatre," by Augusto Boal, translated by Adrian Jackson, is excerpted from Augusto Boal's *Games for Actors and Non-Actors* (London: Routledge, 1992) and is published by permission of Routledge, the author, and translator.

Some previously published essays in this volume make use of gender language common when first authored. Some essays also do not include full citations or bibliographical references. Unless revised by the author, gender language and occasional incomplete citations appear as when initially published.

GENERAL INTRODUCTION
Between theory and practice

Phillip B. Zarrilli

> Scientists of the body speak in figures, teachers of acting speak in images, artists speak in words, theorists speak in propositions. To speak in any of these forking tongues is to be split from the others. It is necessary, though perhaps not possible, that we describe a line that will join these several points. The gap between performance and thought is not simple, but is composed of subgaps on either side, between the pedagogical imagery of performance and the flesh which performance possesses, between thought about the theatre and the metathought which plays through theatre ... The performer and the thinker could momentarily meet in the sign's provisional and already receding closure. The two might be – is it too much to ask? – the same person.
>
> **(Hollis Huston 1984: 199)**

There are many languages and discourses of acting, each written/spoken from a particular point of view. Theorists often speak only to theorists; practitioners only to practitioners. Too seldom do they speak to each other. This book invites us to try to speak and listen across these gaps and boundaries to each other and to those parts of our "selves" which might practice theory or theorize practice.

Like the seminal book of Toby Cole and Helen Krich Chinoy, *Actors on Acting* (1970[1949]), this collection, by juxtaposing historically diverse and often contradictory views of acting, invites the reader to (re)consider both acting and discourses on acting. I use (re)consider to mark clearly the implicitly processual nature of "considering." This view invites us not only to see performance as processual but also to see that "both society and human beings are performative, always already processually under construction" (Drewal 1991: 4).

From this point of view, theatre-making is a mode of socio-cultural practice. As such, it is not an innocent or naive activity separate from or above and beyond everyday reality, history, politics, or economics.[1] As theatre historian Bruce McConachie asserts, "theatre is not epiphenomenal, simply reflecting and expressing determinate realities and forces" (1989: 230); rather, as a mode of socio-cultural practice theatre is a complex network of specific, interactive *practices* (directing, designing, acting, dramaturgy, promotion, management, etc.) which helps to constitute, shape, and affect "selves" as well as historical events and relationships. The relationship between any of the doers and the done (directors, designers, actors, etc.) is *always* actualized within a specific network of relationships and material circumstances which, as a process and a practice, impinges on all those doing what is being done.[2]

For the contemporary actor who is exposed to and/or expected to perform in a wide variety of types of theatre/performance, the actor's perception and practice of acting is a complex, ongoing set of intellectual and psychophysiological negotiations. These negotiations are between and among one "self" and a variety of (explicitly or implicitly) competing paradigms and discourses of acting/performance. The actor encounters these as a part of folklore, mass media, and stage shows; in manifestos and/ or scholarly treatises (on acting, feminism/s, neo-Marxist thought, etc.); and in the specific training or "formations" through which these negotiations are constantly (re)figured. Teachers and theorists alike experience times when their perceptions of acting, and/or its practices, are altered.

For the actor, moments of (re)consideration are times when practice and thought crystallize in an insight which clarifies his or her (embodied) performance practice and technique. Yoshi Oida, in his 1992 book on acting, describes one such moment. Before joining Peter Brook's international company in 1968, Yoshi had been well known in Japanese films and theatre as a Western-style actor. But he had also been trained in nō, kabuki dance, and bunraku. While on tour in rural Iran, Brook's company gave a performance of a work-in-progress.

> After the show, Peter said to me, "Your acting is too concentrated and strong for this style of work." I realized that I was still performing in accordance with the principles of *nō* theatre where the actor's concentration must be extremely intense. But popular theatre requires another approach. And I realized that just as there are many levels of performance, there is no one "right" way to act.
>
> (Oida 1992: 72)

Or, there are moments when the actor's relationship to his or her practice is altered in a way that makes clear that there can be no "neutrality" in art. As Eelka Lampe reports in this volume (Chapter 22), performance artist/ feminist Rachel Rosenthal's (re)consideration of acting was prompted by her attendance at a conference of women artists at the California Institute of the Arts in 1971:

Because she had been taught a history of art that considered only the contribution of male artists, and because she thought of herself as an artist, she identified with men. "Then I came to this conference, and I saw slides of extraordinary work. . . . And so for the first time in my life, I began to shift my identification, and began to see that I could be an artist and be a woman."

Any (re)consideration is simultaneously personal, socio-cultural, and ideological, and therefore includes both idiosyncratic as well as collective/social dimensions. What may or may not prompt (re)consideration depends upon one's "historical circumstances." For the nineteen year old student of acting from New Glarus, Wisconsin, whose experience of acting theory and practice was limited to American versions of Stanislavskian-based acting, studying an historical account which clarifies the differences between the later Stanislavsky's method of physical actions and Strasberg's notion of affective memory may lead to a profound (re)consideration of acting. So might encountering a performance (in the flesh or via type or tape) by Dario Fo, Rachel Rosenthal, David Warrilow, a Tadashi Suzuki-trained actor, or a performance of *kathakali* by Gopi Asan. Whatever prompts a particular (re)consideration, the reverberations of that encounter have the potential to affect not only one's acting but also one's understanding of "self," society, ideology, politics, etc.

Acting (Re)Considered invites students of acting, actors, and theorists alike to put aside parochial preconceptions and points of view that propose acting as *a* truth (that is, one system, discourse, or practice). This book invites instead a pro-active, processual approach which cultivates a critical awareness of acting as multiple and always changing. Of course, in the moment of performance, the actor *must* embody a specific set of actions *as if these were absolute*. But every "absolute" viewed historically and processually is part of a multiplicity.

(RE)CONSIDERING CONTEXT AND ENVIRONMENT

The critical awareness and reflection which (re)considerations can prompt does not occur in a vacuum. Teachers of acting, professional actors, directors, and producers have control over, and therefore responsibility for, the working/learning environments we create. To what degree are we actively making an environment which encourages critical inquiry and reflection, not only about "art" in the narrow sense but also concerning the material circumstances and issues implicit in the art we make? How theatre is made – from scene work and exercises, to rehearsals, to productions – includes attention to issues of race, gender, class, and ethnicity. Failing that, we abrogate our responsibility not only to train students' acting skills but also to educate them about what they are being trained to perform.[3]

THEORIES, META-THEORIES, AND ACTING (RE)CONSIDERED

Every time an actor performs, he or she implicitly enacts a "theory" of acting – a set of assumptions about the conventions and style which guide his or her performance, the structure of actions which he or she performs, the shape that those actions take (as a character, role, or sequence of actions as in some performance art), and the relationship to the audience. Informing these assumptions are culture-specific assumptions about the body–mind relationship, the nature of the "self," the emotions/feelings, and performance context.[4] Enacting these assumptions is as true for the student as it is for the likes of Sarah Bernhardt and Yoshi Oida. Each embodies specific theories and practices of acting locatable within a set of historical, socio-cultural, and aesthetic/dramaturgical circumstances. Likewise, genres have specific theories and practices of acting which are also historically and contextually specific.[5]

In addition to the specific theories and practices of acting, there are meta-theories reflecting more generally on the nature, practice, and phenomenon of acting. To bridge some of the gaps between specific theories and practices of acting and the meta-theoretical discussions, I have organized the essays in this collection into three parts, each with its own introduction and suggestions for further reading. In Part I, "Theories of and Meditations on Acting," the reader is asked to reflect "meta-theoretically" on acting, while Parts II and III focus on the specifics. The essays in Part II (re)consider "The Body and Training" and those in Part III (re)consider "The Actor in Performance." Internally, the essays within Parts II and III have been organized in roughly chronological order. For readers who want to defer theory, reading Part II or Part III first makes as much sense as beginning with theory. I have selected essays not only from different parts of the world but also by practicing theorists, that is, that ever-expanding number who (thankfully) eschew the oversimplistic dichotomies between theory and practice.

Phillip B. Zarrilli

PART  I

Theories of and meditations on acting

2

INTRODUCTION

Phillip B. Zarrilli

During the 1980s numerous scholarly studies of acting began to make use of a wide variety of critical methodologies including phenomenology (States Chapter 3 [this volume], 1985; Wilshire 1982), Derridean decon-struction (Auslander Chapter 5 [this volume]), cultural, contextual, and intellectual histories (Roach 1980, 1985; Worthen 1984; Burns 1990; Schmitt 1990), semiotics (Elam 1980; Aston and Savona 1991; Fischer-Lichte 1992), feminist reconsiderations of acting process, theory, and history (Jenkins and Ogden-Malouf 1985; Diamond 1988; Davis 1991), among others.[1]

The essays in Part I invite readers to take a step back from considering any specific theory or practice of acting and to reflect more generally. The essays by States and Auslander are meta-theoretical in that they help us to (re)consider the performances of particular actresses such as Sarah Bernhardt and the work of Stanislavsky, Brecht, Grotowski, etc., while Kirby prompts us to reflect on how we differentiate between "acting" and "not-acting."[2]

Bert O. States' "The Actor's Presence: Three Phenomenal Modes," along with his longer book-length phenomenology of acting (1985), approaches theatre as a "speech act" in order to explore how the actor's relationship to the audience may shift "keys" during a performance or within a culture over time. States explores three "pronominal modes": the self-expressive in which the virtuosity of the actor predominates, the collaborative in which the actor's direct interaction/communication with the audience predominates, and the representational in which the actor's function as the vehicle of signification predominates.

Michael Kirby's "On Acting and Not-Acting" describes a continuum from non-matrixed activities, such as those in Happenings ("not-acting"), to character acting ("complex acting)." Kirby considers "not-acting" to include a wide range of "non-matrixed" performances in which what the performers do onstage has no representational function within a dramatic narrative. Kabuki stage attendants (*kōken*) are onstage, but assumed to be "invisible" as they assist the performers or move properties. Performers in Happenings do simple "tasks." Both types of activities are "not imbedded, as it were, in matrices of pretended or represented character, situation, place, and time." Kirby's descriptive continuum prompts us to consider carefully how and what we define as "acting" and/or "not-acting."

In "Just Be Your Self" Philip Auslander gives a deconstructive reading of the acting theories of Stanislavsky, Brecht, and Grotowski in terms of the "metaphysics of presence" which lies behind the commonplace ideas of self, identity, and presence. Auslander points out the (limiting) metaphysical assumptions on which modernist theories of acting have been based.

THEORY AND THE PRACTICE OF ACTING

The Metaphorical Languages of Acting

Too often, when we think and talk about acting, we do not examine either our language or the assumptions that lie behind it.[3] Increasingly over the past 75 years, following Ferdinand de Saussure's assertion that language does not provide us with access to *the* "Real," but rather with a *version* of reality (1966), scholars from numerous disciplines began to question the typically non-reflexive, positivist ways in which people think, talk, and write. James Clifford argues that all narratives (including those about acting) are "constructed, artificial ... cultural accounts" (1986: 2) which are not representations of *a* truth or *a* reality, but rather "inventions of culture" in Roy Wagner's sense (1981). Edward M. Bruner said the same thing in a slightly different way – that all texts are formed around implicit stories constructed according to who receives the narrative (1986). If we accept the premise that all narratives are "inventions," then the discourses of acting/performance are locatable within a particular historical, socio-cultural context, that is, each narrative – including this one – has one or more implicit stories that were written for *particular* audiences in *particular* contexts.

Many discourses about acting assume that they are expressing *the* truth. Most narratives foreground neither the process of constructing this "truth" nor the voice or specific position from which this (version of) "truth" is being constructed. To do so would reveal the fact that *this* "truth" is a particular version authored by a particular person for a particular audience in a particular place and time, and is thereby open to question and revision. Consequently, the epistemological assumption that a discourse of acting is *the* truth remains in the background, untold. One name given to these implicit stories and sets of assumptions is "ideology." British culture theorist Graeme Turner summarizes Althusser's definition of ideology as

> a conceptual framework "through which men interpret, make sense of, experience and 'live' the material conditions in which they find themselves." Ideology forms and shapes our consciousness of reality. For good or ill, the world it constructs is the one we will always inhabit.
>
> (Turner 1990: 26)[4]

Languages of acting, like other propositional modes of linguistic construction, mask not only their positionality and ideology but also their referential, signifying nature. As Mark Johnson explains,

> because of the limitations of our propositional modes of representation, we have a hard time trying to express the full meaning of our experiences.... So while we must use propositional language to describe these dimensions of experience and understanding, we must not mistake our description for the thing described.
>
> (Johnson 1987: 4)

Long ago, Nietzsche called our attention to the epistemological problem implicit in the "truth" claims of language. Nietzsche asked, "What therefore is truth? A mobile army of metaphors, metonymies, anthropomorphisms ... truths are illusions of which one has forgotten that they are illusions" (cited in Spivak 1976: xxii).

Take, for example, the assumptions behind one commonplace set of metaphors used to talk about acting, that of "believability" and "honesty." Several years ago, at the University of Wisconsin, a male undergraduate acting student became very confused when told by an acting teacher, "I don't think you believe what you are doing." The use of "believe" or its commonplace synonym "be honest" by many acting teachers and directors stems from the predominant viewpoint implicit in realistic acting that a character when enacted must conform to ordinary social reality as constructed from the spectator's point of view. The audience needs to be convinced that the character is behaving as s/he would in "ordinary life" within the "given circumstances" of the scene. The student explained that his confusion stemmed from the fact that although he felt as if he were being totally honest in the moment, that is, he "believed in" what he was doing, the teacher/spectator was not convinced.

In this case, what does "believe" signify? Why are such apparently simple ideas so confusing for young actors? First, "believe" makes an implicit truth claim which disguises its metaphorical construction. The request for "believability" collapses the character as a fictive construct and sign system into the actor-as-person. The teacher seems to ask the actor to *be* "believable." The actor is not asked to create those psychophysiological relationships to specific actions that might be *read by* the director/

spectator/teacher as signs of honesty. The language of "believability" is problematic because in its propositional mode it appears to make truth claims which mask the referential, signifying quality of any linguistic statement about acting. It also masks its ideology of identity – the collapse of the "person" of the performer into the role.[5] The implicit "truth" claim in the proposition, "you must believe in order to make me believe," is mistakenly understood by both teacher and student alike as an apt description for "the thing described" – acting. A second problem with this particular metaphor is that "believe" is devoid of any reference to the body; there is no assertion that "believability" needs to be embodied.

The student in this situation is faced with two choices: first, by understanding that *all* languages of acting are metaphorical, he can attempt to fill in the gaps between this particular language and what he needs to do as an actor, that is, he can translate the confusing language into terms that are more actable and thereby make choices which appear to the teacher/ director as "believable"; second, if he finds the underlying philosophical assumptions which inform this language and paradigm of acting problematic, he may actively and openly problematize the language and the paradigm it assumes, and search for more appropriate alternatives.

Linguistic philosophers Lakoff and Johnson title their seminal study of the metaphorical nature of language, *Metaphors We Live By* (1980). This title is an apt metaphor of the relationship between actors and the discourses of their practice. If propositional language can never fully represent acting, then actors have no choice but to "live by" metaphors. The question is not whether languages of acting can/should be metaphorical, but what specific "metaphors" are actors to "live by"?

Body–Mind Dualism and the (Supposed) Resurrection of the Body

Given the powerful optimism generated by the achievements of science during the nineteenth century, late nineteenth and early twentieth century theatre theorists labored under the modernist illusion that there *was* an absolute, objective, "scientific" practice and language of acting. Delsarte, Stanislavsky, Meyerhold, and a host of their disciples each developed "systems" which used languages of acting based on the assumption of an objective science (of the mind and/or body).[6] On the other hand, German Expressionists, Artaud and others rebelled against rationalism and/or "the word." They assumed languages and metaphors of acting which romantically reified the subjectivity of the actor, thereby making the intensely "personal" the source of "truth." Objectivism and subjectivism remain two sides of the same problematic, dualistic coin.

To explore both sides of the body–mind problem for actors, I will first re-read Sonia Moore's *Training an Actor: The Stanislavski System in Class* (1979), and then re-read Maurice Merleau-Ponty's seminal attempt to "resurrect" the body, the *Phenomenology of Perception* (1962). I have selected the texts by Moore and Merleau-Ponty, not because I wish necessarily to single out either for "attack," but rather because each narrative represents the general contours of the body–mind "problem" still commonplace among many students of acting.

Moore views the body along with "voice, speech, his powers of observation and imagination, his constant control over the 'feeling of truth,' his spiritual movement" as part of the "actor's apparatus" or "instrument" (1979: 35). One looks for students whose instrument is "trainable." Although Moore says that she wants to redress "one of the gravest distortions of Stanislavski in the American theatre" by reasserting the important place of "the actor's physical training" in the Stanislavski System (1979: 35), she never articulates a process by which the actor's corporeality is central to the training, other than to call for physical training to make the body "responsive." Of the relationship between the body and mind, Moore states that "an actor's control over his body should be as complete as that of a dancer" (1979: 16). Dualism intact, the mind controls the body. Moore quotes without explaining that "the physical excellence that Stanislavski demands is intimately related to the psychological side of the technique" (1979: 16). Although Moore says that the goal of the System is "reincarnation" and that "the body must begin the action and it must finish it" (1979: 15;38), she never explains how bodily action is incarnated or how the body initiates action. Moore's overriding concern is not with the particulars of the process by which one embodies action, but with the construction of the psychology of a character's motivations.

Giving instructions in an exercise, Moore tells one of her students, "Let your body express what you have *in* your mind," (1979: 36, emphasis added). She tells students to take an image *in* mind, and then "make sure that your body expresses it" (1979: 37). She instructs people to "think, think and make your body project what is *in* your mind" (1979: 42, emphasis added). The mind is represented as a container of images etc., separate from the body. Whatever is "in mind" can be transferred to the body. This mind-as-container is a place where the "emotions" are "stored" (1979: 65) to be re-lived in the act of performance. For Moore the mind asserts "conscious control" over the body – an assumption illustrated when Moore concludes that the System permits the actor "consciously to control his entire apparatus of experiencing and incarnating" (1979: 34). For Moore the actor's mind is an all-knowing entity controlling *all* experience and embodiment.

The System provides a certain means of control based on a stimulus–response model imposing order on disorder. Moore assumes a nature/culture dichotomy where culture (male/mind/texts) controls, shapes, and tames nature (female/emotions/the body). Control is provided by what

Moore variously calls "thinking," "logic," or "conscious control" – the Cartesian rational mind. Moore tells her students, "We stop thinking in life only when we are unconscious or dead, and the character is dead when you stop thinking as the character" (1979: 81). The actor's mind becomes an all-knowing entity, separate from the body, controlling all experience and embodiment.

As Sherry Dietchman so astutely observed of her own experience as an actor in training,

> Until I began training I thought that my focus problems were just mental. The fact that they may be physical as well simply never occurred to me.... Very often, I think the body is ignored or "cut off" in actor training. Most of my classes emphasized things such as emotional reality, script analysis, substitution, and memory recall. Body training is either kept separate or ignored altogether ... I wonder what it is in our culture that perpetuates that split. More importantly ... I need to find how that separation can be overcome during performance.
>
> (Dietchman 1990)

Moore's language and Dietchman's training reflect the Euro-American experience of the dichotomy or gap thought to exist between the cognitive, conceptual, formal, or rational and the bodily, perceptual, material, and emotional. The consequence of this split is that all meaning, logical connection, reasoning, and conceptualization are aligned with mental or rational operations, while perception, imagination, and feeling are aligned with bodily operations (Johnson 1987: xxv). This version of body–mind dualism can be traced back to Plato who asserted that the mind (*psyche*) had an independent and superior metaphysical status capable of participating in the knowledge of the world of forms. The body was part of the physical world and therefore a deterrence or hindrance to a person's epistemic and spiritual development (Shaner 1985: 42).

In 1949 philosopher Gilbert Ryle summarized this split:

> every human being has both a body and a mind. Some would prefer to say that every human being is both a body and a mind. His body and his mind are ordinarily harnessed together but after the death of the body his mind may continue to exist and function.
>
> Human bodies are in space and are subject to the mechanical laws which govern all other bodies in space. Bodily processes and states can be inspected by external observers. So a man's bodily life is as much a public affair as are the lives of animals and reptiles and even as the careers of trees, crystals and planets.
>
> But minds are not in space, nor are their operations subject to mechanical laws. The workings of one mind are not witnessable by other observers; its

career is private. Only I can take direct cognisance of the states and processes of my own mind. A person therefore lives through two collateral histories, one consisting of what happens in and to his mind.

(Ryle 1949: 11–12)[7]

American psychological realism's approach to constructing the theatrical character is particularly susceptible to body–mind dualism. The rhetoric and semantics used to represent "creating a character" all too often give the impression that the character is an object logically constructed by the mind and then put into the body. There is little if any discussion of the process by which the character so constructed gets in-corporated. But if the physical body is lost in many of the discourses and practices of American method acting, the physical was never lost to Stanislavsky and a number of his best known students. The master developed his "method of physical actions," admonished his actors to understand their work as a craft recognizing the character as a physical score to be specifically crafted:

> Extra gestures are the equivalent of trash, dirt, spots. An actor's performance which is cluttered up with a multiplicity of gestures will be like that messy sheet of paper. Therefore before he [sic] undertakes the physical inter- pretation ... he must rid himself of all superfluous gestures ... Unrestrained movements, natural though they may be to the actor himself, only blur the design of his part, make his performance unclear, monotonous and uncontrolled.
>
> (Stanislavsky 1949: 69)

As Jean Benedetti reports, late in his life Stanislavsky sought, through the method of physical action, to overcome what divided "mind from body, knowledge from feeling, analysis from action" (1982: 66; also see Gordon 1987: 206ff).

Stanislavsky's brilliant, if wayward student, Michael Chekhov, devel- oped an approach to the creation of character based on an active use of the imagination, not as an image *in* the head, but as an act of engagement of the entire bodymind. The actor explores the creation of a character by physicalizing a "psychological gesture" through which "the soul of the character and the physical body of the performer meet" (Gordon 1991: xxxi).

Given the resilience of mind–body dualism, students often experience a "real" *disjuncture* between their minds and their bodies. They have great difficulty "freeing" themselves to work out from their bodies. They often have a "mental block" which they must overcome before they are free to allow themselves to explore how to get acting *into* their bodies. I read this disjuncture not as an example of an acting problem, but as part of an ongoing cultural reconsideration of the paradigms, discourses, and relationships between the body, mind, and experience in the constitution of meaning, knowledge, "self," and our daily practice(s) of life – including acting. A parallel reconsideration is manifest in "new age" and popular alternative body therapies, systems of healing, and regimes of producing the healthy/fit body, as well as in the widely divergent discourses of the body and experience by philosophers, social scientists, and feminists.[8]

Historically, the 1962 appearance of the English translation of Merleau-Ponty's *Phenomenology of Perception* marks a paradigmatic shift in thinking about the role of the body in the constitution of experience. Merleau-Ponty articulated the fundamental philosophical problem of the body's role (or lack thereof) in constituting experience. He critiqued the heretofore static, objective nature of most representations of the body and experience.

> [T]hinking which looks on from above, and thinks of the object-in-general, must return to the "there is" which underlies it; to the site, the soil of the sensible and opened world such as it is in our life and for our body – not that possible body which we may legitimately think of as an information machine but that actual body I call mine, this sentinel standing quietly at the command of my words and my acts.
>
> (Merleau-Ponty 1964: 160–1)

Moore's formulation of acting, and my student's confusion over "believability", clearly assumed thinking which looked "on from above." While they both acknowledge the body, neither knew how to account for what Merleau-Ponty calls the "actual body I call mine," that is, the body as "an experienced phenomenon ... in the immediacy of its lived concreteness," and "not as a representable object ... for the abstractive gaze" (Schrag 1969: 130).

Merleau-Ponty challenged the Cartesian *cogito* and asserted the primacy of lived experience in the constitution of meaning. His phenomenology eloquently (re)claimed the centrality of the body and embodied experience as the locus for "experience as it is lived in a deepening awareness" (Levine 1985: 62). He rejected the exclusive assumption of the natural sciences and modern psychology that treated the body as a thing, object, instrument, or machine under the command and control of an all-knowing mind.

By the early 1960s in America, experimental avant-garde theatre and "happenings" prompted a radical rediscovery of the body by foregrounding the (supposedly) unmediated body/acts of the performer (Kirby Chapter 4 [this volume]). Artaud's *The Theatre and Its Double* (1958) and Grotowski's *Towards a Poor Theatre* (1968) led the way toward giving the body its due. For Grotowski the total psychophysical engagement of the performer was a "holy act." Some experimenters threw out "character" altogether as inimical to the immediacy of communion "in the moment" between performer and spectator. Richard Schechner overtly rejected objectivist assumptions about the body which treated it as an instrument, asserting that "nothing is worse for the performer than 'movement exercises' or abstract 'body work.' Don't treat your body as a thing. *Your body is not your 'instrument'; your body is you*" (1973: 145). Schechner called for an in-body process by means of which the performer might realize an organic connection between the body and mind:

> All performance work begins and ends in the body. When I talk of spirit or mind or feelings or psyche, I mean dimensions of the body. The body is an organism of endless adaptability. A knee can think, a finger can laugh, a belly cry, a brain walk and a buttock listen.
>
> (Schechner 1973: 132)

Such thinking assumes the bodymind as a *gestalt* to be developed through appropriate training exercises for immediate expressivity and "presence" in the theatrical moment.[9]

However, this "resurrection of the body" has not been unproblematic. If and when the body, experience *per se*, and/or "self" are reified as an essential "real," it problematically assumes that the subject or "self" is a stable location, and that a particular experience or transcendental self exists as an ideal or originary construct or essence. In some improvisational, bodily and/or experientially saturated approaches to acting where "being in the moment" is emphasized, a Cartesian dualism is simply reinscribed in the form of an overly simplistic and monolithic subjectivity often described as the actor's "presence," or as an "organic" or "natural" state of being.[10] A reified subjectivist notion of "presence" is as complicit in a dualist metaphysics as is the Cartesian "mind." Neither provides an adequate account of the "body" in the mind, the "mind" in the body, or of the process by which the signs read as "presence" are a discursive construct.

I am too often reminded of the mystification which a subjectivist indulgence of "experience," the "body," or "presence" has when a student comes to a class where I use Asian martial arts to train actors and initially "spaces out," *trying* to "feel" the connection, to focus or establish some "mystical" relationship to his or her body. Or when a student does not begin to discover the sharp edge of a perceiving consciousness (the mind-aspect) implicit in a fully in-corporated experience of movement as he or she gropes through some culturally-projected romanticized image of "Asia."[11] Blau's perceptive recollection of this problem should give all students of acting and any bodily-based discipline (such as the Asian martial arts) pause for thought:

For all the justifiable devotion to love's body, we still need a deeper reverence of the mind's passion. ("Training! Training! Training!" cried Meyerhold. "But if it's the kind of training which exercises only the body and not the mind, then no thank you! I have no use for actors who know how to move but can't think.") If it becomes easier for actors, or performers or shamans, to be possessed, it becomes harder for them to be intelligent – and, especially intelligent *in* the act of performance . . . The critical faculty, for all the dissidence, had been abused. All things waste from want of use. "Use your head, can't you, use your head," raged Hamm, "you're on earth, there's no cure for that."

(Blau 1976: 22–3)

I want to summarize my argument thus far by rephrasing several of the questions I have been asking. How are we to think and talk about acting if we cannot make "truth" claims about acting and if many of our languages of acting are often rife with dualistic assumptions? First, we can begin by understanding that *all* languages of acting are highly metaphorical. We should not mistake a discourse *about* acting as a representation of the thing that the discourse attempts to describe – the practice of acting. Second, given the impossibility of ever fully describing acting, all languages of acting are necessarily inadequate and therefore provisional. Thus, all languages of acting need to be constantly (re)considered in relation to the particular context of their use and the degree to which a language can help us to make sense of the complexities of the bodymind's relationship to action/acting, and to the ideology implicit in any kind of acting. And finally, rather than despairing, as did Copeau when he remarked under the weight of scientific objectivism, "At present, I can use only metaphors that my students will not understand, that do not get through to them" (1970: 221), we can celebrate the freedom of not having to find a "universal" language once and for all. Rather we can spend our energy on the continuing challenge of searching for languages of acting which best allow one to actualize a particular paradigm of performance in a particular context for a particular purpose.

Signification, Structure, and the "Problems" of The Subject and Character

One place to begin a search for a more complex way of thinking and talking about acting is semiotics. Semiotics is not a theory of acting *per se*, but a theory of a system of signs. Although the actor cannot *act* on the basis of understanding theatre as a semiotic system, nevertheless, in an era which some define as postmodern,[12] an actor will be ill-equipped even for character acting unless he or she is able to understand not only the relation between semiotics and acting but also what is required in productions where one plays moments which are not motivated psychologically –

moments in which an actor's action/gesture/posture might be said to "stand on their own." From a semiotic perspective, in the moment of performance the actor makes meanings (impressions, images) available through the complex network of signs which he or she produces (along with the costumes the actor wears, the space/setting within which he or she acts, etc.). The actor's task is *creating* signs (images etc.) through voice and body. If meanings are created, they are created in the play of signification between the signs produced by the actors and interpretations of those signs made by the spectators.

Since meanings are made collaboratively by the performers and spectators, the actor does not *have* to produce logical, behaviorally motivated, psychological signs for an action to have "meaning" for an audience. Perhaps the best way to illustrate this is by example. When directing Euripides' *Hippolytus* a number of years ago, I instructed the actor playing Hippolytus to open his first scene kneeling, chopping wood with a hatchet. I explained that in the darkness he should take up his kneeling position, grasp the hatchet in his right hand, and the log in his left, and then simply engage himself completely and fully in the act of chopping wood. I further explained that he should use the hatchet in a rhythmically measured but focused manner so that each blow would have a "heavy" quality, and that, once he began to deliver his opening speech, he should set the rhythm and tone of his speech to the chopping. Since, like most American actors at his level of experience, this actor's primary training had been in various forms of Stanislavskian-based method acting, I was not surprised when he asked what his motivation might be for chopping wood. Although either of us could have invented a motivation for Hippolytus which might have allowed the chopping to "make sense" in motivational terms, we resisted using such language. We worked toward clarity about what the actor's task was at this moment – "simply" chopping wood.

Were the actor to have insisted on having a psychologically based motivation, his relationship to the action would have had a behavioral inflection giving the action a different signification than what I wanted: a decided act of chopping wood. My intention was for the chopping to be placed before the audience along with the words of his speech. And for the audience to assemble meaning from the words and the physical action. Whether Hippolytus' chopping "read" well for the audience and whether the meanings and associations that the audience created were those I had intended, are open questions. What the actor and I worked on in this moment was developing a specific energy, focus, and timing in his wood chopping. The actor had to negotiate between his own understanding/ expectations of what acting is or is not, and the demands of this particular production. He had to develop a network of relationships-in-action between the three sets of demands which any production potentially places on the actor's approach: (1) the structural, dramaturgical demands of the dramatic text and/or the particular genre of performance (happenings, performance art, etc.); (2) the structural demands of the performance text – how the director (or whoever is shaping the work) determines the *specific* structure of *this* particular performance text; and (3) the relationship between the actor and what the actor does.

Semiotics alerts the actor to the intricacies of the relationships among the performed actions that generate meanings. But, as Dorrine Kondo reminds us (following Derrida), these potential meanings "can never be fixed, for there is no transcendental signified that commands authority and exists without signifiers or beyond signification. Rather, signification involves a play of signifiers, linked in chains of substitution within systems of difference" (1990: 36). And just as linguistic "truths" and performative "meanings" cannot be "fixed," so too the actor needs to be aware of the double "problem" of the subject and the character. A positivist metaphysics which assumes the stability of "truth" and "meaning" also assumes the stability of the "subject." As Kondo points out, in this view, identities are

> fixed, bounded entities containing some essence or substance that is expressed in distinctive attributes. This conventional trope opposes "the self" as bounded essence, filled with "real feelings" and identity, to a "world" or to a "society" which is spatially and ontologically distinct from the self.
>
> (Kondo 1990: 33–4)

Studies which critique this point of view highlight the fact that the notion of the "individual personality" as a bounded self is peculiar to post-Cartesian (male) history and is culturally-specific to the West.[13] Such critiques also attack the common sense notion

> that human nature determines identity, that as human beings we are the authors of all that we think and speak, and that as such we shape the world around us and the knowledges which structure that world. Common sense, then, assumes that the nature of human "being" is given in some way – that it exists *prior* to language simply to label the world of its own experience. Within this framework, the human individual is conceived as a unified center of control from which meaning emanates.
>
> (Easthope and McGowan 1992: 67)

Critics argue that "self" and "identity" are not "god-given human nature," but are negotiated socio-culturally through time. What is called into question by the problem of the subject is the "hegemonic American assumption about identity and selfhood as a bounded essence containing inner, true feelings" (Kondo 1990: 34).

There are two levels at which the "problem" of the subject is important for the actor: (1) at the aesthetic/structural level – understanding how and why the problem of the subject is altering the way dramatic texts are written, the way characters in novels, films, and plays are represented: how the presumably stable, psychologically whole character is no longer the paradigm of action governing what the actor is asked to perform;[14] (2) understanding how a critique of the "truth" of "inner feelings" throws into question acting theories which either reify personal feelings as the "organic truth and essence" of the actor's art (Strasberg) or reify the actor's "presence."[15]

The destabilization of the realistic, psychologically "whole" character has come from numerous directions. Many productions since the 1960s attempted to dispense with "character." Ironically a metaphysics of "presence" which reifies the immediate actor/audience interaction helped to destabilize the "normative" fictional character. In addition, American method acting has been openly defied by the many successful actors (Spalding Gray, Ron Vawter, David Warrilow, Rachel Rosenthal, Meredith Monk, Willem Dafoe, Anna Deavere Smith, etc.) not trained in the method (Savran 1988: 2; Martin, 1993; Schechner 1993a, 1993b).

As long ago as 1972, Michael Kirby (Chapter 4) attempted to describe the changes taking place in American acting during the 1960s. He argued that, under the influence of happenings, a shift away from character acting toward the not-acting/non-matrixed end of the continuum took place.[16] Keeping in mind Kirby's continuum, realist productions of realist texts by Chekhov, Ibsen, Williams, etc. assume that the actors play specific roles using a specific technique (usually Stanislavsky-based) to create "fully rounded" characters. As John Harrop says, the text is "a map to action" (1992: 54). Actors trained in the American method often approach characterization by "living the role," that is, erasing distinctions between "self"/"the real" and the fictional role. Alternatively, a character may be considered a "*dramatis persona*," a "mask," or a "fictive construct necessary to the plot structure, [thus] free[ing] the actor from the limiting idea that theatre *is* reality, rather than a reflection on, or an illusion of, reality" (Harrop 1992: 69).

For those who reject the dramatic text as the "map to action," the playtext (if used at all) is a point of departure from which the director, collective, and/or actors devise and develop their own performance text which *becomes* the map to the set of actions that the actors will perform either as "themselves" or as fictional characters. Productions of non-realist texts, non-realist productions of realist texts, and/or non-realist genres of performance often assume some variation on, or alternative to, the paradigm of the Stanislavskian actor/character structure. Several examples should clarify the range of possibilities.

My 1989 *(Playing) The Maids* was an adaptation/production of Genet's

The Maids. The production was played between and among four casts/ stages/styles, all of whom were onstage throughout the performance. One was a high baroque style played in bald-caps and sumptuous gowns, the second played in grand *kabuki* style, the third with a chic slicked-back "leather"-MTV-watching cast, and the fourth a roving band of rod puppeteers subversively commenting on the action and/or mockingly quoting the high-seriousness of the play and our production. The assistant director and I were seated in the midst of the semi-environmentally located three stages linked by runways. From this obvious spot, I cued the actors with kabuki-style clapper blocks when it was their turn to play a scene. At least four actors played each role. The actors' approach to sharing roles required that they develop not only their own version of the character but also a "collective" character. "Playing" *The Maids* meant that sometimes one actor "passed" the role of Solange on to *another* stage and actor – requiring the ability to "give" the role to another actor. These and other conventions obviously made specific demands on the actors which were very different from the demands of playing a character in a realist production. However, there still were identifiable (if shared) characters, namely Claire, Solange, and Madame, as well as a series of roles which emerged from rehearsals: Madame's Lover, a Bob Barker type of television game-show host, a Vanna White look-alike, a Member of the Audience, and the director and assistant director.

A second example is *kathakaḷi* dance-drama from Kerala, India. In *Kalyana Saugandhikam*, the actor-dancer playing the heroic Bhima sets off on a journey through the jungles in search of the Saugandhikam flower to bring to his beloved wife, Draupadi. The actor-dancer performs an hour-long "interpolation" into the dramatic narrative. Without a change in costume or make-up, the actor serially plays an elephant, lion, and serpent as he enacts what Bhima sees: a ferocious fight between these three animals. In *kathakaḷi*, the paradigm of acting assumes that the actor-dancer not only plays *a* role or character but also can play a series of characters side-by-side as he enacts a story nested within the main dramatic narrative. The work of performers such as Dario Fo (Chapter 18) and Rachel Rosenthal (Chapter 22) is similar to what happens in *kathakaḷi*. These and other monologists enact multiple roles sequentially. What differentiates the *kathakaḷi* actor's sequence of roles from that of Fo, Rosenthal, and the like is that in *kathakaḷi* the sequence remains part of a narrative within a larger narrative, while Fo and Rosenthal self-consciously juxtapose one role/ persona against another for specific political and ideological reasons.[17]

Johannes Birringer, in his study of postmodern theatre and performance (1991), describes the work of a number of performance artists and directors who believe that the actor should not "enact" a character, role, or persona, but rather should perform a series of actions which are signs within the total semiotic and imagistic field of the *mise-en-scène*: Kirby's "non-matrixed" performances. For example, Birringer describes Laurie Anderson's performance body as one through which the spectator's "attention stays on the surface of the staged signs, and as Anderson manipulates the media that can alter her appearance [...] she becomes another surface in a visual–aural design across which indefinite meanings traverse and cancel each other out" (Birringer 1991: 30). The pleasure in Anderson's performances is her ironic use of a "technoscape." Similarly, in Robert Wilson's spectacles, Birringer describes the performances as

> both abstracted – they are pictorial lines drawn onto the surface, moved, and then frozen to be redrawn – and presented as positions or numbers within a visual and auditory configuration ... In this sense, Wilson's theatre effects a radical repositioning of the human body: within the multiple transparent superimpositions of images, the body is not privileged but treated as one material, one cipher, among others.
>
> (Birringer 1991: 224)

Clearly the psychologically whole "character" is no longer (if it ever was) a *necessarily* stable position even for realist dramatic texts – witness the deconstructive work of the Wooster Group (see Chapter 23). What the actor "does" onstage may range from a psychologically motivated realist character, through a character-structure into and out of which the actor steps on a moment-to-moment basis, to the sequential playing of multiple roles, to the playing of roles or sequences of action which require the development of a specific relationship to the audience as a part of one's score, to the playing of multiple personae, to the enactment of tasks without any characterlogical implications. For the actor, whatever the actions to be performed, these actions are the "material" conditions of his or her work. By means of these material conditions not only are meanings created for, by, and with the spectators but also the actor's "who I am" cannot be divorced from the "who *we* are." Individual and collective identities form a negotiable dialectic within the arena of performance practice.

3

THE ACTOR'S PRESENCE

Three phenomenal modes

Bert O. States

One way of approaching the phenomenology of the actor is to consider him as a kind of storyteller whose speciality is that he *is* the story he is telling. Presumably, the transitional "voice" between the true storyteller and the actor would be the rhapsode who tells his story (or rather someone else's) directly to the audience, simulating the more exciting parts of it in the manner of the First Player in *Hamlet*, who gets so carried away by the plight of Hecuba. With the actor, of course, the narrative voice ("Anon he finds him striking too short at Greeks") disappears entirely, and we hear only the fictitious first-personal voice ("Now I am alone," or "Now, mother, what's the matter?") – rather, we *over*hear it, since the voice is no longer speaking to us. The audience is now an implicit or unacknowledged "you," at least in the more naturalistic styles of acting. This is, of course, what bothered Rousseau so much, that the actor was the final step in the disintegration of presence and direct discourse.[1]

I cite this familiar evolution only so that we might regain some sense of the narrator hiding in the actor, just as there is an actor hiding in the rhapsode. What distinguishes the First Player in the Pyrrhus speech from the complete actor he will become that same evening in *The Murder of Gonzago* is simply that in one case he is carried away *by* a fiction and in the other he is carried away *in*, or *as*, a fiction: in one case he envisions, in the other he *becomes*. In either case, the indispensable personal pronominal order of all discourse holds: speaker (I), spoken to (you), and spoken of (he). We can make better sense of this idea if we put it in the form of a chart opposing the world of the theatre and the fictional world of the play along the pronominal axis. Since Jiri Veltrusky has already given us terms for these two "worlds," let us refer to them as "the acting event" and "the enacted event" (1978: 572):

THEATRE (Acting event)				PLAY (Enacted event)
Actor	=	I	=	Character
Audience	=	you	=	Other characters or self
Character	=	he (it)	=	Absent character or events

The Play column speaks for itself: characters in a play speak, as we do in life, to each other (dialogue) or to themselves (soliloquy) about events or about people (usually absent). The Theatre column, however, requires a shift in perspective on the speech process. In sum: the actor (I) speaks to the audience (you) about the character (he) that he is playing. By extension, the ensemble of actors in any play would constitute the plural number of this same order of speech (we-you-they). But how is this possible? How does the actor speak to the audience *about* the character he is playing?

Immediately we see that the *I* of the actor is not at all the *I* of the character he is playing, the voice that keeps saying "I, I, I" throughout the play. The actor's first person is what appears before us *as* the character, the being that has, in effect, no voice of its own but whose very presence and way of appearing constitute the act of direct speech within the indirect speech in the enacted event. It is visible in the effortless hard work that produces on the actor's brow beads of perspiration that may not belong to the character. But the *I* is not simply the actor's real body. It is rather the *unnatural* attitude of the body, the thousand different means and behavioral peculiarities by which the actor unavoidably remains just outside the character he is playing. He is always slightly "quoting" his character, though not as Brecht's actor practices quoting – that is, not as a consciously estranged style. Even if he is quoting in the Brechtian sense there is a quotation beyond this quotation. No matter how he acts, there is always the ghost of a self in his performance.

This idea of theatre as an act of speech allows us to see how the actor's relationship to the audience may shift "keys" during a performance or, on the longer range, as culture makes different demands on the theatre as a reflection of its concerns. In effect, the actor has three pronominal modes in which he may speak to the audience, and they are modes – not styles – that cover all possibilities simply because they are all that discourse contains. Our chart would now look like this:

I (actor)	=	Self-expressive mode
You (audience)	=	Collaborative mode
He (character)	=	Representational mode

Before defining and exampling these modes I must emphasize that in treating the actor as a speaker I also have in mind the audience as listener. Any speaker–listener relationship is a two-way street, and the listener may hear *selectively* what he *wants* to hear or what he *thinks* he hears. In other words, it is not a simple matter of following the "intention" of the speaker but of abandoning one's senses to the shifting appeals of the speech (and the actor's speech, of course, should be understood to include gesture, presence, and all the aspects of his performance of the role). Above all, I want to avoid any suggestion that my modes have anything *at all* to do with style, or *necessarily* to do with sudden and conscious shifts in the actor's deportment whereby we now perceive him in one mode of listening and now in another. We are interested only in trying to approximate the range of the actor/audience relationship; and it is simply not sufficient to say that the actor performs in various styles (declamatory, naturalistic, Romantic, estranged, etc.) or, beyond style, that the audience's perception of the actor is exhausted in his "dual" nature as actor and character. But I can make this clear only by examining the modes themselves.

THE SELF-EXPRESSIVE MODE

Let us begin by treating them as *pure* modes of performance. In the self-expressive mode the actor *seems* to be performing on his own behalf. He says, in effect, "*See what I can do.*" One might say that certain roles encourage the self-expressive tendency (Cyrano, Faust, Falstaff, Hamlet, Lear, Medea), either because they are so demanding or because they have been deliberately designed as vehicles for the release of the actor's power (the part of Cyrano, for example, was written as a showpiece for Coquelin). Moreover, certain authors (usually the "classic" poets of the art) encourage the self-expressive mode. There is no better way to illustrate this idea than to quote Hazlitt on the occasion of Kean's appearance in *Richard II* in 1815:

> It may be asked, then, why all great actors choose characters from Shakespeare to come out in; and again, why these become their favourite parts? First, it is not that they are able to exhibit their author, but that he enables them to show themselves off. The only way in which Shakespeare appears to greater advantage on the stage than common writers is that he stimulates the faculties of the actor more. If he is a sensible man, he perceives how much he has to do, the inequalities he has to contend with, and he exerts himself accordingly; he puts himself at full speed, and lays all his resources under contribution; he attempts more, and makes a greater number of brilliant failures; he does all he can, and bad is often the best.
>
> (Hazlitt quoted in Archer and Lowe, n.d.: 51)

Converting Hazlitt to our own purposes, we might interpret the actor's decision to play "big parts" such as Lear or Richard as a self-expressive act in which he "bets" the audience that he is actor enough to fill the character's shoes. On its part the audience goes to the theatre to "see Kean," Hazlitt continues, rather than to see the character Kean is impersonating. I am not suggesting that this is the only motive in playing and playgoing, only that the great "classical" plays (particularly in the eighteenth and nineteenth century, when they are more frequently on the boards) seem to charge the theatrical event with the electricity of competition between actor and character. In other words, they invited the actor to put himself "at full speed," and to the extent that one went to the theatre to see Kean or Macready or Mrs Siddons at full speed one would be "listening" in the self-expressive mode.

As another variation, a play might be deliberately converted into a self-expressive vehicle – as in the "star system" or in the *Hamlet* productions of Charlotte Cushman, Sarah Bernhardt and Judith Anderson. Certain speeches in plays call for a high degree of self-expressiveness (the opening of *Richard III*, Hotspur's Popinjay speech, Mercutio's Mab speech). In this sense, opera, dance, and mime are the major self-expressive forms of theatre. Whatever they are *about* is always less important than what they display. The best-known example is the opera soprano who is not expected to "disappear" into her role as a dying tubercular because it is impossible to sing properly and die properly at the same time. Likewise, in dance, what story there is exists less as an illusion than as a display case for a series of demanding solo variations. The secondary role played by verisimilitude in these forms is confirmed by the fact that the performer steps completely out of the illusion and bows to the audience's applause when the solo is over. And so with mime, which is essentially an act of defining an invisible world in terms of the visible body. We do not see the walls of Marcel Marceau's prison or the stairs he ascends or the wind he leans into; his body opens onto the structure of these things in a display of the artist's ability to do without them.

In dramatic theatre, putting aside the great roles and the great poetic arias, self-expressiveness asserts itself in the form of vignettes, cameo "moments," *lazzi*, or, more generally, in the actor's particular stylistic signature: Garrick's kaleidoscope of facial expressions, Edward Alleyn's thunder, Edmund Kean's "flashes of lightning," Mrs Siddons' majesty, Duse's restraint, Bernhardt's Bernhardt, finally Brando's (then everyone's) realer realism. Veltrusky mentions the passage in *My Life in Art* where Stanislavsky talks about the Russian actor, Sadovsky, who had a particular piece of "business" that contains the essence of the actor's self-enlargement of his role: he "suddenly stopped in the middle of a sentence to portray the character feeling in his mouth for a hair from his fur collar, and went on for a long time moving his tongue around and 'trying to take the hair out' with his fingers while the sentence he had begun remained unfinished" (Veltrusky 1978: 57). What is the interest in this search for a hair? In life it would be unremarkable, if not vulgar; on the stage, memorable. It is exactly the revelation of something hitherto sub-theatrical, not simply "realism" but an audacious display of the actor's power to be "real" on the micro-level. In such a moment (assuming it is well done) the actor says, in effect, "You have all searched for a hair: let me show you, comically, what this search amounts to." I suggest it is the essence of the actor's self-enlargement for another reason: here the sentence the actor is speaking might be said to stand for the conventional flow of theatre action; everything is going along "as written." But suddenly the flow is broken, a fissure opens, and out pops a new delight, a slice of human behavior that exists, in cameo, for its own sake. It is not that the actor steps out of character in such moments but that he finds the fissure in the text that allows him to make his unique contribution: he self-creates the real ground of his character's ideality.

It is plain that the self-expressive mode cannot be contained in stylistic terms. It is our awareness of the artist in the actor. The rationale for positing such a mode of performance is that there ought to be a word, or a way of isolating, something as powerful as the pleasure we take when artistry becomes the object of our attention. In opera, dance, and mime the artist is almost constantly this object. In view of theatre's strong illusionary mission, the actor is less so: he comes in and out of focus as an artist; now we see the character, now the artist in a "moment of genius" or, conversely, the unshielded actor in a moment of flaw. But even in theatre there are degrees of artist-presence. We always recognize Olivier in Hamlet or Olivier behind the dark paint of Othello. But this is not what is meant by artist-presence; this is simply actor-presence. The distinction is roughly that between *doing* and *being*: when the artist in the actor comes forth, we are reacting to the actor's particular way of *doing* his role. Our awareness of the artist is likely to surface at certain "peaks" in a performance when the character given to the actor by the dramatist is endowed with its perfect personality. It is not that the personality is less perfect elsewhere, simply that a character of almost any kind, from Osric to Hamlet, contains countless openings for "solo variation." There is always a potential interstice in the text. A character, Diderot says, is an "ideal type." Within the range of a certain typology one can imagine Hamlet doing and being many things that are not written into his character. What a dramatic text offers the actor is an ideal portrait, an abstraction, that can be made real in a thousand ways.

Let us take two instances from theatre history that will dramatize the range of the actor's self-expressiveness. There are actors whose genius rests in the fact that they "play themselves." This is not entirely the metaphor it may seem. Kean was obviously such an actor, an idea that Sartre develops very wittily in his play about Kean. Another was Sarah

Bernhardt and I can think of no better way to document the self-ostentatious side of the self-expressive mode than to quote Arthur Symons' brilliant description of Bernhardt at work:

> The art of Sarah Bernhardt has always been a very conscious art, but it so spoke to us, once, that it was difficult to analyse it coldly. She was Phèdre or Marguerite Gautier, she was Adrienne Lecouvreur, Fédora, La Tosca, the actual woman, and she was also that other actual woman, Sarah Bernhardt. Two magics met and united, in the artist and the woman, each alone of its kind. There was an excitement in going to the theatre; one's pulses beat feverishly before the curtain had risen; there was almost a kind of obscure sensation of peril, such as one feels when the lioness leaps into the cage, on the other side of the bars. And the acting was like a passionate declaration, offered to some one unknown; it was as if the whole nervous force of the audience were sucked out of it and flung back, intensified, upon itself, as it encountered the single, insatiable, indomitable nervous force of the woman. And so, in its way, this very artificial acting seemed the mere instinctive, irresistible expression of a temperament; it mesmerised one, awakening the senses and sending the intelligence to sleep.
>
> (Symons 1927: 151)

Who could go to see *Phèdre* or *La Dame aux Camélias* and become lost in the illusion in the presence of this energy? "It is all sheer acting," Symons says. What is it, then, that Bernhardt *does* to the text? Where does she find its interstices?

> The first thing one notices in her acting, when one is free to watch it coolly, is the way in which she subordinates effects to effect. She has her crescendos, of course, and it is these which people are most apt to remember, but the extraordinary force of these crescendos comes from the smooth and level manner in which the main part of the speaking is done. She is not anxious to make points at every moment, to put all the possible emphasis into every separate phrase; I have heard her glide over really significant phrases which, taken by themselves, would seem to deserve more considera-tion, but which she has wisely subordinated to an overpowering effect of ensemble. Sarah Bernhardt's acting reminds me of a musical perform-ance.... [She] is always the actress as well as the part; when she is at her best, she is both equally, and our consciousness of the one does not disturb our possession by the other. When she is not at her best, we see only the actress, the incomparable craftswoman openly labouring at her work.
>
> (Symons 1927: 154–5)

On the other end of the same spectrum we find Eleanora Duse who, on occasion, played the same roles as Bernhardt in different theatres of the same city, and nightly she performed only the miracle of her own disappearance. Overall, as a stylist, Duse's acting would be best studied as an example of the third-personal, or representational mode of performance. But she had her moments, her crescendos, in which the disappearance was so complete that the artist reappeared on the other side of the "illusion" – that is to say, stunned the audience with the fidelity of the artifice. Shaw relates such a moment in her performance of Magda in Suderman's *Home*. In the third act Magda must face the unexpected arrival of the father of her child in her own father's living room. It is a moment of extreme tension and she (Magda, the character) gets through it "pretty well," Shaw says, but just when her composure seems to be returning and she seems safely over the embarrassment and shock,

> a terrible thing happened to her. She began to blush; and in another moment she was conscious of it, and the blush was slowly spreading and deepening until, after a few vain efforts to avert her face or to obstruct his view of it without seeming to do so, she gave up and hid the blush in her hands. After that feat of acting I did not need to be told why Duse does not paint an inch thick. I could detect no trick in it: it seemed to me a perfectly genuine effect of the dramatic imagination. In the third act of *La Dame aux Camélias*, where she produces a touching effect by throwing herself down, and presently rises with her face changed and flushed with weeping, the flush is secured by the preliminary plunge to a stooping attitude, imagination or no imagination; but Magda's blush did not admit of that explanation; and I must confess to an intense professional curiosity as to whether it always comes spontaneously.
>
> (Shaw 1931: xxiii, 162)

What occurs to one while reading these two reports of "great moments" in the theatre is the marvel of our sensitivity to that zone of behavior within which the act of acting takes place. To recognize the natural progress of a blush as a "feat of acting" one must be able to hold in mind two categories – that of the real and that of the imaginary – that are fused in a single phenomenon. How does one see it as art when the art consists precisely in making it real? Of course Shaw is hardly an average theatregoer, but surely he is describing something about Duse that brought audiences to the theatre to see her. In fact, here we have a direct window into "the end of playing": Duse does not fool us into taking her for Magda any more than Bernhardt, for the simple reason that a theatre is not a palace of illusion. Sartre puts it neatly: the actor "draws his pride in the fact that he would not be admired for 'being' the character so well unless everyone, starting precisely with himself, knew that he was not" (1976: 165–6). So we do see style at all times; it simply emerges more "beautifully" at certain times than others. Symons and Shaw were stunned by Bernhardt and Duse. They are both "great actresses" not because they draw us perceptually into the imaginary but because they present the real in nearly pure form, the fictions of Magda and Phèdre being a means to this end. It would be wrong, of course, to dismiss the imaginary element of performance, and it is true that both Symons and Shaw could easily have written about the characters being played by Bernhardt and Duse without reference to the means through which they were communicated. But, as it happens, they were describing the art in the actress and how it exists as the object of our attention: Duse quietly hides herself in the character; Bernhardt converts the character into "the expression of a temperament." In Duse's case the wonder is that the woman understood the character so well, and could force her soul so to her own conceit that she could become the woman she played without, so to speak, selling her soul in the process. In Bernhardt's case the wonder is that the woman could elevate artificiality ("sheer acting") to such an intense level that she herself devours the imaginary and "substitutes" herself (as Shaw says) for the character.

THE COLLABORATIVE MODE

I would prefer a less clumsy term than collaborative for the second personal mode of performance, but it suggests the main idea: to break down the distance between actor and audience and to give the spectator something more than a passive role in the theatre exchange. The invitation to collaborate varies, of course, from the implicit to the explicit, and from the token to the literal; the guiding characteristic is that the stage uses some form of the "you" address in its relation to the audience. One could think of this as a "we" voice in the sense that the audience joins the actors in the stage enterprise, but I prefer to retain the strict sense of "you" as the *spoken to* in the act of speech. In short, if "we" speaks to itself, it subdivides into "I" and "you." In general, this mode may be symbolized by the comic "aside" which presumes that the audience is complicitous in the setting of traps and deceits – or, to put it another way, the actor plays a character who lives in a world that includes the audience. For the most part, this is only a fictional assumption the play now and then indulges through certain characters (typically the clever servant), since it would be difficult for comedy to get anything done if it had to include the audience in all the developments. Besides, the actor who plays *to* the audience in the aside or the monologue is usually well within the play world, since the audience he addresses is only the idea of an audience. The audience actually has the status of a *confidant* character in neo-classical tragedy, unlike the *real* audience that modern participation theatre tries to involve quite literally in the play. But the comic aside, together with the conventional prologue and epilogue, suggests a generic liberty that most comedy takes with its audience. The current of this liberty is not simply reference to the audience, but the comic project itself: the production of laughter.

A useful way to discuss the collaborative mode of performance is to contrast the relation of comedy and tragedy, as polar opposites, to their audiences. We often say that comedy arouses laughter and tragedy tears. The fact is, it is melodrama that arouses tears: tragedy arouses silence. The point of the distinction is that tragedy is a non-collaborative form, as usually performed. Tragedy creates an empathic experience wherein we are dissolved in what could be called a magnificent loneliness, felt most deeply in the absolute stillness of the auditorium when tragic characters say such things as "Thou shalt come no more." What the audience shares in such moments, and in the play at large, is less important than what isolates each spectator vicariously in the experience. Each spectator may be feeling roughly the same thing, and the actors may know that the whole house is, as Hamlet says, "wonder-wounded," but it is a private thing, as metaphysical experience usually is, and the tragic play makes no non-representational provision for exploiting it. What tragedy tends to give us, at the end, is a surrogate audience of survivors on stage who act out the emotion occurring in the auditorium. A line such as Kent's "Break, heart; I prithee, break!" serves as a lightning rod that grounds our own emotional investment in the play.

Obviously it is wrong to say that tragedy does not openly acknowledge its audience. In its evolution out of the morality play Elizabethan tragedy never gave up its theatrical self-awareness. Characters such as Aaron, Edmund, and Iago talk easily to the pit, or at least to the convention of the pit. But it is notable that they are all villains and planners of deceit and that they have much in common with the clown in the tragic subplot. In fact, the only characters in tragedy who "work" with the audience seem to be clowns and villains. This practice, moreover, is not restricted to Elizabethan drama. Humor and treachery seem to gravitate naturally toward the footlights – humor because it is incomplete without the audience and treachery because it is not necessary to waste good play time motivating it if the villain can have the audience's blessing. The Elizabethan villain, like his descendant the nineteenth-century landlord villain, is what Kenneth Burke calls the playwright's playwright. He seems to say to us, "Pretend I'm just plain evil. If I am not interesting myself, I will be the cause of your interest in the others." Apart from Shakespeare's master-villains, who could hardly be called uninteresting, it is hard to feel anything for characters who are on such easy terms with us because they do not seem to be undergoing anything but a play. They exist, one might say, in a limbo on the audience side of tragic seriousness. It would be unthinkable for a character such as Lear or Macbeth – or even Hamlet, who is brother to the clown – to peer familiarly into the pit because there is something in the abridgement of aesthetic distance that gives the lie to tragic character and pathos. A character who addresses the audience immediately takes on some of the audience's objectivity and superiority to the play's world. This is true even of modern narrator-protagonists such as Arthur Miller's Quentin and Williams's Tom Wingfield. They have survived tragedy, like Horatio, and as the line goes in *Lear*, it is not the worst as long as you are alive to say it was the worst.

In cathartic terms, laughter is the dialectical opposite of tragic silence. As everyone knows, it is hard to laugh in a half-empty theatre, and it is even harder to act the comedy that is supposed to release the laughter. In one of his letters to B, Kierkegaard asks his friend, "Answer me honestly . . .: do you ever really laugh when you are alone?" He concludes that you have to be "a little more than queer" if you do (1959: Vol. II, 331–2). It follows that the genre that produces laughter for its living is the most social of all the dramatic forms, except possibly the masque, just as tragedy is the most non-social, at least from the standpoint of emotional logic. Tragedy, the early Lukács says, is "a science of death-moments, of conscious last moments when the soul has already given up the broad richness of existence and clings only to what it most deeply and intimately owns" (1974: 161). Comedy, one might add, is a science of life-moments, of assurance that the broad richness of existence is all that really matters and that death can always be deferred. I am not assigning the performance of all comedy to the collaborative mode but suggesting only that comedy, as an extension of its theme, encourages the rapprochement of art and audience in a way that tragedy, as an extension of its theme, does not. This social principle does not stop with comedy proper: comedy's nextdoor neighbors are realism and irony, and what energizes both irony and realism is the critique of social life that rests at the base of comedy. For example, I originally thought of the Brechtian actor as performing primarily in the self-expressive mode because he was, to a noticeable degree, *still* a performer standing just outside of his role. But this is not really self-expressiveness in the sense that the performance, the virtuosity, is the center of attention; this detachment, or coming forth, of the Brecht actor is a strategy for keeping the spectator on the objective wave-length in his "hearing" of the play. Moreover, the Brecht actor, as Paul Hernadi writes, "must no doubt identify with the author or the director at least as much as he identifies with 'himself,' the psychophysical substratum of the character he is playing" (1976: 133). In other words, if he remains a performer, he is a *company* performer. Obviously, the Brecht actor can find all sorts of self-expressive fissures in the Brecht text, but as an actor who has a distinctly non-representational relation to the audience, he works primarily in the collaborative mode.

By an obvious association, we might draw an analogy between the second-personal voice and the epic, which we would oppose to the first-personal (or self-expressive) lyric. Perhaps Frye's term *epos*, or a work of oral address, is more appropriate. But I am thinking of epic as the form in which the poet speaks to his countrymen about national matters. He usually uses the third-personal, or narrative, point of view ("Then Hector rose up and slew them all"), but implicit in the manner of the exchange is the familiarity and "sacredness" of the matter. The epic addresses an audience of the initiated, for there would be little point in an epic poet singing about the heroic feats of another nation. As a form we have adapted to the theatre, we would probably have to assign most epic acting (of, say, Shakespeare's Roses octology) to the third, or representational mode, along with tragedy. But Brecht's actor is peculiar in that he wants to speak to his countrymen about "national" matters they *should* hear about but, for the most part, *not emulate*. In other words, he wants to expel something from national character. So he speaks to them, as we have said, schizophrenically, with a self-criticism about what he is doing as a character. Hence he aligns the audience empathically with his critical self, not the self he is portraying. It is a strategy similar to that of the preacher who says, "I stand before you a sinner," the confession itself serving to "alienate" him from his sin. As Brecht uses it, this strategy is substantively ironic: it is a way of denouncing your sin in the act of performing it. But comedy is never far off in Brecht's world.

Is it possible to have theatre by speaking directly to the audience, bypassing the entire pretense of representation and self-expression? This is the assumption of Peter Handke's *Offending the Audience*. Ostensibly, this "play" denies that it belongs to any category of theatre performance. The four "speakers" are not actors; they act nothing, they do not speak to each other, and they do not speak for themselves, as characters ("Our speaking is our acting"). There is no plot, no scenery ("These boards don't signify a world. They are part of the world"). There is no lighting arrangement that isolates the speakers from the audience. Everything that typifies and nourishes theatre has been eliminated except the structure of the actor/audience relationship, and the content of the play is devoted to reversing even this vestige of theatre. In effect, the purpose of the play is not to offend the audience but to make the audience the hero, the event, and the topic.

Can this be called a play? The answer is: of course. The actors have not departed the stage to be replaced by "speakers." The actors are simply representing speakers who are denying they are actors. And there is scenery in the conspicuous absence of scenery. And there is lighting that is perfectly adequate to the purpose of shedding light on the master peripety of the play: the audience's "recognition" that it has, in old-fashioned tragic-comic terms, had the tables turned on it. In short, there is pretense all over the piece. If a Handke actor were to forget his lines he would be in the same pickle as the Brechtian or any other actor. And

Handke is wonderfully aware of all this. In fact, one of his speakers says, "this piece is classical," without spelling out just how classical it is.

The originality of the play lies in what we might call its "you-ness," or the particular level on which the rapprochement of audience and actor is effected. I doubt very much whether Rousseau would have appreciated Handke's project, but there is a passage in Derrida's essay on Rousseau that is as descriptive of what *Offending the Audience* is up to as it is of Rousseau's longing for a spectacle of "presence":

> But what is a stage which presents nothing to the sight? It is the place where the spectator, presenting himself as spectacle, will no longer be either seer [*voyant*] or voyeur, will efface within himself the difference between the actor and the spectator, the represented and the representer, the object seen and the seeing object. With that difference, an entire series of oppositions will deconstitute themselves one by one. Presence will be full, not as an object which is *present* to be seen, to give itself to intuition as an empirical unit or as an *eidos* holding itself *in front of* or *up against*; it will be full as the intimacy of a self-presence, as the consciousness or the sentiment of self-proximity, of self-sameness [*propriété*].
>
> (Derrida 1980: 306)

And, in fact, the you-ness turns out to be a kind of me-ness. The strange thing is that the speakers do not become intimate with the audience in *manner* but in *matter*. They always treat the audience as an assembled group but they increasingly refer to those aspects of individual privacy – blinking, breathing, swallowing, sitting, smelling, sweating – that are irresistible attention-getters because speech has become a kind of anatomical probe ("Why, how terribly self-conscious you are"). In other words, if someone says to you, "You've got food on your chin," the body instantly drops whatever else it is doing and deals with that problem. This is the most "offensive" part of the show, but as the speakers say, being offensive, in any context, is a good way to "tear down a wall."

The whole process of the play is a disgorging of theatre into the world. The play is a prologue, it tells us, to the rest of the audience's life:

> It is not the prologue to another piece but the prologue to what you did, what you are doing, and what you will do. You are the topic. This piece is the prologue to the topic. It is the prologue to your practices and customs. It is the prologue to your actions. It is the prologue to your inactivity. It is the prologue to your lying down, to your sitting, to your standing, to your walking. It is the prologue to the plays and to the seriousness of your life. It is also the prologue to your future visits to the theatre. It is also the prologue to all other prologues. This piece is world theatre.
>
> (Handke 1969: 28)[2]

The logic here is much like that of Brecht's theatre of alienation: to send the audience back to the world with a new awareness. But there is nothing political about Handke's program. What his play has attempted to do, as prologue, is to transfer the audience's normal attentiveness to the theatre event back upon itself, back into the world of pre- and post-theatrical life. It is not a program that is likely to work beyond the trip home, any more than Brecht's or any other socially revisionary program. But that is not what concerns us here. *Offending The Audience* carries the collaborative principle to an intricate extreme, and it is an excellent tool for opening up the nature of the theatre process and experience to students who have not thought much about the phenomenal relation of theatre to living or of play to audience. For Handke's play defines theatre as it dismantles it, and it creates theatre as it claims to devastate its premises. As Douglas Hofstadter might say, there is a "strange loopiness" about it. That is, as the speakers strip away one level of theatre after another, leaving the audience in this state of self-enlightenment, "we unexpectedly find ourselves right back where we started" – in the theatre (1980: 10). Handke, like Gödel in mathematics, is using theatre self-referentially, as an explanation of what it is and how it works. With the right performers – and certainly the right audience – it might do to one's emotions what the Epimenides paradox ("This sentence is false") does to the head.

THE REPRESENTATIONAL MODE

The general idea of the representational mode is implicit in much of what we have said about the others. In effect, the self-expressive and the collaborative modes of speaking and listening display theatre in its extraverted personality or what we might call its courtship plumage. In one case, the performer comes forth and astonishes us with the possibilities of virtuosity; in the other, theatre says to the spectator, "Why should we pretend that all this is an illusion. We are in this together. We are doing this for you." Perhaps the more persistent source of theatre's seductive power is the drama of its subject, or, to use Aristotle's term in a very loose sense, its *praxis*. Theatre's endless mission is to be "about" something, not about men but about their actions, wherein they are happy or unhappy. Theatre is, after all, representation, and all that I have said here by way of adjusting our perspective on the mimetic principle does not reduce its importance, even in the case of opera or the mime. One could argue that dance, in some of its modern forms, does not require a subject to-be-imitated: for example, a dance called "Variations on Sphericality." But the success of your argument would depend on how well you could prove that sphericality itself, as a pattern of organization the body submits itself to, was not a subject of representation.

Behind the representational mode of performance, and our perception of it, is the shared sense that we come to the theatre primarily to see a play, not a performance. Continuing my analogy of the self-expressive with the lyric and the collaborative with the epic, we might describe the representational as the *dramatic* key of theatrical presentation – the key of *he, she, it*, and *they* – in which we look in objectively on a "drama" with a beginning, middle, and end that is "occurring" before our eyes. All of the actor's artistic energies now seem to be bent toward "becoming" his character and, for the audience, they cease to be artistic energies and become the facts of his character's nature. It has nothing to do with credulity; the audience simply sees through the "sign language" of the art to the "signified" beyond. The play is not a text, classic or brand new, out of which theatre "magic" can be made; it is now an enactment of significant human experience. Even if the play is the most trivial comedy, it is something we can "disappear into" because it is *about* people (who are, now and then, both trivial and funny). So the virtuosity now lies in the power of the subject, the collaboration in the mutual agreement by actor and audience on the value and appropriateness of the subject to the community of men.

Before moving into the representational mode, I should emphasize that my treatment of these three modes as if they occurred *purely* is strictly a convenience of definition. It is precisely our ability to integrate them or to arrest one or another of them in our perceptual attention that lends the unique depth and texture to the theatre experience. Theatre is not simply an interesting fiction being performed; it is a *collaboration*, a set of mannerly assumptions about our being present at these other "two" things (this is why a rehearsal is not a performance). So there is no incompatibility among the modes: they co-exist continuously (at some level) on the same stage; one may "hear" them together or in succession, somewhat as one may choose to hear the oboe or the violin or the full orchestra. Perhaps some elaboration of the point is in order. Suppose a character speaks directly, collaboratively, to the audience (without, of course, stepping out of character): is the representational aspect of the moment diminished? Perhaps, but not necessarily. It is really a question of the *kind* of representation that has been established by the play (or by the production). One of the assumptions of "straight" realism, for example, is that there is no acknowledgement of the audience's presence because the play is dead serious about being real, and it would hardly have served the interests of a play such as *Awake and Sing* if Morris Carnovsky had played some of his lines to an audience that was not supposed to be there. But a "violation" of this principle, properly prepared, is not incompatible with all forms of realism, as we see in Tom Wingfield's "This play is memory" speech at the beginning of *The Glass Menagerie*. The purpose of the collaborative principle here, of course, was to embed the "drama" in the wider frame of Tom's reflective consciousness, no less realistic for being outside or beyond the action. In other words, when the collaborative mode is invoked for thematic purposes it is no more destructive to the stage illusion, even a highly realistic one, than iambic pentameter or song in opera. It is simply a means of adjusting the audience's *illusionary* nearness to the action.

As a way of widening the idea, let us look briefly at a symptomatic example from the theatre of Shakespeare. When Edmund collaboratively lets us in on his plan to undo his brother, we are still well within the illusionary world of *King Lear* which includes (for certain characters at least) access to an imaginary listener. We are, in fact, only one short step beyond soliloquy, in which the character tends to speak as much *about* himself as *to* himself. Hence the illusionary realness of Shakespeare's theatre, which offers actors such wonderful opportunities to "show themselves off," always contains a subtle collaborative element, or at least an option to address the audience. I suspect that the function of this option was not simply to allow the play to acknowledge its own fictionality but to keep one theatrical "eye" on the very palpable crowd ringing the stage. It is well to remember that realism, as we know it, is substantially a product of the indoor "evening" theatre, the ideal stage for treating the audience as an unsuspected voyeur rather than as an invited guest. But Shakespeare's stage had a built-in "PR" problem in the sense that its audience, drawn from a relatively wide social base, was very visible, very near (if not on) the stage, and probably very vocal. Part of it loved Termagant and Herod and part of it must have loved Viola and Cordelia. I am not suggesting there was a discipline problem, only a diplomatic one – in fact, one of the oldest problems in communication: how to suit the manner of speaking to the manner in which the listener listens. For such a case, the rule of thumb might be: the more sociable the audience the more sociability must somehow be built into "the act." No doubt this whole speaking relationship came about naturally and unproblematically (and could be attributed to many other influences); I am simply trying to illustrate how the collaborative element may be said to adjust the play to its social scene.

Given the emphasis on the subject matter in the representational mode, our problem becomes one of leaving the actor *per se* and looking more closely at how subjects get into the theatre and how they behave once they are there. Before doing so, however, it must be stressed that the representational mode of performance does not imply a "realistic" style of acting, singing, dancing, or production. Or, to put it accurately, what we call realism is no closer to reality than many forms of representation we would call stylized. It is hard to believe the anonymous biographer of Aeschylus when he says that the chorus of *The Eumenides* "so terrified the crowd that children died and women suffered miscarriage" (in Nagler

1952: 5). What we do learn from the reference, however, is the basic fact beneath all representation: the "suspension of disbelief" does not depend in the least on what we would today call a photographic likeness of the image to reality. It depends only on the power of the image to serve as a channel for what of reality is of immediate interest to the audience. In effect, this brings us to the study of conventions, and it might occupy an entire book. Here I want only to illustrate briefly how *the subject* of the representation "comes forth" and commands our interest. The fact is, most theatre, in Roland Barthes' term, "prattles"; that is, it drifts on the current of fashion, content with predigested food, with "what the public wants." This is not in any sense an indictment of theatre (the same could be said of any art), but an acknowledgement of one of its several responsibilities. But it is self-evident that any image – even a prattling one – has a life cycle we might characterize as a movement from innovation to convention to cliché, often with a final stage of self-parody. The new image explodes with life and ends up struggling for life, wearing out. Again, the simple fate of all art images is the curse of familiarity. "After we see an object several times," Victor Shklovsky says, "we begin to recognize it. The object is in front of us and we know about it, but we do not see it" (1965: 13). Thus all images gravitate toward invisibility. To become accustomed to something means that one no longer sees it as "self-given."

The innovative stage of an image is characterized by enthusiastic over-statement. The new image, like new fashions, "goes too far." This is not a fault but a characteristic of enthusiasm and discovery, though, techni-cally, it is observable as such only retrospectively, from the standpoint of later refinement. For example, in O'Neill's early plays the discovery of "psychology" led to what we now perceive as embarrassing excesses in unrealistic devices (the long asides of *Strange Interlude*, over-explicit self-psychoanalysis) or to over-realism (the use of regional dialect and street slang, long drunk scenes). Many of these same enthusiasms had already become refined in continental realism, but images tend to be reborn *ad ovum* for new audiences. To take another image, virtually at its source, one can imagine how in the early 1890s London audiences who had just seen Ibsen's daring *Hedda Gabler* or *A Doll's House*, or had read Hardy's scandalous *Tess of the d'Urbervilles*, would have reacted to a "big scene" such as Paula Tanqueray's exit from Pinero's play. What probably interested the audience most is her closing speech, which is unfortunately too long to quote. But it may be summarized as a young wife's prophetic vision of the day when age will have taken her beauty and she will be seen by her husband "under a queer, fantastic light at night or in the glare of the morning." This is the last we hear from her, for, like Hedda and so many of her sisters in misery, she rushes off to her suicide. If the speech does not provide a motive (she has more immediate ones), it dramatizes graphically the "physical revulsion" that might make suicide a reasonable option. For flavor, here is a sample of what is in store for her in a few short years:

> A worn-out creature – broken up, very likely, some time before I ought to be – my hair bright, my eyes dull, my body too thin or too stout, my cheeks raddled and ruddled – a ghost, a wreck, a caricature, a candle that gutters, call such an end what you like!

She may even, she says earlier, "drift the way of the others" and resort to cosmetics "and those messes." This speech is probably a good example of what Shaw meant by the word "Pinerotic" insofar as it seems to be more interested in caressing its subject than in getting Mrs Tanqueray into a suicidal mood. Hearing the speech today, an audience familiar, for example, with Blanche DuBois' violent fear of the light bulb, would certainly be amused that a character so beside herself with anxiety would become such an eloquent raconteur of her own decay. But the image value of the speech in 1893 lies in the fact that it sounded a more or less unspoken concern that had not yet had its moment on the London stage. The lot of the ostracized woman had been a theme of realism since Dumas fils and Hebbel, but it was not until Ibsen and the new "sexual" novel that it took on such a private "psychological" complexion; and the important thing was to hold it up to the strong candlelight of the stage and turn it, ever so slowly (like those slow-motion blood baths in Peckinpah's early films) until its anatomy was fully displayed. The common principle of innovative imagery from Seneca's journeys through Hell to realism's journeys into the causal past to Absurdity's absurdities seems to be that if something is good, more of it is better. Little is left to the imagination because the eye and the ear have not yet had their fill.

The innovative obviously gives way quickly to the conventional phase of the image. Conventions, Harry Levin has said, "are seldom recognized until they have been nearly outgrown" (1950: 66). Another way to say this is that function disguises form: when content is interesting you are apt not to notice the container (for example, only when an actor becomes boring do you notice that he has habits). The conventional phase of an image is what we might term the semiotically strong phase. By semiotically strong I am referring to the inrush of memory on perception that allows the new image to begin its work of linking the stage to the world of meaning outside. As an image becomes phenomenally weaker it becomes (for a time) significatively stronger – which is to say that it no longer stands in its own way.

The semiotically vital stage of an image is marked by a drive that might be characterized in two ways. On one hand, the image strives to become more efficient or streamlined: this is one way in which it guards itself against the audience's growing familiarity. An image's relation to its audience, if we can speak in such terms, is like the conversation of married people: it needs to say less and less in order to communicate. But on the other hand, it faces the task of escaping its own streamlined stereotype. Hence its migration to new contents. This is the stage in which it "names" all of the things in society it can express: first adultery in the city, then adultery on the farm, then aboard ship, and so on. Once the theatre is armed with a paradigm, it will not be satisfied until it has tried out every available content. Ideally, the progress will be from surprise to surprise; that is, the next variation should contain an unexpected numerator that will display the denominator (adultery) in fresh accents.

There is no way to be more specific about the evolution of the image because images vary in their resistance or submissiveness to conventionalization, in their potential for combination and permutation, and in their durability. It is only a matter of the time it takes an image to fill up with emptiness. An image might have its season in the sun and die of old age (Charlotte Cushman and Sarah Bernhardt playing Hamlet), only to be resurrected in another age (Judith Anderson playing Hamlet). Or it may achieve "immortality," or such immortality as history permits. For example, in 1830 the actor playing Hugo's Hernani stood downstage with his back to the audience through most of the opening act. It does not matter whether this was the first instance of "the theatre of the back," though it does matter that the scene is France – in England it would have been less memorable because, as Voltaire once put it, an Englishman says what he will, a Frenchman what he can. In one gesture this production of *Hernani* articulated the root principle of naturalism long before its time. Implicit in "the back" is the whole concept of the "fourth-wall convention" and all the uses and abuses of the idea that the stage is a replica of the real world and not a palace of virtuosity from which the real world was kept at bay by firm rules, among them the rule that the actor played *to* his audience at all times. "The back," however, was apparently slow to catch on and only began to flourish in the later century with the Naturalists and Antoine. In other words, it needed the kind of play that would justify it. In fact, by the turn of the century it had passed from the status of a convention to that of an annoyance, a little like swearing in the plays of the 1960s. But the back obviously survived because it was not so much an image as *a way of being* on the stage. Today, we no longer perceive it as a convention but as normal stage posture. It is natural, not naturalistic. Today's naturalistic parallel might be frontal nudity – which began, we might recall, as a "back" view – now well on its way into the conventional stage and, barring a moral revolution, destined for permanent service.

It would perhaps be more convenient to talk in broad terms of image systems, or subjects, rather than in terms of individual images, since all images in the theatre occur in an "informational polyphony" (Barthes

1972: 261), or a dense context in which they interact and give life to each other. As a typical model we might take the evolution of villainy in English drama of the Shakespeare period. Everyone will recognize the phrase "Be ruled by me," which occurs regularly, especially in those scenes in which villains are meeting "in hugger-mugger" and one of them must be persuaded to dirty business by the other. But one notices that the reasons *why* someone should be ruled by someone else become more telegraphic as we progress through the period. That is, the phrase becomes a substitute, or shorthand, for any or all of the standard motives the audience knows from past plays (in somewhat the same way that the sign "Keep off the grass" is shorthand for a set of known motives pertaining to the sociology of landscaping). But this short-cutting in the display of persuasion is only a symptom of a gradual shift in the sensational emphasis of on-stage violence itself. If I may amend a proposition from Kenneth Burke: the growing fascination with the forms of violence leads to a corresponding atrophy in the motivational psychology behind violence.[3] On the whole, Elizabethan drama was very casual about motivating anything, but the spectacle of arousing and plotting revenge (or motivation) is much more central in early drama. For example, Hieronimo is plunged into grief by the murder of his son, is driven mad by grief, and kills sensationally in his madness late in the play. And so with Hamlet. Whereas, in later plays (for example Webster) motives are murky and it is usually sufficient to hate someone to have him dispatched. In sum, long simmering revenges such as Hamlet's or Othello's fell out of fashion, and attention shifted to the interesting things one could do to victims once revenge was set in motion. Now Elizabethan drama, from start to finish, is probably the bloodiest in theatre history. It is hard to top early plays such as *The Jew of Malta*, *The Tragedy of Hoffman*, *Selimus*, and *Titus Andronicus* for pure gore: but these plays are naive when compared to some of the death scenes of Tourneur, Webster, and Massinger. Here the theatrical shock falls not only on the number of deaths or on the brutality but on the ingenuity of the murderers, whose devices remind you of Rube Goldberg machines in their intricacy. In fact, some characters seem to have been admitted to the play only for the spectacle of their departure through someone's "witty cruelty," as one of Massinger's characters puts it. Massinger's best contribution to this spectacle is a play in which a Roman actor (who has been doomed by Caesar) is mercifully allowed to die "on the job" while acting out a death scene with Caesar.

The cliché stage of the image speaks for itself. The vein has, temporarily at least, run dry. The spectator sees not only through the signifier but also through the signified. For example, the benevolent characters of eighteenth-century sentimental drama eventually cease to remind one of benevolence or anything else; they are simply ciphers in a boring formula that no longer accounts for life satisfactorily. Hence Goldsmith's cry – *enough* of the virtues and distresses of private life! The more interesting stage is that of self-parody where the drama pokes fun at its own ossifications. Let us imagine a moment in history in which by some Borgesian fluke the theatre becomes enamored of plays with ticking clocks, running fountains, and child actors with pet dogs. This is, so to speak, the winning combination, and no play is really safe unless it contains at least one or two of these attractions. But in time this winning combination becomes a standard "formula" and things reach a crisis. Audiences begin seeing through everything: they see only the signs of a weary stage. The crisis might temporarily arrest itself in self-parody which injects into the formula the in-joke of its own immanent suicide. This is a highly collaborative moment in which stage and audience share an understanding about plays *as* plays. It is probably very brief and the *coup de grâce* may occur (homage to Chekhov) when an adult character in a new and innovative play enters and says to another adult character, "Let's sit down here and talk. Thank god there are no dogs or children about." And the audience cheers. This seems far-fetched until one remembers that this is how Euripides "finished off" poor Aeschylus in the recognition scene of his *Electra* and, more generally, the "matter of Troy" itself in plays such as *Helen* and *Orestes*.

To sum up: we should think of these pronominal modes as points of reference rather than as discrete phases in our perception of the actor. In other words, having separated them out we should probably allow them to fall back together into a perceptual synthesis, bearing in mind that even when they "upstage" each other they are as much cooperating as competing. The advantage of thinking about the actor in such terms is not that we learn anything new about him but that we have a better basis for seeing how his performance awakens our interest, not only as individuals "sitting at a play" but as members of a social species that "commissions" the actor to enact plays about our various concerns and addictions. There is probably no such thing as a "period" in which one mode dominates the others, though certainly in the era of the star system the actor's virtuosity – or at least his reputation for virtuosity – drew the audience to one kind of theatre more so than the subject of the play. And in the 1960s something in our culture gave rise to a rash of collaborative plays, or what we might call a return to Rousseau natural-ism in which the actor strived, with our consent, to make theatre once again an enterprise that included the audience. Finally, we might point to moments in theatre history when the play itself became the instrument through which we examined emerging veins of social behavior or revived old viens: the new social drama of the late nineteenth century, the American Agit-prop theatre, the various revivals of romantic and poetic drama, "realistic" plays about drug addiction, homosexuality, deranged children, and so on. But even such emphatic moments do not circumscribe theatre's various appeals at any particular time. And so it is with the appeal of the actor, who is probably as complex a phenomenon as the theatre he serves. The problem with the actor, in fact, is that he is *there*, before us, *all at once*, doing artificially what the rest of us do naturally – in one sense the primary medium of theatre, in another its end and purpose. My intention here is not to offer a complete phenomenology of his art but to treat it as an act of speech – a discourse, one might say, on *our* behavior – that can be broken down into the pronominal triad that is the basis of all speech. The actor acts out our way of referring to the things of the world. Or, translated into the terms of our perception of his art: he does this by becoming, in part, a thing himself, in part by doing a thing, and in part by sharing it – that is, allowing us briefly to live another life, peculiarly inserted into our own, which produces an entelechial completion, dimly like the effect of an out-of-body experience.

4

ON ACTING AND NOT-ACTING

Michael Kirby

To act means to feign, to simulate, to represent, to impersonate. As Happenings demonstrated, not all performing is acting. Although acting was sometimes used, the performers in Happenings generally tended to "be" nobody or nothing other than themselves; nor did they represent, or pretend to be in, a time or place different from that of the spectator. They walked, ran, said words, sang, washed dishes, swept, operated machines and stage devices, and so forth, but they did not feign or impersonate.

In most cases, acting and not-acting are relatively easy to recognize and identify. In a performance, we usually know when a person is acting and when not. But there is a scale or continuum of behavior involved, and the differences between acting and not-acting may be small. In such cases categorization may not be easy. Perhaps some would say it is unimportant, but, in fact, it is precisely these borderline cases that can provide insights into acting theory and the nature of the art.

Let us examine acting by tracing the acting/not-acting continuum from one extreme to the other. We will begin at the not-acting end of the scale, where the performer does nothing to feign, simulate, impersonate, and so forth, and move to the opposite position, where behavior of the type that defines acting appears in abundance. Of course, when we speak of "acting" we are referring not to any one style but to all styles. We are not concerned, for example, with the degree of "reality" but with what we can call, for now, the amount of acting.

NOT-ACTING   **ACTING**

There are numerous performances that do not use acting. Many, but by no means all, dance pieces would fit into this category. Several Far Eastern theatres make use of stage attendants such as the Kurombo and *kōken* of *kabuki*. These attendants move props into position and remove them, help with on-stage costume changes, and even serve tea to the actors. Their dress distinguishes them from the actors, and they are not included in the informational structure of the narrative. Even if the spectator ignores them as people, however, they are not invisible. They do not act, and yet they are part of the visual presentation.

As we will see when we get to that point on the continuum, "acting" is active – it refers to feigning, simulation, and so forth that is done by a performer. But representation, simulation, and other qualities that define acting may also be applied to the performer. The way in which a costume creates a "character" is one example.

Let us forsake performance for a moment and consider how the "costume continuum" functions in daily life. If a man wears cowboy boots on the street, as many people do, we do not identify him as a cowboy. If he also wears a wide, tooled-leather belt and even a western hat, we do not see this as a costume, even in a northern city. It is merely a choice of clothing. As more and more items of western clothing – a bandana, chaps, spurs, and so forth – are added, however, we reach the point at which we see either a cowboy or a person dressed as (impersonating) a cowboy. The exact point on the continuum at which this specific identification occurs depends on several factors, the most important of which is place or physical context, and it undoubtedly varies from person to person.

The effect of clothing on stage functions in exactly the same way, but it is more pronounced. A performer wearing only black leotards and western boots might easily be identified as a cowboy. This, of course, indicates the symbolic power of costume in performance. It is important, however, to notice the degree to which the external symbolization is supported and reinforced (or contradicted) by the performer's behavior. If the performer moves (acts) like a cowboy, the identification is made much more readily. If he is merely himself, the identification might not be made at all.

At this stage on our acting/not-acting continuum we are concerned with those performers who do not do anything to reinforce the information or identification. When the performers, like the stage attendants of *kabuki* and *nō*, are merely conveyed by their costumes themselves and not embedded, as it were, in matrices of pretended or represented character, situation, place, and time, they can be referred to as being "nonmatrixed." As we move toward acting from this extreme not-acting position on the continuum, we come to that condition in which the performer does not act and yet his or her costume represents something or someone. We could call this state a "symbolized matrix."

NOT-ACTING		**ACTING**
Nonmatrixed	Symbolized Matrix	
Performing		

In *Oedipus, a New Work*, by John Perreault, the "main performer," as Perreault refers to him rather than calling him an actor, limps. If we are aware of the title of the piece and of the story of Oedipus, we might assume that this performer represents Oedipus. He does not pretend to limp, however. A stick has been tied "to his right leg underneath his pants in such a way that he will be forced to limp." When the "main performer" operates a tape recorder, as he does frequently during the presentation, we do not think that this is a representation of Oedipus running a machine. It is a nonmatrixed performer doing something. The lighting of incense and the casting of a reading from the *I Ching* can be seen as a reference to the Delphic Oracle; the three lines of tape that the "main performer" places on the floor so that they converge in the center of the area can be seen as representing the place where, at the intersection of three roads, Oedipus killed his father, and the limp (and the sunglasses that the "main performer" wears throughout the piece) can be considered to stand for aspects of Oedipus. The performer, however, never behaves as if he were anyone other than himself. He never represents elements of character. He merely carries out certain actions.

In a symbolized matrix the referential elements are applied to but not acted by the performer. And just as western boots do not necessarily establish a cowboy, a limp may convey information without establishing a performer as Oedipus. When, as in *Oedipus, a New Work*, the character and place matrices are weak, intermittent, or nonexistent, we see a person, not an actor. As "received" references increase, however, it is difficult to say that the performer is not acting even though he or she is doing nothing that could be defined as acting. In a New York luncheonette before Christmas we might see "a man in a Santa Claus suit" drinking coffee; if exactly the same action were carried out on stage in a setting representing a rustic interior, we might see "Santa Claus drinking coffee in his home at the North Pole." When the matrices are strong, persistent, and reinforce each other, we see an actor, no matter how ordinary the behavior. This condition, the next step closer to true acting on our continuum, we may refer to as "received acting."

NOT-ACTING			ACTING
Nonmatrixed Performing	Symbolized Matrix	Received Acting	

Extras, who do nothing but walk and stand in costume, are seen as "actors." Anyone merely walking across a stage containing a realistic setting might come to represent a person in that place – and, perhaps, time – without doing anything we could distinguish as acting. There is the anecdote of the critic who headed backstage to congratulate a friend and could be seen by the audience as he passed outside the windows of the on-stage house; it was an opportune moment in the story, however, and he was accepted as part of the play.

Nor does the behavior in received acting necessarily need to be simple. Let us imagine a setting representing a bar. In one of the upstage booths, several men play cards throughout the act. Let us say that none of them has lines in the play; they do not react in any way to the characters in the story we are observing. These men do not act. They merely play cards. They may really win and lose money gambling. And yet we also see them as characters, however minor, in the story, and we say that they, too, are acting. We do not distinguish them from the other actors.

If we define acting as something that is done by, rather than something that is done for or to, a performer, we have not yet arrived at true acting on our scale. "Received actor" is only an honorary title. Although the performer seems to be acting, he or she actually is not. Nonmatrixed performing, symbolized matrix, and received acting are stages on the continuum from not-acting to acting. The amount of simulation, representation, impersonation, and so forth has increased as we have moved along the scale, but, so far, none of this was created by the performer in a special way we could designate as "acting."

Although acting in its most complete form offers no problem of definition, our task in constructing a continuum is to designate those transitional areas in which acting begins. What are the simplest characteristics that define acting?

NOT-ACTING			ACTING
Nonmatrixed Performing	Symbolized Matrix	Received Acting	Simple Acting

They may be either physical or emotional. If the performer does something to simulate, represent, impersonate, and so forth, he or she is acting. It does not matter what style is used or whether the action is part of a complete characterization or informational presentation. No emotion needs to be involved. The definition can depend solely on the character of what is done. (Value judgments, of course, are not involved. Acting is acting whether or not it is done "well" or accurately.) Thus a person who, as in the game of charades, pretends to put on a jacket that does not exist or feigns being ill is acting. Acting can be said to exist in the smallest and simplest action that involves pretense.

Acting also exists in emotional rather than strictly physical terms. Let us say, for example, that we are at a presentation by the Living Theatre of *Paradise Now*. It is that well-known section in which the performers, working individually, walk through the auditorium speaking directly to the spectators. "I'm not allowed to travel without a passport," they say. "I'm not allowed to smoke marijuana!" "I'm not allowed to take my clothes off!" They seem sincere, disturbed, and angry. Are they acting?

The performers are themselves; they are not portraying characters. They are in the theatre, not in some imaginary or represented place. What they say is certainly true. They are not allowed to travel – at least between certain countries – without a passport; the possession of marijuana is against the law. Probably we will all grant that the performers really believe what they are saying – that they really feel these rules and regulations are unjust. Yet they are acting. Acting exists only in their emotional presentation.

At times in real life we meet people who we feel are acting. This does not mean that they are lying, dishonest, living in an unreal world, or necessarily giving a false impression of their character and personality. It means that they seem to be aware of an audience – to be "on stage" – and that they react to this situation by energetically projecting ideas, emotions, and elements of their personality, underlining and theatricalizing it for the sake of the audience. That is what the performers in *Paradise Now* were doing. They were acting their own emotions and beliefs.

Let us phrase this problem in a slightly different way. Public speaking, whether it is extemporaneous or makes use of a script, may involve emotion, but it does not necessarily involve acting. Yet some speakers, while retaining their own characters and remaining sincere, seem to be acting. At what point does acting appear? At the point at which the emotions are "pushed" for the sake of the spectators. This does not mean that the speakers are false or do not believe what they are saying. It merely means that they are selecting and projecting an element of character – emotion – to the audience.

In other words, it does not matter whether an emotion is created to fit an acting situation or whether it is simply amplified. One principle of "method" acting – at least as it is taught in this country – is the use of whatever real feelings and emotions the actor has while playing the role. (Indeed, this became a joke; no matter what unusual or uncomfortable physical urges or psychological needs or problems the actor had, he or she was advised to "use" them.) It may be merely the use and projection of emotion that distinguishes acting from not-acting.

This is an important point. It indicates that acting involves a basic psychic or emotional component; although this component exists in all forms of acting to some degree (except, of course, received acting), it, in itself, is enough to distinguish acting from not-acting. Since this element of acting is mental, a performer may act without moving. This does not mean that, as has been mentioned previously, the motionless person "acts" in a passive and "received" way by having a character, a relationship, a place, and so on imposed on him by the information provided in the presentation. The motionless performer may convey certain attitudes and emotions that are acting even though no physical action is involved.

Further examples of rudimentary acting – as well as examples of not-acting – may be seen in the well-known "mirror" exercise in which two people stand facing each other while one copies or "reflects," like a mirror, the movements of the other. Although this is an exercise used in training actors, acting itself is not necessarily involved. The movements of the first person, and therefore those of the second, might not represent or pretend. Each might merely raise and lower the arms or turn their head. The movements could be completely abstract.

It is here, however, that the perceived relationship between the performer and what is being created can be seen to be crucial in the definition of acting. Even "abstract" movements may be personified and made into a character of sorts through the performer's attitude. If the actor seems to indicate "I am this thing" rather than merely "I am doing these movements," we accept him or her as the "thing": the performer is acting. But we do not accept the "mirror" as acting, even though that character is a "representation" of the first person. He lacks the psychic energy that would turn the abstraction into a personification. If an attitude of "I'm imitating you" is projected, however – if purposeful distortion or "editorializing" appears rather than the neutral attitude of exact copying – the mirror becomes an actor even though the original movements were abstract.

The same exercise may easily involve acting in a more obvious way. The first person, for example, may pretend to shave. The mirror, in copying these feigned actions, becomes an actor now in spite of taking a neutral attitude. (We could call the mirror a "received actor" because, like character and place in our earlier examples, the representation has been "put upon" that person without the inner creative attitude and energy necessary for true acting. The mirror's acting, like that of a marionette, is controlled from the outside.) If the originator in the mirror exercise put on a jacket, he or she would not necessarily be acting; if the originator or the mirror, not having a jacket, pretended to put one on, it would be acting, and so on.

As we have moved along the continuum from not-acting to acting, the amount of representation, personification, and so forth has increased. Now that we have arrived at true acting, we might say that it, too, varies in amount. Small amounts of acting – like those in the examples that have been given – would occupy that part of the scale closest to received acting, and we could move along the continuum to a hypothetical maximum amount of acting. Indeed, the only alternative would seem to be an on–off or all-or-nothing view in which all acting is theoretically (if not qual-itatively) equal and undifferentiated.

"Amount" is a difficult word to use in this case, however. Since, especially for Americans, it is easy to assume that more is better, any reference to amount might be taken to indicate relative value or worth. It would be better to speak of "simple" and "complex" acting with the hope that these terms can be accepted as objective and descriptive rather than evaluative. After all, "simple" and "complex" are terms that may be ascribed easily and without implied value judgment to other performance arts such as music and dance. A ballad is relatively simple compared to a symphony; the ordinary foxtrot is much less complex than the filmed dances of Fred Astaire. Let us apply the same analysis to acting, remembering that simple acting, such as in the mirror exercise, may be very good, whereas complex acting is not necessarily good and may, indeed, be quite bad.

Complex acting, then, would be the final condition on our acting/not-acting continuum. What do we mean by complex acting? In what ways can acting be simple or complex?

NOT-ACTING				ACTING
Nonmatrixed Performing	Symbolized Matrix	Received Acting	Simple Acting	Complex Acting

The simplest acting is that in which only one element or dimension of acting is used. Emotion, as we have seen, may be the only area in which pretense takes place. Or, as in the mirror exercise, only an action such as putting on a jacket may be simulated. Other acting exercises attempt to isolate various aspects of acting, and they are proof that behavior, which is complex, can be broken down into simple units.

The simple/complex scale also applies to each individual aspect of acting. Emotion may be generalized and unchanging, or it may be specific, modulating and changing frequently within a given period of time. Inexperienced actors, for example, often "play an attitude," "telling" or indicating the single emotion the spectator should have toward the scene or the character rather than the changing feelings of the character. An action may be performed in a simple or a complex way. In the game of charades, for example, we may only indicate that we are putting on a jacket. As long as our team understands what we are doing, the acting is successful. The same action becomes more complex as details such as the resistance of the material, the degree of fit, the weight of the jacket, and so on are acted.

(The word "indicate" that was just used in connection with charades has negative connotations in the technical vocabulary of American method acting. Practitioners of the method cannot accept an element of acting that exists in relative isolation and is not totally integrated by being "justified" and related to other elements. In other styles, however, isolated acting elements are perfectly acceptable and are used, among other things, to focus attention.)

Acting becomes complex as more and more elements are incorporated into the pretense. Let us say that the performer putting on a jacket is part of a scene: the performer may choose to act emotion (fear, let us say), physical characteristics (the person portrayed is old), place (there is a bright sun), and many other elements. Each of these could be performed in isolation, but when they are presented simultaneously or in close proximity to each other the acting becomes complex. In like manner, it is obvious that when speech is added to mime the resultant acting is more complex than the mime alone; the acting involved in a staged reading will, in all likelihood, be less complex than the acting in a fully staged production of the same script; and so forth.

In part, complexity is related to skill and technical ability. Some styles make use of a highly specialized, complex vocabulary. This does not contradict my earlier statement that the acting/not-acting continuum is independent of value judgments. It is not a question of whether a performer can do certain complex acting well but whether he or she can do it at all. Anyone can act; not everyone can act in a complex way.

Yet the analysis of acting according to simple/complex does not necessarily distinguish one style from another, although it could be used to compare styles of acting. Each style has a certain range when measured on a simple/complex scale, and in almost all performances the degree of complexity varies somewhat from moment to moment. It would be impossible to say, for example, that the realistic style of acting is necessarily more complex than the "Grotowski style" of expressionism. Realism, in its most complete and detailed form, would certainly be considered relatively complex. Yet there are many approaches to realism; some – such as those used in many films – ask very little of the actor and would be considered relatively simple. The film actor may do very little; the camera and the physical/informational context do the "acting." A nonrealistic style such as that developed by Jerzy Grotowski, however, can also be extremely complex. In *The Constant Prince*, the acting was very complex. The impression was not one of overacting but of many things taking place simultaneously in the work of a single actor. Frequently, actors will do nothing when another actor is speaking; they will act less so as to help focus the speaker. In Grotowski's staging, this did not happen. During the Prince's long monologues, the other performers did not decrease the complexity of their acting; their bodies were frequently involved in numerous, detailed, small-scale movements. In part, at least, this complexity may be explained by Grotowski's exercises that are designed to develop the ability of the actor to express different, and even contradictory, things with different parts of his body at the same time. Some companies, however, that use what may be recognized as Grotowski style act very simply.

Thus we have arrived at a scale that measures the amount or degree of representation, simulation, impersonation, and so forth in performance behavior. Although the polar states are acting and not-acting, we can follow a continuous increase in the degree of representation from nonmatrixed performing through symbolized matrix, received acting, and simple acting to complex acting.

Belief may exist in either the spectator or the performer, but it does not affect objective classification according to our acting/not-acting scale. Whether an actor feels what he or she is doing to be "real," or a spectator really "believes" what is seen, does not change the classification of the performance; it merely suggests another area or parameter.

Various types and styles of acting are, indeed, seen as more or less realistic, but, except as an indication of style, the word "reality" has little usefulness when applied to acting. From one point of view, all acting is, by definition, "unreal" because pretense, impersonation, and so forth are involved. From another point of view, all acting is real. Philosophically, a nō play is as real (if not as realistic) as a Chekhov production. Pretense and impersonation, even in those rare cases when they are not recognized as such, are as real as anything else.

Most plays, of course, even the most naturalistic ones, do not attempt to fool the observer into thinking that they are "real" – that they do not involve acting. Illusionary stagecraft and realistic acting do not intend or expect to be taken for real life any more than an illusionistic painting is intended to be mistaken for what it represents. In almost all performances, we see the "real" person and also that which the actor is representing or pretending. The actor is visible within the character.

To say that no performance can deceive a spectator would not be true, however. True and complete illusion is possible in theatre; acting may actually "lie," be believed, and be seen as not being acting at all. This happened in Norman Taffel's *Little Trips*.

Little Trips began with an enactment by two performers of the story of Cassandra, who was captured by the Greeks when Troy fell. After acting out several incidents – the entry of the Trojan Horse, the rape of Cassandra, among others – the spectators, who were standing around the performing area, were asked to join the actors, if they wished, and to play the same incidents, which would be repeated. At some point in the first or second repetition, while some spectators watched and others participated, the play began to break down. Perhaps one of the spectators protested against spitting in "Cassandra's" mouth, for this was one of the carefully selected images. Perhaps the performers began to argue, and the spectators took sides. At each performance, there was an argument; the play, as it had been described to the spectators in a preliminary introduction, never ended. But this is the way the presentation had been planned. By talking to and exploiting the feelings of the participating spectators, with whom they were able to talk more or less informally, the actors were often able to make them, unknowingly, part of the planned breakdown of the performance. The entire performance was designed to move from the context of art to that of life. Many people actually believed it; indeed, some never discovered that what they thought was a real argument that destroyed the performance had actually been acted.

(During *Little Trips* the two performers changed from a rather simple form of acting that could be more or less copied by participating members of the audience to a conversational style, the realism of which was, perhaps, heightened by the contrast. In terms of our previous discussion of acting, however, it is important to note that the effect of reality did not depend entirely on the acting. It is not only the behavior of the performers but the total performance experience that determines the spectator's response. What creates an illusion in one context will not necessarily do so in another, and in other frames of reference the same acting would have remained "acting.")

There is another type of performance in which the spectator does not recognize the acting for what it really is. An Argentine architect told of her experiences at an all-night religious ceremony on the northern coast of Brazil. At one point, costumed performers appeared who were thought to be dead ancestors. This caused panic among the believers because the doors were locked, and they thought if these ghost-beings touched them they, too, would die. Although belief of this kind obviously affects the quality of the experience, it does not mean that pretense, impersonation, and so forth were not involved in the performance. The appearance of the "dead" ancestors was acted. They knew they were still alive.

Even if the performers believed themselves to be dead, acting would have been involved. Belief would not change the objective fact that something or someone was being represented. This is not to say that belief cannot be an important aspect of acting in certain styles. A principle of the method that achieved the stature of a cliché was the attempt by the actors to believe what the character was doing. If they were successful, the audience would really believe, too. There is no question that this approach has frequently been successful. The attempt to believe undoubtedly attains or approaches with some certainty and predictability the goals that are sought, and it well may be the best approach to these particular problems. At the same time, it is just as clear that belief is not an acceptable criterion for an actor. Many times the actor, when faced with a certain lack of "belief" by the audience, protests that he or she really believed. The important point, however, is that when belief is present or is attained by a performer, acting itself does not disappear. The acting/not-acting scale measures pretense, impersonation, feigning, and so forth; it is independent of either the spectator's or the performer's belief.

Nor can sincerity or commitment be used to define acting. There is the story of the incredibly successful young actor who returns from Hollywood for a visit to his home town. "How do you do it?" his friends ask. "What's the secret?" "There's only one thing you need," the actor answers. "Sincerity." He pauses. "Once you learn how to fake that, you've got it made." As the story indicates, sincerity, too, may be acted. Indeed, the behavior of a person who pretends to be sincere and committed – or underlines theatrically these personality aspects in public presentation – may be seen as another example of simple acting. The story also implies that many people use the appearance of sincerity and commitment as a standard of evaluation. This remains a subjective judgment, however. There is no objective way to measure sincerity and commitment. Nor are these characteristics limited to actors and acting. Everyone – painters, writers, even doctors and teachers – may be sincere about their activities and committed to them. A nonmatrixed performer may be just as committed as someone involved in complex acting.

During the last ten or twelve years, theatre in the United States has undergone a more complete and radical change than in any other equivalent period in its history. At least this is true of the theatre considered as an art rather than as a craft, business or entertainment. Since, in the past, almost all of American theatre has been craft, business or entertainment, this may not be a very startling fact, but the changes have been striking and extensive. Every aspect of performance has been affected, including acting. In 1964, the *Drama Review* devoted two complete issues to Stanislavsky; now the "method" no longer has the absolute dominance it once did in this country, and certain alternative approaches are attracting great interest. Everyone now seems to realize that "acting" does not mean just one thing – the attempt to imitate life in a realistic and detailed fashion.

Thus eclecticism or diversity in the approaches to acting is one aspect of the recent change in American theatre. In terms of our theoretical acting/not-acting continuum, however, we can be more specific: there has, within the last ten years, been a shift toward the not-acting end of the scale. This means not only that more nonmatrixed performing has been used but also that, in a number of ways, acting has grown less complex. A brief review of recent developments will allow us to examine how this has come about while also providing additional examples of the various areas on the acting/not-acting scale.

The most important single factor in the recent changes in performance has been the so-called "Happening." Happenings, of course, are now a part of history. The term is best used in a historical and sociological way to refer to those works created as part of the international Happenings movement of the early and mid-1960s. (The first piece called a Happening was done in 1959, but other generically similar works preceded it, and the term is important only as a reference and as a popular catch-phrase.) The necessary point, however, is that works that, on completely formal grounds, could be called Happenings continue to be done and that almost all of the many innovations produced by Happenings have been applied to narrative, informational, acted theatre. Although I have no wish to perpetuate the name, those who think that Happenings were unimportant, or that the theatre form characterized by Happenings is no longer alive merely because the word is no longer used, do not understand the nature of the form. At any rate, the Happening can help to explain much about current developments in acting.

Under the direct influence of Happenings, among other things, every aspect of theatre in this country has changed: scripts have lost their importance and performances are created collectively; the physical relationship of audience and performance has been altered in many different ways and has been made an inherent part of the piece; audience participation has been investigated; "found" spaces rather than theatres have been used for performance and several different places employed sequentially for the same performance; there has been an increased emphasis on movement and on visual imagery (not to mention a commercialized use of nudity); and so forth. It would be difficult to find any avant-garde performance in this country [USA] that did not show the influence of Happenings in one way or another. But Happenings made little use of acting. How, then, could they have anything to do with the recent changes in acting? One way to see their influence is to examine the historical relationship between Happenings and the more prominent United States theatre groups. The history is not very old, but apparent fads are forgotten very quickly.

The last play that the Living Theatre produced before going into its self-imposed exile in Europe was *The Brig*. It was a realistic play with supposed documentary aspects, and it emphasized the "fourth wall" – a high wire-mesh fence closed off the proscenium opening, separating the spectators and the performers. When Le Living opened its next production in Paris in October 1964, the style and form, if not the sociopolitical nature of the content, had changed completely. *Mysteries and Smaller Pieces* was a Happening. (The group would later do another piece, *Paradise Now*, that could also have been called a Happening.)

Of course, *Mysteries* was not called a "Happening" by the Living Theatre, and few, especially in Europe, recognized it as such. (Claes

Oldenburg, who was the first one I knew to see it, identified it, but this might be expected. He had seen quite a few Happenings.) At any rate, the performance was without plot, story or narrative. It was divided into sequential scenes or compartments – one emphasized movement, another sound, another the smell of incense and so forth. Some even involved acting. The performance was apparently put together on rather short notice and was the work of the group rather than any one writer. (Almost all of the major Happenings were the product of one artist's imagination, but Happenings often were created by a group, each of whom contributed his specialty – music, design, poetry and so forth – and, among other things, the form gained the reputation of being group creations, thus inspiring those who were dissatisfied with working from an author's previously written script.) Certain images in *Mysteries and Smaller Pieces* came from *The Brig*, but much of it was taken from outside the group and was identical or similar to various Event and Happening images.

In one of the later sections of *Mysteries*, all of the members of the cast died. That is, they pretended to die. Death can be symbolized, but they chose to act it. No acting of this sort was taking place in the Happenings; the Living chose to use elements of acting within the Happening structure. But the acting did not involve character, place or situation – other than, perhaps, the conditions of the Artaudian plague that was the cause of death. The actors were only themselves "dying" in the aisles and on the stage of the theatre.

This simplification of acting is typical of much of the work in the new theatre. Indeed, the movement toward the nonmatrixed or "reality" end of our acting/not-acting continuum made some wonder when death itself would become real rather than "merely" acted in performance. In Happening-like presentations, Ralph Ortiz – and others before him – had decapitated live chickens. Peter Brook included the burning of a butterfly in *US*. (Live butterflies were seen flying out of a box, but there is some doubt whether the burned butterfly was indeed real. Cutting the head off a chicken makes death obvious; a butterfly can be "faked." "We cannot tell," reads the script of *US*, "if it is real or false.")

One of the scenes in *Mysteries and Smaller Pieces* was a sound-and-movement exercise taken from the Open Theatre. Two lines of performers face each other. A performer from one line moves toward the other line making a particular sound-and-movement combination. A person from the second line "takes" the movement and sound, changing them before passing them on to someone in the first line, and so forth. Like the mirror exercise that was discussed earlier, this use of an acting exercise as an actual performance is one way to simplify acting by concentrating on one or a limited number of elements. Exercises, often more integrated into the action than was this example, were frequently used in the new theatre for their performance qualities and expressiveness rather than for their training values.

This was probably the same exercise that opened the first public performance of the Open Theatre. These presentations, which began in December 1963 and continued into 1965, combined various exercises and short plays on the same bill. It would be foolish to claim a kinship with Happenings for these "variety" programs, but one wonders whether the similarity between the exercises and certain "game" and task-oriented work by, among others, the Judson Dance Theatre did not suggest the possibility of presenting the exercises, which were designed to be done privately, to the public.

Yet another company that showed exercises and made them part of a longer piece is the Performance Group. In its first public presentation, on a 1968 benefit program with other groups, it performed an "Opening Ceremony" composed of exercises adapted from Jerzy Grotowski with certain vocal additions. This "Ceremony" was in *Dionysus in 69* when it opened.

The effect of Happenings on Richard Schechner's work predated the Performance Group, however. The New Orleans Group, which he organized in late 1965, produced a large and spectacular Happening in 1966 and then adapted the various technical means and the audience/performance relationship of the Happening to an "environmental" production of Eugene Ionesco's *Victims of Duty* in 1967. The use of real names, personal anecdotal material, and so forth in *Dionysus in 69* can be seen as an attempt to move away from complex acting toward the nonmatrixed performing of Happenings.

Happenings somehow gained the reputation for exhibitionism; some certainly had "camp" aspects. It was probably their use of the untrained performer – the "found" person/actor – that had the most influence on the Theatre of the Ridiculous. John Vacarro, who performed in at least one of Robert Whitman's Happenings, has explained how important the experience was to him. The unabashedly home-made quality of many Happenings was also an inspiration to many people who did not have an inclination toward slickness, craft, and technique.

This is not to suggest that the general movement toward simplification of acting resulted entirely from the direct influence of Happenings. There have been many factors, all interdependent to some extent: Viola Spolin's improvisations; Grotowski's emphasis on confrontation, disarming, and the *via negativa*; an interest in developing ensembles; the early desire of the Open Theatre to find techniques that were applicable to the Theatre of the Absurd.

Yet influence can also be indirect. Happenings have contributed their share to the creation of a state of mind that values the concrete as opposed to the pretended or simulated and that does not require plots or stories. The most original playwright of recent years, Peter Handke, has worked in this area. Although his plays are quite different from most of the new theatre in this country [USA], many of them illustrate the same concern with simplification of acting.

Offending the Audience and *Self-Accusation* by Handke are unusual plays, if they can be called plays at all. Handke refers to them as "speak-ins" (*Sprechstücke*). They do not employ any matrices of place or character. They take place on plain, bare stages; the actors do not relate to or refer to imaginary locales. The performers are themselves; they are not dressed in any unusual way, nor do they portray characters. In fact, Handke has written dialogue for performers who do not necessarily have to act. The scripts require no pretense or emotion.

The performers speak. They have memorized what Handke has written, and they have rehearsed. But this does not, in itself, make a person an actor. People recite poems and speeches without acting. Musicians rehearse, are concerned with timing, respond to cues. None of these factors defines acting.

What the performers say are, almost entirely, direct statements that would be true no matter who was speaking them. In *Offending the Audience* they speak about the performance situation: "You are sitting in rows ... You are looking at us when we speak to you ... This is no mirage ... The possibilities of the theatre are not exploited here." In *Self-Accusation* the two "speakers," as Handke calls them rather than "actors," talk about themselves: "I came into the world ... I saw ... I said my name." There is no need to act in order to perform this material.

If *Self-Accusation* were played by a blind "speaker," however, the statement "I saw" would be untrue. Or, to take a somewhat less facetious example from the later passages that are no longer so universally applicable, certain people could not say, as if they believed it, the line "I came into the world afflicted with original sin" without feigning. But even a blind person could use the word "saw" metaphorically, and Handke does not suggest that each of the lines has to be given as if the speaker believed it. There are interpretations that would avoid any kind of acting during the performance.

These observations are based only on the script, and there is no script, including Handke's "speak-ins," that can prevent acting. Let us say that a performer creates an emotion. In *Offending the Audience*, for example, the performer pretends to be angry at the spectators when, actually, he is glad they are there. An element of acting has been added to the performance. The presentation would then be using what I have called simple acting. Under a certain director, each of the actors might even create a well-rounded characterization; the acting could become complex. Given the eagerness of actors to act, it is doubtful whether there has ever been a production of these scripts that did, in fact, avoid the use of acting.

Handke's *My Foot, My Tutor* makes use of simple acting by reducing the performer's means: the two characters do not talk, they wear neutral half-masks, and, for the most part, they perform ordinary movements (that sometimes seem extraordinary because they contradict expectancies and do not "fit" the context). The play does involve characters – a Warden and a Ward – but much of the action provokes the question, "What is acted, and what is real?" There is a cat in the play. A cat cannot be trained and does not act. In the performance, "The cat does what it does." Timing depends on the will of the actor, but the length of one scene depends on the length of time it actually takes water to boil in a tea kettle. The Ward eats an apple just as he would if he were not acting, "as if no one were watching." Yet he fails, for no reason, to slice a beet with a large and powerful beet-cutting machine: obviously he is only pretending.

These scripts by Peter Handke show, among other things, that the playwright, too, may use an awareness of the acting/not-acting continuum. Although the playwright's control – exerted only through the written word – over the complexity of acting is limited, he or she may still deal with the nature and degree of acting as an element in the script. And Handke's early work is another illustration of a general, but not universal, shift among contemporary theatre artists toward simple acting and the not-acting end of the scale.

It must be emphasized that the acting/not-acting scale is not intended to establish or suggest values. Objectively, all points on the scale are equally "good." It is only personal taste that prefers complex acting to simple acting or nonmatrixed performing to acting. The various degrees of representation and personification are "colors," so to speak, in the spectrum of human performance; artists may use whichever colors they prefer.

5

"JUST BE YOUR SELF"

Logocentrism and difference in performance theory

Philip Auslander

Among the terms Jacques Derrida employs in his deconstructive critique of Western philosophy, of what he calls the "metaphysics of presence," are *logocentrism* and *differance* (1978: 279–80). Logocentrism is "the orientation of philosophy toward an order of meaning – thought, truth, reason, logic, the Word – conceived as existing in itself, as foundation" (Culler 1982: 92).[1] Derrida, who denies the existence of such a foundation, points out that every mental or phenomenal event is a product of difference, is defined by its relation to what it is not rather than by its essence. If nothing can legitimately claim to possess a stable, autonomous identity, then there is nothing which can be invested with the authority of *logos*. In his discussions of language and linguistics, Derrida refers frequently to Saussure's double hypothesis that because the relationship between signifier and signified is arbitrary, the production of meaning derives from the interaction of linguistic units, not from additive arrangements of nuggets of meaning contained in words.[2] "The difference which establishes phonemes and lets them be heard remains in and of itself inaudible" (1982: 5); meaning is produced by the action of something which is not present, which exists only as difference. Derrida demonstrates that meaning is generated by a productive non-presence he calls *differance*, defined as "the playing movement that 'produces,' but does not precede, differences" (1982: 11). The purpose of signification produces its own significance; there is no transcendent *logos*, no order of meaning which grounds the activity of signification, no presence behind the sign lending it authority.

Derrida's critique has broad applications to performance theory. In discussion, we often treat acting as philosophers treat language – as a transparent medium which provides access to truth, *logos* or a grounding concept which functions as *logos* within a particular production.[3] Such grounding concepts are: the playwright's vision, the director's concept or, more interesting, the actor's self. We often praise acting by calling it "honest" or "self-revelatory," "truthful"; when we feel we have glimpsed some aspect of the actor's psyche through her performance, we applaud the actor for "taking risks," "exposing herself." One example must stand for many: Joseph Papp was recently quoted as saying: "With Brando in 'Streetcar' or Olivier in 'The Entertainer,' the actor exposed himself in such a way that it was a kind of revelation of soul" (quoted in Kakutani 1984: 1).

With what authority can such a statement be made? As semiotists who have studied acting have discovered, the performing actor is an opaque medium, an intertext, not a simple text to be read for "content." We arrive at our perception of a performance by implicitly comparing it with other interpretations of the same role (or with the way we feel the role should be played), or with our recollection of the same actor in other roles, or with our knowledge of the stylistic school to which the actor belongs, the actor's private life, etc.[4] If our perception of the actor's work derives from this play of differences, how can we claim to be able to read the presence of the actor's self back through that performance?

The problematic of self is, of course, central to performance theory. Theorists as diverse as Stanislavsky, Brecht and Grotowski all implicitly designate the actor's self as the *logos* of performance; all assume that the actor's self precedes and grounds her performance and that it is the presence of this self in performance that provides the audience with access to human truths. Their theories are aptly summarized by a sentence of Joseph Chaikin: "Acting is a demonstration of self with or without a disguise" (1980: 2). For Stanislavsky, the disguise must be based on the actor's own emotional experience; Brecht wants the disguise to be separable from the actor's own persona. Grotowski believes that the actor must use the disguise by her role to cut away the disguise imposed on her by socialization and expose the most basic levels of self. An examination of acting theory through the lens of deconstruction reveals that the self is not an autonomous foundation for acting, but is produced by the performance it supposedly grounds.

Stanislavsky's discourse on acting is inscribed firmly within logocentrism: he insists on the need for logic, coherence and unity – the "unbroken line" – in acting and invokes the authority of such theological concepts as soul and spirit in his writings (1936: 237). There is no question but that the presence of the actor's self as the basis of performance is for him the source of truth in acting: he defines good acting as acting based on the performer's own experience and emotions. He privileges the actor's self over his or her role by stating on the one hand that actor and character should fuse completely in performance (196) and, on the other, that an actor can never play anyone but herself, since she "can't expel [her] soul from [her] body and hire another to replace it" (188). The merging of actor and character thus results exclusively in a fresh presentation (or representation) of self.

This privileging of self is also manifest in another aspect of Stanislavsky's theory. He treats actor and character as autonomous entities, each with its own soul. Because it is impossible for the actor either to divest herself of her own soul or to penetrate fully into another's, she can only hope to find emotions of her own that are analogous (Stanislavsky's word) to the character's (166). The most important terms of that analogy, the choices that make one actor's interpretation of a role different from another's (an essential aspect of the appearance of self-revelation in acting) are determined by the difference between the actor's emotional repertoire and the character's. The uniqueness of the interpretation is a function of this difference, not of the actor's self-presence emanating from her performance.

The actor's self, the basis for an unbroken line of characterization, is itself fragmented. Stanislavsky divides the self into consciousness and the subconscious, identifying the latter as the source of truth, the seat of "emotions that are dearer to [the actor] than his everyday feelings" (166). As Timothy Wiles notes in his excellent study, *The Theater Event*, Stanislavsky "uncritically equates 'meaning' with psychological 'inner truth,' the imprecise term he uses throughout his work" (Wiles 1980: 20).[5] Paradoxically, although Stanislavskian performance is grounded in subconscious materials which cannot be perceived or known consciously (13), the (perceived) presence of those materials behind a performance is the only valid criterion for truth in acting. The paradox necessitates the adumbration of a psychotechnique designed to help the actor's conscious self "fool his own nature" (85), the subconscious, into providing inspiration. Stanislavsky posits the presence of self in performance as the highest good, but his psychology is based on the idea that true self-presence is impossible.

Stanislavskian acting can be seen as a form of "writing" in the expanded sense of that word which Derrida uses to describe psychic functions as well as the recording of language. In his reading of Freud, Derrida asserts that the making conscious of unconscious materials is a process of creation, not retrieval: "There is then no unconscious truth to be rediscovered by virtue of having been written elsewhere" (1978: 211). The process of recording unconscious materials itself creates those materials which exist only as traces in the unconscious, not as fully formed data. Thus, "Everything begins with reproduction" (211) and "we are written only as we write" (226). The unconscious is not a source or originary truth – like language, it is subject to the vagaries of mediation.

For the most part, Stanislavsky treats the subconscious as a repository of retrievable data, as in his famous metaphor of the house through which the actor searches for the tiny bead of a particular emotional memory (1936: 164). He acknowledges, however, that memory distorts, that the information we retrieve is not the same as the data we store, adding that distorted memories are of greater use to the actor than accurate ones because they are purified, universalized, and therefore, aesthetic in nature (163). Furthermore, he suggests that it is advisable at times for an actor consciously to alter her experiences prior to recording them in memory so as to make them "more interesting and suited to the theatre than the actual truth" (88). Despite his commitment to the ideal of self-presence, Stanislavsky seems to realize that the self does not exist independently of the processes by which it is revealed to itself and others, that the self which is supposedly exposed through the medium of acting is in fact produced by the mediation of psychotechnique between the conscious and the unconscious levels of the actor's psyche. Earlier I pointed out that the individuality of an actor's interpretation of a role derives from the difference between the actor's emotional repertoire and the character's. It now seems that the actor's emotional repertoire derives in turn from the process of acting itself which necessitates the distortion of emotion memory. The play of difference which produces a particular characterization is produced by the play of difference that defines the acting process. It is not surprising, then, that when Tortsov, Stanislavsky's alter ego in *An Actor Prepares*, is asked by a student whether the actor's subconscious "inspiration is of a secondary rather than a primary origin" (165), he is unable to answer.

Brecht[6] overturns Stanislavsky's central priority: he privileges the conscious mind over the subconscious because even that level of the psyche has been poisoned by social indoctrination: "it is almost impossible to extract the truth from the uncensored intuitions of any member of our class society even when a man is a genius" (quoted in Willett 1964: 94). Brecht wants the actor to "Demonstrate [her] knowledge ... Of human relations, of human behavior, of human capacities" (26) by not allowing herself to be "raped" (93) by the character but by keeping the character at some distance from herself and showing it to the audience. John Rouse indicates that Brecht engaged his actors in a tripartite rehearsal process. After an initial period of acquainting herself with her character and its motivations the actor goes on to a "Stanislavskian" phase of empathetic character work from the "inside." Finally, the actor takes a step back from the character and "examines it once again 'from outside, from the point of view of society'" (see Chapter 17) and incorporates this point of view into the "gest of showing" which underlies Brechtian performance (Willett 1964: 136, 203). Brecht privileges the actor over the character, but for a different reason than Stanislavsky: in order that the actor's commentary on the character be meaningful to the audience, the actor must be present as herself as well as in character and her own persona must carry greater authority than the role.

But what is this actorly persona? Roland Barthes suggests that "the [Brechtian] actor must present the very knowledge of the play's meaning ... The actor must prove ... that he guides meaning toward its ideality" (1977: 74–5). Timothy Wiles enlarges on this description by indicating that the Brechtian actor "feigns to inhabit a position of knowledge that is superior to the audience" (1980: 82); the actor "speaks from the position of a Marxist utopia in which the problems of the play that Brecht suggests *can* be solved *have been* solved" (80). To guide the play's meaning properly, the actor must pretend to possess knowledge which, historically, he or she cannot possess. The persona that the Brechtian actor presents alongside of the character that she portrays is a fictional creation.

What is the basis for this fictional persona? Barthes and Wiles both indicate that this persona is in service to the play's meaning, an observation which leads us by a circuitous route back to a basic form of logocentrism. Wiles suggests convincingly that the actor's pretended persona is an ironic stance adopted partly as a gesture of hostility toward the audience (82). In the *Short Organon*, Brecht himself proposes another view:

> Without opinions and objectives one can represent nothing at all. Without knowledge one can show nothing; how could one know what would be worth knowing? Unless the actor is satisfied to be a parrot or a monkey he must master our period's knowledge of human social life by himself joining in the war of the classes.
>
> (Brecht 1964b: 196)

Brecht implies that in order for the actor to possess the authority to comment on her character and the play from the proper sociological perspective the actor must be able to ground her commentary in personal social experience, the kind of experience that is as important for Brecht as private emotional experience is for Stanislavsky. Brecht's exhortation of the actor is not all that different in spirit from Tortsov's declaration to his students that "a real artist must lead a full, interesting, beautiful, varied, exacting and inspiring life" (Stanislavsky 1936: 181).

The dilemma of Brechtian performance is that for all of Brecht's emphasis on rationality and the undermining of theatrical illusion, the actor must convincingly portray something that she is not, the persona Barthes calls the "master of meaning" (1977: 75). Brecht's solution to this dilemma is to ground the actor's persona as actor in the actor's life experience as a social being. Unlike Stanislavsky, Brecht does not detail the technique by which the actor translates experience into performance (Rouse points out that Brechtian acting has more to do with an overall approach than with a specific methodology) but it is clear that the presence of the social self in performance is important to Brecht, who has as little use for the parrot-actor and the monkey-actor as Stanislavsky has for the representational actor. Although the ideological gap between Brecht and Stanislavsky is wide, the ethos behind their respective theories of acting is the same: performance can be truthful only if it invokes the presence of the actor's self. Brecht is more overtly aware than Stanislavsky of the nature of the theatre as 'writing'; he defines a number of concepts which expose the mechanics of theatrical signification, but he does not escape the seemingly inevitable grounding even of this exposure in presence.

Grotowski's privileging of self is more radical than either Stanislavsky's or Brecht's. He is concerned with the relation of the "mask of lies" we wear in everyday life to the "secret motor" behind the mask (1968: 46, 52). By confronting the everyday self with "its deep roots and hidden motives" (52), Grotowski hopes to produce revelation, "an excess of truth" (53). The actor uses the "role as if it were a surgeon's scalpel, to dissect himself . . . The important thing is to use the role as a trampoline, an instrument with which to study what is hidden behind our everyday mask – the innermost core of our personality – in order to sacrifice it, expose it" (37). This act of self-exposure and sacrifice is an invitation to the spectator to do the same thing on a less extreme level, to discover and confront the truth about herself (37). Grotowski privileges the self over the role in that the role is primarily a tool for self-exposure. Also, the self is not simply determined by the "secret motor" Grotowski wishes to uncover: "While retaining our private experiences, we can attempt to incarnate myth, putting on its ill-fitting skin to perceive the relativity of our problems, their connection to the 'roots,' and the relativity of the 'roots' in light of today's experience" (23). To some degree, Grotowski privileges the self over archetypal experience and truths to which the self is answerable but which are also answerable to the self. The Poor Theatre is not only of the self but for the self – its purpose is to serve as therapy for both actor and spectator (46).[7]

What is the language of self-revelation? Derrida writes that the self "is inscribed in language, is a 'function' of language, becomes a *speaking* subject only by making its speech conform to the system of the rules of language as a system of differences" (1982: 15). The self is inseparable from the language by which it expresses itself: it is a function of and does not precede that language. Grotowski proposes to eschew dependence on verbal language in the theatre, preferring "an elementary language of signs and sound – comprehensible beyond the semantic value of the word even to a person who does not understand the language in which the play is performed" (1968: 24). This language is made up of ideograms, physical expressions of basic psychic movements: "we attempt to eliminate the [actor's] organism's resistance to this psychic process. The result is freedom from the time-lapse between inner impulse and outer reaction in such a way that the impulse is already an outer reaction. Impulse and action are concurrent: the body vanishes, burns and the spectator sees only a series of visible impulses" (16). Grotowski suggests that a physical language could surmount the mediation of difference by becoming transparent and making psychic impulses directly visible to an audience. He grounds self-presence in physical presence, a seemingly irrefutably originary presence.

But even if the time-lapse which Grotowski describes is eliminated, it is not clear that the body transcends the play of difference that constitutes language. Derrida, through his reading of Artaud, points out that the body too is constituted by difference:

> Organization is articulation, the interlocking of functions or of members . . ., the labor and play of their differentiation. . . . The division of the body into organs, the difference interior to the flesh, opens the lock through which the body becomes absent from itself, passing itself off as, and taking itself for, the mind. . . . The organ welcomes the difference of the stranger into my body: it is always the organ of my ruin, and this truth is so original that neither the heart, the central organ of life, nor the sex, the first organ of life, can escape it.
>
> (Derrida 1978: 186)

Because it is organized, the body is not an organic, undifferentiated presence. The internal division of the body means that we are "several" to begin with, to paraphrase another passage from Derrida (1978: 226), and permits confusion between self and other, mind and body. The body is not more purely present to itself than is the mind and is therefore no more autonomous a foundation for communication than is verbal language. Grotowski would like to see the body vanish and burn in the communication of psychic impulses, but such a neat division between psyche and body is not possible if the body "passes itself off as, and takes itself for, the mind." Pure physical expression of and by the body is impossible for a body which is differentiated within itself and not present to itself. The mind cannot communicate the body without being defined by "the rules of language as a system of differences" and the body cannot express the mind without being defined by its own system of differences. Pure self-exposure is no more possible on a physical level than on a verbal level because of the mediation of difference.

It has not been my purpose to discredit the theories under discussion here. I want to indicate their dependence on logocentrism and certain concepts of self and presence. Stanislavsky states that the actor's self is the basis of performance, but his own working out of this idea leads him to posit that the self is produced by the process of acting. Brecht would have the actor partly withhold her presence from the character she plays in order to comment on it. To do so, however, the actor must endow another fictional persona with the authority of full presence, a theoretical movement which makes Brecht's performance theory subject to the same deconstructive critique of presence as Stanislavsky's. Grotowski proposes the actor's body as an absolute presence which banishes difference, but does not take into account the action of difference within the body. It is not a question of discarding these theories or of ironing out inconsistencies within them, but of recognizing that they are subject to the limits of the metaphysical assumptions on which they are based. If we are to use them, we must realize that, like metaphysics, they demand that we speak of acting in terms of presence, we are referring metaphorically to the creation of "self" from the play of difference which makes up theatrical discourse.

Derrida's philosophy is descriptive and analytical, not prescriptive or programmatic: deconstruction cannot exist independently of the thing it deconstructs. We cannot build a philosophy on *differance*, for to treat *differance* as originary is a contradiction in terms: "To say that *differance* is originary is simultaneously to erase the myth of a present origin" (1978: 203). Derrida acknowledges that *differance* is itself a manifest term for something which properly has no name and does not exist (1982: 26–7). He therefore resorts to such measures as coining some words and crossing out others to indicate, in the first case, the need to refer to conceptual non-entities and, in the second, the inescapable use of terms the validity of which he denies.

In a well known essay on Levi-Strauss, Derrida writes that there are two responses to the realization that all is difference, to "the lost or impossible presence of the absent origin." One is the "saddened, *negative*, nostalgic, guilty" response which "dreams of deciphering a truth or an origin which escapes play and the order of the sign" (1978: 292). It seems to me that most performance theory falls into this category. Having lost what we still suspect was the only valid theatre, the theatre of communal ritual, we either rhapsodize about theatres of other times and places or attempt to ground theatrical activity in versions of presence which bear the stamp of secularism, psychology or political analysis in the place of religion. The other response is what Derrida describes as the response "which is no longer turned toward the origin, affirms play and tries to pass beyond man and humanism, the name of man being the name of the being who . . . throughout his entire history, has dreamed of full presence, the reassuring foundation, the origin and the end of the play" (1978: 292). "Play is the disruption of presence" (292); an affirmation of the play which makes meaning at once possible and impossible is the alternative to the yearning for presence.

There is no need for a poetics of acting based on play: for Derrida, the play of difference is all there is; the question is whether or not we choose to acknowledge it. Acting, like any form of "writing," can express the two responses Derrida mentions: the actor can either hanker after presence or indulge in play which affirms the interdeterminacy of meaning. Performance equivalents for Derrida's practice of writing "under erasure," using language bound up in the metaphysics of presence and crossing it out, might simultaneously use the vocabularies of conventional acting methods and styles and undermine them. Brecht obviously moved in this direction, but although his theory allows for the creation of many, even contradictory meanings in a performance, the implication is that a resolution of these conflicts is possible and desirable since that would imply the resolution of social conflicts. Another interesting example is the practice of "transformational acting" pioneered by the Open Theatre. The "style Transformation" is an exercise in which "the theatrical or sociological style of a scene is transformed (restoration comedy to soap opera to Brechtian *lehrstücke* to Hollywood melodrama) in the course of an improvisation" (Pasolli 1972: 21). To some extent, performance in which the actor moves from style to style from role to role self-consciously dramatizes the construction of the actor's self from the language of theatre. In practice, however, these tactics, like Brecht's, produce polysemy, multiple meanings which imply the presence of an "horizon" of meaning not the open, ungrounded play of signification to which Derrida refers (Derrida 1981b: 350). The one example I can think of which might illustrate "post-Derridean" acting comes from Diderot's *Paradoxe sur le comédien* (c. 1773). Diderot describes a party stunt for which David Garrick would place his head between folding doors and run through a gamut of facial expressions associated with particular emotions. As Diderot realized, Garrick's dissociation of signifier and signified raised vital questions on the relation of the actor's self and her expressive means (1970: 168). Importantly, this example is an instance of literal play: Garrick's performance was not grounded in any meaning; it was a gratuitous demonstration of pure signification.

How far one could extend Garrick's game and still create satisfying performance is probably a matter of opinion. (It may be an historical issue, for our period forms part of the history of logocentrism and of the "metaphysics of presence.")

Perhaps the actor can deconstruct her own work only to a limited extent within that work and it is the audience which makes the fundamental decision of whether to search for presence and determined meaning in a performance or to revel in the play of ungrounded signification.[8] Deconstruction, fundamentally, is the perception of *differance*. Whether or not the person who inevitably records the play of difference in art can also point it out is an open question.

"I am afraid of falling into philosophy ..."

– Tortsov in *An Actor Prepares*

Figure 5.1 Ryszard Cieślak in *The Constant Prince* by Jerzy Grotowski (1965). Adapted from the Polish translation of the play by Calderon. Directed by Jerzy Grotowski. Designed by Jerzy Krygler. Polish Lab Theatre, Breslau.

PART II

(Re)Considering the body and training

6

INTRODUCTION

Phillip B. Zarrilli

Although the actor's body has always been "there" as the actor's sole means of expression in live performance, the degree to which the body and/ or a self-consciously constructed system of training toward performance is foregrounded, is variable since both are culturally, socio-economically, and historically specific. In the popular/public *commedia dell'arte* and Elizabethan theatres, actors did not "train" for the stage in the way that we "train" actors today. How the actors prepared to perform was less important than that they perform well. Similarly, many of today's stand-up comics get their "training" on the job.

Most self-conscious systems of preparation or training have evolved under some form of patronage which frees the actor from the necessity of responding to changeable popular tastes to concentrate on developing a particular body for a particular craft and style of acting – usually a craft and style which brings pleasure, merit, and/or respect to its wealthy and/or politically powerful patrons. For example, the Japanese *nō*, Indian Sanskrit drama, and Western opera were traditions of performance which required specialized training and "bodies" which flourished only after gaining court patronage.

In the Japanese *nō* theatre, there is no specific separate method of training toward performance; rather, when the student learns what Richard Schechner calls the "whole performance sequence" to be performed onstage (1985), he "trains" toward performance (Bethe and Brazell 1982–3, 1990). As is clear from Zeami's treatises on *nō* acting (1984) and Mark Nearman's commentaries on these traditionally secret family texts (1978, 1980, 1982–3), implicit in this process of practice are a set of cultural assumptions about the body, mind, performer's energy which are particular to Japan. In contrast, India's *Nāṭyaśāstra* tells us that as early as the Sanskrit theatre of which Bharata writes (2nd century BC to 2nd century AD), there was a special system for body preparation which included a complex set of preparatory exercises as well as full body massage (Ghosh 1961, 1967) – a paradigm of preparation practiced in Kerala's *kathakaḷi* dance-drama (Zarrilli 1984a) which originally received patronage from Kerala's landholding rulers. Implicit in this process of training is a set of assumptions about the body based on the indigenous medical system of Ayurveda (Zimmermann 1983, Zarrilli 1989a). And as theatre historian Joseph Roach has shown, the eighteenth century *castrati* performers gave their bodies over to a transformative regime of the body for performance (1989). As Roach explains, each of these modes of disciplining the body is an example of how "power touches people's lives through social and cultural practices more than through centralized state organizations or systems of belief. Power is diffused at the 'capillary' level in the micropolitics of daily life" (1989: 101).[1]

Our contemporary Euro-American notions of training are peculiar to the development of new forms of drama/performance (including film/ television), the modern repertory stage, the avant-garde and experimental theatre, as well as to institutional training within the college and university setting where students, often under the patronage of the state and/or parents, are "free" to pursue training in the arts. As is clear from this list, it is impossible to speak of actor training as if it were *one* thing, separate from the particular context within which training takes place, and without reference to the type of performance toward which one is preparing.

Similarly, as anthropologist John Blacking reminds us, "there is no such thing as *the* human body, there are many kinds of body, which are fashioned by the different environments and expectations that societies have of their members' bodies" (1985: 66). Particular modes of training and particular genres of performance demand specific bodies fashioned in a particular environment for a particular set of performative expectations. Therefore, acting, like any other technique of disciplining the body such as aerobics, weight training, contact improvisation, military drills, etc. might be considered "technologies" of the body in Foucault's sense, that is, practices through which "humans develop knowledge about themselves" (Foucault 1988: 18). As cultural theorist Richard Johnson asserts, "subjectivities are produced, not given, and are the objects of inquiry, not the premises or starting points" (1986: 44).[2] The techniques which constitute a particular technology of the body cannot be divorced from the discourses and assumptions which inform how that set of techniques is understood and/or represented. For example, for a devoutly Buddhist Japanese *nō* actor, the subjectivity produced through his practice and experience of *nō* acting assimilated through the tenets of Buddhist religio-philosophical thought, may lead toward aesthetic and personal enlightenment of the sort that Zeami discussed as the ultimate flowering of one's life-in-art; what Nearman calls a "psycho-spiritual process" (1982–3).

HISTORICAL (RE)CONSIDERATIONS OF TRAINING

Mel Gordon's (Chapter 7) historical and contextual discussion of Meyerhold's Biomechanics traces the development of this set of exercises as one part of the actor's training along with other popular early twentieth century training activities including fencing, boxing, Dalcroze eurhythmics, etc. Given the turn of the century predominance of a popular belief in the miracles of modern science and engineering, Gordon's discussion of Taylorism, reflexology, constructivism, and William James' theory of emotion, helps us to understand how any training system is informed by the political, intellectual, scientific, and ideological milieu in which that system of exercises and training develops.[3]

THE "NEUTRAL" STATE AS A PRIMARY METAPHOR

If scientific and mechanistic metaphors were dominant in the development of Meyerhold's vision of training and performance, the essays by Sklar (Chapter 8), Eldredge and Huston (Chapter 9), and Zarrilli (Chapter 14) focus on various strands of an alternative primary metaphor through which methods of actor training developed – training toward a state or condition of "neutrality." As Zarrilli explains at length, Jacques Copeau and his collaborators retired to the countryside in 1913 to develop a system of helping the actor to realize a state of motionlessness or simplicity in silence – what is usually called a "neutral" state today. Eldredge and Huston report how Copeau introduced his students to work with masks, thereby sowing the seeds for Etienne Decroux's development of Corporeal (Promethean) Mime discussed by Sklar, the neutral mask work developed by Jacques Lecoq, and A.C. Scott's use of Asian martial arts in actor training. Although Eldredge and Huston emphasize the paradox and problem with use of "neutral" as a primary metaphor – "the actor cannot be neutral; he can only hope to attain moments of neutral action" – neutral mask work, corporeal mime, and martial arts help the individual to discover what Copeau defined as that moment of motionlessness to and from which the actor moves.

Inspired by Copeau's vision, implicit in the use of the word "neutral" is the notion that the actor in training passes through a process of development and transformation which is artistic, but can also be interpreted as personal. As Sklar suggests, for Decroux, the personal could also very much be *the political*, that is, social transformation begins with disciplining the self.

The emphasis upon (artistic/personal) transformation often led, as with Copeau and Decroux, to the sequestering of companies, ensembles, and students in countryside retreat centers, restrictive enclaves, or conservatories where "intensive" work could be carried on and whose justification was the activity and process of training *per se*. During the 1960s Jerzy Grotowski and Eugenio Barba combined the notion of training/transformation with the scientific metaphor of the research laboratory as they founded centers where their ensembles of actors could train as well as conceive and worshop productions relatively unencumbered by the constraints of time. For Grotowski and Barba, this quest for transformative exercises, focused at first on developing "psychophysical techniques," that is, techniques which equally engaged the actor's mind (psycho) and body (physical) in a "total" intensive engagement in the moment. In Grotowski's most recent "para-theatrical" work (Lendra, Chapter 11) personal transformation has completely subsumed the artistic.

NON-WESTERN AND INTERCULTURAL (RE)CONSIDERATIONS

Throughout the twentieth century, the search for alternative paradigms and techniques of training through which to (re)consider theatrical structure and form, acting, the body, as well as training led many Western practitioners, if not at first to the use of Asian techniques *per se*, at least to an alternative vision prompted by encounters with non-Western, and in particular Asian performance traditions. Between the 1920s and 1960s Yeats (Quambar 1974), Meyerhold (Braun 1969), Claudel, Artaud (1958), Brecht (1964a), Grotowski (1968), Barba (1972; Barba and Savarese 1991), Christoffersen (1993), Watson (1993), Brook, and Schechner (1985) among many others were inspired by their encounters with non-Western performance to forge alternative dramatic forms, techniques, and/ or discourses of acting.[4] As James Brandon points out, the early encounters of Brecht and Artaud with Beijing opera and Balinese performance in Europe were fleeting, surface encounters which may have stimulated their own theatre practice and led to the crystallization of some of their concepts, but accomplished little in terms of helping Westerners to understand the complexities of these genres within their cultures of origin (1989: 32–3).[5] Grotowski, Barba, Brook, and Schechner all traveled extensively throughout Asia, and reformulated their approaches to production and training in part through these intercultural experiences. Most recently a new generation of practitioners and practitioner/scholars have not only visited Asia but also undertaken extensive training in specific performance or performance-related disciplines, gaining accomplishment in techniques and performing (Snow 1986, Brandon 1989).

Intercultural interaction has by no means been a one-way street from the West to non-Western cultures. Some of the foremost non-Western dramatists, directors, and actors, such as Wole Soyinka from Nigeria, Tadashi

Suzuki from Japan (Brandon 1978, 1990), Yoshi Oida from Japan (Oida 1992), I Wayan Lendra from Indonesia (Chapter 11), and Putu Wijaya from Indonesia (Rafferty 1989), have forged new dramatic forms and modes of performance which meld indigenous cultural concepts and techniques with what they self-consciously borrow from Western mythology, drama, theatrical theory, and/or techniques of performance. Brecht's theories in particular have helped to vitalize activist theatre throughout the third world (Rotimi 1990). Eugenio Barba describes this interaction in his reflection on "Eurasian Theatre:"

> In the meeting between East and West, seduction, imitation and exchange are reciprocal. We have often envied the Orientals their theatrical knowledge, which transmits the actor's living work of art from one generation to another; they have envied our theatre its capacity for confronting new themes, the way in which it keeps up with the times and its flexibility that allows for personal interpretations of traditional texts which often have the energy of a formal and ideological conquest.
>
> (Barba 1990: 32)

Experiencing an-"other" can lead to a profound (re)consideration of one's own paradigms and models of drama as well as performance practice; however, as Edward Said (1978) has shown, it can also lead to an equally profound and disturbing form of colonial appropriation of techniques and/ or misrepresentation of another culture. Although intercultural interaction is an inevitable part of what Arjun Appadurai and Carol Breckenridge identify as the "transnational flows of global culture" in which theatre participates today (1988), the nature, terms, and practice of intercultural interaction is open to debate.[6] Critic Daryl Chin expresses the double-edged prospect and problem:

> Interculturalism is one of the ways of bringing previously suppressed material into the artistic arena, by admitting into a general discourse other cultures, cultures which had previously been ignored or suppressed or unknown. But the general discourse (which we must define in terms of the dominant culture) must not deform other cultures by making them speak in the language of the dominant culture.
>
> (Chin 1991: 95)

For practitioners who would work with specific techniques from another culture, James Brandon pointedly states the case, "The problem is having superficial knowledge and applying Western standards to everything" (1989: 37). In this post-colonial era, "artistic freedom" can no longer be used as a naive narrative which "frees" the artist from responsibility, but neither can nor should exclusivity and/or censorship be willy-nilly employed on any kind or type of exchange.

Actor trainer Robert Benedetti's 1973 essay reflects the historical moment when images of non-Western, and especially Asian performance were becoming primary visions through which the state or condition of the performer was being re-defined. Although Benedetti never trained in a non-Western performance tradition, like both Brecht and Artaud he nevertheless saw in a demonstration performance by Chinese actors a vision of embodiment and of the "total" actor which he read as displaying the actor's "dynamic essence" – a moment of "stillness at the center" which he interprets as arising from the actor's total engagement in the moment (1973: 464). As Benedetti expresses it, this is a vision of the "whole performer" and not one who "artificially separate[s] skills of voice, body, and mind" (ibid). For Benedetti, Brecht, Barba, A.C. Scott, and many others the Asian performer *per se* has become a metaphor of the type of performance practice they wish their own actors to actualize in the performative moment.[7]

Chapters 10 and 11 focus on the closely related work of two of the most important figures to have used techniques and principles distilled from non-Western cultures in their work with actors – Eugenio Barba and Jerzy Grotowski. Ian Watson's essay (Chapter 10) details the melding of Asian and Western influences on performer training at Eugenio Barba's Odin Teatret in Holstebro, Denmark, as well as the evolution of this process and set of techniques over the years. Early in his work with the Odin Teatret, Eugenio Barba inherited from his work with Jerzy Grotowski a search for a foundational psychophysical process for the actor which took account of observations, insights, and techniques from non-Western performance traditions. Eventually Barba abandoned his own quest for a specific psychophysical training technique, leaving it to the Odin Teatret actors with whom he still works, to develop their own process as a state of constant "self-revelation," and thereby to ensure that their techniques would not be the imposition of some external technique (1972). In place of developing a specific training technique, Barba began a long-term collaborative commitment to an exploration of what he calls "Theatre Anthropology" by periodically holding "International School(s) of Theatre Anthropology" (ISTA) at which he gathers an interdisciplinary team of scholars, an intercultural group of professional performers, and a number of observers/participants which varies from school to school. To gain a fuller appreciation of Barba's reflections on the dynamics and principles of the actor's art from an intercultural perspective, the reader should explore Barba and Savarese's *A Dictionary of Theatre Anthropology* (1991), which is simultaneously a document of ISTA's research and workshops up to 1991, and a valuable, if eclectic, resource book for actors, scholars, and practitioners exploring the phenomenon of acting. Here Barba clearly defines his purpose:

> Theatre Anthropology is not concerned with those levels of organisation
> which make possible the application of the paradigms of cultural anthro-
> pology to theatre and dance ... Nor should Theatre Anthropology be
> confused with the anthropology of performance ... Theatre Anthropology
> is the study of the behaviour of the human being when it uses physical and
> mental presence in an organised performance situation and according to
> principles which are different from those used in daily life.
>
> (Barba and Savarese 1991: 5)

Collected and arranged alphabetically in the *Dictionary* are those cumulative "bits of good advice" (1991: 8) for the actor's "work on himself"
which focus on what Barba describes as the "biological" and "empirical"
bases of the actor's creative process – such phenomena and performative
circumstances as the actor's "anatomy," "balance," "dilation," "energy," or
"rhythm." Barba's focus is on "the principles of this extra-daily use of the
body and their application to the actor's and dancer's creative work"
(1991: 5). The *Dictionary* can be an invaluable, if sometimes problematic,
place to begin to explore the phenomenon of the creative art of the
performer beyond the narrow confines of a Euro-American male point of
view.[8] As Watson shows, Barba has applied the principles distilled from
this research to his own practical work and dramaturgy with the Odin
Teatret.

Jerzy Grotowski's theatrical and paratheatrical work has been widely
documented (Grotowski 1968; *TDR* 1991, 35, 1, *passim*). In the particular
exploration of Grotowski's intercultural paratheatrical "Objective Drama"
project, undertaken at the University of California at Irvine, which is
included here, Balinese performer I Wayan Lendra discusses his own
perception of the parallels he experienced between Grotowski's project
and his own training and experience of Balinese performance. Lendra is
among a new generation of accomplished performers trained in an
indigenous tradition of performance who has chosen to come to the West
to pursue an academic degree, and who has also chosen actively to explore
the process of performance between cultures. Lendra traces the similarities
in the state of being between his own experience of Balinese performance
and Grotowski's project – a state he describes as one of total "alertness."
In his work with Grotowski this state is realized through a set of exercises
known as "the Motions," which Lendra demonstrates. Lendra constructs
his description and observations between his experience of Balinese
performance in a traditional ritual/religious context, and the experience of
commitment and "hard work" required of participants in Grotowski's
work.

Grotowski's work in "Objective Drama", like his earlier paratheatrical
projects, has moved completely away from any concern with performance

as a fiction, to a (hypothetically) irreducible and nonrepresentational mode of experience. Grotowski's use of "objective" suggests the search for an absolute state beyond the Western dualistic separation of the fictive from the real – a movement from theatre to ritual/transformational process where he locates a "real" beyond the representational.[9]

If Grotowski and Barba alike eventually turned away from developing a specific discipline of training, internationally known contemporary Japanese director and actor trainer Tadashi Suzuki has developed a strict discipline practiced not only by his own company (Suzuki Company at Toga, SCOT) in a rural Japanese village but also by a number of actor training programs in the West. In his essay, "Culture Is the Body" (Chapter 12), Suzuki reflects upon the purpose, practice, and philosophy behind his method of training which emphasizes the actor's relationship to the ground through his feet – a subject which he explores in more depth in his book-length set of essays (1986). Suzuki calls his method a "grammar of the feet" since "consciousness of the body's communication with the ground leads to a greater awareness of all the physical junctions of the body." James Brandon explains how in Suzuki's rigorous training disciplines (*kunren*)

> actors are pushed to the ultimate in the interests of *dépaysement*: holding excrutiating physical positions, they sing unrelated songs. The actor is therefore forced into a powerful and deep self-encounter from which will come the ability to act the self, whatever the character. The disciplines themselves are derived mostly from *kabuki* and *nō* acting. Powerful stamping, forceful and rhythmic gestures, total concentration of energy in the pelvis (*koshi*), and a complete physicalization of acting are the major aims of training, and these concepts and specific physical postures and movements derive either directly, or indirectly, from Japanese traditional theatre forms.
>
> (Brandon 1990: 92; see also 1978)

Suzuki explained to Brandon the type of engagement he expects of the actor while doing the exercises:

> Any time an actor thinks he is merely exercising or training his muscles, he is cheating himself. These are *acting* disciplines. Every instant of every discipline, the actor must be expressing the emotion of some situation, according to his own bodily interpretation. That's why I don't call them exercises (*undo*) or physical fitness teachers don't go on the stage. We do.
>
> (Brandon 1978: 36)

For Suzuki's actors, training exists to "make the whole body *speak*, even when one keeps silent." For Suzuki "the body" becomes the primary metaphor for the optimal state of the actor in performance. For Suzuki "Culture *is* the body."

THE CULTURE OF THE BODY

In many non-Western cultures the body served as a vehicle for cultivating extra-ordinary religio-philosophical sensibilities whether through meditational, martial, ritual, or performance disciplines (Yuasa 1987). Consequently, traditional mythologies of the body adopted by Asian practitioners do not simply assume a "physical" body which is separate from the mental, emotional, cosmological, and philosophical modes of existence, but rather a "body" which instantiates all of the above. As East Asian scholar A.C. Scott explains:

> the body of the Asian actor is creative in the manner of a musical instrument and where the actor in the West uses his body to represent reality, the Asian actor's body becomes reality ... Only by conditioning the body in this way can it become a medium of response to every nuance of suggestion enabling the actor to immerse himself within the cosmic force which in Asian thinking defines the inner reality.
>
> (Scott 1975a: 211)

The essays of both Lendra and Suzuki implicitly assume this notion of the body as a medium through which the actor develops a hyperawareness and sensibility which is a *total* psychophysiological engagement of the bodymind/spirit in the activity. Kathy Foley's account of the performer's body and training in West Java (Chapter 13) makes explicit what is usually implicit for the West Javanese performer – the cosmological assumptions which inform the experience of the performer's body.

Kathy Foley is one among the recent generation of Euro-American practitioner/scholars to have immersed herself in training and performance in a non-Western culture. A gifted performer of Sundanese *wayang golek* (rod puppet theatre), Foley's essay is written between her own experience of practice in West Java, her position as teacher of acting in the United States, and her scholarly interest in a careful articulation of indigenous concepts of the body in performance. In terms similar to those used by Lendra to describe his experience in Bali, Foley relates how the Sundanese performer comes to "embody the whole cosmos." In describing the West Javanese performer's journey through training, Foley relates how training first "... creates distance between the performer and what is performed. Moving away from real life is the first step of training ..." Foley astutely points out how different this is from American method-based actor training:

The *topeng* and *wayang* theatre radically separates the performer (power) and the performed character (individual manifestation of power). That is why the training moves first away from the performer's personality only to reintegrate it later in the new system developed through continuous practice. It is interesting to note that the American actor trained in the Stanislavsky system usually begins by drawing closer to the self; early acting assignments are often characters close to the performer in age and type, certainly in gender, race, and species.

In West Java training begins with the "refined character whose slow, measured movement and melodious, centered voice are considered furthest from the ordinary 'self,'" but moves the performer through "multiple personae" each with its own quite different use of voice, energy, and space so that ultimately the actor inhabits "different 'bodies.'" Ultimately the performer is capable of playing a "repertory of beings ... that are emotionally different aspects of one's soul, the social order, the life cycle."

The final intercultural (re)consideration of the body and training is my own account (Chapter 14) of training in the Asian/Experimental Theatre Program of the University of Wisconsin–Madison, founded in 1963 by well known East Asian scholar and director, A.C. Scott. Out of his desire to actualize the vision of both Copeau and St Denis of the actor achieving a state of "expressive stillness which contains the embryo of the action to follow" (1993: 56), Scott began to use the Chinese martial art, *t'ai chi ch'uan*, to train American actors.[10] Scott became interested in learning *t'ai chi ch'uan* after witnessing performances by the best Chinese actors, including Mei Lan Fang:

> The sheer physical command, vibrant presence, yet consummate restraint of the Chinese actor or actress seemed to lay bare the very essence of the theatrical process and compelled consideration of the art of acting in a new light.
>
> Interest in Chinese acting led naturally to a deeper exploration of training methods and principles. From there it was a short step to learning *t'ai chi ch'uan*, both as a personal discipline and an essential guide to understanding some basic working principles of activities which have had an immense influence on stage techniques.
>
> (Scott 1993: 51)

Scott eventually began to use *t'ai chi ch'uan* in training American actors when faced with students "whose bad habits on the stage were reinforced by their confusion in perceiving that acting is not simply the duplication of life" (1993: 52). This essay outlines a way of training through the Asian martial arts, as well as a psychophysiological paradigm of the bodymind relationship and acting which draws upon the underlying principles and metaphors of the (Asian) bodies-in-practice, as well as the ideas of Copeau and Artaud.

BEYOND THE "NEUTRAL": THE INNER (PSYCHOPHYSIOLOGICAL) DYNAMISM OF CHARACTERIZATION AND ACTING

For those making use of the primary metaphor of the beginning state of the actor as "neutral," there is always the problem that students will misinterpret "neutral" to mean a state of relaxation rather than a state of dynamic readiness, that is, students may miss the *something more* that lies behind the apparent surface "neutrality" of a state of motionlessness – it is the "flame" that is "underneath the stewpot."[11] Throughout these essays are references to this "flame" burning beneath the surface, that is, to the hyperawareness of the body and its internal "energy" that is sometimes achieved. As most teachers of acting know, one cannot light this "flame" in a student – one can only enable a student to discover the flame, and then gain the accomplished ability to modulate its intensity in a manner that is appropriate to particular performative circumstances.

The "flame" as a sign of the actor's internal modulation of his or her energy in performance is particularly apt for theories and metaphors which focus or elaborate on acting as a psychophysiological process, and particularly the role that the breath/energy/life force plays in creating the dynamism of the performative moment.[12] As I explain in detail in my own essay, Asian disciplines of practice, including acting, are implicitly understood to be a psychophysiological means to effecting a fundamental transformation of the individual through the repetitious practices of exercises and/or forms (*kata*, Japanese). Mastery of embodied forms, when combined with the ability to fix and focus both the gaze and the mind, frees the practitioner/artist from "consciousness about" for entry into a state of "concentratedness." Each culture has its own particular version of the psychophysiology of exercise; what is shared is a common concern with cultivation through the body.

Such concerns are at the heart of traditional Asian systems of health and medicine, and therefore the psychophysiological dynamics of any disciplined use of the body implicitly assumed a special relationship between breath, energy, and the body in space and time. As I explain at length in Chapter 14, as the actor gradually cultivates the skills of modulation of the breath and internal energy, this ability is applied in the literally nuanced manipulation and use of one's body in performance to express a character's emotional states or conditions within the context of the drama.

The essays by Lendra, Foley, Suzuki, and me reflect non-Western assumptions about the material, psychophysiological basis of acting as a dynamic, "vibratory" process. Foley reports that Sundanese training prompts "a change of consciousness ... activated by hyperstimulation of the nervous system." It is an exercise of "changeability." Similarly, Lendra explains how the exercises he has practiced "help the body to generate innate physical power" through which he becomes hyperaware of his body, that is, "it absorbs what I see and hear. The surroundings become one with my body, and I feel as if my body is hollow and is being lifted. The more I see and hear, the more I sense my body." Lendra found that such hyperawareness was generated especially when performing "the Motions" through which he would "feel the vibration of my energy through my body and I feel the pulses of my heart in my feet." From this psychophysiological perspective, characterization and the expression of the dramatic states or conditions within which a character "lives" onstage are accomplished not through a psychological understanding of motivations, but through the dynamic psychophysiological process.

Regarding Suzuki's exercise, James Brandon observed how he noticed a "sense of great tension" in their performance, to which Suzuki responded:

> Suppression is fundamental to traditional Japanese theatre. What do I mean? Expression in Japanese theatre isn't natural or real. There is nothing natural about a *mie* or the leaping *roppo* exit in *kabuki*. They are extremely unnatural. So there is this almost unbearable tension in the actor, because he is using unnatural movements and voice to express natural emotions ... The secret of this kind of acting is instantaneous release of suppressed action, then suppression (that is, nonaction), release again, and so on ... I suppose you call it tension, but it is not muscular tension. It is psychological tension.
>
> (1978: 40)

Therefore, Suzuki's training develops "concentration of the body through controlling the breathing." Similarly, as I explain, training in traditional Asian martial arts develops the practitioner's intuitive ability to control the circulation of the breath/energy through the entire body.

Although the religious/cosmological dimensions of this "total" process of engagement are specific to non-Western traditions, a psychophysiologically based understanding of the actor's internal process has not been the sole province of the Asian actor. As E.T. Kirby suggests, melodramatic acting, and Delsarte's codified system were developed to allow maximal affect through the complete training of the actor's body precisely in order to allow him to display the effects of the virtuosic ability to modulate inner intensity through the body and voice (1972). As discussed at length in Chapter 14, Antonin Artaud, who was inspired by his interactions with esoteric non-Western religious traditions, envisioned the actor as a "crude empiricist" who, through control of the breath, would be able to place the breath in specific locations in the body in order to cause psychophysiological "vibrations" which would "increase the internal density and volume of his feeling" and "provoke ... a spontaneous reappearance of life," that is, of emotional states (Cole and Chinoy 1970).

Sklar (Chapter 8) describes how the actor trained in Decroux's Promethean mime has feet which stay "rooted to the ground while the upper body fights against the uplift of gravity to perform expressive attitudes," thus creating an internal dynamic tension between the full torso and the feet not unlike that which Tadashi Suzuki emphasizes in the development of a "grammar of the feet" through which his actors become rooted to the earth. Sklar describes the development of internal tensions "between adjacent body parts" – what Decroux called *"dynamo rythme"* which "combines duration and speed with degrees of muscular tension." Not surprisingly, Sklar uses an analogy from the playing of the violin to explain one of Decroux's *dynamo rythmes*, the *fondu* or "the sustain", where "like a note held on the violin, the *fondu* involves continual slow movement at constant velocity with a constant degree of muscular tension."

For Western actors who self-consciously create their art with a sense of full body engagement – whether Meyerhold's Biomechanics, Decroux's mime, a Copeau-inspired use of the mask or martial arts, Dario Fo (Chapter 18), Rachel Rosenthal (Chapter 22), or David Warrilow (Chapter 24) – an awareness of the body's internal psychophysiological dynamics of creating the particular is foregrounded whether that is applied to creating a psychologically "real" character or to some other set of actions.

SCIENCE, THE PSYCHOPHYSIOLOGICAL BASIS OF "EMOTIONAL" EXPRESSION, AND TRAINING THE BODY

The final essay in which the body and training are (re)considered by Bloch *et al.* (Chapter 15) represents a small but significant portion of scientific research on the nature of emotional expression and affect in the actor, and which, in its regard to the neuro- and psycho-physiological basis of the actor's art of emotional expression, focuses scientific attention on the interior dynamics of the actor's art discussed above.[13] Since Darwin and William James focused on the nature of emotional expression, studies of emotion became the province of ethologists, psychologists, and most recently neurophysiologists. Going considerably beyond the research of Paul Ekman (1984) on facial expression,[14] Bloch and her collaborators have attempted not only to study the neurophysiological dimensions of emotional expression but also to construct a psychophysiological system for training actors in emotional expression which includes, for each particular emotion to be inhabited and expressed: (1) a characteristic breathing pattern; (2) activation of a particular set of muscular patterns when assuming a complete posture of the body; and (3) activation of specific patterns of facial muscles.

In the seminal essay included here which summarizes the basic methods and findings of their long-term research and practice, Bloch and her associates clearly assert that "real-life" emotions and artistically created "emotional" expressions have a physiological correspondence, yet nevertheless are different. Taking their general model of the actor from Artaud, as an "athlete of the heart" (*athlète affectif*), they define the techniques as a psychophysiologically based set of "instrumental techniques for learning how to express [voluntarily] an emotion."[15] In contrast with the commonplace assumption that stage and everyday emotions are the same, Bloch and her associates insist that they are different. Unlike the experience of a "real-life" emotion, the actor is able to move freely from one emotional state to another.

Key to their technique is the priority given to a complete psychophysiological training for the actor which emphasizes the development of breath control, as well as control of the body's musculature, both of which allow the actor the freedom to modulate the intensity and location of the breath in the voluntary creation of emotional states – a view of the physiological basis of acting and emotional expression implicit in many of the earlier essays. Helpfully, they see the "set" of patterns that they have identified not as a restrictive set of patterns to be replicated but "as a tool, that is, as a technical support for ... acting behaviour so as not to depend almost exclusively on their own personal experience and/or limitations."

The description by Bloch and her associates of the psychophysiological process of breath control and muscular contractions basic to inducing each effector pattern is strikingly similar to that of the interior psychophysiological processes of some traditional Asian actors and to Artaud's ideas outlined above. Bloch's research establishes a scientific basis for understanding how the "flame" underneath the stewpot can be modulated in a neuro- and psycho-physiological way by the trained actor to produce dynamic affects both in the actor and presumably in an audience enculturated to a particular mode of emotional expression.

7

MEYERHOLD'S BIOMECHANICS

Mel Gordon

In my Biomechanics, I was able to determine altogether twelve or thirteen rules for the training of an actor. But when I polish it, I'll leave perhaps no more than eight.

(Vsevolod Meyerhold)

Biomechanics was a system of actor-training that Meyerhold devised shortly after the Revolution.[1] Although not always clearly understood, it received wide attention during the twenties and thirties owing to Meyerhold's unique position as the foremost revolutionary avant-garde director. Curiously, Meyerhold's own conceptions about Biomechanics, which were almost unchanged throughout his career, appeared to be both grandiose and seemingly modest. While maintaining that the mastery of Biomechanics afforded the actor all the essential skills necessary for scenic movement – skills that would take the ordinary actor nearly a life-time to learn, he relegated his own class in Biomechanics at the Meyerhold Workshop to a status equal to that of the other studies in body movement that were taught there, such as acrobatics, modern dance, or *eurhythmics*. Partly because of this apparently paradoxical attitude and partly because of the similar theoretical foundations of Meyerhold's training program and his early post-revolutionary systems of acting, Soviet and Western critics were frequently confused as to the theatrical function and application of Biomechanics.

THE SIXTEEN ETUDES IN THE MEYERHOLD STUDIO

Meyerhold's first work in schematic actor-training predates the Revolution and at least goes back to his course in stage movement at the Meyerhold Studio in St Petersburg in 1914. There, with Vladimir N. Soloviev, an expert on the *commedia dell'arte* and the Spanish theatre of the seventeenth century, Meyerhold developed a series of Sixteen Etudes and pantomimes, which he and Soloviev abstracted from various theatrical cultures. Purportedly, each of the sixteen exercises was designed to teach the students a number of particular principles of scenic movement, such as how to move in a circle, square, or triangle; how the alternation of the numbers of even and odd characters on stage affect the style of acting; the relationship between movement and the shape of acting platforms or proscenium boundaries; the traditional "antics appropriate to the theatre," involving the contrast between the space-and-time realities of the stage and life; the relationship between the metric basis of music and movement (including the idea of pauses in movement); working with stage properties; and generally the effects of acting on the spectator (the difference between large and small gestures). These exercises, some of which were performed publicly on 12 February, 2 March, and 29 March 1915, in conjunction with other plays and sketches, resemble the later Biomechanics in several ways.

Meyerhold, in these Sixteen Etudes, attempted to create a limited and precise system of exercises that contained all the fundamental expressive situations that an actor would encounter on the stage. They differed from Biomechanics in a purely functional manner – the Sixteen Etudes, mainly, pertained to Meyerhold's pre-revolutionary studio work, which was a synthesis of many traditional theatre conventions, while Biomechanics was designed as a more universal system for many kinds of theatre. No doubt the failure of Soloviev and Meyerhold to discover actual Elizabethan or *commedia* training techniques heavily influenced their decision to create such a system. Yet, even beyond their format, the Sixteen Etudes bear other resemblances to Biomechanics; for instance, in the circus buffonades or in the use of shouts and cries instead of words.

Although the only detailed documentation we have of the *études* are those few that were demonstrated in 1915 and described in Meyerhold's theatrical journal, *Love for Three Oranges* (Braun 1979: 149–51), the titles and brief generic descriptions themselves provide the reader with some information as to their possible use in actor training:

1 Two Baskets, or Who Got the Better of Whom. An *étude* composed of "antics appropriate to the theatre."

2 Two Jongleurs, an Old Woman with a Snake, and the Bloody Climax Under the Canopy. Pantomime composed by Meyerhold and Soloviev.

3 Ophelia. An *étude* of the mad scene from *Hamlet*.

4 The Story of the Page Who was Faithful to his Master and of Other Events Worthy of Presentation. An *étude* treated in the style of a sentimental, late seventeenth-century story (performed on the main stage; training in slow motion).

5 Harlequin, the Vendor of Bastinadoes. A pantomime in the style of the French harlequinade of 1850 ("antics appropriate to the theatre").

6 Fragment of a Chinese Play – "The Catwoman, the Bird, and the Snake." A pantomime by Meyerhold and Soloviev (use of Chinese

scenic conventions as might be interpreted by Carlo Gozzi; use of *mise en scène* to create illusion of more characters than actually appear).

7 The Two Esmeraldinas. A sketch from a *commedia* scenario.

8 Collin Maillard. An *étude* performed in profile in the manner of Lancret's paintings.

9 The Street Jongleurs. A pantomime in the style of the popular performances of the late eighteenth-century Venice (use of stage audience to guide emotions of real audience; acting on two levels; "antics appropriate to the theatre").

10 From Five Chairs to a Quadrille. An *étude* by Meyerhold and Soloviev in the manner of the 1840s.

11 The Baker and the Chimney Sweep. An *étude*.

12 The Loss of the Handbags.

13 The Cord.

14 Three of Them.

15 Three Oranges, the Astrological Telescope, or What One's Love for the Stage Masters May Lead To. A circus buffonade (use of trick properties; "antics appropriate to the theatre").

16 How They Carried Out Their Intentions.

Four years after the revolution, with the demise of the mass spectacle movement, an apparent decline in the general quality of the proletarian theatres became obvious. Meyerhold, who placed the utmost importance in the development of these amateur and semi-professional workers' troupes as both an educational and social tool for the masses and as a bulwark against the bourgeois academic theatres, was deeply dissatisfied with their clumsy and ineffectual attempts at acting. Lacking any formal training, many of the new mass actors simply mounted the stage and gracelessly declaimed speeches, very much in the manner of provincial melodrama protagonists without regard to the *mise en scène*, stage size, or audience. The irony lay, Meyerhold felt, in the fact that the theatre, whose social function was to educate and promote the socialist and scientific reconstruction of Russia, had retreated to archaic and basically rural forms, whereas other sectors of Soviet society were already going through a process of rapid collectivization and industrialization.

If the theatre were to survive and play a dynamic part in the future Soviet culture, Meyerhold thought, then it too would have to be transformed by the same factors that were guiding the rest of Soviet life. Thus, drawing on the scientific methodologies that were then current in Soviet industry and culture (Taylorism) and in Soviet psychology and education (reflexology), Meyerhold began to formulate his own scientific, and therefore indisputable, foundations for actor-training, "the laws of Biomechanics."

TAYLORISM

The work of Frederick Winslow Taylor (1856–1915), the American inventor who pioneered the study of *scientific management* at the turn of the century, became widely known throughout Europe in the early 1910s. In 1918, Lenin himself held up Taylor's principles of scientific management, or Taylorism, as a primary example of those achievements of capitalism, which, however brutal and exploitive in intent – the augmentation of work output and resulting profits – represented a grand and revolutionary approach to the entire work process worthy of Soviet emulation.

Investigating each work unit on a production line, Taylor came to the conclusion that the workers' physical movements were among the least efficient in the entire factory. The worker, while performing his prescribed task, would often engage in superfluous and awkward motions, causing a premature strain in his muscles and generally lowering his work output. Taylor, analyzing the execution of each task according to precise motions, which he timed and regulated within fractions of a second, sought to find the most efficient movements and gestures for each kind of work. Calling his study *motion economy*, Taylor had soon to take into account such nonlinear and unmechanical factors as work-rhythms, balance, muscular groupings, fatigue, and "rest minutes." Through trial and error, Taylor developed a system of *work cycles*, each involving a whole network of movements and pauses, allowing the worker to produce the greatest work output with the least amount of strain.

Although Taylor seemed to relish the variance and multiplicity of detail in his movement analyses, many of his American followers sought to delimit and abstract certain principles from his study of motion economy in order to make them more universal. (Frank and Lillian Gilbreth had already discovered in 1912 sixteen fundamental hand movements [*therbligs*] that were cross-occupational.) After Taylor's death in 1915, several such generalized tables began to appear. From these, seven fundamental Taylorist principles on the use of the human body in the work process evolved:

1 Smooth continuous curved motions of the hands are preferable to straight-line motions involving sudden and sharp changes in direction.
2 Both hands should begin and complete their actions simultaneously.
3 The two hands should never be idle at the same time, except during work pauses.
4 Motions of the arms should be made in opposite and symmetrical directions, and should be made simultaneously.
5 Hand and body motions should be confined to those muscles that require the least amount of exertion (usually the fingers, forearm, and shoulder).

6 Movements involving the single contraction of a positive muscle group are faster, easier, and more accurate than movements caused by sets of antagonist muscles.

7 Rhythmic movements are, generally, the most efficient.

A.K. Gastev (1881–1941), the foremost Soviet Taylorist, went even further than his American counterparts in the reduction of Taylor's principles. He maintained that once the worker attained perfect mastery over the handling of (a) the hammer, (b) the knife, and (c) the pick, he would be able to run any piece of machinery, no matter how complex. This basic idea – the single, outwardly simple, yet complex and difficult pedagogical device – was to have a special appeal for Meyerhold.

REFLEXOLOGY

Shortly before 1900, several schools of "objective psychology" arose independently in America and Russia. While differing in their findings and temperament, they shared similar sentiments toward the introspective trends in psychology, which they vigorously attacked. Rejecting the notion of the soul outright and minimizing the significance of the intangible unconscious, the "objectivists" looked for other ways of explaining behavior.

William James, the American psychologist (1842–1910), who was unable to exorcise his states of severe depression through his own mental faculties, began to investigate the actual visceral nature of emotion. Many of the folk maxims that prescribed seemingly irrational, secondary actions for the reduction of unpleasant emotional states "such as, 'Whistle when you pass a graveyard' or 'When you're so angry that you can't speak, just count to ten'" he surmised were nothing more than the application of effective reflex reactions. Experimenting on himself, James concluded that emotional consciousness and its transitory states were directly linked to the physical body; in fact, the body's automatic response to stimuli itself was the emotion, preceding the mental perception of the emotion. Using the dictum, "I saw the bear, I ran, I became frightened," James attempted to demonstrate the physiological basis of his theory: to trigger the sensation of fear, a person would only have to run – with his eyebrows raised and pupils dilated. Regardless of what the person was stimulated by or thinking, an automatic reflex signifying fear would be felt throughout his body. Surprisingly, James shied away from any formalized theory or system, believing that while certain patterns of muscular activity elicited certain emotional states, each of these states varied with the individual body and were, therefore, infinite and unclassifiable.

In Russia at this time, Vladimir Bekhterev (1857–1927) had already begun his research toward the discovery of the precise laws that govern human reflexive action and behavior, or reflexology. Like James and Pavlov, whose studies of conditioned reflexes in animals were linked to his own, Bekhterev rejected the old subjectivist psychology as intuitive and unscientific. Working with children and groups of criminals, he formulated his theory of "associated motor reflexes": all human behavior can be explained by the pattern of reflexes produced by the environment in the individual's nervous system. Once fully developed, Bekhterev maintained, the science of reflexology would eventually replace psychology since all human motivation and behavior could then not only be understood and predicted according to immutable laws of biology and sociology but also be instantly changed under laboratory conditions. Although Bekhterev himself was unable to provide a large body of supportive data, his theories were widely circulated among physiologists, psychologists, and educators after the Revolution.

CONSTRUCTIVISM AND THE "LAWS OF BIOMECHANICS"

Constructivism in the Soviet theatre, of which Meyerhold was a chief exponent, was a scientifically based movement that embraced many kinds of theatres that shared particular ideas about staging, design, and function from 1922 to 1926. Since Taylorism and reflexology formed part of the ideological cornerstones of both Constructivist acting and staging and Biomechanics, critics expected them to be closely alike. After having been told that the Taylorization of the theatre would make it possible to perform a four-hour play in one, they were quite bewildered to find few working gestures and many slow motion ones in the biomechanical *études* performed at the public exhibitions. One critic, Ippolit Sokolov, dismissed Meyerhold's Biomechanics as anti-Taylorist and rehashed circus clowning.

In Meyerhold's mechanistic vision of the theatre as factory and schoolroom – the use of the fastest and most efficient methods (Taylorism) to produce a predetermined audience reaction (reflexology) – we find a total emphasis on work output, that is, the manufacture of effects in the spectator, creating a desired state of mind. Allowing for the fact that there was a finite number of effects and states of mind, the Constructivist director/engineer was free to calibrate the theatrical components at his disposal (dramatic text, staging areas, scenery, properties, costuming, lighting, styles of acting, speech, music, tempo, etc.) in nearly inexhaustible combinations, toward a single goal. In this, the Constructivist director worked much like Taylor, who approached each task differently, seeking a unique strategy for the execution of economic and efficient movements.

On the other hand, Meyerhold, like Gastev, was searching for certain core movements that would train the new precision worker in the efficient execution of all of his prescribed tasks. Even the training system itself would have to be a model of economy: a concise, but comprehensive, program that would require a minimum amount of time to learn. (The number of *études* in Biomechanics varied from seven to more than twenty, generally staying at twelve or thirteen.) Just as Gastev had created a whole series of paradigmatic working movements from the perfect execution of a seemingly unsophisticated task such as swinging a pick, which was unlike any of the complex machinery Gastev's workers were being trained to operate, Meyerhold fashioned each of his biomechanical *études* to contain complex bundles of physical activity that superficially appeared to be simple and unrelated to the Constructivist acting styles. Yet, every *étude* was to be a fountainhead of lessons in the development of expressive movement, culminating in a system that had utilized every essential principle in scenic movement that an actor might encounter.

Taking stock of his extensive theatrical background, Meyerhold selected and refined the biomechanical *études* from a host of sources that he found most dynamic or "theatrical" – circus, music hall, boxing, gymnastics, military discipline, the Chinese theatre, and *kabuki*, as well as those theatrical cultures in his pre-revolutionary career from which he devised his Sixteen Etudes. Dividing each gesture of the *études* into exact movements, Meyerhold was able to apply both Taylorist principles of motion economy and James' emotion theory to the actor, causing him automatically to experience an entire gamut of emotions owing to a constantly changing arrangement of his musculature. This would also enable the actor to establish precisely the relationship between his physical appearance and his own inner nervous feelings. As Meyerhold told Harold Clurman in 1935, "Each exercise is a melodrama. Each movement gives the actor a sense of performing on the stage."

Other elements of Taylorism and reflexology were directly incorporated into Biomechanics. Meyerhold's conception of the *acting cycle* (Intention; Realization; and Reaction, Refusal, or Point of Repetition) was closely modeled after Taylor's *working cycles* and functioned similarly. Also Pavlov's conditioning experiments were employed with mainly sound stimuli to perfect the actor's state of "reflex excitability," his ability to realize an externally prescribed task with the minimum amount of forethought.

ROLE OF BIOMECHANICS

Except in its developmental stage, Meyerhold conceived of Biomechanics as having a lesser importance in his theatre than in almost any other. The goal of Biomechanics was to instruct the new actor in all the essentials of scenic movement, and Meyerhold had hoped that his own actors would go far beyond that. Biomechanics was created as a standardized, but minimal, program for the training of the revolutionary actor. For instance, in a Ukrainian Proletkult troupe, the actors might study medieval Ukrainian military drills, gymnastics, modern dance techniques, choral speech, diction, and Biomechanics. In an amateur workers' club theatre, where the actors might be severely restricted in time and training space, only machine movements, verse reading, and Biomechanics might be practiced. Bio-mechanics was to be the common training link and, however high in comparison with the bourgeois theatres, the lowest standard of actor-training in the proletarian and Constructivist theatres.

In Meyerhold's own workshop, besides Biomechanics, the actors were schooled by professionals in fencing, boxing, Dalcroze *eurhythmics*, classical ballet, floor gymnastics, modern dance, "tripod positioning," cabaret dance, juggling, diction, speech, music, and many other disciplines that Meyerhold thought would be useful to the actor for a particular production or for his general education, such as practice in *pre-acting*, theatrical history, economics, biology. Clearly, the greater amount of movement skills at the actor's disposal, the more efficiently he could carry out a variety of tasks. Still, because of the difficulty of training instructors, and Meyerhold's private feeling that it was not yet wholly perfected, Biomechanics, with few exceptions, remained the sole property of the Meyerhold Theatre.

BIOMECHANICS IN THE MEYERHOLD WORKSHOP

Occasionally assisted by Meyerhold, the biomechanic instructors Valeri Inkidjinov, Mikhail Korenev, and later Nikolai Kustov each designed their own daily one-hour sessions for every group of actors, which varied from eight to nearly thirty members. Typically, a single session consisted of the practice of supplementary biomechanical exercises, which were keyed to the physical execution of the *études*, and two biomechanical *études* separated by one fifteen-minute rest period.

The actors were asked to wear light uniforms – blue shirts and shorts for the women, and shirts and trousers for men. Many of the *études*, which were designed to teach the actor maximum movement in space through exact coordinates, necessitated that the actor be aware of certain lines and creases in his costume.

Most of the Biomechanics were performed to the accompaniment of piano music, which guided the actor in setting an emotional tempo that sometimes conflicted with the natural rhythmic organization of the *étude*. This technique was diametrically opposed to Boris Ferdinandov's use of the metronome in actor-training at his Experimental Heroic Theatre. The music itself, which varied from classical and romantic melodies to a kind of vaudevillian type, functioned differently in each *étude*, frequently correlating body rhythms to melody; at other times, notes and tempos were played against rests and breathing spans. The biomechanical exercises, unlike the *études* – since their purpose was a purely physical adjunct for the psycho/physical *études* – were performed without music.

The first movement the actors learned was the *dactyl* (not illustrated), a signaling exercise that signified the precise moment of initiation for most, and the completion for some, of the biomechanical *études*. There were two kinds of *dactyls*, a complete and a simple form. In the complete form:

(a) The actor, beginning with a complete relaxation of all muscles,

(b) suddenly claps his hands twice in a short upward motion which

(c) his body follows until he stands on the balls of his feet.

(d) Then, bending his knees,

(e) he immediately claps his hands twice in a violent and downward motion,

(f) throwing his arms back as they separate after the last clap.

(g) This abrupt movement is transferred to the actor's entire body in a forward and downward motion as the momentum of energy is conveyed to his calves and feet. The actor is now prepared to perform the *étude*.

The simple *dactyl* eliminated the steps (b) and (c).

The *dactyl* aided the actor in establishing an exact instant of concentration and provided him with a timing device to coordinate his actions with the other participants before the execution of the *étude*.

13 BIOMECHANICAL ETUDES

The following partial reconstruction of thirteen of Meyerhold's Biomechanics was derived from published and unpublished accounts by participants and observers of Meyerhold's acting workshops.

1 Shooting the Bow

(a) The actor executes two *dactyls*; the second *dactyl* is performed at a very fast tempo (*not illustrated*).

(b) The actor falls to the floor.

(c) He draws his legs and arms together.

(d) Rising on his right foot, he slowly draws up an imaginary bow.

(e) The actor advances with his left shoulder forward and his right foot back.

(f) Spotting an imaginary target, he transfers his weight from his right foot to his left and back to the right foot.

(g) Describing an arc with its center at his right shoulder, the actor's balance is shifted from the right leg to the left and back again to the right.

(h) He draws an imaginary arrow from his belt, or imaginary quiver.

(i) Very quickly he bends his upper torso toward the floor.

(j) Now, slowly the actor straightens up, holding his extended arms in a rigid position. The left arm is drawn out toward the front and the right arm is thrown back to a slightly lower level (*not illustrated*).

(k) He slowly loads the imaginary bow and draws it back.

(l) The actor aims.

(m) He fires with a shout.

(n) His body immediately contorts like a sprung bow into positions of "refusal."

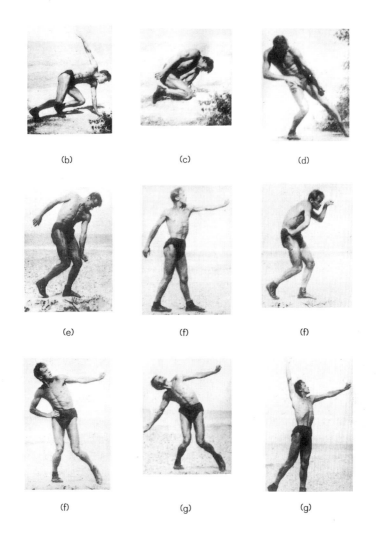

(b)   (c)   (d)

(e)   (f)   (f)

(f)   (g)   (g)

(g) (h) (i)

(k) (l) (m)

(n) (n) (n)

Objectives
Example of Acting Cycle: Intention, Realization, Refusal of the Action, Development of free, broad shoulder and arm movements. Use of horizontal extensions of the body for finding centers of gravity. Use of feet in establishing balance. Practice of falling and lifting gestures.

Comment
According to Alexei Gripich, this *étude* probably had its source in Meyerhold's pre-revolutionary actor-training work. It was also later utilized by Stanislavsky in his studio work.

Figure 7.1

Multiple sequence

Shooting the Bow.

2 Throwing the stone

(a) Actor executes a *dactyl*.

(b) He then leaps, turns to the right, and lands with his left foot forward. His knees are bent with his right hand in front, the left behind.

(c) The actor runs.

(d) He jumps again, landing on his left foot with his left shoulder forward.

(e) He straightens his body. Both arms hang loose and are perfectly symmetrical to each other.

(f) He rises on his toes, then drops to his right knee. His body is swayed backward and forward.

(g) Picking up an imaginary stone in his right hand, the actor rises, swings his right arm around in a wide arc to the left, across to the front and back, behind his body, where it hangs. His left shoulder is high, the right low with the right hand at knee level. The knees are slightly bent.

(h) He steps backwards.

(i) With the imaginary stone still grasped in his right hand behind the body, the actor begins to run. His left shoulder is raised.

(j) He stops with a slight jump, landing with left foot in front.

(k) After his right arm is swung across the chest, the left hand grips the wrist.

(l) The body weight is transferred to the right foot. Still clasped by the left hand, the right arm is swept back and is swung in an arc with its base at the shoulder. The actor releases his left hand, permitting the right arm to form a wide, complete circle.

(m) Arresting the circular movement, the right arm is held out in front while the actor searches for an imaginary target.

(n) He runs a few steps forward and jumps.

(o) Preparing the throw, he swings his right arm and leg back.

(p) He throws the imaginary stone, twisting his right side forward, left back.

(q) Kneeling on his right knee, the actor claps his hands, then cups his right ear as if listening for the result.

(r) (The imaginary mark is hit.) He points with his left arm and leans back with the right arm on the right hip.

(s) Rising, he executes a *dactyl*.

Objectives

Example of a complex Acting Cycle with multiple preparations, actions, reactions, and pauses. Development of free curved motions and balance. Use of arms and shoulders in establishing the center of gravity while in movement. Exercise in reflex excitability to sound stimulus (q).

Comment

Etude is performed in alternating tempos.

Note

This description is taken from André van Gyseghem's *Theatre in Soviet Russia*, 1943, the only published detailed account. Although the *étude* was a basic part of Biomechanics, no photographs were made available.

3 The Slap in the Face

(a) Two actors stand facing each other at a distance of three feet. Their feet are parallel with the toes firmly planted and slightly to the right. Standing on the balls of their feet, their heels are almost off the floor. Their heads are tilted forward with the shoulders raised. The knees and arms are bent.

(b) Both actors execute a *dactyl*.

(c) The first actor steps forward with his left foot, placing it directly in front of the right. It points to the right, perpendicular to the right foot.

Figure 7.2
The Slap in the Face (d).

Figure 7.3
The Slap in the Face (f).

He rotates his upper torso to face right. His face is directed toward his partner. The knees are bent with the weight forward on the left foot. Meanwhile, the partner has stepped forward on his left foot, which is placed six inches from the axis of his right foot. The partner's chest is on a 45° diagonal from his original position.

(d) Simultaneously, both actors lean backward, transferring their weight to their right feet. The first actor, with his right arm outstretched and hand open, shifts farther back until his left foot is almost off the floor.

(e) Moving his right arm in a wide circular path to the right side, the first actor twists his body to the right as his weight is transferred forward to the left foot, which is moved back. The partner also moves forward and to the center.

(f) The partner tilts his head to the right as first actor's upward-pointing hand slowly approaches.

(g) The first actor quickly throws his left hand to the lower right side of partner's face. He jerks down his right arm, catching his own right hand and creating a slapping sound.

(h) Sound signals a return to position (a). (*Etude* is repeated with partners exchanging roles.)

Objectives
Example of Acting Cycle: Preparation, Action, and Point of Repetition. Coordination with partner in changing action tempos. Use of feet and lower trunk movements to establish balance. Division of left and right sides of body. Development of reflex excitability to sound stimulus (h).

Comment
Etude performed at alternating tempos although never as slowly as "Shooting the Bow."

Figure 7.4
The Stab with the Dagger (e).

4 The Stab with the Dagger

(a) Two actors face each other at a distance of six feet. They execute a *dactyl*.

(b) His open hands behind his back, the first actor bends his legs and jumps up before his partner, who slightly recoils backwards.

(c) Landing on his right foot which is on a 45° angle to his partner, the actor clenches both hands.

(d) With his weight on his right foot, the first actor draws an imaginary dagger from an imaginary sheath held in his left fist, forming an arc which crosses his face at a 45° angle and ends to the right and over his head.

(e) Very slowly, he begins to plunge the dagger into the space occupied by the recoiling body of his partner. As the first actor initiates his stabbing motion, his weight is shifted to his left foot, and his upper left and center torso is forward. The partner, whose legs are well established with the left leg bent and evenly balanced at the foot base and the right foot tensed at the calf and inner area of foot, throws his head back and arcs until he has formed a half bridge, thrusting his arms downward. His shoulders are parallel on a horizontal plane.

(f) At the extreme point of contact between the partner and imaginary

dagger, the partner jerks up with a cry originating from the diaphragm.
(g) This signals the first actor quickly to withdraw his right arm and
body to the original position.

Objectives
Example of Acting Cycle. Coordination with partner. Example of automatic psycho/physical states caused by changes in equilibrium and
muscular tension (clenched fists, contraction of lower back muscles).
Development of strengthening lower trunk for center of balance. Development of reflex excitability from outside sound stimuli (f) + (g).

Comment
Etude performed in extremely alternating tempos.

5 Building the Pyramid
(a) Two actors stand at a distance of three feet facing each other. They
execute a *dactyl*.

(b) The partner bends his knees, with the left foot forward. He then
extends his right leg back and to the right, creating a stable platform
between his hip and left knee. The partner presents his left hand to the

Figure 7.5
Complex Pyramid used
in *Roar China* (1926).

first actor, who, taking it in his left, places his left foot on his partner's left lower thigh.

(c) The right hand of the first actor is grabbed by the partner's right, which is held high over his head.

(d) As the partner pulls the right hand of the first actor in a wide circle behind the partner's head to the partner's right, the first actor quickly swings his hips to the right, while pushing his left foot against the "platform" and swings his right foot and body up and to the right until his right foot lands on the partner's right shoulder. The partner assists in this action by pushing his hands upward and to his right.

(e) Facing the same direction as his partner, the first actor pushes his right foot against the partner's right shoulder, and steps up to his left shoulder. He is supported by the upward push from the partner's hands, which are grasped in his own.

(f) One hand at a time, the partner releases the first actor's hands and uses his to grasp on the first actor's ankles.

(g) The first actor straightens his body and spreads his arms horizontally, forming a T.

(h) Once his balance is perfectly established, the first actor bends his knees and claps.

(i) Swinging his arms back, like a diver, he leaps from his partner's shoulders. He jumps in a diagonal direction to his left.

(j) In the air, the actor twists his upper torso to the left and his lower torso to the right.

(k) This torquing action has caused his body to swing around, allowing him to land in his original position, facing his partner at a distance of three feet. His knees are bent.

(l) First actor performs a *dactyl*. (*Etude* is then repeated with partners exchanging roles.)

Objectives
Practice in rotary motion, torque movements against gravity. Strengthening of wrist, leg, and back muscles. Development of balance in space and on impact. Coordination with partner.

Comment
Essentially a simple acrobatic feat, Meyerhold added numerous steps to this *étude*. In advanced classes, actors performed forward somersaults instead of rotary jumps and built towers and complex pyramids with many partners.

6 Strike with the Feet

(a) Two actors face each other at a distance of six feet. They execute a *dactyl*.

Figure 7.6
Strike with the Feet (c).

(b) The partner with his knees bent and feet pointed slightly inward forms a stable base. With his body slightly forward, he makes taunting sounds at the first actor.

(c) The first actor, his eyebrows raised and eyes focused on his partner's, slowly lifts his right leg, which is bent at the knee, until it reaches its extreme height. His head is forward. The actor's body is balanced by the weight of his arms, which are tensed at the shoulder and behind his back. The actor's right foot is on a 45° angle to his body.

(d) Slowly bending his right foot and tilting his body backward, the first actor thrusts his body forward, feet first, at the nose of his partner, whose upper torso recoils.

(e) Once in the air, the actor kicks his legs up and forward, landing gently on his left shoulder.

(f) Partner falls backwards to his right side.

Objectives
Development of reflex excitability and response. Establishment of balance on one foot. Movement against gravity. Learning to fall. Coordination with partner.

Comment
Meyerhold claimed that he learned this *étude* from Giovanni di Grasso, the Sicilian actor who visited Russia before the Revolution.

7 The Leap on to the Chest

(a) Two actors standing at a great distance execute a *dactyl*.

(b) First actor, running at a great speed,

Figure 7.7
The Leap on to the Chest (e).

thrusts from his right foot and leaps at his partner, whose balance is firmly fixed.

(c) In the air, the first actor directs his knees at his partner's chest.

(d) Landing against his partner, the first actor hooks his elbows behind the partner's shoulders.

(e) The partner leans his upper torso backward to support the weight of the first actor, who holds the back of the partner's neck in his left hand.

(f) Then, the first actor slowly pulls an imaginary dagger from his belt with his right hand.

(g) He stabs his partner drawing the imaginary dagger across his throat.

(h) The partner slowly begins to bend his body backward, and makes a sound as if dying.

(i) Releasing his grip from the partner's neck, the first actor begins to slide down his partner's body, continually stabbing it with his imaginary dagger.

(j) They both fall to the floor at the same time.

Objectives

Exercise in precisely estimating distances. Supporting weights against chest cage through positioning of legs. Development of reflex excitability through complex stimuli.

Comment

This *étude* was also inspired by Grasso, who reportedly bit the neck of his partner, drawing blood.

8 Dropping the Weight

(a) The first actor stands directly behind his partner.

(b) At the sound of a whistle, the partner draws both of his legs together over the first actor's left foot, forming a perfect vertical.

(c) The first actor holds the right side of his partner's waist with his

Figure 7.8
Dropping the Weight (d).

right hand and, bending his left elbow, grasps his partner's left hand in his own in the manner of a hand shake.

(d) Planting a slightly bent right leg to his right side with the foot facing outward, the first actor slowly drops the rigid body of his partner, whose right arm is allowed to swing downwards.

(e) Keeping his feet in the same position, the first actor drops his partner's body using only the muscular contraction of his thighs.

(f) When the partner's left hand touches the floor, the action is reversed until the partner is once again vertical.

Objectives
Practicing purely linear movements. Learning to support weights and falling.

9 The Horse and Rider

(a) At the sound of a whistle, the first actor begins a short run and leaps on the back of his partner, straddling his shoulders and wrapping his arms across his partner's neck.

(b) Receiving the weight with bended knees, the partner holds on to the first actor's legs and begins to run with a long, carefree, loping stride.

(c) When the whistle is blown again, he stops in a well-balanced position.

(d) The whistle is blown for a third time, and the partner begins again to run, turning on a perpendicular axis to his left.

(e) Sequence continues until two blasts of the whistle are heard.

Figure 7.9
The Horse and the Rider (b).

Objectives
Use of shoulders to support weight. Development of reflex excitability.

Comment
In advanced classes, many groups of "horses and riders" were drilled in more complex sequences based on alternating tempos and geometric schemes.

Note   The drawing seems to illustrate a variation on the standard execution of the *étude*.

10 Tripping Up

(a) Two actors face each other as in "The Slap in the Face." They execute a *dactyl*.

(b) The partner's hands clench into fists.

(c) The first actor grasps the partner's right wrist with his left hand and violently pulls it to the side. This causes the partner's body to lose its balance as his left foot is jerked off the floor.

(d) The first actor then pushes the partner's left side with his right arm, causing his partner to step backward on his left foot.

(e) The first actor grasps the throat of his partner with his left hand, causing the partner to cry as if wounded.

(f) That sound signals a return to the original position.

(g) They execute a *dactyl* and repeat the *étude* after exchanging roles.

Objectives
Development of rhythmic balance. Extremely fast reflex excitability.

11 Carrying the Sack

(a) From a distance, two actors execute a *dactyl*.

(b) The first actor, holding an imaginary dagger, pursues his partner.

(c) Switching his direction, the partner still cannot escape the first actor, who stabs him in the back.

(d) The partner slowly falls to the floor.

(e) The first actor bends down to his knees and very slowly lifts his partner's rigid body.

(f) Then, suddenly, he throws the body over his shoulder.

(g) The first actor begins to run wildly in a wide circle.

(h) He stops and slowly lowers the body.

Figure 7.10
Carrying the Sack (e).

Objectives
Development of reflex excitability. Exploration of psycho/physical emotional states.

Comment
Etude seems closely to resemble a standard clowning action.

12 The Leap from the Back

(a) Two actors facing each other execute a *dactyl*.

(b) The partner turns to the right and squats in a low stable position that is perpendicular to the first actor who, with his arms high in the air, places his right foot on the right side of his partner's back.

(c) As his partner slowly leans forward, the first actor pushes his left foot against the floor, thrusting his body upward. In a twisting motion

Figure 7.11
The Leap from the Back (e).

with his arms brought down and knees bent, the first actor climbs on the partner's back, facing the same direction as his partner.

(d) Moving slightly upward and sliding his right foot back and to the right, the partner creates a flat, stable "platform" with his back. With his knees bent, arms behind him, and upper torso bent forward. the first actor calibrates his movements to those of his partner.

(e) First actor and partner hold a motionless, balanced position.

(f) At the sound of a whistle, the partner begins to slowly walk forward.

(g) At the sound of the next whistle, the first actor leaps from his partner's back.

Objectives
Development of many forms of balance and reflex excitability. Coordination with partner.

Comment
In advanced classes, Meyerhold added other steps such as forward somersaults instead of simple leaps and jumping from one back to another.

13 The Circle

(a) A number of actors in multiples of three perform a *dactyl*.

(b) They march around the room in a circle with long loping strides.

(c) At the sound of a whistle, the second actor of each threesome places his hands on the first actor's shoulders. The third actor leaps forward landing on his hands and one knee on the platform created by the first two actors.

(d) With each change in music tempo, the third actor executes a different balanced position on the shoulders of the first two actors, who are marching in stride.

Figure 7.12
The Circle (c).

(e) In the final balanced position, the third actor sits on the arms of the second actor.

(f) At the sound of a whistle, the third actor leans forward grasping the shoulders of the first as the second actor slides his hands away from the shoulder of the first actor. This allows the third actor to land in an upright position in the march.

(g) The three actors continue to march until the whistle is blown.

Figure 7.13
The Circle (e).

Objectives

Development of many forms of balance. Reflex excitability. Coordination with many partners. Supporting weights on the back and arms.

8

ETIENNE DECROUX'S
PROMETHEAN MIME

Deidre Sklar

> Even if his work does not turn out to be the principal, central theatrical work of our time, it can resemble the work of some small, strict holy order from which the whole church benefits.
>
> **(Eric Bentley 1953)**

Eric Bentley, reviewing a Corporeal Mime performance by Etienne Decroux and his company, recognized the value of Decroux's work but also its strangeness. Jean-Louis Barrault, who helped Decroux to formulate the principles of Corporeal Mime in the 1920s, called him a puritan revolutionary who cultivated the more-than-perfect. During my own apprenticeship with Decroux in Paris from September 1967 through December 1968, a legend circulated about how Decroux used to stop performances to repeat a passage until he got it perfect. This kind of stage behavior did nothing for Decroux's popularity with audiences. The feeling was mutual. Concerned less with entertainment than with purity of execution, Decroux eventually refused to perform for more than a small and select group of friends. His ultimate concern has been pedagogic rather than performative; his goal has been to train actors to be in perfect control of their bodies.

While Bentley's idea of a cloistered holy order accurately describes Decroux's iconoclasm, it misrepresents his message. Shunning religion, Decroux claims that "[m]ime is a political art, but not political in the way that some would like me to say it is – in the way of Trotskyism, Stalinism, or anarchy. It is political or Promethean as opposed to religious" (Decroux 1978). When Decroux calls his art Promethean, he is claiming the right to rebel against the limitations of the body and against socially accepted esthetic images. "I don't want to stay as I am," he writes. "I want to become what I desire to be" (1963). The ideal of the Promethean actor who is more beautiful than the one God made is the image underlying Decroux's Corporeal Mime.

> Promethean art [is] an art in which man does things. Man was not content to live in a cave. He is the rival of God in that he makes things. He makes statues. It's as if he said to God, "The man you made is not beautiful. I'm going to make another. The cave you made is not beautiful. I'll make a monument."
>
> (Decroux 1978)

Prometheus is for Decroux what anthropologist Sherry B. Ortner calls a summarizing key symbol. A summarizing key symbol condenses a network of ideas and beliefs into one image, which then stands for the whole complex. In the Greek myth, Prometheus challenged the Olympian gods by stealing the fire of sun and lightning. He gave this "raw" heavenly fire to human beings as "cooked" or domesticated hearth fire. Since it enables cooking, heating, smelting and other industry, domesticated fire separates humans from animals. Because the use of fire suggests that humans must work to live, it separates us from gods who do not. Symbolizing reason, artifice, culture, labor and suffering, Prometheus' gift thus defines the human condition.

In an alternate Roman version of the myth, Prometheus creates mankind out of clay after the Olympians have decided to abolish the human race. In either version, Prometheus defies the gods, creates or re-creates the human race and is punished for his defiance. Likewise for Decroux, human beings must perpetually struggle and inevitably suffer as a result of their actions. The key themes of self-creation, rebellious and heroic action, struggling and suffering, manual labor and choice based on reason form the core of Decroux's world view, esthetic and physical technique.

This idea was popular in nineteenth century European thought. Goethe in his Prometheus poem addresses Zeus:

> Here I sit, shaping man
> After my image,
> A race that is like me,
> To suffer, to weep,
> To rejoice and be glad,
> And like myself
> To have no regard for you!

Goethe's Prometheus is the "immortal prototype of man as the original rebel and affirmer of his fate" (Kerenyi 1963). Similarly, Nietzsche sees Prometheus as the titanic individual or *übermensch*. He writes in *The Birth of Tragedy* that "what distinguishes the Aryan conception is the notion of active sin as the properly Promethean virtue." This active sin is uniquely masculine as opposed to the feminine Biblical sin of suggestibility.

Promethean *hubris* is necessary for Nietzsche's titanic individual who purchases his own heroic suffering.

For Decroux, as for Nietzsche, the Promethean actor instigates action and purchases suffering. When Decroux writes about action, the verb he uses is not *faire*, which is "to do" in the sense of "make." He uses *agir*, which is "to do" in the sense of "agitate." "No longer hesitating before taking action, man anguishes in action," Decroux writes. Suffering is Decroux's "subject of subjects" (1963). He claims for his art the right to paint portraits of life in black, to depict sorrow the way the great dramatists, sculptors and poets have done.

> One must live, one must suffer, and one must struggle before expressing oneself artistically. One must have something to say. Art is first of all a complaint. One who is happy with things as they are has no business being on the stage.
>
> (Decroux 1978)

Like Prometheus chained to the cliff or like a "butterfly nailed alive to the board" (Decroux 1963), the Corporeal Mime actor expresses the contradiction between what we are and what we would like to be. This opposition between aspiration and limitation is exemplified in the physical technique. The foot, "proletarian of the esthetic," stays rooted to the ground while the upper body fights against the pull of gravity to perform expressive attitudes. Unlike the dancer who, according to Decroux, is "free and soaring," the Corporeal Mime actor is "struggling and earthbound." Unlike dance, the kinesphere of Corporeal Mime action tends to be limited; rarely does the actor traverse large distances in space. He is like a "Greek statue changing form under a glass bell" (1963).

Paralleling the struggle between upper and lower body, in Corporeal Mime a relationship of tension is maintained between adjacent body parts. For example, in order to achieve the position shown in Figures 8.1 and 8.2, the chest bends while the waist struggles to remain upright. This means that the muscles of the waist exert a contradictory pull in the opposite direction to the chest. Similarly, to achieve a smooth backward curve of the spine, the chest must be trained to bend more than its natural inclination, while the waist is trained to curb its naturally large capacity for bending.

In addition to the opposition maintained between parts of the body, struggle is expressed in Corporeal Mime through general muscular tension. Tension and release create the dynamics of movement. Decroux's concept of *dynamo rhythme* combines duration and speed with degrees of muscular tension. The results are somewhat similar to Rudolf Laban's Effort qualities. For example, the two most basic *dynamo rhythmes* are the *secousse* and the *fondu*, or the shock and the sustain. In the *secousse*, force-in-place is generated by tensing the muscles and then releasing them in a

Figure 8.1 Decroux's Promethean Mime.

Figure 8.2   Decroux's Promethean Mime.

powerful and quick movement. Like a note held on the violin, the *fondu* involves continual slow movement at constant velocity with a constant degree of muscular tension. Either dynamic can be performed with the whole body or with any isolated part. Decroux illustrates the combination of *secousse* and *fondu* with the image of a fish which first darts and then glides.

"The Antenna of the Snail," an important exercise that was performed frequently while I was a student of Decroux, demonstrates the principle of *dynamo rhythme*. It begins with the tensing of the neck muscles. The head then turns slowly as the tension is released. As the head reaches the 45° angle, the neck tenses again, causing the head to rotate back in the opposite direction. The tension and recoil imitate the sensitive snail's antennae as they near an obstacle, vibrate and recoil.

The struggle symbolized by Prometheus and enacted in Corporeal Mime technique is also reflected in Decroux's political philosophy. In spite of his denial that he embraced any one political system over another, Decroux characterizes himself as having a "socialist temperament." He explains that he is moved by the struggles of people, the spirit filtered through stone (as in statuary), large masses gathered around large monuments or sports events, singing choirs, processions and group protests.

> A revolution is constructive. It's active. It rises up. It takes energy to make a revolution of whatever kind. And one must suffer for that. A revolution is not a liberation from chains, it's a changing of chains. It consists of breaking with obligations that seem bad, and adopting other obligations that seem better. I would even say that liberty is the right to choose one's restraints. That's what liberty is.
>
> (Lust 1974)

Decroux was particularly inspired by the Russian Revolution. "One felt that at the moment Russia was not falling but rising up," he said (1978). The idea of "rising up" corresponds with Decroux's image of the Promethean actor.

> When an actor in shorts is lying on the ground, it's a whole nation lying down. And when he slowly rises up, you see the play of his muscles. After that he comes and goes, lifts things, throws them. He's self-reliant man, and there's his rapport with Promethean art.
>
> (Decroux 1978)

A simple exercise demonstrates the transition from inaction to "rising up," or from mental sleep to wakefulness.

1 You sit in a chair. You are asleep.
2 Still sleeping, you stir. The head shifts to center.

3 The eyes open, but you do not see.
4 You see, but do not register what you see.
5 Registering what you see, your interest is aroused.
6 You take action; stand.

For Decroux, the human struggle to rise up is epitomized in activities of manual labor and sports. The sight of the lightweight boxing champion Georges Carpentier first inspired Decroux to devote himself to an esthetics of the body. At 15, Carpentier was small, strong and beautiful. His "vigor and grace; force, elegance, flash and thoughtfulness; a taste for risk and for the smile" became an esthetic ideal for Decroux (1963).

"Mime is the champion of manual laborers," Decroux wrote in *Paroles sur le Mime*. The muscular action of manual labor and sports provides the subject matter for many of Decroux's pieces, such as *The Carpenter, The Washer Woman, Ancient Combat, The Factory, The Discus Thrower* and others. Actions such as sustained force, shocks of effort, resistances and counterweights underlie even those pieces that are not concerned with manual labor or sports. Like the laborer's work, the technique demands strength, endurance, force, weightiness and sustained energy. For Decroux, the worker's or athlete's movements are harmonious, logical, efficient and beautiful. When the actor moves with the harmony, logic and efficiency of the worker or athlete, Decroux finds him *beau*. The Corporeal Mime must be an "esthetician who is also a carpenter" (Decroux 1978).

Born in 1898, Decroux had worked as a mason, a hospital orderly, a factory worker and a dock worker before he was 25. He enrolled at Jacques Copeau's Ecole du Vieux Columbier at the age of 25 in preparation for a career in political oratory. Without losing his political orientation, Decroux became a man of the theatre. As Annette Lust, an ex-student of Decroux, writes, "All Decroux's political passions – rigorous, idealistic and visionary – were transferred to the theatre" (Lust 1974). Decroux's home and studio are now in the Boulogne–Billancourt district of Paris, an area distinguished for its car factories and revolutionary politics. Thus, in his life as well as his art, Decroux has remained close to the worker.

Decroux's Promethean actor, self-created in his own image, rebellious against the gods, rising up with political passion in the name of humanity and firmly grounded in the esthetics of manual labor, acts according to the laws of reason. The "chains" Decroux chooses are the rules of rational thinking. The hero's struggle to create himself is equivalent to the mime's struggle to rule the body according to the mind's will. The mind is free, according to Decroux. It can move at constant speed, slow down, speed up, stop or change direction at will. It can take precarious jumps, return to review an idea or hold one in abeyance while examining another. It is not limited in time, space or the mechanics of the body. Therefore, we "want the body to regulate its step to that of thought" (1963).

> I desire theatre in which the actor … is an instrumentalist of his own body, and everything he does, he does as an artist, and not just as an exposition of his personal nature.
>
> (Decroux 1978)

By contrast, the actor whose actions are based on impulse or emotion is embarrassing or ridiculous to Decroux. The actor's personal nature manifests itself spontaneously and easily in facial expressions and hand gestures, according to Decroux; therefore, face and hand gestures must be suppressed.

> If I've been impressed by all the arts, if not equally impressed by all of them, there is one that frankly displeases me. And that is pantomime. Pantomime: that play of face and hands which seemed to try to explain something but lacked the needed words. I detested this form.
>
> (Decroux 1974)

For Decroux, it is the trunk, the largest and most difficult part of the body to articulate, that expresses what is universal. Large movements of the trunk demonstrate a "hunger to speak to people," and therefore Decroux gives them primacy over the hands and face.

Like Edward Gordon Craig, Decroux sought to rid the theatre of the actor's personal idiosyncrasies. Craig thought the director's will and spirit could be most faithfully represented by the marionette-actor. Decroux disagreed, saying that the human body is more suitable than the puppet for expressing life's struggle. Still, Decroux's ideal actor – unhampered by stage paraphernalia and ruling his body by will and reason the way a puppeteer manipulates a marionette – owes much to Craig's genius.

Geometry is the substance of reason for Decroux. To have the body "regulate its step to that of thought" means that all movement must be inspired by geometric principles. The body segments must be isolated and "played" like a keyboard.

> What exactly have I done? One day a student of mine said to me, "The day you said 'head without neck' you found your whole system." I wouldn't have thought of that definition, but I think that's it: the head without the neck, the neck without the chest, the chest without the waist, the waist without the pelvis, the pelvis without the legs … So we consider the keyboard as something that should inspire us. Nothing should happen in the body except what is desired and calculated.
>
> (Decroux 1978)

Head, neck, chest, waist, pelvis and legs can be isolated and "played" in three dimensions – sagittal (side-to-side) inclinations, frontal (back-and-forth) inclinations and rotations. Each part is trained to move in all three ways and in combinations called single, double and triple designs (*dessins*). A single design is movement on one plane or dimension; a double design is in two dimensions; and a triple design is in three dimensions. For example, if the head leans to the left, or if head, neck, chest and waist all incline left, this is a single design. If the head leans right and then rotates in either direction, it is a double design. If it leans right, bends forward and then rotates right, the head creates a triple design. Figure 8.1 shows a triple design in which head, neck, and chest have rotated right, inclined right and inclined back. Figure 8.2 shows the head, neck and chest rotated right, inclined right and inclined forward. The resulting combinations, or attitudes, can be arrived at by moving each part separately or all at once. Moving from one attitude to another, the Corporeal Mime actor creates an itinerary (*itinéraire*) or moving statuary (*statuaire mobile*).

This kind of abstract geometric analysis is also applied to everyday actions. For example, to throw a ball with the left arm, the Corporeal Mime moves into the position of head, neck, and chest rotated right, inclined right and inclined back. To release the ball, the attitude is reversed into the position of rotation left, inclination left and inclination forward. The arm simply "echoes" the movement of the chest, preparing to throw on the first move, extending on the second. Decroux applies this kind of geometric analysis to a range of everyday actions from sitting down on a chair to pushing a cart or sweeping the floor.

Decroux's concept of the rational actor who rules his body with his will is epitomized in his work on the *Meditation*, an improvisation piece whose subject is reasoning itself. The improvisation begins with a transition from vacuity to wakefulness similar to the preparatory exercise that has been described. In the *Meditation*, however, the actor begins standing and distills the entire sequence into one instant of transition from inaction to attention. This moment represents the awakening of thought.

Thought awakens in the eyes and head. The head then begins an investigation, a research of logical movement possibilities. For example, if the head inclines to the right, it then returns to rectilinear and repeats the movement, or it executes a symmetrical inclination to the left. The neck follows to the right or else contradicts the head and inclines to the left. The choices are limited by the logic of geometry.

Growing interest produces expanded physical involvement. The chest is pulled into action. Perhaps the head and neck explored only the sagittal plane, and now a second "idea," originating in the head, pulls the neck and chest into an exploration of the frontal plane. The possibilities of two dimensions are explored. The chest must be able to move with as much force and weight as the head. Normally fused to the waist, it struggles to articulate while the waist stays fixed.

Perhaps the head has led the neck and chest into an inclination to the left and forward. Holding this "idea," it begins a new exploration in rotation, still inclined to the left and forward. Continuing to rotate, the waist is engaged, and finally, pulling the legs and hips to an extreme rotation, a new plateau is reached, a new starting point.

The search begins again. The head starts out in a new direction, following a new thought, constructing a new geometrical design. An itinerary begins to unfold, a map carved out by the moving statuary. Seeking a harmonious line, a uniformity of execution, obedience to the logic of mind, the body struggles to keep step with thought. Moments of stillness are juxtaposed with moments of shock and reverberation. An action may repeat and accelerate, then unfold in a new direction. It is like an animal searching for food or a Greek statue transforming in stone. The whole process has taken perhaps three, perhaps ten, minutes.

The *Meditation* can also be performed as a group piece, and it is then called *Research Scientists in a Laboratory*. The principles are the same as for the solo *Meditation*, except that while "thinking," each person is expected to respond to all the other "scientists." For example, person A might be exploring an inclination to the right and bump her head against the chest of person B who is in the middle of a descent to the ground. Both would be expected to incorporate the interference. B might join A's inclination, and the two would continue inclining together to the right. Perhaps B would receive A's head in the hollow of his waist, or he might recoil from the contact and set out on an entirely new exploration. In this way the entire group would be constantly in and out of interaction.

The *Meditation* and *Research Scientists in a Laboratory* can be performed as concert pieces or, in the studio, as demonstrations of the students' mastery of Corporeal Mime principles and technique. While I was a student, although we practiced the group piece for a year, we performed only at weekly Friday night improvisation sessions for other students and under Decroux's critical surveillance. These Friday night performances are highly charged in-group events that substitute for public performance.

In the basement studio, students set up a semi-circle of folding chairs facing a table and chair where Decroux will sit. He appears wearing his red and blue velour robe and formally greets the students. Sitting at the table, he delivers a talk on some aspect of Corporeal Mime philosophy, such as the difference between mime and dance or the subject of the "thinking" mime. After Decroux's talk, table and chair are removed and students improvise in hierarchical order – the newcomers first, and the *anciens* last. While students are sometimes asked to improvise on other themes, the primary subject while I was a student was the *Meditation* or its group version, *Research Scientists in a Laboratory*. Decroux's responses can be ecstatic or scalding. His most scathing comments are reserved for people who try to be spontaneous or clever, or who try to express themselves emotionally.

Only students are permitted to observe the Friday night improvisations, except for one regular visitor: an older woman who sat silent in the corner and sketched the proceedings. Both performers and audience are therefore initiates, so to speak, in Corporeal Mime. All share an understanding of the specialized vocabulary and underlying theoretical principles of the form. When students are not performing, they are scrutinizing and evaluating each other's work. The separation between skilled performer and non-skilled spectator that characterizes most European theatre is absent.

In the absence of public performance, Friday night sessions are like formalized rituals of initiation into Decroux's esoteric order. Richard Schechner distinguishes between preparation and rehearsal in the theatre, saying that the more attention paid to the preparation rather than rehearsal, the closer theatre comes to ritual.

> Rehearsal is a way of setting an exact sequence of events. Preparations are a constant state of training so that when a situation arises one will be ready to "do something appropriate." Preparations are what a good athletic team does.
>
> (Schechner 1977)

Weekday classes in technique prepare students to "do something appropriate" at Friday night improvisations. Schechner also suggests that the more the audience is integrated into the performance, the closer theatre comes to ritual. Both the criteria of preparation versus rehearsal and that of integration of the audience into the event apply to the Friday night performances in Decroux's studio. Decroux's system of codified communication is itself a kind of ritualization, a transformation of natural sequences of behavior into composed sequences.

Not only Corporeal Mime technique and Friday night improvisation sessions but Decroux's lifestyle and pedagogical style suggest ritual and initiation into an esoteric order. Entering Decroux's home is like walking into another era. He refuses to accept normative technological life. After students knock on the front door, Madame Decroux ushers them into the kitchen where she has been cooking or doing the wash by hand. The smell of French cheeses and pastries comes from under glass covers. Students must remove their shoes and place them under the stove before ascending the stairs to the second floor drawing-room to change clothes.

If Decroux has not already emerged to greet students in the kitchen, he now rings a brass hand-bell signaling students to file back down through the kitchen and down another flight of stairs to the basement studio. There he formally greets each one, offering his hand to the men, sometimes kissing the women's eyes, or embracing men and women alike.

Greetings are followed by an elaborate and prescribed ritual of handing out four-foot-long ropes. (From 1973 to 1978 Decroux replaced the rope ritual with another in which students had to pull him across the floor on his buttocks. Apparently, this was a serious joke about his age: he was over 80.) One by one, students approach Decroux. Holding the ropes by one end in his left hand, he transfers them one at a time to his right hand and steps forward toward a student, who at the same time steps forward to receive the rope. The exact movement of arm, hand and chest are codified and must show respect. If performed improperly, the entire sequence must be repeated. Once the ropes are all handed out, Decroux and the class perform the exercise called *Statuette d'Automobile* 25 times. This exercise establishes the correct body position for all subsequent work.

Decroux teaches by modeling the figures of Corporeal Mime, the moving statuary, counterweights, walks, turns and studies of everyday movement. While he explains the principles, tells jokes and stories and demonstrates movement, students are told to sit down. Then, at Decroux's signal, everyone gets up to imitate what he has done. Decroux sings an accompanying *dynamo rythme* and scrutinizes execution of the movement. He may then single out a student to perform the movement next to him or next to an *ancien*. The rest of the class must compare the two versions and point out differences. These critiques develop the capacity for minute observation and awareness of the fine points of technique.

Comparison between students clarifies the hierarchy of the classroom. *Anciens* who have been with Decroux for several years are models for the others. Among those who have been with Decroux a year or less, rank depends upon both skill and promise, which includes seriousness about studying, respect for Corporeal Mime and a strong and graceful body. Students who show promise and remain long enough to master the rudiments of technique are invited to join the *équipe*.

Decroux's *équipe*, while I was a student, consisted of seven to ten students who shared Decroux's research work in daily three-hour sessions (and twice on Thursdays). In addition, they attend the hour-and-a-half daily classes for all students. An invitation to join the *équipe* is considered a privilege and is taken very seriously by Decroux, his wife and the students. In my own case, I was warned several times by Madame Decroux that skipping classes was jeopardizing my chances for an invitation. When my attendance improved, I was asked to join.

Once inside the inner circle, although the hierarchical ordering of students continues, the tension releases and research goes on in a less formal atmosphere. Research includes analyzing new movement sequences, learning choreography, and revising and perfecting Decroux's repertory of abstract and representational movement sequences. In addition, the *équipe* works on the group improvisation, *Research Scientists in a Laboratory* and new pieces that are based on the body types and personalities of the members. The *équipe* was in the process of preparing for a public performance when it disbanded.

The disbanding came as a result of clashing values. The *ancien* of the group announced his intention to leave for several months to study with Jerzy Grotowski in Poland. This broke the rules inherent in Decroux's "holy order." Decroux denounces what he calls the "5 and 10" approach to art in which students sample bits and pieces of many techniques. He expects students to train exclusively with him in the old European master–apprentice system and then remain with him as journeymen after they have completed their apprenticeship. The *ancien*'s announcement was deplorable and unforgivable to Decroux. The announcement occurred during the 1968 "revolution" in Paris, and after Decroux had forbidden the young man to return to his studio, the others declared "solidarity" with the renegade. In spite of attempts to assure Decroux that no disrespect was intended, outbursts and recriminations followed. Several students eventually returned to classes, but the *équipe* fragmented, and no public performance was ever given.

Corporeal Mime is not a secret study, yet it has never been a popular form. Decroux's "puritan revolutionary" personality discourages the merely curious, and his art seems esoteric to many. Decroux's "small, strict holy order" remains outside the mainstream because he is less concerned with entertaining spectators than with transforming students – mind and body – into his image of the Promethean actor or ideal Everyman. This ideal is achieved through mastery of the physical technique of Corporeal Mime and through assimilating its theoretical principles. Students who remain with Decroux long enough to master the system have undergone a deconstruction and reconstruction process that more closely resembles ritual initiation than theatre.

9

ACTOR TRAINING IN THE NEUTRAL MASK

Sears A. Eldredge and Hollis W. Huston

During the first World War, in Paris Jacques Copeau developed the idea of a severe and simple form of theatre, neither classical nor topical, but versatile through the economy of its means. In 1919 he remodeled the stage of the Vieux-Columbier in accordance with his new ideas, and over the next two years he founded a school for the training of actors, the Ecole du Vieux Columbier. Both in design and in acting, Copeau wanted to make large statements with simple gestures. The pursuit of simplicity made him eliminate distractions, to create the still ground against which a movement or a form could be seen. His bare architectural stage was meant to magnify the evanescent statements of the drama. "I want the stage to be naked and neutral," he wrote, "in order that every delicacy may appear there, in order that every fault may stand out; in order that the dramatic work may have a chance in this neutral atmosphere to fashion that individual garment which it knows how to put on" (in Sergeant 1917). The simplicity that Copeau sought required a neutral atmosphere.

Copeau built that atmosphere into the theatrical space of the Vieux-Columbier, but to realize it in the spaces and rhythms of the actor's body was another, less tangible problem. The actor would have to be stripped as bare as the stage; only then could he express himself clearly and simply. Otherwise, the movement would be lost against a ground of temperament or convention. To find the neutral atmosphere within himself, therefore, the actor would first have to give up deeply ingrained but superficial habits. "The actor always starts from an artificial *attitude*, a bodily, mental, or vocal *grimace*. His attack is both too deliberated and insufficiently premeditated" (Copeau 1970). The starting point was to be not an attitude but a silence serving as a resting state, a condition without motion but filled with energy, like the condition of a runner in the moment before his race. All impulses were to arise from that state and return to it. "To start from silence and calm. That is the very first point. An actor must know how to be silent, to listen, to answer, to remain motionless, to start a gesture, follow through with it, come back to motionlessness and silence, with all the shadings and half-tones that these actions imply" (1970).

To lead actors into familiarity with a neutral atmosphere in their own bodies, Copeau assigned his students to work with masks. In Copeau's use of the mask to rid the actor of temperamental habits, Etienne Decroux found the germ of his severe and abstractive corporeal mime. Decroux noticed that the mask reveals the personality of the wearer. In commonplace actions as well as dramatic ones, the actor's idiosyncratic way of moving tended to drown the movement itself; under the mask *how* becomes more important than *what*. "So we're relying on masks to fix things up, are we? But it's just the contrary! Masks make things worse.... It's like lightning. We see everything you do clearly. And the moment you wear a mask, especially [a neutral] mask, we see the quality of what you're doing" (in Leabhart 1975). If the mask could reveal the "attitude" or "grimace" that controlled the untrained actor, then it could also amplify and objectify the "neutral atmosphere" when the actor found it. Therefore, the neutral mask became an important tool for Copeau and for a later generation of teachers.

Copeau's school did not survive, but the influence of his mask training has been carried on in two main channels. One of those channels was defined by Michael Saint-Denis, Copeau's nephew; the other, by Jacques Lecoq, who trained under Jean Dasté, Copeau's son-in-law, from 1945 to 1947. Teachers from both traditions have worked in or founded actor training programs in the United States. The Saint-Denis teaching stresses the actor's service to text, and uses only character masks, though some of those are closer to neutrality than others. Lecoq's teaching, on the other hand, is concerned in its initial phase with matters that precede speech and character. Before wearing character masks, Lecoq's students are made familiar with the *masque neutre*, which is designed to rid them of conditioned attitudes in favor of an economical use of the body. More than any other person, Lecoq has defined the neutral state for the performer, as it is realized in masks.

NEUTRALITY

Jacques Lecoq speaks of the neutral mask as tending toward a "fulcrum point which doesn't exist." As the actor approaches this fixed point, he becomes "a blank sheet of paper, a 'tabula rasa.'"[1] For Bari Rolfe, "the two words, 'appropriate' and 'economical' together almost add up to the term 'neutral.' The student executes any action, like walking, with only the expenditure of energy and rhythm, in space and in time, that the action requires" (Rolfe 1972). Richard Hayes-Marshall speaks of neutrality as "a condition such that, if the actor finds himself there, he doesn't know what he will do next. ... When you are there, you don't know what it is; if you did, it wouldn't be neutral." Andrew Hepburn writes that "Neutrality means responding to stimuli in a *purely sensory* way."

A neutral organism expends only the energy required by the task at hand. Personalities expend that amount of energy and something else besides; personalities are distinguished from each other by the nature of what they add. *Therefore, to be a personality, to be oneself even, is not to be neutral.* Yet one cannot avoid being oneself. An actor can hope to perform a neutral action, but he cannot be neutral – neutral is a "fulcrum point that doesn't exist." To approach neutral action, one must lose oneself, denying one's own attitudes or intentions. At the moment of neutral action, one does not know what one will do next, because anticipation is a mark of personality; one cannot describe how one feels because introspection intrudes on simplicity; one reacts in a sensory way, because when the mind stops defining experience, the senses still function. Economy demands that both motion and rest be unpremeditated. Neutral activity withholds nothing; it is an energized condition, like the moment of inspiration before speech. The neutrality that the mask seeks is *an economy of mind and body, evidenced at rest, in motion, and in the relationship between them.*

CHARACTERISTICS OF THE MASKS

The personality of the maskmaker threatens the neutrality of the mask. One must devote many trials and experiments to the research of neutrality. Hayes-Marshall has redesigned his neutral masks seven times. "There is no such thing as a neutral mask," he says, "it has to be designed by somebody."

Neutral masks are at rest: they do not gesture, frown, smile, or grimace. The masks are symmetrical. Though the neutral mask is never used for speaking, the lips are lightly parted, as if the mask were about to speak. The masks are usually designed in pairs, male and female. Since the male and female bodies have different centers of gravity, the masks that will be carried by them must also differ. The leather mask designed for Lecoq by Sartori is brown, but celastic or papier mâché masks used in other studios are often white. A white mask reflects light well, and therefore shows its expression clearly; brown masks, on the other hand, are closer in appearance to skin tones. Leather is the best material for simulating the textures of living skin, but there are few people capable of making leather masks. Amleto Sartori of Padua reconstructed the craft from Renaissance sources, and made neutral, expressive and *commedia* masks of leather for Lecoq and for Carlo Mazzone-Clementi. His son Donato carries on the work today, but the masks are expensive and slow to produce. Papier mâché or celastic masks are easier and cheaper.

Styles of sculpting vary according to the amount of personality considered proper in the mask. The Sartori mask used by Lecoq, which is dominated by a pair of sharp lines that define the nose and continue upward to form the brow line, seems to some observers rather abstract. The Hepburn mask is softer in outline and more naturalistic: detailed contours in the nose, eyes, cheeks, and brows, give an impression of flesh and muscle. The tragic masks of the Saint-Denis tradition, which are used for some of the same purposes as the neutral mask, are simple and harmonious masks that represent the four ages of man (Saint-Denis 1969). At the extreme of abstraction is the metaphysical mask of Mazzone-Clementi (Figure 9.1). The metaphysical mask is defined only by a centerline, a browline, and one circular and one triangular eyehole. An abstract mask leads the actor beyond psychology to the intrinsic qualities of movements and body shapes. A personalized mask is less remote from dramatic characterization.

EXERCISES FOR THE ACTOR USING THE NEUTRAL MASK

Most teachers of the mask believe that training should be a *via negativa*: they will not tell the student what to do, but they will point out mistakes after they have been made. "By blocking the path taken by the actor," writes Rolfe, "you oblige him to look for another.... Each restriction placed on the actor forces his imagination to seek ways to get around it" (1972). The teacher cannot provide a model or a set of rules. The student must look for the condition of neutrality within himself. Since bodies are unique, each person's neutrality is his own: there is no single pattern. Hayes-Marshall says that "if a student's work creates fire, I'm not interested in saying it's not fire." Yet in the pursuit of neutrality, a lapse into psychology is perceived as an error. To see such lapses, and to train his students to see them, the teacher must have experienced them in himself.

A period of training, often as long as a year, is required before students attempt the mask. The training period is devoted to acrobatics and conditioning, to developing an awareness of the body's articulations and of the images that the body can project into space. The mask then becomes a way of learning the meaning of those articulations and images.

Most teachers introduce the mask with a talk on its design and significance. Then the actor studies the mask: at the Ecole Lecoq, that study lasts for eight days. The moment of putting on the mask is crucial, since the body will immediately begin to accept or reject the mask. The actor may feel the urge to impose a movement or a body image, but he must inhibit that urge, allowing his own thoughts, his breathing, and his stance, to be replaced by those of the mask. Lecoq does not allow his students to view themselves in a mirror at this point, but some teachers find that the mirror can help a student see the change in his condition. The mask is treated with the respect due to a human face. It is handled by the sides or

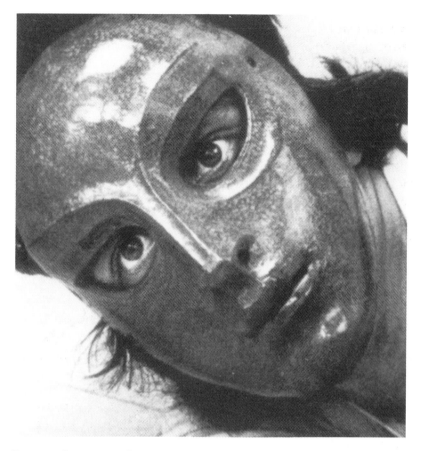

Figure 9.1 Carlo Mazzone-Clementi's metaphysical mask.

by top and bottom; one never grabs it by the nose or places the hand over its eyes. There is no speaking in the neutral mask; if the student needs to say something, he must first raise the mask onto the forehead.

The first exercises begin from sleep, the most fundamental of resting states. The study of neutrality starts with simple activities such as standing, walking, sitting, or picking up an object, as performed in the mask. The first level of error is gratuitous movement. In walking, one student will bounce, another will sway, another will take extra steps after the forward movement has stopped; one will look at the ceiling, another will look at his feet. In standing, one will scratch his head, another will put his hands on hips. One student will take hold of an object several times before lifting it, another as he picks it up will make gestures to show how heavy it is. Such movements are imposed on the action; the student must find a way to do the action without them. By making mistakes, however, a student begins to learn how his habits lead him away from neutrality.

A second level of error has to do with the tempo of movement. The actor may seize an object abruptly, without preparation, or he may wait so long that when he picks up the object, the need to do so is gone. Either error will leave questions in an observer's mind. "Why so fast?' Or "why so slow?" If the question arises, the action is not neutral – an attitude has intruded on the movement. There is a moment when the body is ready to move, and if the movement happens at that moment, no question arises.

A third level of error is marked by the imposed attitude. The student performs a single action, but in a manner that creates the image of a character with prior experience of the action. The hands may be so stiff that they seem fearful or hostile. The chest may be sunken, expressing fatigue or cunning, or expanded, showing curiosity. The student must examine his customary self-use, because neutral action is performed as if for the first time. No one part of the body, nor the mask itself, can draw attention; in neutrality, the entire body and the surrounding space are perceived with equal weight. To focus on a part of the space – to expand the chest, for instance – is to be dramatic and not neutral.

The initial exercises introduce the student to a process of experiment, perception, and change. Each error brings discovery of a new approach to the task. The new approach is questioned, in its turn, bringing the student closer to a condition that he can fully achieve only for brief moments. The research of neutrality never ends, for every level of knowledge, if accepted rather than questioned, becomes a technique imposed on the mask. The advantage for the performer is that each new technique is stronger than the old, because it is closer to the body's natural functioning.

After exploring simple actions in the mask, the teacher may assign extended scenarios, in which the person wearing the mask encounters elements or objects. Some of the common exercises are:

1 The figure wakes and moves toward light.
2 The figure wakes in the desert and walks into a city.
3 The figure wakes in the desert; goes to a river and enters it, perceiving its flow and its source; finds a tree, from which a bird flies.
4 The figure encounters another figure, of the opposite sex (man meets woman).
5 The figure wakes and stands in a fog; explores the fog; finds himself at the edge of the sea, as the fog clears: throws a stone out to sea.
6 The figure walks along a beach; goes to the end of a pier; sees a boat moving across the water, and waves to a person in the boat.
7 The figure walks to the end of the pier and pulls in a sailboat; punts the boat away from the shore, raises sail, and rests at the tiller; lowers sail and throws out the anchor; casts a net and pulls it in full of fish; lifts the anchor, raises sail, and rests at the tiller.

The teacher looks for simplicity and clarity in the actor's imagery. Lecoq has said that "If the Neutral Mask looks at the sea, it becomes the sea." Does the actor accept the environment, or does he establish a dramatic conflict with it? Does he show us the sea, or his own impression of the sea? Are the imaginary objects established in their weight and texture as well as in their shape? Is each experience – touching the earth, entering the river, casting the net – finished before another is begun? Does the actor show awareness of another person, or is he only compelled in a social way to look at him? Does he show awareness of objects and elements, or is he only compelled in an intellectual way to touch them? Is his breathing quiet and regular, or jagged and dramatic? Does the stone continue its flight after it leaves the actor's hand? "How can I discover without curiosity?" protests the student, and in asking the question, he defines the assignment.

In the exercise called "Discovery," the actor carrying the mask assumes a position of sleep, while the teacher places around him objects of various shapes, weights, and textures. The assignment is to wake up, to explore several of the objects as if one had no experience of them, and to return to sleep. Familiar objects are treacherous; it is tempting to hold a knife by the handle, to pick up a book and read the print, to open an umbrella, to bounce a ball, but these familiar actions may assume a history of interaction with the object. The neutral mask might discover the working of the umbrella, but only as the result of an exploration; and that discovery, if it comes, has no psychological or intellectual purpose. The mask does not impose a concept on the environment, but accepts the experiences contained within the environment.

Not all neutrality exercises cast the actor as a human figure. Rolfe asks her students to identify with animals in the neutral mask; or to recreate the images of a *haiku*. Hayes-Marshall gives assignments in the elements: earth, air, fire, and water. By asking the student to carry the mask in a nonhuman image, the teacher extends the student's ability to enter a condition without imposing personal associations on it.

BENEFITS OF THE TRAINING FOR THE ACTOR

The neutral mask is a way of understanding performance, not a way of performing. The mask is a tool for analyzing the quality of the body's action. The mask hides the face, but reveals the attitudes and intentions, the nuances, the feeling tones, that are otherwise only dimly sensed in a person's motion or stillness. When he carries it, the actor must communicate through his whole person; and the spectator must perceive the expression of the whole person. The experience can be frightening, because it is like being, or perceiving, a second person within the familiar body. Because the neutral mask is empty to begin with, it fills with whatever expression is perceived in the body. Hayes-Marshall says that "a good neutral mask looks like the person who puts it on." Trained observers know the expression of the face before the student takes off the mask. The mask draws attention to the body's points of resistance, and demands, as the price of comfort, that the body be integrated in a single image. Carrying the mask is internal and external, analytic and holistic. The dichotomies of physical and emotional technique are united in a single experience. The neutral mask allows the quality of a movement to be seen; it takes that quality on itself and magnifies it.

Because it requires participation in an image different from oneself, the mask attacks mumble-and-scratch naturalism. Peter Frisch has described the kind of actor who says, "Oh, I know that character, that character is just like me," when the truth is that "the character is nothing like they are. They see it through their own neurotic self-image." The neutral mask can lead an actor to reject his habitual identifications in favor of a deeper, simpler understanding of his powers of expression.

The neutral mask teaches simplicity in stillness and in activity. When an actor throws a stone, each part of his body should throw the stone, and no part should do anything else. The action should be allowed to complete itself before it is terminated, and it should terminate either in stillness or in the incipience of the next action. Bad movement training confuses activity with commitment; in the hands of a good teacher, the mask shows us that many details of our movement are parasitic behaviors, caused by resistance to the task at hand. When the actor clears himself of habitual assumptions and attitudes, he becomes a finely tuned instrument, capable of recording the subtle phases of perception and intention. An actor who is comfortable in stillness and activity, who commits to both, and who moves easily from one state to the other, is an actor who commands the stage. The neutral mask provides a way for the teacher and student momentarily to grasp and hold on to the intangible quality called "presence."

The actor cannot be neutral; he can only hope to attain moments of neutral action. Yet the pursuit of neutrality purifies him, making his very errors more commanding. Shedding personal clichés and habitual responses, he looks deeper into himself for images that are truly his own. After experiencing the neutral mask, he moves on to expressive masks, to the speaking masks of *commedia*, and finally to the clown nose and the discovery of his personal clown. Beneath these masks, however, is the state of near-neutrality: in a sense, the actor wears the neutral mask beneath every other mask and every other character. Lecoq likens the neutral masks to "the bottom of the sea," whereas "the Expressive Mask is like waves."

The neutral mask is not a way of performing; there is no neutral "style" of acting. The mask helps to identify a resting state for the actor, a condition of presence from which all things are possible, and to which all actions return at completion.

10

EASTERN AND WESTERN INFLUENCES ON PERFORMER TRAINING AT EUGENIO BARBA'S ODIN TEATRET

Ian Watson

Despite the fact that Eugenio Barba and his company, Odin Teatret, are not particularly well known in the United States, they, along with Jerzy Grotowski's Theatre Laboratory, are generally regarded as one of the most important influences on the modern European group-theatre movement.

The Odin Teatret, which continues to produce new and exciting works, was originally formed in Oslo, Norway, in 1964. In 1966 the company moved to Holstebro, a small town near the west coast of Denmark, where it has been based ever since. In its 23-year history the company has mounted productions ranging from intimate studio pieces, for audiences as small as sixty or less, to huge street spectacles encapsulating whole villages at a time. The Odin has traveled extensively in Europe, South America, and Asia. It has established a major theatre center in Holstebro, where it publishes books, makes and rents films, and mounts workshops in collaboration with artists such as Jerzy Grotowski, Dario Fo, and Jean-Louis Barrault; and it is the only state-supported pedagogical institute devoted to theatre research in Western Europe.

Barba, the founder and artistic director of the Odin, began his theatre career as an assistant to Grotowski in the early sixties, long before Grotowski became known in the West. In fact, Barba was instrumental in introducing Grotowski to the world by organizing the Theatre Laboratory's first European tour, and through books and articles, including *Towards a Poor Theatre*, which Barba edited, and the famous *Tulane Drama Review* articles of 1965, written by Barba and Ludwig Flaszen, which were among the first materials published on Grotowski in the United States.

Barba, unlike Grotowski, has remained in the theatre and is recognized today as a major director, theorist, and pedagogue. Apart from Odin productions directed by Barba – such as *Feria* (first performed in 1969),

Figure 10.1
A group training session
at Odin Teatret in the
early 1980s. (Photo
by Christoph Falke.)

My Father's House (*Min Fars Hus*, first performed in 1972), and *Brecht's Ashes 2* (first performed in 1982), he has written extensively on the social role of theatre and esthetics of performance. In 1979 he founded the International School of Theatre Anthropology (ISTA), which is devoted to a study of the connections between performance in the East and West.

A major focus in all of Barba's work is the performer. His productions are based on actors' improvisations in rehearsal and much of his writing centers on the acting process. Even his sociological concerns revolve around performer interaction, as individuals in a group and as a group within the greater society. This emphasis on the actor is nowhere more evident than in the performer training of Barba and the Odin.

Members of the Odin have trained regularly, six days a week, since the company was formed, and over the years the training has undergone many changes (Figure 10.1). At times it has been physically demanding and rigorous, lasting between eight and ten hours per day for months on end. At other times it has been much less intense, and for periods some actors have not trained at all.

During the summer of 1985 the company was completing final rehearsals for its latest production, *Oxyrhincus Evangeliet*. Despite the focus of attention on the production, the actors still held two one-hour training sessions daily – the first devoted to physical training, which most performers attended, and the other to vocal training, in which everyone participated.

The division between physical and vocal training is one that the Odin has basically maintained since its formation. But, regardless of this division, both forms of training have been influenced by performance techniques from different cultures. This influence is most clearly evident in the group's physical training.

If one watches an Odin physical training session today, it does not appear to be what one might commonly think of when one thinks of training. The following is a quote from notes I made while observing a training session in the summer of 1985:

> Barba is not present. There are five actors in the room, three women and two men, all working separately. Following a brief warm-up, consisting of simple stretch exercises, the actors begin to work on their individual activities. Actress 1 is sitting in a deck chair. She moves her right arm across her body, then her left arm. She moves her head from right to left, then up and down. All actions are slow, precise, and punctuated with a brief pause. She sits up in the deck chair, she sits back, she sits up again, then repeats this up and down action several more times. During these actions her trunk appears to move as one unit, with no curve in the spine or separation between chest and waist.
>
> Meanwhile, Actor 1 moves to the back of the room and begins to do a tap dance-type shuffle. He raises his arms in the classical ballet position and spins around several times. He lowers his arms and begins what appears to be a simple dance. The top half of his body does not seem to be engaged in the dance. He stops suddenly and does several shoulder stands, returning to the upright position each time. He lunges into the shoulder stands, but has great control and executes them precisely. He returns once more to a simple dance and moves around the room, occasionally breaking into the tap dance shuffle he began with.

From this brief description, which typifies the hour-long session, various things are obvious. There are no teachers; there are no clearly identifiable skills being learned; the actors are not doing scenes from a play, nor do they seem to be exploring characterization. Despite the fact that people are together in a room, each is focused on his or her own work. To a casual observer, it could easily appear that the Odin's so-called training is a sham, a one-hour period per day where people meet in a room with no intention beyond physical exercise.

There are a number of hints, however, which indicate that more is going on than mere gymnastics. If you watch the performers carefully you realize that their attention is focused, and that even in the simplest of sequences most of them sweat profusely, suggesting that they are working very hard despite the undemanding nature of the task at hand. If you follow the training for any length of time you see the actors repeating the same sequence of actions in every session, indicating that the exercises are not as arbitrary as they may appear. And the high standard of performance in Odin productions is legendary; no matter what one's opinion of productions such as *The Million* (first performed in 1978) or *Brecht's Ashes 2*, the ensemble performances are superb. The intensity, the physical precision, the mastery of skills such as acrobatics, stilt walking, and dancing, as well as the vocal work, are of the highest order. It is clear that the actors are very well trained.

So what is happening? What role do the training sessions, which appear to have little to do with training, play in preparing actors for performance? In order to answer these questions, one has to consider the evolution of training at the Odin in light of Barba's studies of Asian theatre.

As noted above, the Odin's training has gone through many changes since 1964. The single most important change, however, has been the gradual evolution of individual training. When the company was first formed, the actors trained collectively and everyone learned the same basic skills, including acrobatics, gymnastics, pantomime, and voice. During this period Barba, though rarely the teacher, was always present, and he came to realize the importance of individual rhythm in the training process. This realization led to a gradual change of focus in the exercises, from an emphasis on skill to an emphasis on the individual actor's pace and rhythm (Barba 1979: 65). At the same time as this shift in emphasis was taking place, the company began to develop composition exercises and to change the way in which it used improvisation.

Composition at the Odin, no doubt influenced by Grotowski, does not consist of specific exercises such as body rolls or head stands.[1] In fact, it can involve virtually any series of movements, since the focus is not on the movements themselves but rather on the physical ideograms created by the composition of body elements during the movements. These ideograms can have their source at a purely technical level, as in dividing the body so that one half moves rapidly while the other half moves slowly in order to express an inner tension, or they can involve physical expression of a mental association, such as using the image of a flower's growth, from germination to maturity and death, to influence how one moves through space. In a composition exercise the actor concentrates on the balance of muscular tensions and/or psychophysical association, rather than on executing a task correctly. These concerns emphasize process over product – that is, doing the exercise rather than learning a specific skill.

The shift toward process at the Odin was accompanied by an increased use of improvisation in training. The Odin has used improvisation to develop performances during rehearsals since its first production, *The Bird Lovers* (*Ornitofilene*, first performed in 1965). However, until their production of *My Father's House* in 1972, almost ten years after the company was formed, these improvisations were based on texts written prior to rehearsal. *My Father's House* was the first production developed entirely – from its inception through to the performance text – by Barba and his actors during rehearsals. This increased emphasis on improvisation placed the creative responsibility entirely upon the performers and the director since they no longer had a single, cohesive literary source to guide their rehearsals. Inevitably this change in the use of improvisation fed back into the training where, combined with the focus on process in composition and the emphasis on individuality in rhythm, it led to the creation of a new type of training altogether.

In the latter stages of rehearsal for *My Father's House*, one of the actresses, Iben Nagel Rasmussen, began to develop her own training. This training consisted of an improvised series of physical and vocal exercises that she felt best challenged her own skills and limitations. Despite the fact that the collective training continued during this period, her experiments did not go unnoticed, and there was a great deal of discussion between her, Barba, and her fellow actors. Gradually everyone began to develop his or her own training, and eventually collective training was abandoned altogether. Each actor now explored what he felt was important for him or her, but within the supportive environment of a single room where others were engaged in similar research.

Barba, while following these changes in the Odin's training, maintained contact with traditional Eastern performance, which had interested him from his earliest days in the theatre. This contact consisted mainly of visits to Asia and of invitations to masters of forms such as *nō, odissi* dance, and *topeng* to work with him in various workshops which he organized in Holstebro, at International Theatre Institute (ITI) conferences which he directed, and at ISTA.

According to Barba, his fascination with Eastern performance stems from the ability of its actors to project a powerful presence on stage. This fascination prompted him to begin a systematic study of Oriental theatre, with the express aims of discovering the source of this presence and exploring its possible relevance for Western actors (Barba 1986a: 115).

From the beginning of his research Barba rejected the idea of Western actors merely reproducing Eastern forms. He reasoned that Westerners could study forms such as *kathakaḷi* or *nō*, but since these, like most other traditional genres, involve a lifetime of study begun at a young age, the results would be poor imitations of the original. He further reasoned that the greatest value for people training in the West would be derived from using Eastern ideas to explore their own training (Barba 1985b).

Barba's interest in cross-culturalism was further stimulated by the Theatre of Sources Project mounted by Grotowski, with whom Barba remains in close contact. The intercultural nature of the project, in which Grotowski explored the connections between ritual and ceremonial practices in different cultures, inspired Barba to draw direct parallels between Eastern forms and the Odin actors' training (Barba 1986a: 156). Through this comparative study Barba was able to conceptualize two of the fundamental elements of Oriental forms that contribute to the actor's commanding stage presence: the use of learned body techniques designed to break the performer's automatic daily responses, and the codification of principles which dictate the use of energy during performance.

In daily life much of our physical action is automatic because of constant repetition. Our bodies "know" how to accomplish relatively complex tasks, like walking and climbing stairs, without having to think through the various muscular adjustments involved, because we have done them so often. In Eastern traditional forms such as *kathakaḷi* and *nō*, on the other hand, the body is intentionally distorted, particularly through the positioning of the feet and legs. In *kathaka ḷi* the performers stand on the outer edges of their feet with their legs in an open position, and in *nō* the actors lock their hips and bend their knees, altering the line of the spine and the distribution of weight. These "distortions" constitute what Barba refers to as extra-daily technique – that is, learned technique which establishes a pattern of performance behavior which is different from daily behavior. According to Barba, this extra-daily technique is a major source of actor presence during performance since it establishes a pre-expressive mode in which the actor's energies are engaged prior to personal expression (Barba 1986a: 19–20).

Personal expression in traditional Eastern performance is rigidly codified and can vary greatly from one form to another. Barba's studies revealed, however, that despite these differences the codes incorporate similar principles which dictate the body's use of energy – principles such as the use of opposing body tensions to create a dynamic on stage, a balance between energy expended through space (i.e., motion) and energy expended through time (i.e., dynamic inertia), and the use of distorted equilibrium to alter muscular tensions during performance.[2] An example of distorted equilibrium may help to clarify Barba's point. In *nō*, *odissi* dance, and Balinese dance drama the performers use precarious balance to engage their performance energies. As noted above, in *nō* the hips are locked, the knees bent, and the actor walks by sliding his feet across the stage without lifting them. This changes the normal position of the spine, alters the center of balance, and engages the trunk as a single unit – all of which create opposing tensions in the upper and lower parts of the body that require the performer to find a new point of equilibrium. In *odissi* dance the *tribangi*, which is a major component of the form, requires the dancer to manipulate her body as if the letter *S* were passing through the hips, trunk, and neck. This position, which distorts the line of the spinal column, affects the performer's balance and thereby alters the normal relationship between body weight, center of gravity, and the feet. Similarly, in many Balinese forms of dance drama the performer pushes down on the soles of the feet while at the same time lifting the toes, thus reducing contact with the ground. To compensate, the dancer widens his gait and bends his knees, which alters the center of gravity and the normal position of the spine. These adjustments increase the level of muscular activity, which, as in similar distortions in *odissi* dance and *nō*, produce a dynamic, rather than static, physical state.

Through his knowledge of the few similarly codified Western forms, such as mime and ballet, Barba realized that many of the principles in Eastern performance are shared by their Western counterparts. The principle of opposing body tensions, for example, is a major component of mime, and the alteration of normal equilibrium is a fundamental element of ballet. He further realized, in observing the individual training of his Odin actors, that they were employing similar principles – without being aware of them.

Barba began to publish the results of his research, which, combined with the influence his discoveries had on his work and on his discussions with his actors, led to a further change in the Odin's already individualized training. There was a gradual shift in emphasis from composition, with its focus on physical expression, to an exploration of the principles underlying performative action.

The Odin actors continue to develop their own training, but as one actress describes it, "training is improvisation structured by the application of principles" (Carreri 1985). A simple example, quoted by another company member, clarifies what she means:

> To stand on one's head involves mastering particular technical skills such as placement of the hands, legs, and head, and the adjustment of body weight and balance. It also involves the principle of shifting the body's weight quickly so that one is off-balance, finding a point of equilibrium which is held for a period, and returning to the normal body position. Standing on one's head is a skill that has to be learned; the principle underlying it, meanwhile, can be applied to many situations, including walking, sitting, and working with a requisite.
>
> (Wethal 1985)

Physical training at the Odin focuses on exploring this and similar principles, rather than on mastering skills. For example, the actress working with the deck chair in the training session quoted from my diary above told me after the session that during her training that day she had worked with several principles at different times – including moving with one part of the body at a time, leading all movement with the eyes, and segmenting various sections of the body. What appeared, then, to be haphazard movements were, in fact, movements strictly monitored by adherence to consciously chosen principles.

The exploration of performance principles is an endless process. Actors work with one or several related principles for extended periods, applying them to a wide variety of activities, ranging from walking, to running, to dancing, and even to gymnastic exercises such as somersaults and shoulder stands. Once actors feel that they have mastered the particular principles they are working on, however, it is time to move on to another cycle of exploring new principles – otherwise, there is a danger that mastered principles will lead to mechanical actions. Just as our daily activities lack physical dynamism because they are habitual actions learned through constant repetition, without the support of a codified structure which incorporates principles in its codes – such as one finds in traditional Eastern forms – so performative action based on the mechanical application of principles can lead to a "lifeless" presence on stage.

It is this very "lifelessness" that Barba has rejected since he began his work in the theatre. He has explored several paths to this end, including rigorous physical exercises based on his experience as Grotowski's assistant and the extensive use of improvisation to develop individualized training. His research has finally led to a training based on a synthesis of Eastern and Western approaches to performance, and it is this synthesis that constitutes the major component of the Odin's training today.

11

BALI AND GROTOWSKI

Some parallels in the training process

I Wayan Lendra

The Objective Drama Project (November 1983–June 1986) was a special research project conducted at the University of California–Irvine (UCI), sponsored by the Department of Drama with Dr Robert Cohen as its principal promoter. The project was formulated and directed by Jerzy Grotowski as an extension of his previous Theatre of Sources. The direction of the project was to isolate the performative expressions of several traditional cultures and introduce them to performers outside of their original cultural contexts. Once the technical aspects of a form were internalized, the effects of the relationships among performer, form, group, and environment were the subject of observation. A 1984 "Research and Development Report" by Cohen described the project:

> "Objective Drama" is Jerzy Grotowski's term for those elements of the ancient rituals of various world cultures which have a precise, and therefore objective, impact on participants, quite apart from solely theological or symbolic significance. Mr Grotowski's intention is to isolate and study such elements of performative movements, dances, songs, incantations, structures of language, rhythms, and uses of space. Those elements are sought by means of a distillation process from the complex through the simple and through the separation of elements one from the other.

Each cultural form was taught by an expert performer native to that culture. The traditional cultural forms included: Haitian voudoun ritual, whirling dervish, Korean shamanistic dance and songs, Balinese incantation and mantra, hatha yoga, and Japanese karate. A number of exercises were also developed throughout the project. Literary texts such as the Gospel of Saint Thomas and some literature from Hinduism were used in the newly created songs.

Two traditional practitioners from Haiti, Maud [Robart] and Tiga [Jean-Claude Garoute], worked intensively with us for several months. They

Figure 11.1   The author as the old man Topeng Tua, a character from Topeng dance theatre. (Photo by Chris Hrusa.)

taught the movements and songs of Haitian voudoun accompanied by traditional drums. A karate master from Japan and a master performer of the Sufi dervish tradition taught for short periods. A number of new exercises were developed by "technical specialists" from traditional material Grotowski had worked on during his Theatre of Sources in Poland. In addition to all of these exercises, we worked intensively on our individual or group pieces called *Mystery Play*, a work that was not intended to be performed for the general public. Through *Mystery Play* we explored our personal artistic possibilities, applying our insights and experiences gained from the work and the creative energy generated by the exercises. This intensive work was directed by Grotowski. *Mystery Play* was performed at marathon sessions – two days and two nights of work.

Four of us technical specialists worked with the project continuously: Du Yee Chang from Korea, Jairo Cuesta-Gonzales from Colombia, Wei-Cheng Chen from Taiwan, and myself from Bali, Indonesia (Figure 11.1). The four of us were accomplished artists in our own cultural traditions, with backgrounds in experimental modern theatre. We learned and recorded the materials of the traditional practitioners and helped Grotowski to formulate new exercises. We then taught and guided the 18 participants in both the traditional forms and the new work. These participants included some students from UCI. Other participants, selected by audition, worked with us for set short periods of time. They came from different countries, many from cities and universities in the United States. For example, 15 students from Yale University were invited for a two-week period and 10 from New York University joined for another session.

Throughout the three years of work, Grotowski's role was manifold. On the administrative side he was assisted by Marion Barnett. This allowed him to focus on his primary function as director of the research activities in the workplace. During the exercises Grotowski observed and made notes, taught, and commented. He intervened with either physical or verbal directions. The energy of his presence was an essential contribution to the working process.

The project took place on the southern edge of the campus of UCI, in an isolated area of rolling hills populated only with horses, cattle, and field rabbits. Our center of work was two buildings: an old historic building known as "the barn," renovated into a studio theatre for the project, and a new hexagonal, one-room, redwood structure called "the yurt." Both buildings had wood floors and many windows that allowed in natural light. The color of the walls in the barn was light blue while the yurt was natural wood. At night we used kerosene lanterns for light, although electricity was available. The hills behind our studios were as much a part of the workspace as the buildings, and much of our group work took place outdoors.

The work itself was very rigorous. It required not only physical dexterity and stamina but also mental perseverance. Grotowski imposed uncompromising discipline. There were many requirements that we had to observe. Grotowski prescribed some rules which were difficult to perform, in the same way he chose participants, chose to work in nature, and isolated the essential elements of ancient performative rituals. In addition to all these, he proposed to work long hours. Most of the time we worked between five and six days a week. Each exercise would last approximately two hours or longer depending on the development of the action. Our sessions, which usually began in the early evening, often extended for eight hours, sometimes through the entire night.

The work affected my perceptions on many levels simultaneously. There was a change of consciousness and awareness, a change of physical impulses and behavior, and an intensity which developed throughout the work. Generally I felt my body was awake even though I was working long hours almost every day. I was very much connected with myself and certainly with my native culture, Bali. There seemed to be a close similarity with the trance situations I had seen in Bali, or the trancelike quality of Balinese performing arts.

In the summer of 1984 I went back to Bali for a break from the project. During this visit I witnessed a calonarang performance, a trance dance drama featuring Barong (a mythical dragonlike figure of benevolent nature) and Rangda (an awesome masked figure of demonic quality), performed during the anniversary celebration of the temple, Bukit, in my village, Bitra. About 20 of my friends and relatives, men and women, went into trance. The following days I interviewed some of the performers, focusing on a specific question: whether or not they were aware of the spectators and surroundings during the trance. Each of them answered "yes." They added that their bodies became sensitive and they felt a burning and itching sensation in different parts of the body, particularly in the chest. Their awareness became more acute than in normal everyday life. They said that if they were not totally alert they could hurt someone with the sharp *kris* (a dagger) they carried. Yet, it was remarkable that they were not at all aware of stabbing their chests or cheeks with the sharp steel daggers, or of eating live chicks. During the violent moment of stabbing, the performers were carefully watched by assistants in case of an unexpected mistake.

Jane Belo, in *Trance in Bali* (recorded in the late 1930s and published in 1960), quoted trance performers who reported that during the perform- ance they "were in and out of trance" (1960: 254). She reports that during the convulsions going in and out of trance, the performers were unaware of their beings and surroundings; the trancers I interviewed reported a similar state. She also writes that during the performance the trancers were often playful, stealing each others' chicks, eggs, or liquor and challenging each other in the action of stabbing. I also observed the childlike playfulness or behavior of the trancers in several different trance forms in Bali.

The point I am making here is that during the state of trance, the Balinese trancer experiences both a state of acute awareness, a state of the true self (*inget*) and a state of being unaware (*engsap*). In the state of inget the trancer is very much her- or himself and can be very playful, like a child, while in the state of engsap the connection with the surroundings is cut, during which time the stabbing may occur.

I am convinced that there are a number of similarities between Balinese trance performers, Grotowski's words concerning trance, and my experi- ences in the project. Grotowski once said, referring to the Haitian trance tradition, that when a person is in trance he is "highly aware of his surroundings." During this time the person is deeply involved with what he is doing and at the same time he is capable of sensing and incorporating the events in his environment without being affected by them. This may be similar to the state of being of a powerful actor, whose "presence" deeply affects the spectators as well as absorbs his or her surroundings. Her art is organic, a phenomenon generated not by his or her intention to "show," but by her honest and sincere motivation to "do" what he or she is doing.

My interest in this research in Bali was to relate it to my experience with

Grotowski in California. From the beginning of the project I felt that there was something very Balinese about Grotowski's work, even though the nature of the theatrical work exercises was not Balinese. I felt that the project was more than a theatre project. I realized what Grotowski meant by "yes but not only" when he was asked in a 1983 interview for the *Los Angeles Times* if this was a theatre project.

The project certainly had a spiritual dimension even though Grotowski never referred to it as spiritual work. This is similar to the spiritual nature of the Balinese theatre that I have been doing since I was a child. Through the work of the project. Grotowski helped to deepen my insights into the spiritual nature of Balinese arts. He brought me back to my own sources. Through my research and knowledge of the Balinese performing arts and my interviews with religious practioners in Bali, I found that there is a parallel between Grotowski's work and Balinese theatre in the training process as well as in its impact on the actor and the spectator.

To analyze and highlight Grotowski's work based on my interpretation as a direct participant and as a Balinese artist, I would first like to consider three elements basic to the Balinese way of life and art. The first is the intimate relationship between people and nature, which is similar to Grotowski's high regard for working in a natural setting. The second is the routine of religious rituals and custom, essential elements which have a close relationship with Grotowski's specific selection of traditional discipline and teaching methods applied in the project. And last, the way the Balinese people consider art, besides being an entertainment, as a medium of true inner expression, connecting the gods to their worshipers. This is similar to Grotowski's work, in the manner in which he examines how performative arts have the potential to generate higher awareness.

It is important to note that these three major elements are woven into Balinese daily life. The daily application of these elements throughout the stages of life allows a Balinese to express his respect for nature, to realize his humanity, and to shape him into a Balinese. As Belo accurately says in her book:

> The Balinese are people whose everyday behavior is measured, controlled, graceful, tranquil. Emotion is not easily expressed. Dignity and an adherence to the rules of decorum are customary. At the same time they show a susceptibility and a facility of going into states of trance, states in which there is an altered consciousness, and a behavior springing from a deep level of personality is manifested.
>
> (Belo 1960: 1)

I believe that Belo's statement about the Balinese has a parallel with what I experienced and observed in the Objective Drama. What do the traditional Balinese do that has inspired Belo to make such a statement? We should first examine the interrelationship between the essential nature of Balinese arts and the Balinese ways of life in relation to religion and nature.

Traditional Balinese arts, whether music, dance, theatre, painting, sculpture, or food offerings always have a religious function as well as an entertainment or worldly function. The "essence of the true effort" in doing the arts serves as an offering to the gods and goddesses, while the "form and energy" generated from and stimulated by the arts or artists entertain, touch, and bring harmony to the spectators. Whether the art is sacred or secular, if it is true art coming from the deepest heart of the artist, the process of the making and the presentation of the arts in Bali always involves a religious commitment. Balinese consider the arts a tool for bringing out the expression of the inner spirit, our true nature. The artist's skill and the true and honest way of doing (*ngayah*) are the mediums for that expression. Because of this attitude, the arts should be handled with care and respect. This should be reflected in one's thoughts and actions.

Care and respect are performed not only to create a sense of humbleness necessary in the arts and in life, but also because what is being cared for and respected has a definite meaning. Precise technical skills, for example, should be acquired through learning and through conforming to the traditional forms. These forms are difficult to master and, therefore, require a strong motivation and dedication. Even though they vary slightly from region to region and master to master, the basic forms – such as the *agem* (basic body positions) – are a physical structure that has a physical and psychological impact. In a precisely performed agem, the creation and flow of energy is nurtured (this will be further described below). Of course there are other technical elements involved in creating these effects of energy. These have an impact on the performer and the spectator: a heightening of awareness and a sense of well-being. A performer may say that s/he feels complete after ngayah, performing a true act.

However, the awakening of higher awareness cannot be fully accomplished only through the mastery of techniques. Observing religious and traditional ways of conduct constitutes the other half of the effort. In Bali, skilled activities, especially those which are going to be exposed to the public, such as the performing arts, are always preceded by a presentation of an offering to the gods or the lower spirits. This is a form of protecting oneself against any unexpected danger. Making offerings is a form of contemplation which results in a self-assurance, an alertness of the body and mind.

To the Balinese, life is wonderful, it is precious. The Balinese believe that an individual is a reincarnation of her or his ancestor, therefore, life is a special thing to have and care for. Balinese also believe that we are not alone in this world. There are higher energies and spirits around us. These others cannot be seen, except occasionally by special eyes, heard by special ears, and understood by unsuppressed instincts. They are unknown to the brain, therefore they are a mystery. The mystery of the unknown and the belief in it create a wonder. This leads to our "humbleness," a state of being that is free, honest, and respectful. This is opposed to an "arrogant" manner – an attitude that a person "knows" is not considered refined and proper.

The Balinese believe that the higher energies (gods) and the lower energies (demons) exist in nature and in us. A Balinese *dalang* (puppeteer) told me: "Pray to your god inside you before you pray to the gods in the temples. If you cannot find it, try to find it while you pray to the gods in the temples." The Balinese believe that gods and other higher and lower energies live at the peak of the sacred mountains, in sacred spots, in sacred objects, in the ocean, in trees, and in animals. Each of these natural elements has its own life and energy. It is no wonder that the Balinese celebrate *tumpek uduh*, a ceremony for trees and animals, every 210 days; *tumpek wayang*, a ceremony for puppetry and performing arts, during which time costumes, headdresses, and masks are given offerings; and *tumpek landep*, a ceremony for sharp objects such as the kris. To the Balinese, their island is full of gods and both good and bad spirits. Their presence is felt instinctively and the vibrations of these energies are overwhelming. It is a magical place.

The Balinese built thousands of temples, shrines, and altars almost everywhere on the island. On this beautiful island, the view is wonderful during the day, while at night and during transitional times the place becomes awesome. The night belongs to the spirit world and to the gods, while the day belongs to the living and also to the ever-present gods. Life and death are one in Bali. Life is a beauty and death is a danger that creates a subtle undertone of fear. Yet, when death must come it is willingly accepted and even celebrated.

To avoid danger, the gods should be consulted and asked for their blessings whenever a person is doing any activity, especially a skilled activity. The lower spirits also have their place, and should be appeased. *Banten* – ornately decorated offerings of food, fruits, flowers, and incense – are usually presented to the gods for their blessings and to the lower spirits to assure that they will not disturb the activities. In the performing arts, the powers of gods or demons may be invoked if they are needed. When an actor is performing the character of a demon, the energy of the demon may be called. Similarly, the god may be invoked if an actor is performing a deity or simply invited to witness and to bless the performance.

The banten physically acknowledges the existence of the gods and spirits of nature and expresses the spiritual commitment of the performer. If the believer does not do this preliminary ritual, he will have a feeling of guilt which leads to anxiety and perhaps incompetence. He may even fail. The Balinese are afraid of this state of imbalance, which could lead them to be mis-oriented (*paling*), and if prolonged, could lead to mental derangement (*buduh*). "Brought up in fear of supernatural danger, there was a persistent need for assurance" (Belo 1960: 251).

RELIGIOUS PREPARATIONS IN TRAINING

When a group of children are chosen to become actors and dancers, an auspicious day from the Balinese calendar is selected for the very first rehearsal. Selecting a special day for the beginning of an activity is a common practice in Bali. The selection of the day is based on the cycle of the planets and the vibration of nature. This special time to start an activity is called *menuasen*, which literally means "to mark with the auspicious day.' On another special day soon after menuasen, the children will undergo a ceremonial initiation called *meperascita*, which literally means "the purification of body and mind." The children may be taken to a temple to ask for a blessing from the gods. Preceding each rehearsal, small offerings (*banten canang*) are made and incense burned at the shrine for the god or guardian of the crossroads where the community center is located. The gamelan orchestra that accompanies the rehearsal, as well as the rehearsal space itself, are also given small offerings. Even though the degree of elaborateness and the frequency of this ritual differs from village to village, or family to family, it is customary in Bali to observe this process properly. An unsuccessful activity would be blamed on the failure to observe the ritual routine, if only in its simplest form. The Balinese would say, "*Sing taen nang ngai canang kenkenan men bisa dueg,*' which literally means, "Just a simple offering you never make, how can you be successful?"

Pasupati is the next ceremony that the children go through once they have achieved a satisfactory level of technical precision. The function of this ceremony is to transform raw materials – the costumes, headdresses, and masks – into powerful art objects by infusing them with spiritual energy. This process, carried out by a priest and blessed by the gods in the temple, transforms these ordinary materials into carriers of sacred power. The performers, who are also present at this ceremony, are further purified as well. In a parallel symbolic sense, the performer's art of dance or acting is transformed from raw learned technique into a spiritually internalized artistic expression. After this purification, the artists are united with the sacred objects and materials that will be used at the moment of their premiere performance and thereafter. From this time onward the performer is ready to seek *taksu*, the ultimate spiritual power that allows the performer to present his or her art in its truest form.

This process of religious ritual occurs not only in the performing arts but also in other skilled professions. To become a priest and/or a diviner, for example, one must go through several steps of ritual purification (*mewinten*) and adhere to an increasing number of behavioral restrictions that distinguish one from ordinary others. Only after these rituals are performed can a priest learn sacred texts such as mantras, sacred chants. The individual must also go through a ceremony called *mesakapan dewa*, a ritual "marriage" to the god of the temple in which he or she officiates as priest or acts as a diviner.

Religious ritual is a necessity in Bali. It is like a need to breathe. It is rejuvenating, a renewal of energy – it becomes a way of life. For this reason, ritual operates in every facet of Balinese life. It is practiced by priests and by lay people. And, of course, it is also practiced by artists. To Balinese, a ritual activity is fun. The ritual is not only the time for the renewal of spiritual energy but also a time of celebration, of good food, of good clothes, and of a good time. It is a time to connect one's self to natural phenomena, and to rediscover one's own inner nature.

The main purpose of a purification ritual is to help the individual to discover the meanings of her or his duties. It also creates a context for attention to appropriate behavior and respect for the occupation one has chosen. Consequently, a person establishes an identity that is valued by the community. This mental cleansing prepares the body and mind to concentrate fully; and through repeated practice it deepens one's dedication and insights. Ritual also generates alertness in the person, a higher awareness necessary in life and the arts. In Bali, this awareness is reinforced by beliefs; its meaning is nurtured by nature; and its continuity is assured through repetition and the training process. Proper traditional training is necessary for effective art, art that functions not only as entertainment, but also as a means of uniting one's true self with the infinite power of nature.

In the Objective Drama Project there were no religious practices, like those in Bali, performed by participants. Even though we worked on exercises which derived from rituals of various traditions, Grotowski never referred to these exercises as religious. They were simply exercises that had special values. However, the manner in which this work was conducted and organized played an important role in the successful result and effect of the work. Like the religious practices that are part of the Balinese training process, the Objective Drama Project was executed in a very distinct manner.

An important word which Grotowski used frequently was "alert;" participants should be alert. In order to be alert the first and most important basic rule to observe is to be silent. This rule permeated every facet of the project. Participants were only allowed to speak when they really needed to express an idea related to the project, or when asked to discuss their reactions to specific activities. During breaks we generally did not speak. This was the time to absorb and internalize the experience. Grotowski called this a "silence of saturation." It was not meant to be a spiritual silence. Those who wished to discuss personal matters were asked to talk outside the project area. Owing to the nature of the work, nobody did this. This requirement was unusually challenging especially for newly arrived participants, as they had to abandon conventional socializing during and between the long hours of work.

Being silent allows many possibilities. Part of the work was to increase the awareness of being in an environment, to settle the mind through silent self-observation. This is closely related to the awareness and alertness resulting from the attentive and respectful manner seen in Balinese religious activities, such as the purification ceremony. By eliminating verbal dialog in the project we reduced the mechanical social interaction of ordinary life. This allowed us to develop an attunement to each other, the group, and the surroundings by sensing their presence or actions. It allowed us to suspend judgments about people and situations and just to be, do, and observe.

There were other specific requirements, such as when one walked in the fields or in the woods one was not allowed to pick up anything or to disturb nature. In Bali, an unnecessary action in nature (*usil*) is a degraded behavior strongly forbidden for Balinese children. In the project we were also told not to make noises with our feet or hum while walking in the field. Similarly, we could not make noises when walking in the rehearsal space. This type of requirement allowed participants to be self-observant, a level of contemplation that leads to alertness. Occasionally Grotowski would spend a long time criticizing those who did not properly observe this way of working. To join the project, a participant had to learn exactly what to do and what not to do, a similar understanding held by believers in Balinese ritual, who know exactly what must be done in order to insure the efficacy of the ritual.

Everything was neatly organized in the project. What needed to be prepared before a work session began was clearly spelled out. Grotowski might ask Du Yee, or Jairo, or me, during the first two hours to discuss his plan for the rest of the session, while the others waited patiently and quietly. During this time some did warm-ups, some simply sat. In the meeting, Grotowski specified what needed to be corrected, who would be correcting whom, where the work would take place, and approximately how long it would take. This was very specific and very orderly. Grotowski never discussed the whole plan of the session, for he did not want people to have expectations that could lead to mechanical work. He wanted to create an organic flow of events, and therefore rearranged the sequence of the work according to the need and flow of each session. He often said that the work should have "new life" at every session. The only exercise with a set time was the exercise called "the Motions." This action was always executed at sunset or sunrise.

We should remember that the project was designed to test the impact of the exercises. The participants were the "guinea pigs," therefore they were not informed of the direction or plan for each session. Probably Grotowski himself did not know what would need work. Even if he knew he did not tell because that would go against the principle of the experiment.

Because of the disciplined nature of the work, the lifestyle in the project was very different from that of normal life. Socialization and an easy-going behavior did not take place. Alleviating one's social problems or complaining was discouraged. Doubt resulting from the rules of working was resolved by quitting the project or participating fully. But even participants who complied with the rules still faced other difficulties of commitment to the work.

This is similar to the commitment in the Balinese training process, except in Bali this commitment is not experienced as hard work, but as a religious commitment. But both the Balinese and Grotowski's style of commitment lead to the establishment of an identity. The religious nature of the traditional Balinese training is more pronounced than in the rigorous work of the Objective Drama Project. In Bali commitment and dedication are internalized; dedication is shown in daily actions, diligent practices. No Balinese actor would practice eight hours a day, or work from early evening until early morning. A Balinese performer might work until early morning when performing but, even so, would not perform everyday. Balinese actors might work hard and adhere to all kinds of rules and restrictions, but these rules and restrictions are tradition – everybody does the same. All are born into this tradition. There is no apparent pressure that an artist experiences, because her or his effort is supported by the society. Commitment and identity are molded by the traditional system, by the natural environment, and by religious beliefs.

Grotowski attempted to recreate this kind of tradition in the project by enforcing ways of working and by working in a natural setting. The experience of the work taught the participants the meaning of the work. Because the project was not intended to be lifelong, but only for three years, Grotowski had to conduct the work very intensively. In the project everything was condensed, distilled, and selected. This ranged from the selection of participants to the strictness of rules and the materials explored in the work.

Working in the evening and through the night with the illumination of only oil lamps, for example, may have seemed unnatural and mysterious to a new participant. But the practical intention of this setting was to make the body and the mind alert. Generally evening is the time most people rest. But if asked to do difficult exercises during these hours and in such a setting, most likely the participant would react organically causing him or her to be alert, and increasing the effectiveness of the work. Grotowski is very fond of the idea of "contradiction," an idea against conventional ways of living and understanding, but with the intention of provoking organic physical and mental responses on the part of participants.

The exercise called the Motions, practiced at sunset or sunrise, also has a practical purpose embedded in the idea of contradiction. Sunset and sunrise are the times when ordinary nature is spectacular. Yet, during the Motions the participant is not allowed to respond emotionally to what she sees. She cannot say the sunset is beautiful, which people normally do; she simply observes what is out there. This is one of the contradictions seen in the Motions, a contradiction that creates alertness and awareness of physical impulses. If this exercise is practised consistently, the alertness resulting from it leads to a sensitivity of the body and, consequently, a spiritual experience.

In an agricultural society such as Bali, a performing art rehearsal usually takes place at night. The training occurs at night because during the day people work in the fields. In the evening their minds are more settled, their bodies are clean, and the temperature is cooler. Religious activities generally occur during transitional times, especially right before sunset. Banten (offerings) are presented to the gods and spirits at this time because this is the moment when the body and mind are alert. To Balinese, transitional times and night time belong to the negative forces and are therefore the times of danger, times to be alert. Any activity conducted during these times must be taken with great care. Thus we see a similar contradiction in the Balinese belief system as that in the Motions.

Another important element of the training process in the project was that Grotowski never described the meaning of or the idea behind any exercise. In the same way, the Balinese (except specialists such as priests) would not know the meanings and symbolism of the elaborate religious rituals. If a Balinese is asked why he performs a religious ritual, the usual answer would be "*Nak mule keto*," meaning "That is the way it has been done." But he knows that he feels a sense of well-being after performing the ritual. Thus the ritual is efficacious. In the project one could only understand the ideas and values of the work by listening to Grotowski, by observing his way, by experiencing the exercises, and by relating them to one's own knowledge. Even so, the understanding was still an interpretation because the meaning of each exercise was not specifically described. Grotowski did not intend to give the meaning or the intended result of the exercises. He did not wish the participants to start working with an "idea." He thought that to work on a physical exercise with an idea would be misleading and deceiving because the mind would be consciously searching for the result of the idea. The action would not be organic and the physical impulses would be blocked.

The rules and the technical precision and strategy of the different exercises were worked out in minute detail. In the workspace or at Grotowski's apartment we often discussed and analyzed them – did they work or not? Changes or adjustments occurred based on reevaluations. Once the criteria and rules were understood and became routine, specific corrections were given, mostly nonverbally. The understanding of the rules and the precision of the exercises were of primary importance. Grotowski and his assistants would always give corrections and criticism. The criticism, which was verbal, could be severe.

Because of the variety of both mental and physical demands encountered in the project, the work was not easy to follow. Grotowski was obviously aware of the difficulties. For this reason, he was very careful in selecting participants. He would look for a particular quality in a candidate. This was not based on technical ability, although technique had a value. It was based more on the "human quality" of the person. I recall when we auditioned 25 students in Pontadera, Italy, Grotowski stated clearly that the selection should first be based on "human quality." What Grotowski meant by "human quality" was a puzzle to me. But during our three years of working together, I somehow understood. My interpretation is a person who is not arrogant, not pretentious, not overly nice, and not talkative; someone who is humble, simple, subtle but bright; a person who seems to have an interest in adventure and a curiosity for life. If this interpretation is correct, then I would definitely see a close relationship with the Balinese ideal of a novice performer.

The Balinese traditional theatre follows a formal structure, with characters that are well known to the people. Characters are divided into three different types: deities, humans, and demons. Actors are chosen for a role according to their personalities, human qualities, and physical types. The qualifications for the selection of a novice in Bali include a refined manner, respectfulness, and tolerance. Being humble is an important qualification because the responsibility of the artist is to become a medium. The artist must be able to invoke the character and allow that character to live through him or her. The spirit of the character would most likely enter the artist who has the qualifications mentioned.

PHYSICAL EXERCISES

Kinesthetic learning is the most important aspect of the learning process in both Balinese traditional training and in Grotowski's training. Verbal communication, describing what is being learned, is not a part of this training process. This is an ancient way in which a novice learns through the body directly rather than through a preliminary mental process. Grotowski says that "the body itself functions like a brain"; it can record and later recall movement patterns and emotion in a seemingly instinctive way, when stimuli are given. Grotowski discouraged learning through verbal explanation, perhaps because the brain does not record the emotional quality of an action when learned through a mental process only. Learning kinesthetically, on the other hand, incorporates both the physical precision and the emotional quality of the action. This is also true of vocal work.

In Bali kinesthetic learning takes place in two distinct ways. In the first, the teacher moves the body of the young student, shaping and giving the flow of the direction of the movement. The body of the child is manipulated as a puppet is manipulated by a puppeteer. When the student is older and more accomplished, the teacher may offer corrections by a light touch or facial and body signals. The student also learns through observing and following the teacher, repeating the voice or movement sequence many times. Repetition is another basic principle of kinesthetic learning through which the body will internalize the physical experience. Repetition may lead to a mechanical quality but a student is instructed to find the life of the action in each repetition.

In the Objective Drama Project, this process of training was highly valued and consistently applied. Throughout the work, the exercises were communicated mostly nonverbally. When verbal direction was needed, the leader or teacher used only limited and precise words. Otherwise the exercises were conducted in silence. If necessary, Grotowski would explain the requirements of an exercise. Occasionally he gave a lengthy instruction, or got up during an action, speaking loudly. Sometimes he screamed, adding energy to a weak action. As in Balinese training, the actions were learned through following the leader; the observation/ physical imitation/repetition formula was used, as in traditional training. However, the Balinese puppet method of shaping the student's body was not applied because the project students were already adults. Using this method with adults is physically impractical and socially inappropriate.

THE MOTIONS

The Motions is a physical exercise that incorporates several elements of training. It is a body-stretching exercise as well as training for mental endurance. The primary purpose of this exercise is to train the body to be sensitive and the mind to be alert. The Motions, executed in a standing position, is a complex exercise, meditative in quality, slowly performed and physically strenuous. It was usually practiced outdoors on the hillside, in silence, and during transitional times, especially at sunset and at sunrise. The exercise always begins facing the sun. The original duration of the Motions was about an hour and a half, but later it was reduced to 45 minutes. It is normally done in a group, in a diamond-shaped formation, in which four leaders stand at the four corners of the diamond. The participants find their places inside the diamond shape with appropriate distances from each other. They should be able to see the leaders at the four directions they are going to face, just as the Balinese novice can clearly see the teacher and follow the action.

Figure 11.2 The *agem*, or basic body position, for Balinese dance theatre. (Photo by Leslie S. Lendra.)

The exercise relates to seven directions: east, west, north, south, up, down, and center. The up and down are performed in connection with body movements, and the imaginary center is associated with the heart and with what Grotowski calls the "primary position." There are three major movements, each of which is repeated at the four directions. The three major movements are connected by several transitional movements. There is also a very slow turning which is used to reach the four cardinal points. The slow turning, executed in place, may take from one to two minutes depending on which direction is being reached. However, there is a basic body position which appears to be one of the most important features of the Motions. This movement is similar to the basic stance of Balinese dance theatre called agem (Figure 11.2).[1]

The primary position is executed standing. The feet are placed parallel, about one fist apart. The knees are slightly bent and the body weight rests on the balls of the feet, as if the performer is ready to move. The torso and the head and chin are gently pulled in, so that energy travels from the bottom of the spine up to the head. The torso and the head are tilted forward, which allows a slight contraction and pull at the bottom of the torso. The pelvic region is tucked in, the abdomen is lifted, and the chest and the shoulders are relaxed. The arms are straight, placed at either side of the body, and the base of each thumb touches slightly the section below the hips. The palms face backward, and the fingers, touching each other, are slightly curved in and relaxed. The eyes see in a panoramic view, a wide-angle vision. In this primary position the body should feel light and ready. This position is intended to develop the sensitivity of the body and to help generate mental alertness.

Grotowski's primary position is similar to the Balinese agem in the alignment of the torso and the head, and in the effect of the position on the body and mind. An exception is the male-style agem for a strong character, for which the legs are turned out and about one step diagonally apart. The pelvic region is slightly thrust out instead of tucked in as in the primary position. Because in Balinese dance the upper arms are generally raised in line with the shoulders, and the lower arms, with hyperextended hands and spread fingers, are bent forward at the elbows, the shoulders tend to be slightly contracted. However, the most important quality of both agem and the primary position is the alignment of the torso and the head, as well as the slight leaning forward of this line of the body. The tilt causes a pull and a contraction which generates energy. This energy flows upward to the head which then causes the intended awareness. This is closely related to the elaborate Indian energy system of *chakra*, in which the energy generated from the bottom of the spine (*muladara*) travels upward to the head (*sahasrāra*), the crown chakra. At this point higher awareness is achieved. Another essential result of both the Balinese basic stance and the primary position, in my experience, is that it creates the feeling of lightness and readiness. There is an essential feeling of energy traveling upward, triggering physical and mental sensitivity.

Another essential requirement of the Motions is that the eyes should see in a wide angle, a panoramic view, and the ears should hear all sounds at once. Grotowski usually said: "See that you are seeing and hear that you are hearing." This is a difficult thing to do and at first it sounds like a crazy thing to do. Participants are instructed not to react to what they are seeing or hearing. Typically, when performing this slow and meditative exercise, our brain begins speaking – a variety of thoughts will come. If thoughts come we must not react to the thoughts or continue to develop the thoughts, but instead simply observe them. We notice the thoughts and let them pass by in the same way we observe what we see and hear. While seeing and hearing, the body must be in the correct position and we must remember the sequence of the action. During this action, the body often slightly changes its position without our awareness. Because of this, Grotowski insisted that we strive always to be aware of the precision of the body position and make self-corrections from time to time.

The rules of this exercise seem to be simple, but to perform the Motions precisely – physically and mentally – is extremely difficult. The brain is occupied with monitoring the minute details of the physical action, thus freeing the inner mind, the subtler consciousness, to "come out" and merge with the environment. The inner consciousness can only do this when the brain is engaged in some directed thinking and so does not interfere. But the purpose of the physical precision of the movements is not just to keep the brain busy. When the movements are performed as designed, they help the body to generate innate physical power. If the brain fails to watch the body, fails to observe the thoughts, and reacts emotionally to what is seen by the eyes and heard by the ears, the inner energy will not manifest itself.

The Motions is a complex exercise. Several elements of technique are performed at once. To see really with panoramic vision is difficult. When we are able to see in a panoramic view, our perception cannot be as focused as when we see only one thing. This is difficult because in daily life we constantly focus, selecting from our perceptions what we want to see or hear. The brain is curious and will follow something of interest, almost automatically. But the requirement of the Motions is that we must not react to any one thing but must fully perceive all that there is to see and hear. To see and hear and not to react, according to the way we normally live, is a contradiction. This contradiction creates "life" and self-awareness.

In my experience, when I see with panoramic vision and hear all sounds – both in performing Balinese dance/acting and in doing the Motions precisely – I become highly aware of my body; it absorbs what I see and hear. The surroundings become one with my body, and I feel as if my body is hollow and is being lifted. The more I see and hear, the more I sense my body. Especially in the Motions I feel the vibration of my energy throughout my body and I feel the pulses of my heart in my feet. Sometimes I hear a high-pitched and continuous noise in my ears. Different parts of my body sometimes move by themselves. As I become aware of all these sensations, it seems that my attention to them diminishes the flow. When this happens, I proceed to correct my body positions. After each session of the Motions, I usually have the feeling of distilled energy and oneness in my body.

CONCLUSION

The Motions is one of the physical exercises practiced in the Objective Drama Project. In my observation and understanding, these exercises have a single, most important purpose: the awakening of innate physical power. This physical power, which the Hindu tradition refers to as the "sleeping energy" (*kundalini*), lies at the bottom of the spine. This innate energy can be awakened through a variety of physical and vocal exercises. Grotowski described what I call innate physical power as the "reptile brain," the spinal cord and brain stem,[2] with the "sleeping energy" at the very bottom of the spine. This unawakened energy source exists in every human being. Grotowski wanted to investigate and find a way to wake up this energy center which, when awakened, can increase our awareness, sensitivity, and perception. The awakened state is necessary not only in life but also in the performing arts. For this reason Grotowski was interested in working on the undulating spinal movement of the Haitian voudoun ritual and the Hindu spinal movement exercise called kundalini, which I studied and practiced closely. Like the Motions, these two exercises have a powerful effect on the body.

In Bali, the study of gaining spiritual energy is still a strong tradition practiced by trancers and diviners. It is also practiced by dalangs, and by *pregina wayah*, highly accomplished artists, usually older performers. In the arts, this ability to awaken innate physical power and invoke this energy is a necessity. The function of artists is to be more than entertainers. They are also considered to be mediums between the people and the gods. For this reason they need to have spiritual knowledge and the ability to invoke this innate energy. An artist who has this ability is considered to have *taksu*, an ultimate spiritual energy that helps the performer project the essence of his or her art.

The knowledge and ability to invoke taksu is not limited to artists. Intelligent individuals can also have this innate or learned ability. Dr I Made Bandem, a Balinese and a scholar in Indonesian performing arts told me that taksu can be referred to as "genuine creativity," an ability acquired through education, practice, and the experience of both worldly and spiritual insights.

In Bali, highly competent spiritual practitioners such as priests, priestesses, diviners and traditional healers – especially those attached to specific temples – are also considered to have taksu. They can invoke innate physical power and receive signs and messages from nature. The diviners belonging to specific temples through their trance states deliver the messages of the gods or goddesses to the people. The messages are oracles which are followed by the people. The messages often contain requests for what is lacking and what needs to be done to restore the balance of life in the community. They can also contain prophecies or predictions which consequently alert the people and direct them to take necessary actions. This tradition remains alive in Bali – and is similar to what Grotowski is investigating.

But the most important part of the research at UCI was the training process. The research of the Objective Drama Project included selecting participants, setting the work in the natural environment, training the participants to be sensitive to nature, applying specific regulations in the workplace, and, most important, using various exercises from traditional performative arts and ancient literatures. All of these elements are parallel to traditional training in Balinese arts and life.

CULTURE IS THE BODY

Tadashi Suzuki

The main purpose of my method is to uncover and bring to the surface the physically perceptive sensibility which actors had originally, before the theatre acquired its various codified performing styles, and to heighten their innate expressive abilities. I first began to think of the method when I was trying to search for ways to examine the differences in physical perception among different peoples, such as are found while the actors on stage just stand still, or have an impulse, take some action. I wished to integrate these differences into something we humans could share as a common property, beyond all differences in race and nationality.

First of all, I felt the necessity of inspecting our human orientation, in sensibility or feeling, toward the ground or floor – the attraction for the ground which the lower half of the body feels. I extracted some basic ways of using the body as perceiving various nuances of feeling, and then arranging them to formulate my method.

Technically speaking, my method consists of training to learn to speak powerfully and with clear articulation, and also to learn to make the whole body *speak*, even when one keeps silent. It is thus that actors can learn the best way to exist on the stage. By applying this method, I want to make it possible for actors to develop their ability of physical expression and also to nourish a tenacity of concentration.

In short, this training is, so to speak, a grammar necessary to materialize the theatre that is in my mind. However, it is desirable that this "grammar" should be assimilated into the body as a second instinct, just as one cannot enjoy a lively conversation as long as one is always conscious of grammar in speaking. These techniques should be mastered, studied, until they serve as an "operational hypothesis," so that the actors may truly feel themselves "fictional" on stage. For actors to realize the images they themselves pursue, they will have to develop at least this basic physical sensibility.

In my opinion, a "cultured" society is one where the perceptive and expressive abilities of the human body are used to the full; where they provide the basic means of communication. A civilized country is not always a "cultured" society.

It is true that civilization originated in connection with the functions of the human body; it may be interpreted as the expansion of basic functions of the human body or the extension of the physical faculties – of the eyes, ears, tongue, the hands and feet. For example, the invention of such devices as the telescope and microscope is a result of human aspiration and endeavor to *see more*, radicalizing the faculty of sight. The accumulated effect of such endeavors is civilization – the product of the expansion and extension of physical faculties.

What we have to consider, then, is the kind of energy required to materialize such aspirations. That leads us to think about modernization. A criterion some sociologists in the United States apply to distinguish between modernized and pre-modernized societies is the ratio of animal energy to non-animal energy. Animal energy here refers to the physical energy supplied by human beings, horses or cattle, etc.; while non-animal energy refers to electric power, nuclear power and the like. One way of showing whether a country is modernized is to calculate how much non-animal energy is used. Roughly speaking, in African and Near Eastern countries, for example, the ratio of animal energy used is very high, compared with such countries as the United States or Japan, where energy derived from oil, electricity, nuclear power is used in all processes of production.

If we apply this thinking to the theatre, we notice that most contemporary theatre is "modernized"; non-animal energy is fully utilized. Lighting is done through electricity. Elevators and revolving stages are operated by electrical energy. The building of the theatre itself is the end-product of a variety of industrial activities from the concrete foundation to the props and scenery.

On the contrary, the Japanese *nō* theatre is a surviving example of pre-modern theatre in which almost no non-animal energy is used. Take music, for example. In the modern theatre, it is recorded and reproduced through amplifiers and loud-speakers, whereas the voices of the dancer-actor and the chorus and the sound of the instruments played on stage in the *nō* theatre are conveyed *directly* to the audience. Costumes and masks for *nō* plays are made by hand, and the stage itself is built based on traditional principles of carpentry. Although electricity is used for lighting nowadays (which I still object to – in the old days it used to be done by candles and tapers), it is limited to the minimum, never like the elaborate and colorful lighting of the "modern" theatre. *Nō* theatre is pervaded by the spirit of creating something out of human skill and effort. So much so that the *nō* can be said to be the epitome of pre-modern theatre! It is a creation of animal energy.

As the theatre, either in Europe or in Japan, has kept up with the times and has come to use non-animal energy in every facet of its activities, one of the resulting evils is that the faculties of the human body and physical sensibility have been overspecialized to the point of separation. Just as civilization has specialized the job of the eyes and created the microscope, modernization has "dismembered" our physical faculties from our essential selves.

What I am striving to do is to restore the wholeness of the human body in the theatrical context, not simply by going back to such traditional theatrical forms as *nō* and *kabuki*; but, by employing their unique virtues, to create something transcending current practice in the modern theatre.

We need to bring together the physical functions once "dismembered"; to regain the perceptive and expressive abilities and powers of the human body. In doing so, we can maintain culture within civilization.

In my method of training actors, I place special emphasis on the feet, because I believe that consciousness of the body's communication with the ground leads to a great awareness of all the physical junctions of the body.

A basic part of my method of training involves actors stomping on the floor for a certain period of time to rhythmic music, or rather, walking around fiercely beating the floor with the feet in a semi-squatting posture. Then, the moment the music stops, the actors relax their bodies totally, falling on the floor. They lie completely still and quiet. After a while, music starts again, but this time it must be slow and smooth. In accordance with the change in the music, they slowly rise to their feet in any way they like, eventually standing upright, back in a natural posture. This training consists of a pair of contrasting movements, that is, the dynamic and static (motion and rest); in other words, emission and repression of physical power. The purpose of this training is to develop concentration on the body through controlling the breathing.

The essential point of the first half of this training is to keep stomping with a constant force, without swaying the upper half of the body. If the actor does not concentrate his consciousness on his feet, legs and hips which must be well-disciplined, it is impossible for him to continue to stomp consistently, however energetic he may be. Moreover, without the spiritual power and will to control his breathing, the upper half of his body gradually begins to sway and then the rhythm of the stomping becomes irregular. If one beats the floor with one's feet, the force naturally influences the upper half of the body to make it sway. As I get actors to stomp as forcefully as possible, a reaction rises upwards so the more strongly they stomp the more the upper half of their body sways. If they try to minimize the sway, they have to repress the force with their hips. They have to stomp while always being aware of the relationship between upper and lower halves of the body which are pivoted together at the hips.

Of course, emphasizing the fact that the construction of the human body and the balance of the forces which support it are centered on the pelvic region is not thinking unique to my method; almost all the performing arts invariably use such thinking. However, I believe it is specific to my training that first of all the actors are made to feel conscious of this by stomping and beating the ground with their feet. This is derived from my belief that the basic physical sensibility of any stage actor depends on his feet. In our daily life, we tend to disregard the importance of the feet. It is necessary for us to be aware that the human body makes contact with the ground through the feet, that the ground and the human body are inseparable, as the latter is, in fact, part of the former, meaning that when we die we return to the earth. We must make the body, which usually functions unconscious of such a relationship, aware of this fact by creating a strong sense of impact through the beating of the ground with the feet.

This idea of mine has often been said to be quite Japanese, but it is not. Even in classical European ballet, in which the dancers seem to aim at jumping from the ground to soar through the air, the basic physical sensibility consists of a feeling of affinity to the ground.

Again, in traditional Japanese theatrical forms, such as *nō* and *kabuki*, the balance of the two vectors leading towards the sky and the earth, towards the heights and the depths, has been very important in physical expression. However, in the traditional Japanese theatrical forms, these two forces with vectors contrary to each other meet at the pelvic region, and the energy derived from this tends to radiate horizontally. Therefore, the higher the upper half of the body tries to go, the lower the lower half of the body tries to sink to balance this movement. The feeling that the feet are planted firmly on the ground is thus increased. This is symbolized in such movements as sliding steps (*Suri-ashi*) or stomping (*Ashi-byoshi*) which express the affinity with the earth.

The late Shinobu Origuchi, a prominent Japanese anthropologist and man of letters, said that when examining Japanese performing arts, he found that the performers invariably stomp at some part of the performance and that appearing on the stage in itself signifies the treading down of evil spirits under the ground; the stomping is called *Hembai*. Seen from this point of view, the sliding steps (*Suri-ashi*) in *nō* plays can be considered as preparatory movement to set off the stomping. According to Origuchi, the essence of traditional Japanese dancing is wandering around the stage, which originally signified sanctifying the place by treading down the evil spirits. The series of movements in my training consists of two parts – first, straining the whole body, concentrating the forces at the hips, stomping to the same constant rhythm; and then, after collapsing on the floor to lie still, getting up again to music like a marionette, by extending a calm strength throughout the body. All is achieved by completely changing the quality of what we might call the raw, unconcentrated body of everyday life. That is why many beginners feel that they are just forced to move mechanically and that the delicate nuances of their own bodies disappear. According to my own experience in giving this training, actors in the United States, who are close to realistic acting, tend to feel like that. Even though they begin stomping forcefully and seriously, they soon lose their concentration and their bodies "loosen." There are some people who watch this and consider my training particularly Japanese; who say that the training is unsuitable for American actors because their legs are long compared with those of the Japanese actors. However, it has nothing to do with the length of the legs or the stamina, but with the discovery of an inner physical sensibility or with the recognition of an inner and profound memory innate to the human body. In other words, it is to do with the ability to uncover this profound physical sensibility and to give it full play. Therefore, it is not necessarily only Japanese actors who are likely to assimilate the aim of my training into their body. Whether in Europe or in Japan, stomping or beating the ground with the feet is a universal physical movement necessary for us to become highly conscious of our own body or to create a "fictional" space, which might also be called a ritualistic space, where we can achieve a personal metamorphosis.

The stomping or beating the floor with the feet originates in ancient Japanese rituals.

Origuchi, in his "Six Lectures on the History of Traditional Japanese Performing Arts," mentions the Opening Ritual of the Heavenly Stone Wall in the Japanese Creation Myth as the origin of the Sacred Dance (*Kagura*), and talks about the rhythmical dancing to calm down the spirits, which a goddess named Ameno-Uzumeno-Mikoto danced, turning over a wooden tub and stomping on it and striking it with the end of a stick. He says:

> Perhaps the tub symbolized the earth. The goddess stomped on it and struck it with a stick while making loud noises; actions supposed to wake up and bring out the soul or spirit that was believed to be under the tub, whether sleeping or hiding, in order to send it to the unseen sacred body of the god nearby.

He infers that the purpose of the action of stomping and striking is not necessarily to tread down or suppress evil enemies but to arouse their energy in order to use it to activate human life. As a result, an effect similar to that of exorcism is brought about, since by acquiring the spirit of evil it is possible to overcome it. The fact that *nō* and *kabuki* actors often stomp on the stage floor can be regarded as a practice related to this tradition.

The ancient Japanese stages were built on graves or mounds where the souls of the dead were considered to dwell. This has led to the custom where, even now, people hollow out the ground or bury a pot before building a *nō* stage over it. This is not only for the sake of technical effectiveness – the hollow ground makes the sound of stomping resound better – but it is a procedure to create an illusion that the actor can conjure up earth spirits or the spirits of ancestors who have returned to the earth, in order to acquire their energy. The resonance enforces the physical feeling of responding to the spirits. Even today such an illusion is necessary for actors on stage: that the energy of the spirits can be felt through the feet to activate our own bodies is a most natural and valuable illusion for human beings. *Nō* is well blessed because it has continued to cherish this idea right up to the present. Graves and mounds can be regarded as wombs from which we have been born. In that sense the earth is a "Mother" herself. Actors can undertake their roles on the premise that they are connected with all humanity as integrating individuals.

Perhaps it is not the upper half but the lower half of our body through which the physical sensibility common to all races is most consciously expressed; to be more specific, the feet. The feet are the last remaining part of the human body which has kept, literally, in touch with the earth, the very supporting base of all human activities.

(Compiled and translated by Kazuko Matsuoka.)

13

MY BODIES

The performer in West Java

Kathy Foley

"The soul changes its abode, the soul changes its abode, changes its garments," sings the *dalang* (puppetmaster) of the *wayang golek*, the Sundanese puppet theatre of West Java, Indonesia. While chanting, the performer replaces one puppet with another; a refined lady becomes a dynamic warrior; a fanged ogre sports the svelte body of Arjuna, playboy of the Eastern World; a fat, hermaphroditic clown appears in the glorious form of a divinity. The Sundanese do not necessarily feel, as I believe most Americans do, that our individual human body and soul are inextricably bound together till death do us part. This lyric on the movable soul, sung for each of the many transformations that may occur in a performance, tells us as much. It would not occur to the Sundanese to worry, as I did in the back rows of my Catholic school classroom, about the age and state of development my body would have reached when Gabriel's horn called it forth for eternal reunion with my soul at the world's end.

Memoirs of a Catholic girlhood may seem an odd beginning to a description of how performers in West Java learn to "multiply" their bodies in performance by learning to play via masks (*topeng*) and puppets (*wayang*). Yet the recollections, I hope, suggest the distance I have traveled in my 15 years of studying the theatre of West Java. Though I speak as an individual, my experiences participate in the cultural distance that exists between a contemporary Westerner's passionate embrace of the individual body, personal identity, and history as the beginning point from which an artist works to sketch her/his view of the world, and the way the Sundanese and Cirebonese people of West Java work against individual mannerisms, personality, and history to find the range these circumstances of life limit. The distance I have traveled, though it seems vast, is no longer than the three-foot trip up the human spinal column: the stylized characters that each performer learns to dance as masks and manipulate as puppets are, I will reveal, ways of introducing the performer to different energies and balance points that are latent in each human body. Through the one body we inhabit in this life we can, with the help of these puppets or masks and the ideas they encode, embody the whole cosmos.

This trip is introduced to the performer via training that may extend over a semiformal learning period of two to ten years, though childhood exposure prepares the way. Through observation of teachers' performances of mask dance and puppetry and the rote physical replication of the teachers' gestures, with little verbal or written explanation, the student lets the new patterns of movement and vocalization enter *daging lan darah*, his "flesh and blood." Thereafter, the student is expected to understand intuitively the meaning of the practice.

I will discuss the performance practice of West Java in three ways: (1) creating distance; (2) introducing the character types of mask and puppet work; and (3) comprehending the system. The order roughly replicates the process that I experienced when learning the dance and puppet theatre of West Java and corresponds to the way Sundanese performers of today articulate their own artistic development.[1]

CREATING DISTANCE

The body of the artist in topeng, wayang, and virtually all the traditional theatre of West Java,[2] is ideologically distanced from the bodies of the characters presented in performance. A conventionalized system of movement and vocal stylization defines the characters' sex, age, and nature. Masks and puppets highlight this separation of character from performer. The training, likewise, creates distance between the performer and what is performed. Moving away from real life is the first step of training. Through emulating the teacher in stylized theatrical movement and voice, the student develops a wide range of types which may include a character analogous to her own as well as other more distant characters.

The preference for set characterizations is sustained by the fact that solo puppetry and mask performances (genres benefiting from stylization) are considered the oldest and most important theatres in West Java, as in much of Southeast Asia. Theatre by multiple performers is considered less important, an innovation of the last two or three centuries, and, except in the modern drama experiments of the university-educated elite beginning in the late 1960s, movement and voice characterization in this human theatre are consciously modeled on conventions of the puppet/mask characters.[3]

As a result of these conventions, the Sundanese do not demand that the gender, age, or even species of the performer and the character coincide – men play women, women play men. Septuagenarians may be singled out for their fine representations of adolescent characters; and demons, gods, and animals are all felt to be splendidly performable by human beings. The proper focus of study in this system is not wo/mankind, but the totality of beings that make up the universe. This system recognizes that the particulars of bodily life change with gender, age, and circumstances, but that souls are more comprehensive and in need of fuller exercise: the individual "soul" participates in the overall cosmic power manifest in all things continuing eternally; material "abodes" – bodies – are limited and temporary containers of this force.

Thus, ideological gender equality is part of the system, and men and women have traditionally had access to the roles of dancer, puppeteer, and actor along the north coast of West Java, performing all the varied parts (Foley 1987). Admittedly more specialization of the sexes does emerge in the highlands which are inhabited by Sundanese-speaking people. In this area women have closer association with mask dance than puppetry, and some genres in which they appear were associated with prostitution in the pre-1945 colonial period (Arjo 1989). Males were and still are the puppeteers in the Sundanese highlands.

Set character types, bodies, masks, or puppets are presented as changeable abodes for the more unitary and enduring power of the performer's soul. This more encompassing energy takes many forms not distinguished by age, gender, or rank. Benedict Anderson's essay "The Idea of Power in Java" is useful for understanding why "object theatre" is so attractive to people in this part of the world:

> Power is that intangible, mysterious, and divine energy which animates the universe. It is manifested in every aspect of the natural world, in stones, trees, clouds, and fire, but is expressed quintessentially in the central mystery of life, the process of generation and regeneration. In Javanese traditional thinking there is no sharp division between organic and inorganic matter, for everything is sustained by the same invisible power.
>
> (Anderson 1972: 7)

This power is not of itself good or evil; human, animal, or divine. Though containers change, the power is the same. Energy that in one manifestation may be a human being, may at other points in time inhabit the body of a tiger, or lodge within a tree or atop a mountain after death. The human soul participates in this power as does everything and our individual bodies are tools whereby we can begin to experience and, gradually, understand this power cycling through the world. The dancer or the dalang who moves many different figures but is not bound forever to a single one, shows how unitary power activates/is active in the universe. By moving away from oneself in puppetry and mask performance, one better understands the potential of the self: the possibility for positive and/or negative actualizations of the power latent within all beings.

The topeng and wayang theatre radically separates performer (power) and the performed character (individual manifestation of the power). That is why the training moves first away from the performer's personality only to reintegrate it later in the new system developed through continued practice. It is interesting to note that the American actor trained in the Stanislavsky system usually begins by drawing closer to the self; early acting assignments are often characters close to the performer in age and type, certainly in gender, race, and species.

The Sundanese or Cirebonese dancer, regardless of personality, begins by learning a refined character whose slow, measured movement and melodious, centered voice are considered furthest from the ordinary self. By starting with the character which stretches the average performer most, the system tries to enfranchise him/her with the full potential range. Although individual performers may exhibit a special aptitude for a particular type of character, most consciously abjure cultivating favorites.[4] I believe this is because they are sensitive to the fact that in mask and puppet theatre performers are not dedicated to any particular type, since this would limit command of the full cycle of characters. The training is designed to give each performer multiple personae, with different vocal, energy, and spatial usages – different "bodies" – so that the performer can ultimately realize that *all* of the masks of the "other" are merely sides of the eternal self. The major masks represent the directions of the world, the ages of life, and the elements of the universe. All of these inhabit each human being.

THE MASKS

The mask and puppet traditions of West Java are based on a sequence of set character types that find their clearest representations in the *topeng babakan* (literally, "masked acts") of the north coast city of Cirebon.[5] Four major masked characters are presented in a storyless, six-hour performance by a dalang. In times past, this dalang would also be the narrator of a masked drama (*wayang topeng*), or sometimes a puppet play using shadow (*wayang kulit*) or wooden rod figures (*wayang cepak*).[6] The creation of both topeng and various forms of wayang is attributed by performers to the Javanese holy man Sunan Kalijaga and his eight companions who converted Java to Islam in the late sixteenth century.[7] Although the exact number of masks that are danced in a performance in any particular village of the Cirebon area varies, the four classes (very refined, semirefined, warrior, and emotionally uncontrolled) are always in evidence. In the masked performance, dancers usually call the four figures by character names – while in the unmasked dances and puppetry of that area, a word categorizing the personality is more often used to identify the type. In the descriptions that follow I will give the mask names used in the village of

Figure 13.1 The refined character mask, associated with Panji, is presented in a topeng dance drama in Cirebon. In this instance, the dalang speaks the dialog through a microphone as the performers dance the story. The seated figure in the half mask is a clown character. (Photo by Kathy Foley.)

Slangit with the name for the Sunda personality type in parentheses. A description of the movement and the vocalization will give a sense of the actual performance of each particular type.

Panji (*lungguh* – very refined) is generally the first mask presented (Figure 13.1). A delicate white mask with an aquiline nose and thin, elongated eyes, this legendary prince Panji is considered by the Javanese to be a great cultural hero. The music that accompanies Panji is complex and the dance, while appearing to be almost stationary when viewed from the outside, demands the most intense internal focus and undivided concentration. In mastering the dance the performer learns subtly to shift the weight of his/her feet from toe to ball so that the character can move imperceptibly toward the audience. The slightest head accents mark the heavy stroke of the gong, while subtle shoulder rolls awaken precise articulations on the spine and activate an unobstructed, if almost unseeable, energy flow that is the character. The otherworldly aura of Panji is immediately apparent to the performer, but not necessarily engaging to the audience. Endo Suanda, a student of Sujana Arja, a major contemporary topeng performer in Slangit, notes, "This dance, it seems to me, is more for the dalang's inner satisfaction or meditation than for the audience's entertainment" (Suanda 1983: 104).

The dancer moves relaxedly in the space defined by his/her natural kinesphere. Panji's visual focus is directed to the ground about a body length in front of him, almost giving the impression of being recycled back into his body. What I will call the center of gravity,[8] by which I mean the area of the body where the dancer places the energy focus, is low, in the umbilical area near the base of the spine. This extension of energy toward the earth and the maintenance of a wide, deep plié allows all the parts of the body above this center to give a floating impression. A sphere of energy is created, but it slows down time, negates space, and is turned back on itself rather than grabbing the audience. It pushes the dancer into the self and urges him/her to savor the slightest movements, especially those originating where the shoulders and head meet the spine. The vocal placement associated with Panji is created by focusing the sound in the mouth cavity while letting the jaw drop and relax even as the upper jaw raises slightly creating extra space. "Masaman" is a tuning word which is used for Panji. The speaker first draws out the syllables, placing the voice comfortably, then continues into the slow expansive sentences of Panji's speeches.[9]

Panji is the most relaxed and economical in his energy and space usage, but this very economy of movement, combined with complexity of music, balanced center, and inner quality make Panji's character difficult to achieve. Ideologically Panji is said to represent the ruler, the direction north, *mutmainah* (peace), the color white, the ancestral origins of the Javanese which are associated with mountain tops (a favored abode for ancestral beings), fertility, rain, and semen. Panji is said to be the child newly entered into the world testing out his senses. It is interesting to note that Panji achieves all of these images associated with high, eternally flowing fertility, by keeping his center low. What goes down, must float up. I associated Panji with the head, since the movement directs the mind up into itself and traditional imagery reinforces this interpretation: north and mountains are associated with the head. The island of Java is perceived as a body with the northern mountains comprising its head and the southern ocean its nether regions.

Pamindo (*ladak* – semirefined) is the second mask, with a white face and curly dark hair. The movement is dynamic, nimble and joyful, while remaining refined and maintaining a center of gravity in the navel region.

Shoulders swivel, floor pattern curves, and wrists undulate with a full sense of flow. The character is said to be adolescent, a coquettish female,[10] rejoicing in the delights of her world. This mask is frequently used to represent princesses. She giggles, fixes betel leaf, combs her hair, pretends to peer into a mirror, using stylized gestures to connote these actions. She sits with legs extended in front and softly jackknifes her body with the arms extended high over her head, and seems to fall asleep. Then, ever so gradually, she rises, unfolds her body and arms until, head up and arms to either side, she seems a bird soaring upward and forward.

Indeed the movements from this seated part to the end of the dance often have names of birds (usually swan or crane) and are felt to be imitative of these creatures. It seems possible that the sequence from sitting to soaring is a vestige of more ritual performances which connect birds and ancestral spirits in a wide area of the Pacific.[11] These bird associations are felt to be significant by performers who relate Pamindo to a bird, saying hers is the oldest topeng dance from which the others derive (see Rogers-Aguiniga 1986).

The character focuses on the audience, looking at the ground about two body lengths in front of herself; she luxuriates in, but does not confront, the viewer's gaze directly. The vocal resonance associated with Pamindo is two notes of the gamelan scale above the rounded vocalization of the Panji character. To create the voice the performer directs the stream of sound toward the hard palate and the upper teeth. The tuning sound which produces this resonance is "ke-ke-ke," and a quick breathless pace is used for delivering the dialog. Pamindo is associated with the west, *supiyah* (possessiveness), the color yellow, and is felt to be the individual wandering here and there looking for her mission in the world. Pamindo is refined like Panji, but her higher center allows for more quixotic use of space and time and for greater audience interaction. While Panji is firmly aligned with the clearest consciousness of self and head, I associate Pamindo's character with possibilities that are slightly dangerous but exciting, the floating possibilities that twisting and turning and total concentration can allow to flow free. The association of Pamindo with the west links her with sunset, death, and the difficult but exciting energy of the left hand.

The next major character type to appear is Tumenggung (*punggawa* – official, warrior), a prime minister whose rose-colored mask has a curling moustache. His use of space and time is more direct and energetic. His visual focus is directly toward the audience. Wide strides are his customary step, and quickly repeating gongs make it easy for the dancer to signal transitions from one movement sequence to the next. The complex patterns of movement (and implied complexity of thought) that characterize Panji and Pamindo are simplified. The deep, throaty, reverberating voice associated with Tumenggung is attained by tightening the folds of the vocal cords and utilizing the chest as the major resonator. The speech is considered, its delivery slow. The center of gravity for this character is higher on the spine, in the back of the solar plexus, and this pulling up of energy allows for freer movement of the legs which swing wide from the hip joint permitting Tumenggung to cover ground quickly. His big movements command wider audience attention. Tumenggung is felt to be a male character of 40, in the prime of life. He is associated with the east, black, *luwamah* (determination), growth, and strength. Though with his high center he is less firmly planted than the earlier characters, his forceful energy gives the impression he accomplishes more in the immediate moment. Tumenggung's connection with the east and forcefulness link him with the power of the right hand.

Finally the mask Klana (*angkara murka* – emotionally uncontrolled) appears (Figure 13.2). His red face and fangs denote the emotional uncontrol that is frowned upon in Java and associated with ogres and demons. Klana is Panji's opponent and is usually enamored of Pamindo. Klana is a man in the throes of death, but longing greedily for life. Short, sharp shocks of movement, jumps, and kicks characterize his dance. His visual focus skims over the audience's heads. Vectors of force radiate from Klana's center of gravity, high on his spine near the top of the chest, and slam into the audience as Klana claims a universe of space. The nasal resonators are activated in creating his implosive, quick voice which rises and swoops over an octave, utilizing a tessitura of *madenda*, a minor key that shares only three notes with the five-toned *salendro* musical scale adhered to by the other characters in their talking. The mood song which introduces Klana's arrival gives a sense of his character:

> The crying of Dasamuka is in the wind,
> a fight in the air,
> his chest was pecked and it cracked,
> Lives again after he dies,
> remembers the incantation of Pancasona.
>
> (Suanda 1983: 142)[12]

Klana's scattershot energy focuses in the high chest. This allows his limbs to move relatively broadly and freely underneath.[13] Much of the movement activates the spine where the neck meets the head. This joint is jerked and wrenched during his dance, especially at the end of the slow opening passage as the dancer prepares to put on Klana's mask. This is the point in the dance that the "warm up" ends and the performer is felt to "put on" this demon king character.

Klana interacts most dynamically with the audience, laughing at them, tossing a cloth to them, touching a child. Klana is associated with the south,

Figure 13.2 Klana, an
emotionally uncontrolled
demon king, is the final mask
presented in each performance.
Sujana Arja dances the role.
(Photo by Kathy Foley.)

the regions beneath, *amarah* (passion), death, menstruation, and fire. Klana's high center of gravity allows explosive energy to pour forth. Klana is the climax of the performance, and the obverse of Panji's eternally recycled conservation of energy. Klana is technically the easiest to perform. His movements are less precise than the prior characters and, since the musical cycles are quick, the dancer can change movement sequences almost at will. But he is ideologically the hardest to control, the most potentially dangerous. While seasoned performers remain in control, unpracticed performers court dangerous trancelike states where the character overpowers the performer. Klana evokes the volcanic and is apt to explode.

Ironically, by activating the top of the spine and shaking the head in

Figure 13.3 Young dancers in Losari village near Cirebon execute Pamindo movements. This refined character is customarily studied first. (Photo by Kathy Foley.)

swift, sharp movements, and by slamming the voice against the top of the head, the deepest emotions can pour forth. Klana is born from the depths and waits until the dancer releases him by opening at the top of the spine.[14] The Sundanese are in no rush to do this. The dancer spends the first hours of each performance as Panji, Pamindo, and Tumenggung. Likewise the early years of topeng learning train the performer to focus on the lower end of the spine.

A refined character related to Panji or Pamindo is introduced first (Figure 13.3). The choice seems odd when compared to much Western training where freeing the natural voice and activating the deep psycho-physical system of the actor often advocates large energy and emotional stretches early in training to break down barriers which prevent the performer from understanding her/his "natural" state.[15] Such training, it seems to me, was especially prominent in the 1970s when Grotowski-influenced physical exercises, Lessac's call, and American variants of Stanislavsky-influenced emotional memory were introduced to me. In Sunda these big movements and emotions are what the performer is asked to activate last — probably because they are considered the easiest to achieve and the most difficult to control. Starting with Klana would leave both the student mastering the system and a performance building toward a climax with no place to go. To begin with Klana misunderstands the significance that the system ascribes to this powerful material. The traditional training system asks the novice to begin with what is most complex, most stationary, most subtle, and most difficult.

In both the past and the present, the mask with its set image of a type, like the unchanging representations in the puppet theatre, are nonverbal tools that release the body to find the movement, voice, and idea of a character. Endo Suanda, a noted dancer of today's generation, discusses his different strategies in learning topeng which progressed from rational analysis, to emotive response, to letting the mask move him:

> Most of the movements that I saw or felt, I could not analyze how to do, as they were too small, too subtle or too quick. So finally I stopped trying to analyse the physical design of the movement, and instead focused my attention on absorbing the sensuality or expression of the whole movement while I was studying or practicing. After a while I knew that I moved my head unconsciously. [...] Because the mask is worn it makes the head of the dancer move. [...] Wearing a mask means having a different face, so it will definitely change his expression and create different movements.
>
> (Suanda 1983: 203–4)

Irawati Durban Arjo, another noted topeng performer, agrees that the mask comes to dance the dancer: "After wearing the mask, I feel stronger. You have to be sensitive to it first and it will expand into everything you move. I can feel more of the character when I wear the mask. Klana is very powerful and can act as he wants" (Arjo 1988). By opening the body to the influence of evocative traditional images and following the prescribed order of characters, the dance and its meaning become part of the performer's body.

COMPREHENDING THE SYSTEM

The cycle of dances is a trip around the periphery of the body, from head (Panji) to left hand (Pamindo) to right hand (Tumenggung) to gut (Klana), while the center of gravity moves directly up the spine from low (Panji) to high (Klana). Opposition is inherent in these simultaneously occurring voyages. Panji is ideologically at the top (head) and actually at the bottom (lower spine), while Klana is ideologically at the bottom (gut) and actually at the top (upper spine). The tension between the two points pushes the mind toward the idea of center which plays an important part in Southeast Asian thinking (see Errington 1983). Pamindo and Tumenggung are closer to the central point on the spinal journey, but not precisely there. Indeed, the dancer is invited to find this point herself, or in some villages in a fifth character, Rumiang, whose movement is between Pamindo and Tumenggung in forcefulness and is introduced to pinpoint the central focus. The reason that the Rumiang mask is lacking in some areas may be that it is redundant, a replication of what the dancer is who knows all his/her powers – centered.

Though different "bodies" in terms of rhythm and movement dynamics seem to appear with each dance, the sum of the characters always adds up to *one* person's moving body. The impact of the training is to create a repertory of beings that force the performer to know his/her many potential bodies. These characters are emotionally the different aspects of his/her soul, peace (Panji), possessiveness (Pamindo), power (Tumenggung), and passion (Klana); different aspects of the social order, the ruler (Panji), the princess (Pamindo), the warrior (Tumenggung), the opponent (Klana); conceptually, an accelerated trip through his/her life cycle from birth (Panji), through adolescence (Pamindo), adulthood (Tumenggung), to death (Klana); a preview of the cycle that each individual will repeatedly pass through in his/her regeneration from a god-ancestor showering benefit on the world (Panji), to a youth dreaming worlds that might be (Pamindo), to a person building worlds that must be (Tumenggung), to a demon-ancestor rumbling dangerously beneath the volcanic earth (Klana), waiting for the eruption which will mark the transition into Panji once more. It is clear that the multiple movement possibilities and layering of imagery provides rich stimulation for the muscles of the performer's body and mind. Traditional performers of topeng or wayang scoff at the need to forge new idioms of movement or theatre and are apt to assert, as did one dalang I interviewed, that "Everything is in the wayang already" (Sukarya 1977).

Rather than explore the many possibilities of this system, I wish merely to note two alternative transformations, animal and ecological, that are implied rather than stated. These permutations are evocative in that they go beyond what Western thinking or acting ordinarily invites as a transformation of the human body and/or social order. Topeng invites us to experience a bird/snake dichotomy by highlighting Pamindo and Klana, and a tree/mountain permutation by dancing the whole sequence. While these changes may seem removed from the human body, actually they begin and end in the body.

Bird and the Snake

Though the system presently yields four character types, this is really an elaboration on what may be an older pairing of two. In many ways, Panji and Tumenggung, while ideologically important as positive images, do not lie at the heart of topeng. The dance really focuses more on the other two characters, Pamindo and Klana, who are more integral to the performance. In villages such as Losari near Cirebon the Panji dance is not done; the Pamindo mask is called "Panji." In a variety of introductory mask dance performances of the Sundanese area, Panji is missing while Pamindo,

Klana, and sometimes Tumenggung remain. Dancers such as Sujana Arja aver that Pamindo's is the oldest dance, the source of the other dances. Indeed, a marked choreographic symmetry exists between Pamindo's and Klana's dances. The former, I believe, shows us our "bird" possibility, while the latter teaches us the energy of the "snake."

As noted before, the Pamindo dance has many movements which are imitative of a bird. This may correspond to the importance of the bird in a wide area (see Holt 1967: 106). Pamindo incarnates the possibilities of the human in motion; the flightlike potentiality of this dance in its extreme becomes the sleep-walking trance of female mediums found in roughly the same area as topeng.[16] The lowered center of gravity, coupled with twisting, turning motions, brings the body as close as it can come to flying. In Sunda and Java the images of birds are often found on dance headdresses. Most characters in dance dramas and many female dances in nonnarrative dances have eagle or peacock designs on their leather headgear. This costume, in addition to marking a now defunct religious heritage which associated the eagle with Garuda, the vehicle of the Hindu god Vishnu, is a performed assertion that when we lower our center of gravity we all can "fly."

The Klana dance exhibits a jerkier whipping of the spine, an energy related to a high center of gravity which stimulates the head–neck connection. I link this Klana dance to *nagas*, mythical snakes that dwell in the earth, which in Indonesian as well as Indian mythology are the opponents of Garuda. Elsewhere I have noted that jumps and jerks characterize male trance performance in this area (Foley 1985); I think a change of consciousness is activated by hyperstimulation of the nervous system. This technique of transformation differs radically from the flightlike feeling of the Pamindo dancer. Klana's jerking spine, with special emphasis on the head–neck connection, while clearly not a trance performance, may be similar to trance in that this movement technique releases the emotions of the gut – sexuality, hunger, greed, power. Such emotions are associated with nagas, coiled beneath the earth creating fertility but, if uncontrolled, threatening chaos. Although not explicit in topeng, the naga theme is implicitly evoked. *Naga seser*, "the naga defeated," is the wide plié position found in the topeng choreography of Losari village. In Arja's Klana, the dancer takes out a dagger (*kris*) worn at the waist and points it in front of him as he reaches a highpoint in the dance. The wavy-bladed knife is patterned to look like a snake, and both naga and dagger are associated with male sexual potency. The floor pattern zig-zags back and forth in this sequence, reiterating the naga theme.[17]

When I do Klana, especially after enjoying the birdlike flight of Pamindo, I have the sense of my subcortical consciousness being jerked to life, as if Klana awakened some sense-memory of my neural column's reptilian prehistory. Klana is naga power incarnate, and yet, paradoxically, this power is activated by pushing the focal point of the dancer up the spinal cord.[18] The bird–snake identification is important to humans far beyond Java. It is widespread through the world and is often said to have shamanic origins. Even Catholicism gave me images of holy ghosts in bird bodies bringing ecstasy to Mary and snakes slithering through Eden seducing Eve. Yet the religious training I received encouraged me to see these mythical creatures outside of me, manipulating me. The study of topeng has given me power over them by showing me that they are parts of me. I dance these creatures to life in my body, identifying myself with the animal world.

The Tree/Mountain

One last figure from the puppet theatre I wish to relate to topeng is the flat leather puppet called the *kayon* (tree) or *gunungan* (mountain) used as a multipurpose tool. Representing the creation of the cosmos, the kayon dance opens each performance. It is placed at the center of the playing space when the dalang narrates between scenes, marking the structural divisions of the story as a curtain might in Western theatre. It is used as an all-purpose set piece in the play, becoming now a rock, next a cloud, then a throne, a gate, a weight. The kayon usually has a winged gate at the bottom which is guarded by two ogres. Behind the gate is a pool; two strong animals (tigers, bulls, etc.) stand facing each other at the base of a tree that grows in the garden. A snake may twine round the trunk which branches where the face or faces of a protective demon, a Kala, appears. High at the top, the tree culminates in a lotus. The imagery and mysticism that surrounds the kayon is very rich and I will merely hint at some of its aspects.

The kayon represents the cosmic whole that makes up the world: the Indonesian version of the world tree and/or mountain found in the iconography of many cultures. It can become all things in a performance because it is all things, and it reminds Javanese viewers that trees and mountains are the abodes of gods and ancestral souls. Even today, banyan trees with their complicated root systems and far-spreading canopies are the focal point of many villages, while sacred volcanos continue to bring fertility and destruction. The kayon invites Indonesians to contemplate participation in larger cycles than humans experience in one life span. It invites them, too, to expand their thinking about the human body in a way related to the idea of power discussed earlier. A tree or a mountain, rooted in the earth, extending through the world we inhabit, reaching to the heavens is an axis binding the different layers of life's eternally circling energy. In death one's body is placed in the ground; in a dream one's spirit soars above. But the experience of these other states is also available at any moment. The energy of the macrocosm – represent by the tree or mountain extending from the underworld to our world to the heavens – is not really different from our own personal energy. The same unseen power uses the tree and the mountain, as it does us, as abodes. Although this perspective might seem mystical and esoteric from the Western point of view, it is an ecology of the mind which the traditional Javanese worldview finds simple and pragmatic.

The figures of topeng appropriately appear on the kayon, this cosmic whole, in nonhuman forms. The winged gate represents the female – associated with both the womb that carries each of us to the world, and the winged bird I have linked to Pamindo. The facing animals are figures of our strength and can be associated with the forceful Tumenggung. The Kala head's demonic representation which often rises above the snake is identified with Klana. The lotus at the top is the mind's fulfillment, associated with Panji the baby who, self-realized, descends into the world again and again. Though the kayon is a tree or a mountain, it is also a human. The tree is our spine and the snake is our kundalini energy rising from the genitals, snapping into consciousness once we can confront that point at the top where Klana, our protective Kala head, prods us to full consciousness.[19] The kayon is the "mask" that the dalang holds in front of him/herself when s/he delivers the narration. It is the "puppet" s/he hides behind. Yet it is also his/her spine; s/he is the tree, the mountain, the multiple bodies/energies at play in the world. Topeng and wayang with their typology of characters are ways of guiding first the performer and then, through that performer, each spectator toward these wider identifications. A simple trip up the spine, moving from a low center using minimal space and a comfortable vocal range toward higher intensities of energy, wider spaces, and exploding vocalities. At the same time topeng and wayang demand a recognition of the different tendencies of different body parts, the Panji in the head, the Klana in the gut, the quirky Pamindo of the left hand, and the powerful Tumenggung of the right.

A mood song that opens most puppet performances alerts us:

> The kayon is a screen that masks the god,
> masks the one who executes the performance.
> The puppets breathe through the soul of the dalang.
> The dalang breathes his soul into the puppets.
> The kayon screens the unseen power behind.

The unseen power is the dalang, the puppetmaster, who is all the puppets at once. How odd that I, who felt bound to one body from here to hereafter, should sing this lyric. The audience does not really know what it means. They see only the bright kayon and the glittering puppets whose faces resemble Panji, Pamindo, Tumenggung, and Klana. They think I am telling stories about long ago and far away – fascinating stories indeed – but not the real story. Topeng and wayang teach me to be the force not bound to my normal body or history. I have many bodies. I participate in both human emotions and volcanic explosions. By exercising my changeability, I am no longer locked into a one-dimensional view of the world – which is associated with an individual puppet, mask, or life. Performance is a way of speeding up my life cycle, or the many life–death–life cycles, so that I can travel from body to soil to reintegration. By speeding up the process I participate actively in the workings of the cosmos. I, the dalang, manipulate the different entities and forces and finally reach an artistic balance.[20] The topeng, the kayon, the cosmos are my bodies.

14

"ON THE EDGE OF A BREATH, LOOKING"[1]

Disciplining the actor's bodymind through the Martial Arts in the Asian/Experimental Theatre Program

Phillip B. Zarrilli

[An] important thing to remember is that an actor must concentrate on . . . his whole body . . .
[J]ust as a musician has to exercise his fingers every day, so an actor has to exercise his
body almost to the point of overcoming it, that is, being in complete control of it.
(Ryszard Cieslak in Torzecka 1992: 261)

As long ago as 1973 Robert Benedetti summed up at least one of the goals of "serious actor-training programs" as attempting to help students to discover "stillness at the center" because it "relates to those most fundamental problems of concentration and relaxation" which the actor must actualize on stage (464, 467). Reflecting on a demonstration performance by Beijing Opera actress Yen Lu Wong, Benedetti noted how the American actor

> often tends to be at the mercy of his [*sic*] own energy because his technique is incapable of encompassing it fully; he has to 'work himself up' to high energy levels, while [Yen Lu Wong] carries with [her] a powerful but balanced energy source which [she] taps freely as needed.
>
> (Benedetti 1973: 464)[2]

Yen Lu Wong told Benedetti how throughout her prolonged training period her "main focus was [. . .] on maintaining 'tranquility'" – a state of performance actualization which A.C. Scott summed up as "'standing still while not standing still'" (Benedetti 1973: 463).[3]

This essay is about both the thought and the actualization in practice of the notion of "standing still while not standing still." It explores both aspects of this seeming paradox in all its complexities, that is, how the actor learns simultaneously to "stand still," yet "not stand still." It specifically traces the practice and discourse of actor training and acting in Asian martial arts as taught in the Asian/Experimental Theatre Program at the University of Wisconsin–Madison founded by Scott in 1963 and currently directed by me. Implicit in this training is a psychophysiological paradigm of acting which, in contrast to the psychological paradigm assumed in most American method-based approaches to acting, approaches the performance of any action *or* the creation of "character' by first "disciplining" the "body."[4]

FROM "IN-DISCIPLINE" TO "DISCIPLINE": (RE)DISCOVERING THE BODY AND MIND THROUGH PRACTICE

To speak of training the actor to be able to "stand still while not standing still" is necessarily to speak of a process which transforms not only the practitioner's relationship to his body and mind in practice but also how one conceptualizes that relationship. I begin such a discussion with my own experience of this process of transformation to illustrate the commonplace confusions as well as the idiosyncracies characteristic of this twofold process. My story takes place between the fields of play on which many middle-aged American males of my age were enculturated to particular practices and paradigms of the body–mind relationship, and Kerala, South India's *kaḷari*s or gymnasia-cum-temples and stages where at least some practitioners of the traditional martial art, *kaḷarippayaṭṭu*, and dance-drama, *kathakaḷi*, are enculturated to a quite different understanding and practice of the body–mind relationship as they undergo their intensive yearly disciplines of body training and perform their arts.[5]

Before I first traveled to India in 1976 I had very little movement or dance training. My experience of my body was based on a variety of sports: baseball, track, wrestling, basketball, soccer, and football. I assumed that they promoted good health while making me assertive and self-confident. But I also intuitively knew that especially my high school football training promoted aggressive and potentially violent attitudes and behavior. While being psychophysically shaped by my training in sports, I was philosophically, ethically, and ideologically becoming a pacifist.

But my body remained separate, that is, it would not be "pacified." It had been shaped by a culture of the body which assumed an overarching and directive "will" which, through sheer determination and/or aggression, could shape the body *per se*, and/or make use of the body to impose that will on someone/something else. Consequently, I unthinkingly either "forced" my body to shape itself to a "discipline" such as football, and/or I tried to use that body as a means to an end, that is, for "winning." My "sports" body was the objective or "neutral" biomedical, physiological body observable from the outside. As a "thing" to be mastered, male culture gave me permission to keep this body sequestered and separate from my beliefs and values. Separate from my biomedical/sports body, I inhabited an-"other" body – the "personal" and private body which was a repository of my feelings. It too existed in a state of tension with my beliefs and ethical values, and also remained separate from my biomedical/sports body.

My (separate) mind was manifest in my "will" to mastery, in my reflexive consciousness which could watch my "sports" body from the outside, and in my beliefs and values which attempted, through my active will, to impose themselves on either or both bodies. None of these fragmented experiences of my body–mind nor their implicitly dualistic paradigms helped me to inhabit and/or understand my body–mind in a way that led me to achieve an integration between them which, at least intellectually, I eventually sought both in performance and in life.

Consequently, when I first went to India in 1976, I was totally unprepared for the psychophysiological experiences I was to undergo. For my first six months I was immersed in studying *kathakaḷi* dance-drama for approximately seven hours of intensive daily training at the Kerala Kalamandalam under M.P. Sankaran Namboodiri. For an additional three months I began four hours of daily training in the closely related martial art, *kaḷarippayaṭṭu*, under Gurukkal Govindankutty Nair of the C.V.N. Kalari, Thiruvananthapuram.[6]

Over the months and years of observing masters of both *kathakaḷi* and *kaḷarippayaṭṭu*, I began to notice the "ease" with which they embodied their incredibly dynamic arts, manifesting an extraordinary focus and power. In *kathakaḷi* that power is manifest in the full-bodied aesthetically expressive forms through which the actor channels his energy as he realizes each mood (*bhāva*) appropriate to the dramatic context.[7] In *kaḷarippayaṭṭu* that focus and power is manifest not only in performance of the fully embodied forms of exercise but also in the fierce and potentially lethal force of a step, kick, or blow.

When masters of either the dance-drama or martial art performed their complex acrobatic combinations of steps, kicks, jumps, turns, and leaps, as Govindankutty Nair liked to describe it, they "flowed like a river." My body did anything *but* flow. The serpentine, graceful, yet powerfully grounded fluidity of movement seemed an unapproachable state of embodiment. My overt physical ineptitude was matched by my equal naivete about how to learn through my body, and how that body was related to my mind. I physically "attacked" both *kathakaḷi* and *kaḷarippayaṭṭu* exercises. I tried to force the exercises into my body; my body into the forms. I was determined to make myself learn each exercise, no matter how difficult. There in the Indian *kaḷari* was my Akron, Ohio, Buchtel Griffin high school football coach yelling at me:

> Zarrilli, hit him harder. Get up off your ass and let's see you move! And I mean really move this time! Get up and do it again – right, this time![8]

Given this approach, my body was full of tension and my mind was flooded with my aggressive attempt to control and assert my will.

Gradually, after years of practice, the relationship of my body and mind in practice and my understanding of that relationship began to alter. When demonstrating the martial art or when acting, I found myself able more consistently to enter a state of readiness and awareness – I no longer "attacked" the activity or the moment. My body and mind were being positively "disciplined," that is, for engagement in the present moment, not *toward* an end or goal. My tensions and inattentions gradually gave way to sensing myself simultaneously as "flowing" yet "power-full," "centered" yet "free," "released" yet "controlled." I was beginning to actualize what Benedetti described as a "stillness at my center." I was learning how to "stand still."

Simultaneously, through the long process of repetition of basic forms of practice, I also began to sense a shift in the quality of my relationship to my bodymind in exercise or on stage – I was discovering an "internal energy" which I was gradually able to control and modulate physically and vocally whether in performance or when extending my breath or "energy" through a weapon when delivering a blow. I was moving from a concern with external form to awareness of the "internal," dynamic dimension of my psychophysiological relationship to my body/mind *in practice*. I was able to enter a state of heightened awareness of and sensitivity to both my bodymind/breath in action, as well as the immediate environment. I was simultaneously beginning to discover how *not* to stand still, while standing still.

In my case, I emphasize *beginning* because every day of practice in India I could watch a master such as Govindankutty Nair actualize this optimal state of "standing still while not standing still." When he would perform the *kaḷarippayaṭṭu* lion pose (Figure 14.1), behind the stasis, that moment of stillness when he fully assumed and held the position, was a palpable inner "fullness" reflected in his concentrated gaze and in his readiness to respond to the immediate environment. A Malayalam folk expression best describes this state of a *kaḷarippayaṭṭu* master for whom, like Lord Brahma, the thousand-eyed, "the whole body becomes an eye (*meyyu kannakuka*)." Simultaneously, I sensed a shift in the relationship between my values and beliefs as they worked their way into my body and behavior.

However, with these changes, I found it difficult to describe my experience in language that neither objectified nor, as in the above paragraphs, romantically subjectified and/or reified my own experience, applying to it a thin gloss of self-congratulation. In face-to-face encounters and/or demonstrations of techniques with students, actors, and/or other

Figure 14.1 Gurukkal Govindankutty Nair of the Thiruvananthapuram, performs one of C.V.N. Kalari, *kalarippayaṯṯu*'s poses, the "lion." Here "the body becomes all eyes."

teachers (more than in narratives such as this), I can display this dynamic "connection" through the bodymind, and then demystify it by stepping out of it, and/or literally commenting on it.

TRAINING TOWARD READINESS IN THE ASIAN/EXPERIMENTAL THEATRE PROGRAM

When A.C. Scott was invited to found the Asian/Experimental Theatre Program in 1963, after his initial encounter with American acting students he observed how

> I was worried by the casual naturalism they regarded as acting, impressed by the vitality they needlessly squandered, staggered by their articulate verbosity on the psychological nature of theatre, and dismayed by their fragile concentration span, which manifested itself in a light-hearted attitude toward discipline that seemed to arise from an inability to perceive that a silent actor must still remain a physical presence on both the stage and the rehearsal floor.

(Scott 1993: 52)

Starting in 1963 and continuing until his retirement in 1980, in an effort to help American students to solve these problems, Scott developed a rigorous year-long training regime built around the daily practice of *t'ai chi ch'uan* "long before the present interest in Asian physical training forms had swept over America" (1993: 52).[9] In 1979 Scott invited me to join him for a transition year before his retirement so that I could learn the training system he had evolved, incorporate my own techniques into the training system, and assume in 1980 direction of the Asian/Experimental Theatre Program. Since my own field work and practical training had been in South Asia, I integrated Scott's own exercises and the short-form Wu style *t'ai chi ch'uan* with *kaḷarippayaṭṭu* and selected yoga exercises. Implicit in Scott's use of *t'ai chi ch'uan* as an actor-training discipline was not only a rejection of American actors' exclusive attention to a psychologically/ behaviorally-based paradigm of acting, but also an attempt to actualize an alternative paradigm.

In this, Scott was inspired by Jacques Copeau, by his own experience of practicing *t'ai chi ch'uan*, and by the religio-philosophical assumptions which inform such traditional Asian practices. In 1913 Copeau, with Charles Dullin and Louis Jouvet in his troupe of eleven, retired to the French countryside to train and prepare a company and repertoire. For Copeau, training must take place prior to whatever leads to performance. It is a period during which the actor should discover an optimal condition or state of "readiness," that is, a state of "repose, calm, relaxation, detente, silence, or simplicity" (Cole and Chinoy 1970: 220) like Benedetti's "stillness at the center." To accomplish this state of motionlessness, Copeau wanted to develop a form of body training for the actor which was not that of the athlete for whom the body remains an instrument or tool, but rather a training through which "normally developed bodies [become] capable of adjusting themselves, *giving themselves over* to any action they may undertake." It is a state in which the actor has mastered "motionlessness" and is *ready* for what comes next. Once a state of motionlessness and readiness has been actualized, actors should begin all of their work from this state of readiness and not "from an artificial *attitude*, a bodily, mental, or vocal *grimace*." Whatever they do should be done with "simplicity and good faith" in a state of "sincerity," that is, "a feeling of calm and power, of identity, that allows the artist ... at the same time to be possessed by what he is expressing and to direct its expression" (Cole and Chinoy 1970: 220).

In addition to giving oneself over completely in the moment to an action, as part of this corporeal training, Copeau hoped that the actor would simultaneously develop "an internal state of awareness peculiar to the movement being done." Barba (Barba and Savarese 1991) correctly calls such abilities "extra-daily" skills. Copeau, despite continuous experiments, remained dissatisfied with the results of his experiments: "I do not know

Figure 14.2 (Playing) The
Maids, the 1989
Asian/Experimental Theatre
Program production in which
students apply the work in
Asian martial disciplines to
performance practice.
Pictured here from the left are
Denise Myers as the kabuki
Solange, Duane Krause as
the kabuku Madame (above),
George Czarnicki as the
Baroque Claire, and Rhonda
Reeves as the Baroque
Solange. For further
discussion of the production
see Krause, Chapter 20.

how to describe, much less obtain in someone else, that state of good faith, submission, humility, which . . . depends upon . . . proper training (Cole and Chinoy 1970: 221). Inspired by Copeau, Jean-Louis Barrault and Etienne Decroux developed Corporeal Mime and Scott began to use martial arts as disciplines of training.

Expanding on Copeau's vision, four general purposes guide training in the University of Wisconsin Asian/Experimental Theatre Program. These aim to provide students with: (1) a repeatable set of psychophysiological techniques (breath control exercises, *t'ai chi ch'uan*, *kaḷarippayaṭṭu*, and selected yoga exercises) through which to cultivate the bodymind toward a state of readiness and through which to discover an alternative psychophysiological relationship to the bodymind-in-action; (2) a special space set aside for this work in which an appropriate atmosphere for serious training can be maintained; (3) sufficient time to begin to discover this new awareness of their bodies in and through "time;" and (4) an opportunity to begin to actualize a non-psychologically based alternative paradigm of acting through the body.

Each fall a group of graduate and undergraduate students gathers in a training space set aside for our daily work where, for 90–120 minutes each day five days per week, they practice a specific set of psychophysiological techniques and performance-related exercises which require them to apply what they are learning to performance practice.[10] After six months of preparatory training, the exercise regime becomes an intensive one-hour preparation for a six to eight week period of rehearsals and performances during which students must apply what they are supposed to have embodied (Figure 14.2).

Even though explanations are kept to a minimum when teaching the basic exercises, instructions and corrections are important. Therefore, the following summary of the process of training includes a brief example of the kind of language I use when introducing students to the breath control exercise which begins their training.

Dressed in loose-fitting exercise clothes to allow them to move freely and keep warm, students enter the training space by stepping with their right foot and touching with their right hand the floor, their forehead, and chest – an act intended to remind them to leave everything outside the training space except the work that is to come. Students begin a series of *t'ai chi ch'uan* and *kaḷarippayaṭṭu* breath control exercises standing with legs at shoulder-width, hands at their sides, eyes focused straight ahead.

> Keeping the knees flexed, and feet rooted to the ground through the soles of the feet, focus the external gaze straight ahead, and allow the "inner eye" to focus on the breath. Keeping the mouth closed, follow the path of the breath on the inhalation, tracking its path through the nose, and down, to the region below the navel. As the breath "arrives" in the region of the navel, let it "fill out" expanding the diaphragm. Keeping the "inner eye" focused on the breath, follow the exhalation from the navel up through the torso, out through the nose, all the time keeping the sense of the breath's connection to the navel region as the diaphragm contracts. If there is a distraction, acknowledge it, then bring focus back to attention by specifically following the breath.

A series of other more complex breath-control exercises follows in which simple movements of the arms are coordinated with inhalations/ exhalations – all the while simultaneously keeping attention fixed on a point of external focus and keeping the 'inner eye' focused on tracking inhalations/exhalations to and from the region below the navel and by extension from the navel region through the remainder of the body, that is, into the ground through the soles of the feet, out through the arms/hands, up along the spine through the top of the head.

Included are selected yoga exercises in which coordination of breath with complex movements is emphasized. Particular attention continues to be paid to the circulation of the breath during exercise, and the necessary

Figure 14.3 Soogi Kim and Kevin Brown perform the elephant pose – one of many exercises which require breath control and abdominal support.

support in the pelvic region; thus, even when extending the leg backward while simultaneously arching the back on an inhalation during perform-ance of an extended yoga sequence (*surya namaskār*), the student must develop an intuitive awareness of and connection to the lower abdomen, to and from which the breath travels and which provides the support necessary in hip/thigh region to perform the exercise correctly.[11]

These simple-to-state but difficult-to-actualize principles of focus/concentration (on the breath *and* on an external point), coordination of breath with movement, and support/centering (in the hips/navel with a natural alignment of the spine) constitute a set of primary discourses of practice. They are applied throughout the two-hour training regime as it progresses through other preliminary exercises, including slow balancing exercises, *kaḷarippayaṭṭu*'s animal poses (Figure 14.3), a cycle of vocal exercises (based on a variety of sources including Japanese *kyōgen*), a twenty minute non-stop sequence of short form wu-style *ta'i chi ch'uan*, *kaḷarippayaṭṭu*'s *vanakkam* or "salutation" exercise (combining breath control with a sequence of poses connected by steps – performed in slow motion similar to the quality of *t'ai chi ch'uan*), and penultimately a full set of vigorous *kaḷarippayaṭṭu* body-control exercises including poses, kicks, steps, jumps, and combined full-body exercises (*meippayaṭṭu*). Each day's work concludes with repetition of selected breath-control exercises as a "cool down."

Making use of both *t'ai chi ch'uan* and *kaḷarippayaṭṭu* allows students to explore two corporeal disciplines which require them to garner and manifest their energy in two qualitatively different modes of expression. The *kaḷarippayaṭṭu*, while beautiful in its flow, has sharp, strong, percussive, immediate releases of energy in some of its kicks, jumps, and steps. In contrast, the *t'ai chi ch'uan* is soft, circular, yet behind that "softness" is "power" and a grounded strength. As students progress through the training, the contrast in the quality of energy in the two disciplines helps them to begin to understand intuitively the potentially rich expressive possibilities open to them through their bodies.

The atmosphere I try to foster is one of quiet focus on the specific work at hand. Students are expected to keep focused and concentrated *in* each moment. I occasionally remind students:

> 1 *not* to "space out," "zone out," or attempt to relax – rather, their task is, through specificity of focus, to enter a state of concentratedness *in* the moment which is not energy-less, but energy-full or *energized*;
> 2 *not* to push or attempt to find some mystical or spiritual "something" in what they are doing, that is, they are to assume that what they "find" will come out of the *specificity* of their embodied relationship to the exercise in the moment of its performance;
> 3 *not* to work so hard at attempting to find or keep focus that they are distracted by their "trying," to allow themselves to acknowledge distractions but learn how to "discipline" their (naturally) wandering attention by bringing it back to a specific point of focus and breath;
> 4 that they are engaged in a *long-term process* which they are likely to find at times frustrating and boring in its repetition, and therefore should not expect immediate, earth-shattering, and/or constant "discoveries," that is, they must be *patient* and work *with and through time*;
> 5 that this work is not for me, their teacher, but for themselves, and therefore they must begin from the first day of class to become their own teachers, that is, to internalize the "discipline" which my outside eye and comments at first calls to their attention. Such attention to the focused and concentrated deployment of their (energized) bodies in space through time must become intuitive.

However, if training through repetition of forms is not to become an empty, habitual technique for the long-term practitioner, the actor must commit him/herself fully to training as an ongoing process of self-definition. As Eugenio Barba explains:

> Training does not teach how to act, how to be clever, does not prepare one for creation. Training is a process of self-definition, a process of self-discipline which manifests itself indissolubly through physical reactions. It is not the exercise in itself that counts – for example, bending or somersaults

– but the individual's justification for his [sic] own work, a justification which, although perhaps banal or difficult to explain through words, is physiologically perceptible, evident to the observer. This approach, this personal justification decides the meaning of the training, the surpassing of the particular exercises which, in reality, are stereotyped gymnastic movements.

This inner necessity determines the quality of the energy which allows work without a pause, without noticing tiredness, continuing even when exhausted and at the very moment going forward without surrendering. This is the self-discipline of which I spoke. (Barba 1972: 47)

This process of *self*-definition and personal justification can never end – the practitioner must constantly (re)discover the "self" in and through the training with *each* repetition.

As with any new experience, the first few classes are often interesting and intriguing; however, within four to six weeks students often are befuddled, confused, disoriented, and/or have doubts about the applicability to acting of their repetitious practice of psychophysiological exercises. As one student observed, "For the longest time I had difficulty imaging how the discipline work could be directly applied to my acting!" In part I attribute these doubts and confusions to the assumptions students bring with them about what acting "is" or "is not," about the relationship (or lack thereof) between them-"selves," "acting," and embodiment, as well as a lack of experience and clarity about how "training" *through the body* relates to "acting."

Richard Schechner calls our attention to "the whole performance sequence, that is, a seven phase progression stretching from training to workshops, rehearsals, warm-ups, performance, cool-down, and aftermath" (1985: 16).[12] For most student actors, their first experiences in the theatre are with the rehearsal process, that is, in junior high or high school one is cast in a specific role for which there are lines to learn, rehearsals to attend, and then performances. Unlike dance, gymnastics, or playing a musical instrument, one is not required to go through any bodily "training" before auditioning and rehearsing. If would-be actors have had "training," it usually is of the method or Stanislavskian-based kind. Consequently, American student actors have little experience or understanding of the difference between a preparatory form of in-body training and rehearsals, at least as Copeau and more recently Schechner have defined them:

Rehearsal is a way of setting an exact sequence of events. Preparations are a constant state of training so that when a situation arises one will be ready to "do something appropriate."

(Schechner 1976: 222)

Consequently, intensive body training must first awaken in the student an awareness of the body which has been missing from his or her experience and understanding of the acting process. MFA acting student Dora Lanier explains why this separation of preparation from rehearsal is important for her: "When I'm in training I can work specifically on each psychophysiological exercise and there is no need to solve specific (acting/dramatic) problems, whereas in rehearsals you have to solve all these problems (of interpretation and choices) to get onstage." But, as Blau reminds us, in Euro-American theatre one is always "working against time" (Reinelt and Roach 1992: 443). As much as it can be, the first six months of training is a "time out" from "working against time." This "time" is intended to become a space in which the student begins to discover an alternative relationship *to* time *through the body.* Since students enter the training process predisposed to "work against time," that is, filled with the necessity of getting to a THERE (somewhere), it is at first difficult to encourage them to settle their bodies and minds into not trying to get there, to staying in the "here."

Some students are in such a rush. Undergraduate acting student Brooke Nustad explains how she gradually arrived at a realization of the importance of allowing herself the time to focus:

> The idea of focusing the "inner eye" on the breath made sense to me, but it wasn't as easy as I thought. Because I had never spent so much time concentrating on my body before, it took a lot of effort. This was a surprise to me. I guess I thought that these things would "happen" to me just by being in the class. Therein was my next obstacle ... I started trying to make [things] happen. Instead of ... concentrating on my breath, I began to think with every move, "How does this make me feel? Am I changing? Is there progress?" ... At some point ... I finally gave up the "trying," and that's when I actually made some progress. I stopped pushing so hard, and it helped. This made me realize that the same applies to acting. When I keep on task without pushing what I'm doing, I do a better job.

Through practice, the student optimally begins to develop a new relationship to his or her own bodymind in space as it is "deployed" through time, discovering a state of calm and repose as well as a heightened sense of awareness of the body-in-exercise. Copeau was precise about the type of embodied awareness that training should develop in the actor: "What is needed is that *within them every moment be accompanied by an internal state of awareness peculiar to the movement being done*" (Cole and Chinoy 1970: emphasis added). With each repetition of each exercise, for the nth time, there is this "something more" that can be found in one's relationship to movement. It is repetition *per se* which leads one, eventually, to the possibility of re-cognize-ing oneself through exercise.

Copeau's vision of training shares several important basic assumptions with training in an Asian martial art. The act of embodiment is present as a mind-aspect ("an internal state of awareness"), and that *progressive development* of such an awareness comes *through the process of corporeal training per se*. These ideas reject the Cartesian body–mind dualism, assuming instead that the body–mind is an integrated whole. As David Edward Shaner explains,

> Phenomenologically speaking, one can never experience an independent mind or body ... "Mind-aspects" and "body-aspects" have been abstracted so frequently that there is a tendency to believe that these terms have exact independent experiential correlates ... Although there may be mind-aspects and body-aspects within all lived experience, the presence of either one includes experientially the presence of the other. This relationship may be described as being "polar" rather than "dual" because mind and body require each other as a necessary condition for being what they are. The relationship is symbiotic.
>
> (Shaner 1985: 42–3)

Consequently, Shaner refers to the "presence of both aspects in all experience as 'bodymind'" (1985: 45). Shaner insists that "in our pre-reflective lived experience one might suggest that we think with our body and act with our mind and vice versa" (1985: 46).

Actualizing a state in which one "thinks with the body" and "acts with the mind" is precisely what Copeau hoped corporeal training would accomplish, and what training through the martial arts has the potential to accomplish. In Asian disciplines of practice, as in Copeau's *vision*, it is assumed that one accomplishes this state progressively through time. As Yasuo Yuasa asserts, such a view "starts from the experiential assumption that the mind–body modality changes through training of the mind and body by means of cultivation (*shugyo*) or training (*keiko*)" (Yuasa 1987: 18, emphasis added). To practice an Asian meditational, martial, or performance discipline under the guidance of a master traditionally meant that one assumed there would be a progressive alteration and refinement in the body–mind relationship which is different from the normative, "everyday" body–mind relationship. As we have seen, such practice begins with the external body and progresses from the outside "inward" toward realization of an ever more subtle and refined relationship to the bodymind in practice. As Yuasa asserts, regarding Zeami's theory of acting in the *Kadensho*, "art cannot be mastered merely through the conceptual understanding, but must be acquired, as it were, through one's body. In other words, it is a bodily acquisition by means of a long, cumulative, difficult training (*keiko*)" (1987: 104–5).[13]

TOWARD ACTUALIZING AN ALTERNATIVE, PSYCHOPHYSIOLOGICAL PARADIGM OF ACTING THROUGH THE BODY

But what, precisely, is "acquired" or "brought to accomplishment" through long-term bodily based training? First, to be "accomplished" is a *certain type and quality of relationship* between the doer and the done. The accomplished practitioner is one who has achieved and is able to manifest *in practice* a certain (internal and external) relationship to the specific acts: the object of meditation for the practitioner of meditation, the target for the martial practitioner, the "score" for the actor. Although the specific discourses used to explain the qualities and nature of this relationship are culture, genre, and period specific, there is the shared belief that practice is palpable, visceral, physiologically based, and felt. From the practitioner's perspective especially powerful is the link between the breath and the body-in-motion. It is also assumed that the practice is observable and correctable, at least to the outsider/master trained to read the signs of its presence.

Consequently, theorists of acting working from a corporeally based process of training and traditional Asian bodily based systems of martial arts and actor training share remarkably similar descriptions of the psychophysiology of practice, all of which are written from the participant's point of view, that is, from "inside" the experience of one's relationship to the body in practice. Copeau said that the actor must develop an "internal knowledge of the passions he expresses" and an ability "to modulate the intensity of his dramatic expression" (Cole and Chinoy 1970: 219). He expected this ability of internal modulation of expression to be accomplished by practicing

> appropriate exercises so that he may learn [the difference between] neutral motionlessness [and] expressive motionlessness ... He will be made to experiment so that he can learn how, in various cases, *the internal attitude*, the physiological state ... will be different.
>
> (Cole and Chinoy 1970: 222)

In a similar vein to Copeau's description of this phenomenon as a palpable "physiological state," theatre visionary Antonin Artaud called for actors to become "crude empiricists" and to examine the "material aspect" of the expressive possibilities of their bodyminds.[14]

Expanding on Copeau's general description of "modulating" the "intensity of the passions," Artaud postulated that the actor, through breath control, would be able to place the breath in specific locations in the body in order to cause psychophysiological "vibrations" which would "increase the internal density and volume of his feeling" and "provoke ... a spontaneous reappearance of life" (Cole and Chinoy 1970: 236, 239). Artaud assumed that these emotional states have "organic bases" locatable in the actor's body; therefore, "for every feeling, every mental action, every leap of human emotion there is a corresponding breath which is appropriate to it" (Cole and Chinoy 1970: 236). The actor's task is to develop an "affective musculature which corresponds to the physical localizations of feelings" (Cole and Chinoy 1970: 235), that is, the actor must cultivate the "emotion in his body" (Cole and Chinoy 1970: 239) by training the breath. As the actor becomes able to localize control of the breath, he will be able voluntarily to "apportion it out in states of contraction and release," thereby serving as a "springboard for the emanation of a feeling" (Cole and Chinoy 1970: 238). Once trained, "with the whetted edge of breath the actor carves out his character" (Cole and Chinoy 1970: 237).

Artaud was never able to develop a psychophysiological technique actualizing this vision of the actor as an "athlete of the heart." Among today's actors those who visibly display Artaud's vision of an "affective musculature" controlled by manipulating the breath is the *kathakaḷi* actor-dancer who literally wears his emotional states "in" his body – most obviously in his facial expressions – and who learns such control through the overt manipulation of his breath.[15]

As I have explained in detail elsewhere (Zarrilli 1990), in performance of *kathakaḷi*'s nine basic emotional states (*navarasas*), breath control with its attendant circulation of the internal energy is combined with manipulation of particular facial muscles and a dynamic posture of the entire body to bring each state to realization in performance. For example, when performing the erotic sentiment (*rati bhāva*) the external manipulation of the facial mask executes the following basic moves, which are closely coordinated with the breathing pattern:

> Beginning with a long, slow and sustained in-breath, the eyebrows move slowly up and down. The eyelids are held open half-way on a quick catch breath, and when the object of pleasure or love is seen (a lotus flower, one's lover, etc.), the eyelids quickly open wide on an in-breath, as the corners of the mouth are pulled up and back, responding to the object of pleasure.

Throughout this process the breathing is deep and connected through the *entire* body via the "root of the navel" (*nābhi mūla*), that is, it is not shallow chest breathing. The characteristic breath pattern associated with the erotic sentiment is slow, long, sustained in-breaths with which the object of love or pleasure is literally "taken-in," that is, the sight, form, etc. of the lotus or the beloved is breathed in. The accomplished realization of any of the expressive states occurs when the mature, virtuosic actor's entire psychophysiology is engaged in this dynamic and intricate "internal" process through which particular tensions are created through the manipulation of the breath as it circulates through the entire body.

Like other traditional Asian arts through which an "extra-daily" virtuosic body of practice is actualized, *kathakaḷi*'s understanding of the psychophysiology of performance is based on indigenous concepts of medicine and physiology – in India this understanding is derived from the physiology of Ayurveda as well as from tantric yoga's understanding of the subtle body (Zarrilli 1989a). Therefore, the *kathakaḷi* actor, yoga practitioner, and *kaḷarippayaṭṭu* martial artist all assume that "the *vāyu* (breath/energy/life force) is spread all over the body" and that "it is how to control [the breath] that is [an implicit] part of the training." Through repetition of daily exercises the breath is eventually controlled as students are instructed to breathe only through their nose, and not the mouth – a simple instruction which, when adhered to along with maintenance of correct spinal alignment when performing a variety of exercises, develops breathing which originates at "the root of the navel." Correct instruction also comes from the hands-on manipulation of the student's body by the teacher. As *kathakaḷi* teacher M.P. Sankaran Namboodiri explained, "Without a verbal word of instruction the teacher may, by pointing to or pressing certain parts of the body, make the student understand where the breath/energy should be held or released." When a student assumes *kathakaḷi*'s basic position with the feet planted firmly apart, toes gripping the earth, it creates a dynamic set of internally felt oppositional forces as the energy is pushed down from the navel through the feet/toes into the earth, while it simultaneously pushes up through the spine/torso, thereby supporting and "enlivening" the upper body, face, hands/arms. This centered groundedness is "behind" all aspects of *kathakaḷi* performance including delivery of elaborate hand-gestures (*mudrā*). In performance, actors literally "speak" with their hands/arms through a complete and complex sign-language. Psychophysiologically, each gesture originates in the region of the "root of the navel" (*nābhi mūla*) as the breath/energy extends outward through the gesture, optimally giving it full expressivity appropriate to the dramatic moment. Finally, it should be noted that *kathakaḷi* teachers, when teaching some of the basic facial expressions, occasionally instruct students specifically to "push the breath/energy" *into* a certain part of the face, for example, the lower lids, in order to create the psychophysiologically dynamic quality necessary to actualize fully an emotional state – in this case, *krodha bhāva*, or the "furious" sentiment.

When compared to *kathakaḷi*'s dynamic mode of displaying the emotions openly in codified facial expressions, supported by a dynamic and fully expressive body, the *nō* theatre seems to epitomize a form in which the actor must literally "stand still." But, behind the surface stillness, the master actor is "not standing still." Commenting on Zeami's treatises on *nō* acting, Mark Nearman clearly explains how Zeami's understanding of the effects of an actor's performance is based on a physiological "vibratory" theory of performance (1982–3). Therefore, implicit in the training of the *nō* actor is the necessity that he be able to modulate his internal energy/breath (*ki/ch'i*) in order to create the affects used in creating a character. Nearman explains how

> the emotions that the portrayed character appears to experience and that are attributed by some spectators to the actor's personal feelings are seen by Zeami to be the product of the trained actor's use of his voice, particularly through his manipulation of the tonal properties of speech. . . . However real these "emotions" of the character may appear to a spectator, they are not truly identical with the personal feelings of the actor. The actor's focus is upon creating these effects. Thus, he cannot permit himself to respond emotionally to his own performance in the same way as the spectator would respond.
>
> (Nearman 1984a: 44)

Nearman goes on to explain that "Zeami's term for this vocally created feeling is *onkan*, "tonal [or vibratory] feeling" (1984a: 44), that is, "character ... arises from the relation of the actor's use of his voice and body to the ambience in which the character appears to exist" (1984a: 46; see also Zeami 1984: 74). Paralleling Nearman's careful exegesis of Zeami's texts, Junko Berberich (1984) has called attention to the palpably dynamic physical *tensions* that the *nō* actor generates when he moves, which create the vibratory affects that Nearman discusses, and which form the basis for the "not standing still" which is behind the actor's surface quietude.

RETURN TO DISCIPLINE: TOWARD ACTUALIZING A PSYCHOPHYSIOLOGICAL PARADIGM OF ACTING

In finding a means to overcome the "separation" between the mind and body, a psychophysiological understanding and practice of acting makes available to the actor an alternative to the too often cognitively based model of the psychological/behavioral creation of the character. Practice of disciplines such as *t'ai chi ch'uan* and *kaḷarippayaṭṭu* allow students to discover the breath-in-the-body and, through acting exercises, to apply this qualitative body-awareness to performance. For example, students work on Samuel Beckett's *Act Without Words I* – a score of physical actions which *requires* the embodiment of a series of actions in the moment. Students first create a "base score," and then variations which require them to inhabit the same score with completely different psychophysiologically based qualities.

Working toward mastery of embodied forms, when combined with the ability to fix and focus both the gaze and the mind, frees the practitioner from "consciousness about," allowing the person instead to enter into a state of "concentratedness" focused on the performer's relationship to his or her breath and its circulation through the body. Training in the martial arts, Decroux's Corporeal Mime, and other intensive bodily based disciplines empowers the actor with a means of making *embodied* acting choices, and not simply choices that remain empty "mind-full" intentions.

It is not that reflective consciousness does not have its place in acting. Copeau clearly differentiated between the nature of the actor's cognitive engagement in preparing a role and performing that role, between what Shaner describes as third and second order consciousness (1985). In contrast to first order bodymind awareness which is a "pre-reflective neutral consciousness in which there is no intentionality," second order consciousness is "pre-reflective, assiduous consciousness as exemplified by an athlete during intense competition or a musical artist during performance," while third order consciousness is the "reflective discursive consciousness" (Shaner 1985: 48).

In workshops or rehearsals, one approach to characterization is for the actor to use third order "reflective discursive consciousness" to direct an interpretive choice suitable for each dramatic moment. Another approach, most evident in Michael Chekhov's (1991) concept of "psychological gesture," is to make use of second order "pre-reflective consciousness" as one explores the possibilities of physicalizing the role. In either case, when the performer performs, what had been the object of preparation "ceases to be an object of study."

Copeau helpfully defined the relationship between the performer and the performed as a state in which the performer simultaneously "directs [the passions] but ... is possessed by them" (Cole and Chinoy 1970: 219). Copeau recognizes the optimal state of performance as a *gestalt* in which the performance score, created during the preparatory period through using both third and second order modes of consciousness, in performance becomes an intuitively present structuring of the actor's score which, although it is present to the actor at the periphery of consciousness, may or may not be foregrounded, depending upon how much the actor wants to display these artistic choices as they are enacted. In either case, whether showing or "hiding" this artistry, the structure of action which guides the performance contains in each specific repetition the horizon or limits of the possibilities of its realization within the dramatic and performance context.

The actor trained through a corporeal discipline learns to "direct" the passions as he or she learns to control the breath. Yuasa's research on the body and bodymind relationship eventually led him to describe the practitioner who develops an experiential sensitivity to the internal circulation of *ki* (breath/energy) as a "*ki*-sensitive person" whose psychophysiological awareness he describes as "a *self-grasping sensation of one's body*, that is, as an *awareness* of the whole of one's body" (Nagatomo, 1992b: 60). Yuasa asserts that the *ki*-sensitive person, through disciplines such as the martial arts, has activated "a mediating system that links the mind and the body" (Nagatomo, 1992b: 59), thereby overcoming Descartes' mind–body dichotomy. For Yuasa the internal flow of *ki*-energy brings into awareness what he calls the "emotion-instinct circuit." The individual who actualizes an intuitive awareness of *ki*-energy and is able to channel this energy throughout the body, is able to control and extend it out from the body, whether through vocal or physical action or into images.

How unimaginatively we have conceived of the imagination. Under the influence of Cartesian dualism, the imagination is too often considered to be simply an "image" conceived of as something *in* the mind. From the points of view of Yuasa and phenomenology, *imagining* is a psychophysiological act of the entire bodymind. For the actor to actualize an image, such as visualizing the seagull in Chekhov's play by the same name, means much more than seeing the gull projected onto the screen of one's mind. The actor trained *through the body*, who has begun to actualize "*ki*-sensitivity," *should* be able intuitively to actualize a full-bodied connection *to* that image which is palpable through the actor's body – from the soles of the feet through the eyes. This is what Barba described as a distillation of "patterns of energy which [is] applied to the way of conceiving or composing a dramatic action" (1985a: 15). This is the "physical aspect to thought" which is the counterpart of "thinking with the body," *both* of which are essential for the actor if he or she is to be a *complete* artist capable of *creating* thoughts with the body.

Blau, who used *t'ai chi ch'uan* in working with his company, KRAKEN, comments on how actors engaged in this type of psychophysiological work which is intended to "physicalize thought" must take their engagement in that work *beyond* "mere experience."

> Thus, *now*, doing nothing but breathing (and *taking* time, take *time*). You are living your breathing. Stop. Think. You are dying in your breathing. Stop. Think. You are living in your dying, dying in your living. (Take time, breathing.) Stop. *Show.* The doing without showing is mere experience. The showing is critical, what makes it theater. What makes it show (by *nothing* but breathing) is the radiance of inner conviction, the growing consciousness that it *must* be seen, what would make the word come even if there were no breath.
>
> (Blau 1982a: 86)

The actor who is unable openly to *display* his or her art while fully engaged in making it is prone to repeating the fundamental ideological mistake that Artaud made by conflating into some imagined real the palpably present, physiologically based vibratory "feelings" that one experiences while acting and the actor's own personal emotions. What differentiates Blau's, Bloch's, as well as the Asian actor's understanding of embodiment is that, as Zeami makes clear, in the moment of performance the actor modulates the intensity of his or her breath/energy through the body for the *artistic* purposes of the moment, that is, to create aesthetic effects *for* an audience, and not to make him/her*self* "feel good."

This takes me back to Scott's observation about the excess energy of American actors and their confusions over the nature of their relationship to them"selves" in creating their art. The "messiness" of the young American actors' problems are as locked up as much in their conceptions of acting, as in their inability to unlock their bodyminds for creative artistry. However, the possibilities of disciplined training through the body, so easy to articulate here, are only grudgingly actualized by the most patient and dedicated students who refuse to "lose" themselves in the discipline from which they can "find" so much. As Blau put it, the wholly trained actor perches "on the edge of a breath, looking" (1982a: 86).

EFFECTOR PATTERNS OF BASIC EMOTIONS

A psychophysiological method for training actors

Susana Bloch, Pedro Orthous and Guy Santibañez-H

INTRODUCTION

Concept of "acting behavior"

From a purely descriptive point of view, the phenomenon of acting can be characterized as a particular form of behavior produced at will by an actor in order to transmit gnostic and emotional information to an audience by word, gesture and posture within an artistic framework. This form of behavior, which we shall refer to as "acting behavior", is the "representation" (playing) of "natural" (spontaneous or "real-life") behavior, from which it differs by its spatio-temporal structure and by its physiological integration.[1]

There are analogies and differences between "real-life" and "acting" behavior. They have similar effector patterns and similar effects on the observer. They differ in the stimuli that trigger them, as well as in the internal physiological and subjective states which accompany them. In a spontaneous emotion, for example, the emotogenic stimulation comes from the "real" world, either external or internal; in the "represented" or "played" emotion, the stimulus comes from a text, and the reaction is performed voluntarily in a predetermined place and at a programmed moment in time. Emotional behavior expressed on the stage cannot, therefore, be equivalent to the spontaneous emotion.

Acting behavior is a learned process and can therefore be taught. A systematic way of teaching someone how to act, that is to say, how to develop the tools and skills necessary for acting behavior, constitutes a training method. Such a method should contain a sequence of psychophysiological exercises which will tend to increase the ability of the actor to "represent," that is, to transmit the gnostic and emotional information contained in a play, thus evoking in the public the corresponding intention of the author. The actor must learn how to use his body in order to express emotions, just as a singer must learn to use his voice or a pianist his hands. This requires mastering a series of technical abilities.

While different schools and methods exist for other artistic disciplines that involve bodily expression such as music, singing, mime and ballet, there are very few methods providing systematic practical training for actors, especially in relation to the expression of emotions. Stanislavski (1922) had already pointed out the lack of practical textbooks. In the Renaissance, actors of the Elizabethan Theatre learned to use specific hand gestures in order to denote different emotional states (Joseph 1951). Meyerhold (1922) proposed that scenic art should be called "bio-mechanics": actors should be light and precise in their movements, and possess athletic qualifications obtained through acrobatic training, carried out even to grotesque and eccentric levels. This was a pedagogic method (see also Brown 1969).

In most drama schools of the European tradition, actors are trained to use their bodies. Is not the actor, after all, a specialist of the body (Barrault 1975)? In fact, a large number of physical training methods are available which are based, to varying degrees, on the "biomechanical" approach. For voice training, too, there exists a wide choice of methods.

What in our opinion is lacking in the curricula of most drama schools are instrumental techniques for learning how to express an emotion. While the gnostic-verbal (literary) and the body-expressive (physical) aspects of acting behavior are quite well covered pedagogically, the emotional-expressive (psychophysiological) aspects are almost entirely left to the intuition, life experience or "emotional memory" of the student actor, with little or no technical support. To become an actor, one must become an "athlète affectif" as Artaud (1964) puts it – an athlete of emotions (see also Esslin 1976). The question is *how*.

In spite of the fact that many prominent contemporary theatre directors (e.g. Brecht 1967b; Brook 1968; Grotowski 1969; Saint-Denis 1982) have dwelt on these matters from a creative, artistic, pedagogic and even sociopolitical (see Brecht) point of view, a psychophysiological approach to acting behavior has, to our knowledge, not yet been attempted.

Acting behavior and neuroscience

We consider behavior to be a psychophysiological process which depends on the integrative function of the neuroendocrine system. In this context, a method designed to teach "acting behavior" should at least fulfill the following requirements.

1 It should provide the actor with a technique for the voluntary control of the body or part of the body involved in the emotional and verbal

behavior to be represented. For this purpose, special exercises involving specific groups of muscles must be developed.

2 It should provide the actor with the techniques needed to control the psychophysiological activation which may interfere with such exercises, that is, with the techniques needed to control the stress which appears during acting behavior, and to obtain an adequate balance of excitatory and inhibitory neural processes.

3 It should teach the actor to 'simulate' an emotion. This means to learn to reproduce at will the respiratory, postural and facial configurations which correspond to 'real-life' emotional behaviors.

Over the years, we have systematized a method for training actors to express emotions (BOS method), based on our findings on the effector patterns of emotions (Bloch *et al.* 1972; Bloch and Santibañez-H 1972; Santibañez-H 1976). Practice with the method has shown that it is sufficient to produce such patterns correctly in order to evoke a particular emotion either in the actor and in the observer or only in the latter. In this article, we shall present the BOS method and show the validity of the above claim through our success in applying our findings to the training of actors.

Effector patterns of emotions

We have found that, in a normal person, for each emotional event there is a unique association between its effector-expressive and its subjective-feeling components. The specific configuration integrated by effector organs (such as muscles and viscera) which allows an observer to recognize one particular emotion as different from another one is what we call "the effector pattern of an emotion." We have previously determined this by direct observation and by electrophysiological recording during emotional recall and reliving of emotional experiences, in normal, neurotic and hypnotized subjects (Bloch and Santibañez-H 1972; Santibañez-H 1976; Santibañez-H and Bloch 1986).

The effector pattern of an emotion is a particular configuration of neurovegetative, hormonal and neuromuscular reactions. From this complex physiological ensemble, we chose for the purpose of our training only the respiratory–postural–facial components because these can be started and modulated at will and carry with them most of the other features that are not directly under voluntary control. Accordingly, we are not considering within our training method physiological parameters such as heart rate, blood pressure, skin resistance, skin temperature and gland secretions which are part of the effector pattern but whose control is not needed for the recognition of an emotion by the observer.

Indeed, we have determined that each basic emotion can be evoked by a particular configuration composed of: (1) a breathing pattern, characterized by amplitude and frequency modulation; (2) a muscular activation characterized by a set of contracting and/or relaxing groups of muscles, defined in a particular posture; (3) a facial expression or mimicry characterized by the activation of different facial muscle patterns.

Emotions and acting behavior

The main finding of our research on emotions was that the subjective component of a particular emotional event can be aroused by the activation of the corresponding respiratory–postural–facial configuration (Bloch and Santibañez-H 1972): by "performing" the emotional "effection," the subjective feeling can be triggered by what appears to be a sensory feedback mechanism. At the same time, we have found that if such retroaction is avoided by training, that is, by the systematic repetition (initiation and interruption) of the effector pattern, the subject may retain the expressive components of the emotion with very little of the subjective involvement. This turns out to be a necessary condition during stage acting, as the actor, required by the different spatio-temporal configurations of the dramatic performance, needs to move freely from the expression of one emotion to another. This is not possible within the time course of a "real-life" emotion.

BASIC EMOTIONS

Definition

We consider as "basic emotions" those types of emotional behaviors which are present in the human infant and in animals (at least in mammals), either as innate behaviors or apparent at very early stages of post-natal development. We are therefore dealing with the basic invariants of emotional behavior in a manner close to the meaning given to emotions by Darwin (1965 [1872]). In the description of the basic emotions, we are not considering the social and cultural aspects which certainly modify such emotional behaviors. Studies on the regulation of emotion in social interaction are currently being investigated among others by Scherer *et al.* (1983). For a review of the psychobiological literature, the reader is referred to Panksepp (1982).

We shall use in the presentation of our training method only the effector patterns of the following six basic emotional behaviors (see Bloch and Santibañez-H 1972; Santibañez-H and Bloch 1986): *happiness* (laughter, pleasure, joy); *sadness* (crying, sorrow, grief, depression); *fear* (anxiety, panic); *anger* (aggression, attack, hate); *eroticism* (sex, sensuality, lust); *tenderness* (filial love, maternal/paternal love, friendship).

In the observation of emotions, one can see that there is a *phasic* (transient, stimulus-bound) reaction and a *tonic* (maintained in time, not clearly stimulus-bound) state. The denominations in brackets in the list

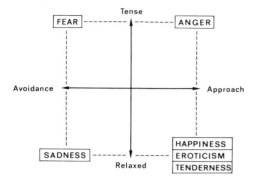

Figure 15.1
A representation of the six
basic emotions in terms of
postural tension/relaxation
and approach/avoidance
parameters.

below belong to the category of the emotion in question and indicate differences in intensity and/or in whether the reaction is phasic or tonic. For example, depression is the tonic state corresponding to the same effector pattern as the phasic reaction of crying; anxiety corresponds to a maintained state of fear and hate, to a chronic state of anger.

The basic emotions can be represented, from a postural point of view, on two axes, namely tension/relaxation and approach/avoidance. Such a representation may contribute to differentiating between the six basic emotions, setting the emotions of happiness, eroticism and tenderness apart from each of the others (Figure 15.1). A finer differentiation among the three is given by the particular breathing pattern, the particular muscular activation within the given postural pattern and by the facial mimicry. Table 15.1 attempts to convey this information schematically with respect to the posture and breathing features, the facial expression not being included.

Table 15.1 Schematic representation of posture for the basic emotions.

Emotion	Posture	Direction	Main breathing trait
Happiness	R	Ap	Saccadic expiration (mouth open)
Sadness	R	Av	Saccadic inspiration (mouth open)
Fear	T	Av	Inspiratory apnea (mouth open)
Anger	T	Ap	Hyperventilation (mouth closed tight)
Eroticism	R	Ap	Small amplitude, low frequency (mouth open)
Tenderness	R	Ap	Small amplitude, low frequency (mouth closed in a relaxed smile)

Schematic representation of the posture in terms of predominant muscle tonus (T, tense; R, relaxed) and of the body main direction (Ap, approach; Av, avoidance) for each of the basic emotions. In the last column, the main breathing trait and mouth aperture are indicated.

It is interesting to observe that though the three so-called positive emotions (joy, tenderness and eroticism) are generally speaking relaxed and of an approaching nature, they clearly differ in their breathing pattern. With respect to eroticism and tenderness, while breathing is quite similar, the magnitude of the mouth aperture is different: open for the first and semi-closed in a smile for the second.

Description of the effector patterns

A brief description of the respiratory–postural–facial components of each basic emotion as analyzed earlier (Bloch and Santibañez-H 1972; Santibañez-H and Bloch 1986) will be given in an attempt to present the rationale behind the different exercises that were developed.

Happiness–laughter. The breathing is characterized by a deep and abrupt inspiratory movement followed by a series of short saccadic expirations which may even invade the expiratory pause. The posture is relaxed; the distribution of the phasic muscular tonus is quite particular, with a tendency to diminish in the extensor muscles, especially in the antigravitational groups. As a consequence, during laughter, subjects tend to sit or even to fall. The mouth is open, and the contraction of the *musculus caninus* and *m. zygomaticus* results in the exposure of the upper teeth. The eyelids are relaxed, and the eyes are semi-closed.

Sadness–crying. The breathing pattern is the opposite of that of laughter: rapid saccadic movements modulate the inspiratory phase in this case. This saccadic modulation may be prolonged into the expiratory phase and into the respiratory pause, but it is essentially the inspiration by saccadic bursts that characterizes this breathing pattern. The posture is relaxed and the antigravitational muscles tend to relax, particularly during the sharp expiratory movements leading the body to a posture in which flexion predominates (the body 'hangs' as it were). The face adopts a particular expression produced by the relaxation of *m. masseter, m. perilabialis* and the palpebral muscles. The eyes are semi-closed or tensely closed, and the brow is contracted by a frown.

Fear–anxiety. The effector pattern of this emotion is relatively complex because there are at least two types of reactions: a passive fear and an active one. Basically, it consists of a reaction of withdrawal from a stimulus, physical or not, which is perceived as dangerous. The effector pattern is characterized by a massive increase of the muscular tonus mainly affecting the antigravitational groups, e.g. those involved in the extension of the head. The respiratory pattern consists of a period of inspiratory hypopneic movements followed by passive incomplete exhalations, and sometimes by an expiratory–inspiratory 'sigh-like' phase. The characteristic pattern can appear during a normal respiratory cycle, and it can be maintained during the time corresponding to several normal cycles. As a result, breathing is very irregular. The facial expression is characterized by an increase in the tonus of the facial muscles, by a large opening of the mouth and the eyes, which protrude with strong midriasis. This effector pattern corresponds to passive fear ("freezing reaction"), the body remaining immobile in a withdrawal or crouching-like position, arms and hands lifted in a protective gesture. In active fear, the pattern is modified by the consummatory reaction of running away.

Anger–aggression. The breathing pattern is characterized by high frequency and high amplitude. The muscular tonus is increased in all the antigravitational extensor muscles of the body, in particular in those muscles related to a posture of attack. The facial muscles are tense, and the lips are tightly pressed together; the eyes are semi-closed owing to the contraction of the superior palpebral muscles.

Sex–eroticism. The principal feature of sexual activation is an even breathing pattern which increases in frequency and amplitude depending on the intensity of the emotional engagement; inspiration occurs through a relaxed open mouth. The face muscles are relaxed, and the eyes are closed or semi-closed. In the female version of the erotic pattern, the head is tilted backwards, and the neck is exposed. The general distribution of tonus corresponds to a posture of relaxed approach; however, the *m. quadriceps femoris* and the *m. rectus abdominis* increase their tonic activity and, depending on the intensity of the emotion, tend to give phasic synchronized discharges. When the pattern is performed in dynamic postures, rhythmic pelvic movements are added, which increase in frequency as the pattern approaches consummatory behavior.

Tenderness. The breathing pattern is of low frequency with an even and regular rhythm; the mouth is semi-closed, the relaxed lips forming a slight smile. Facial and antigravitational muscles are very relaxed, eyes are open and relaxed, and the head is slightly tilted to the side. The postural attitude is one of approach. Softly touching, caressing and sensing with the hands are parts of the active pattern. Vocalization includes a humming type lullaby sound.

TRAINING PROCEDURE

Subjects

The following method was initially worked out in Santiago (Chile) with a group of 12 actors (8 males and 4 females aged between 22 and 26 years), who had just finished their three-year study program at the Theater School of the Universidad de Chile. They worked in groups for three hours twice a week at the university theatre, and also individually in our laboratory for interviewing and for recording different physiological functions. The training period and the experimental application for theatre performance extended over a period of two years.

General techniques

In order to approach correctly the described effector patterns, the actors were first trained to control their posture, to regulate their movements by modulating different degrees of muscular tension, and to work with breathing and relaxation. This was necessary so that they could later learn to simulate those motor reactions and breathing rhythms that take place during natural approach or avoidance behaviors, that is, behaviors leading toward or away from a stimulus (Table 15.1 and Figure 15.1). At the same time, exercises were developed to enlarge and enrich the actors' perceptual capacities and to control stress and inhibition. An up-to-date terminology was employed, and in some instances basic theoretical information was given in order to make the actor aware of certain psychophysiological processes that were taking place during the training.

The following techniques were worked out.

Techniques for controlling stress and muscular tension

Perception of muscular tension.   At the beginning of the training, actors were instructed to contract and to relax different groups of muscles in order to become aware of the degree of muscular tension present. The exercises were done in lying, sitting, standing and walking positions.

Muscular relaxation.   Once the subjects were aware of the different possible levels of muscular tension, a variety of techniques was used to induce relaxation in these muscles. In general, the subjects learned to adopt a slow respiratory rhythm, of which the expiratory phase and the respiratory pause were used to induce an active relaxation of the muscles in different postural conditions. A teacher of yoga led the group in a variety of yoga-like exercises. The Jacobson (1924) method for deep relaxation was used, but in fact any reliable method for inducing relaxation can be employed.

*Respiratory training.*The subjects (Ss) first learned to breathe at a slow rate with the deep complete abdomino–thoracic normal pattern, while lying, standing or walking. Then they would work with different controlled in-breathing/out-breathing tempos. Very gradually, some 'hold' periods were introduced between inspiration and expiration, until breathing could be regulated at will with different timings. Since these are very delicate exercises, great care was taken, and individual surveillance was given in order to detect any possible effects (for example, dizziness owing to hyperventilation). The exercises were first done in supine and prone positions and then while standing or walking. The different breathing rhythms were practiced until they were completely mastered; however, since the breathing pattern is the key point of our method, this basic breathing training was continually reinitiated throughout the work program.

Techniques for controlling motor activity during static and dynamic postures

Tonus modulation of groups of muscles with different postural backgrounds.   Once the actors were able to perceive and control at will the tension of isolated or groups of muscles, they learned to integrate this ability into dynamic or static, bizarre postures. They learned to mimic, for example, different types of paralysis, different kinds of walking steps, different ways to deform, stretch or bend the body or parts of the body.

Vertical and horizontal dissociation of symmetric or asymmetric muscle groups.   Exercises such as tensing one hand while relaxing the rest of the body; or tensing one foot and the opposite shoulder while keeping the rest of the body as relaxed as possible; or tensing the trunk while maintaining the head and extremities relaxed.

Facial musculature.   Control of eye movements and apparent eye size with exercises such as tensing the eyelids with different degrees of eye apertures; working with the muscles of the brow and separate control of each eyebrow; exercises with facial 'masks' in vertical and horizontal asymmetries, as, for instance, just tensing the left cheek and the right eyebrow.

Techniques for controlling inhibition

Exercises of physical disinhibition.   The Ss were instructed to touch themselves and each other, to become aware of their own presence and that of those around them. Then they were told to undress completely while sitting or walking as naturally as possible; then to dress again and to undress, in quick succession. These actions were chronometered and repeated until the timing of both actions was about the same.

Exercises of verbal disinhibition.   Ss were told to express their intimate feelings; to say dirty words or insults; to criticize the others; to express aggressive or tender thoughts; to perform "prohibited actions" or to adopt bizarre positions while saying something difficult or embarrassing.

Exercises of interference.   The Ss were interrupted by the others or ridiculed while performing an action or reciting a poem.

All these exercises, which are particularly important for actors, were done in order to teach them in a very technical way to overcome shyness, to prevent stage fright and to concentrate and avoid distraction. Such exercises help an actor to be in control of what he/she is doing and at the same time to be open for the unexpected. This kind of training necessarily varies for different cultures, but it is always needed for actors whose profession by definition demands personal display.

Exploratory–cognitive exercises

Ss were trained to explore the space and objects around them with different sense organs (touch, taste, sight, hearing, smell) and to become aware of kinesthetic information such as positions of their limbs and body in space. They worked at reacting quickly to sudden noises or signals ("startle" and "orienting" reflexes) in the body-tense or body-relaxed initial state. Exercises of avoidance, simulation of vomiting with stomach contractions and simulation of reactions to unpleasant smells were developed. Every time that it was possible, situations which naturally produce certain reactions were created, so that actors could become conscious of what happens in their bodies under such circumstances and learn to simulate them.

The concept of approach–avoidance behavior (curiosity and rejection) and the paradigm of unconditioned and conditioned reflexes were imparted and worked out with exercises illustrating them.

The general techniques that have been described up to now were preparatory and complementary to the training of performing the emotional effector patterns proper and provided the necessary baseline conditions for this training method. The next step was the training of the specific techniques for learning and executing the effector patterns of the basic emotions.

Specific training of the effector patterns

Technique for "simulation" of emotions

First, the actors were instructed to adopt a particular breathing pattern without being told the name of the corresponding emotion; then the postural component was added and, finally, the facial expression. The complete configuration was always worked out for each emotion in the same order: breathing–posture–face. The pattern was maintained until a stop signal was given. At the beginning, each subject would do the exercise individually, maintaining it from about 15 up to 80 seconds, depending on what was judged prudent by the experimenters. In the early stages of training, the exercise was, on a few occasions, purposely prolonged so that the Ss would begin to experience the subjective activation (feeling) of the particular emotion and could thus recognize what effect the exercise was having on them. This procedure was repeated two or three times, especially with those subjects who had difficulties with a particular emotion (one S, for instance, would say that he did not know the experience of anger, or that at least he was unaware of it). Then a "stop; out" was verbally signaled, and the S had to end the exercise abruptly, immediately following it by two or three complete abdomino–thoracic breathing cycles. The subject was then asked to describe what he/she had felt while performing the exercise, whether he/she had "got into" the emotion, whether particular images had appeared and, as a whole, what his/her impressions were. In the following stages of training, the pattern was initiated, stopped and reinitiated in such rapid succession that practically no further subjective involvement would occur.

The entire procedure was done in a very technical and methodical way in the sense that while the S was doing the required breathing pattern, he/she was asked to tense or relax a particular part of the body and then to add the corresponding facial mimicry. In fact, we observed that the facial expression appeared by itself as soon as the breathing pattern started. No one particular pattern was worked with for more than 2 to 3 minutes. Other general exercises were then intercalated, and the pattern would be tried once or twice again. Great individual care was taken, since controlled breathing and muscle tensing are very fatiguing and demanding on the Ss.

Once each effector pattern was well mastered, different modulations in intensity, different successions of patterns and different mixtures were worked out in order to develop the techniques gradually into a structured method. Actors could later use these techniques for characterizations and the building up of roles.

Modulation of intensity

The patterns were first learned with maximal intensity (that is, with the maximal muscular activation or relaxation) and with the particular breathing pattern in its most intensive, almost exaggerated form. Once the pattern was well practiced at such a level, the intensity was reduced. This was done by giving instructions for modulating (decreasing) the breathing pattern and for reducing, in a very controlled manner, the amount of muscular tension and/or the number of muscle groups involved. In this way, at least three different intensities of the emotional expression were obtained: (1) small; (2) medium; and (3) peak. The actors practiced until they could reproduce all degrees of the emotion, either at will or by instruction.

Emotional modulation of isolated movements, gestures, actions and vocalizations

Once the emotional patterns were well mastered in their basic effector components and in different degrees of intensity, exercises were developed in which an action or speech was modulated by different emotional patterns. Some of the previously described body or muscular symmetric and asymmetric contraction–relaxation exercises, and the exploratory–cognitive exercises were done with the different learned emotional effector patterns. This was done by modulating the patterns with different parts of the body, as for instance doing the "anger" pattern with only the corresponding breathing and the tension in the left arm. Simple actions were sometimes done in connection with an emotional pattern, as for example carrying a chair with "sadness." In other exercises, the actor had to recite a simple poem or speak the lines of a text or sing a song, first in a neutral emotional tone and then while performing each of the learned effector patterns. These exercises prepared for the work with mixed emotions (see below).

"Stepping in" and "stepping out" of an emotional pattern

It is essential in this method to train the actors not only to adopt an emotional pattern at will, with rapidity, precision and adequate intensity, but also to stop the exercise with equal promptness as soon as a signal is given (as when the curtain falls).

The intensity with which the effector patterns are executed at the beginning of training may trigger the subjective feeling of the emotion. In order to avoid this, a strict technique was developed for abruptly ending every exercise where an emotional pattern had been activated, even if it had lasted for only a few seconds. The procedure was to give one or two deep and complete abdomino–thoracic normal breathing cycles and to perform a simple action such as wiping the face with the hands, stretching the body or changing posture immediately after the signal "stop; out" had been given. This instruction was emphasized throughout the training until the actors really learned to do it automatically.

Succession of emotional patterns and "stage games"

The next step was to learn to switch from one pattern to another in quick succession. This was done in the following way: while a pattern was being performed, a signal was given for a quick switch either to a different pattern or to a change of one of the components of the same pattern. This kind of procedure was repeated until the subjects could go easily from one emotional pattern to another. Once this was well mastered, the actors, working in couples or in groups, were each assigned a given pattern with which to start the "game." At the same time, they were instructed to perform an action and to be ready to switch to another pattern at a given signal. At least one brief normal breathing cycle was inserted between each change of pattern.

Procedure to work with "mixed" emotions

The most important repertoire of adult human emotional behavior consists in fact of mixed or blended emotions. By this, we mean that "pure" emotions are rare in everyday life and rare in plays (except maybe in some of the Greek tragedies). In our Western society, more often than not sex is mixed with aggression and fear, and anger gets side-tracked by sadness, only to reappear in disguised mixed forms such as sarcasm or verbal attack.

The method reported here allows actors to work technically with mixed emotions by assuming that these can be split into their component parts. Thus, the execution of a particular mixture may be done by combining parts of the effector pattern of one basic emotion with parts of the effector pattern of another one. A few such mixed combinations were analyzed and worked out during the course of the experimental training.

Pride.   It consists of a particular blending of joy and anger. The actor was therefore trained to put some tension (degree 1) in the body, especially in the muscles of the back and the neck (the head is held high), and then to add a degree 1 of the laughter breathing.

Irony (sarcasm).   It also consists of a mixture of anger and joy except that the proportions are different, so that this time the instruction was a small amount of tension in the legs and arms together with a degree 2 of joy breathing.

Jealousy.   It consists of a blending of anger, fear and eroticism. The actor was told to contract the body, while breathing with the anger pattern and at the same time to open the eyes so as to give part of the facial pattern of fear. According to the situation, a degree 1 breathing of eroticism was alternated with the anger breathing.

Through an understanding of this basic procedure, each mixed emotion can be worked out by finding the right proportions of the "basic ingredients," so to speak.

PHYSIOLOGICAL CONTROL

Trained actor

In order to monitor some of the physiological activation during the performance of the effector patterns, in one fully trained male actor we recorded the electrocardiogram (ECG), the pneumogram (respiratory movements) and the electromyogram (EMG) of the following muscles: *m. quadriceps femoris*, *m. rectus abdominis*, *m. brachioradialis*, *m. orbicularis oris* and *m. masseter*. The actor was lying on a couch in a soundproof, electrically shielded chamber. Contact electrodes (Beckman) were attached for ECG and EMG recording, and a transducer was placed around the chest for recording respiratory movements. The recording apparatus (Grass polygraph) was situated in an adjacent room. In order to obtain a control baseline, the actor was instructed to lie relaxed and to breathe normally, keeping as still as possible. He was then asked to start an emotional pattern, trying not to make overt movements, that is, just to change the breathing, the corresponding muscle tonus and the facial mimicry. The onset signal was the name of the trained basic emotion and the release signal the word "stop." While the actor was performing the

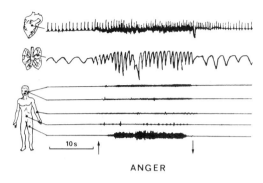

Figure 15.2 A polygraphic recording during the anger effector pattern performed by an actor trained using this method. Upper trace, ECG; middle trace, pneumogram. Lower traces, EMG from top to bottom of *musculus orbicularis oris, m. masseter, m. brachioradialis, m. rectus abdominis* and *m. quadriceps femoris.*

ANGER

pattern, a professional photographer (René Roy) took pictures of his face. A polygraph recording of the above physiological indices during the execution of the anger pattern is shown in Figure 15.2.

No quantitative analysis was done at this point, and the recording should only be taken as a qualitative illustration of the activation patterns. The subject is breathing normally. As the word "anger" is signaled (upwards arrow), he starts to breathe with a higher frequency and a larger amplitude. A few seconds later, he tenses the muscles, mainly of the arms and legs, his face almost naturally following with the corresponding mimicry. When the stop signal is given (downwards arrow), the S immediately relaxes the face and the body, gives a few deep breathing cycles and then returns to normal baseline conditions. Heart rate is increased while the pattern is performed, the tachycardia persisting a few seconds after completion of the exercise.

Comparing physiological activation in the "simulated" emotion (trained actor) and the "natural" emotion, as seen under hypnosis

As seen in Figure 15.2, there is an abrupt initiation and cessation of the activation pattern during the actor's "simulated" emotion, which shows the voluntary control of the pattern. Figure 15.3 depicts the pneumographic recordings during the emotions of anger, eroticism and sadness during the performed trained patterns (a) as compared to the corresponding "natural" emotions as recorded in a female non-actor S under deep hypnosis (b) (adapted from Bloch and Santibañez-H 1972). The experiments were carried out in different periods, and the pneumographs have been lined up only for comparison and illustration. One can see that the breathing of the hypnotized S was also modified as soon as the suggestion to relive an emotional event taken from the S's personal history was given (vertical line). The changes in breathing were accompanied by the corresponding facial expression, muscular activation and subjective activation (report by the S).

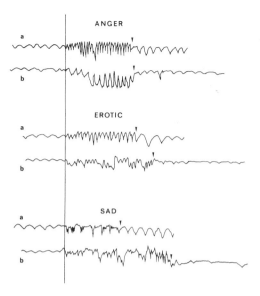

Figure 15.3 Pneumographic recordings during "simulated" (a) and "natural" (b) emotions of anger, sadness, and eroticism (see text). The vertical line indicates the beginning of the actor's execution of the corresponding effector pattern (a) and the emotional revival by a non-actor subject under hypnosis (b); the arrows indicate the end of the pattern. Traces: downwards, inspiration; upwards, expiration.

 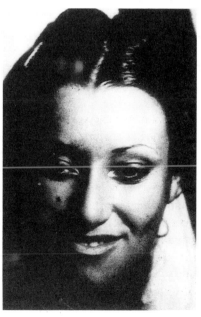

Figure 15.4 Photographs illustrating the facial expression of tenderness. To the left, the face of an actor performing the learned respiratory-postural-facial effector pattern of the emotion; to the right, the expression of a subject (non-actor) to the hypnotical suggestion that she is holding a baby in her arms.

It is interesting to remark that once the hypnotized S was told that the emotional situation had ended, the respiratory rhythm did not quite come back to the baseline rhythm preceding the onset of the suggested emotional revival. This observation would suggest that although the particular breathing pattern can be ended rather abruptly with the hypnotist's instruction, the aroused physiological state somewhat persists for a while. On the other hand one knows by experience that it is not possible to end abruptly the time course of a spontaneous or real-life emotion by simply withdrawing the emotogenic situation: both the physiological activation as well as the subjective arousal take some time to disappear. All of this suggests that an emotion relived under hypnosis has a close though not identical temporal configuration to that of a natural emotion.

Figure 15.4 shows the facial expression of the emotion of tenderness. On the left, the actor is executing the learned effector pattern of tenderness; on the right, the hypnotized S has been told that she is holding a baby in her arms. The remarkable resemblance in the expression of both persons reveals the evocative power of the trained effector pattern.

SOME IMPLICATIONS OF THE METHOD

For the actor

The general training

After working on the basic training for about eight months, the actors developed a perfect control of their breathing and were able to modulate it with different rhythms and intensities. They also learned to control their body musculature with correct, localized tensing/relaxing modulations of different muscle groups.

Considering that the actor's body is his performing instrument, it appeared to us as a surprise to realize that actors of the European tradition [training with this method has since been continued by one of us (S.B.) in Brazil, Denmark, Sweden and France] are quite unaware of their body-expressive possibilities. For example, at the beginning of the general training, actors would very often contract both arms when specifically asked to contract only one shoulder. The capacity to learn to dissociate different muscle groups and to combine such postural modifications with different breathing rhythms is very important as a preparation for the work with the "mixed emotions." The newly acquired skills therefore complement the physical training normally imparted in theatre schools.

This general preparatory work also taught the actors to relax better and to develop the correct balance of excitatory and inhibitory neural processes, which helps them to cope with stress, stage fright and shyness. For example, disinhibition exercises such as undressing were very important for the Chilean actors. At the beginning, undressing took about four times longer than dressing, showing that exposing a naked body is still a repressed behavior within our culture, even in actors.

The specific effector patterns training

Once the effector patterns proper were learned and mastered (the full training takes over two years), the actors could use them at will or under instruction in particular spatio-temporal configurations and with controlled intensities. They could switch from one pattern to another and do different stage actions with different patterns: for instance, taking a cup with a tense hand and then just relaxing the hand without modifying the breathing; or singing a song with the facial expression of joy and then changing the breathing into the crying pattern. The resulting changes in the action were immediately apparent and unequivocal to the observer. Such exercises were also preparatory for the work with the mixed emotions.

As the actors became more skilled in the execution of the patterns, more subtle and finer intensity modulations could be achieved. At the beginning, the patterns were worked at their maximal intensities in order to allow the actors to get well within the emotion. For example, in the case of anger the hyperventilation that develops with the required deep and fast breathing rhythm could be so strong that the subjects would often get dizzy; in such instances the pattern was only practiced for very short periods (15 seconds maximum) and was always interspaced with other exercises, with the strict routine of always ending it with the described "step-out" technique. In this strong form, the performed patterns often looked like "overacting." Later in the training, though, more localized tensions and more subtly controlled changes in the breathing could be achieved, and the actors learned to perform the patterns with smaller degrees of intensity without losing the particular structure of the pattern. In this way, practice with the techniques led progressively to a more artistic framework which is necessary for building up a role. Practice with the patterns developed a kind of sensitization, so that a very slight change in the pattern was later sufficient to produce a change in the modality of the emotional output which was clear for the S as well as for the observer. This is an important point, since on the stage long duration of an emotional state may be required, in which case the most extreme version of the pattern could not be sustained.

When a naive observer, or even one who is acquainted with the techniques, watches the correct execution of an emotional effector pattern, he/she considers the observed emotion as "true" as a spontaneous one. This was particularly striking when watching a sequence of what we have called "stage games," where the trained actors would interact while performing a string of different patterns in swift succession, alternations and combinations. It was a totally arbitrary exercise in the sense that there was no plot; nevertheless, such pure expressive patterns executed in a certain sequence suggested a meaning to the observer. If the performers were then questioned as to whether they had "felt" the particular emotions portrayed, that is, whether they had been subjectively involved, the answer was that they had not "felt" the emotion and had concentrated only on executing as precisely as possible the instructions given by the experimenters.

This is quite good evidence that in order to appear "natural" or "true" on the stage, actors do not need to "feel" the emotion they are playing but must produce the correct effector-expressive output of the emotional behavior. If anything, in our opinion, subjective involvement and identification with the emotions may hinder the theatrical performance. In fact, it is possible that actors often confuse the unspecific excitation they feel during acting with the belief that they are truly "feeling" the emotion that they portray.

If, in the process of learning, a particular pattern was not correctly performed, the conveyed information was ambiguous, and the observer could immediately detect that something was wrong. For example, if during the laughing pattern the subject tensed the body, the perceived emotion was no longer one of joy. Simple correction of the tension allowed the intended message of joy to be conveyed. Interestingly, joy was found to be one of the most difficult emotional patterns to train, the main reason probably being the need for complete relaxation.

It is possible that spectators of a theatre play often feel that something is wrong or unconvincing in an actor's performance because they perceive the lack of organic (psychophysiological) coherence in the expressive components of the represented emotion.

Advantages of the "step-out" technique

This technique is one of the main advantages of the method, as actors very often become identified with the emotions of the roles they play, frequently with neurotic after-effects.

We had frequently observed at the beginning of our work that the subjects tended to stay within the emotion, in other words the subjective feeling was often maintained over a few days. By repeatedly initiating and stopping the patterns using this precise technique, such after-effects could be largely eliminated. Accordingly, the essential rule was always to end any effector pattern exercise with a deep normal breathing cycle, and a change in posture was strictly observed. Such a procedure is a protection against any continuing subjective involvement, since a change in posture and in breathing determines a change in the internal state (subjectivity). Only during the initial stages of training was the pattern intentionally prolonged, in which case, if the pattern had been correctly performed, the actors reported having felt the beginning of the natural emotion.

Psychotherapeutic side effects

A clear benefit with respect to personal emotional problems can also be obtained with the use of the effector patterns. For example, one of the actresses had sexual inhibitions as a consequence of mixing eroticism with fear; this resulted in a great rigidity of her body posture during love scenes. Work was done with her with the fully developed erotic pattern, which helped her to perform such scenes more convincingly. At the same time, she reported to us an improvement in her private sexual life.

This method helps the actors to recognize their own emotions more clearly and to face some of their personal conflicts, which may constitute a professional handicap. At the same time, it enlarges their acting capacities and helps to free them from the exclusive dependence on personal life experience.

The work with mixed emotions

Finally, the effector patterns of the basic emotions can be used for working out the "mixed emotions." If an actor wants to show, for example, despair or impotence, which are a mixture of sadness, anger and fear, he can combine the breathing of sadness, the body tension of anger and part of the facial mimicry of fear. The training of such mixed patterns leads directly to the work of character building and theatre performance. An entire construction of the troll's scene in Ibsen's *Peer Gynt* (Act II, Scene 6), a production directed by Horacio Muñoz in Denmark, was done with grotesque mixtures of this kind.

Possible evaluation of the method as applied to theatre performance

The results of our preliminary experiments in working out this method with professional actors (Bloch *et al.* 1972) will be briefly summarized here. A scene from Chekhov's *The Seagull* (Act III, Scene 5) was prepared. In order to be as close as possible to a scientific methodology and being well aware of the difficulty in judging theatrical output objectively, seven professional theatre directors were invited to see and judge two successive representations of the above-mentioned scene, as performed by a couple of "trained" actors and as performed by a "control" (untrained) couple. The couple of actors naturally less endowed for the roles with respect to type casting was intentionally chosen for the experimental group. All four actors participated in the dramatic analysis of the scene, but only the experimental group was trained in the expression of the emotional sequences. The control group rehearsed the scene with the theatre director (Pedro Orthous) with the classical Stanislavski's method of "physical actions" and "emotional memory" (Stanislavski 1922). The experimental group received only general staging instructions from the same director. The scene was then presented before the selected audience twice by each couple. The directors-spectators had to judge as carefully as possible by rating from 1 to 3 the intensity and emotional quality of the behaviors contained in the scene. They were asked to assess the amount of relaxation and of body tension; the specificity of the reactions of approach and avoidance, and the precision in the expression of the emotions of tenderness, fear, anger and sadness contained in the scene. The observers were not informed as to which group was experimental. The average rating of the questionnaire gave 195 points for the experimental group against 134 for the control group.

The group of actors who worked with the effector patterns proper, as reported in this article, prepared and enacted *Antigone* by Sophocles after the training was finished, again with the artistic direction of Pedro Orthous. The text was analyzed in terms of basic and mixed emotions, and the role building was done by putting the acquired patterns into practice. For example, in the monologue spoken by Antigone to the citizens of Thebes, the mixed emotion of anger and grief was done by speaking the lines with the breathing pattern of crying and then adding tension in the neck and lower extremities. The result was very powerful, as judged by the reaction of the public. No attempt at rating was done this time, and work on possible evaluation of our method as applied to theatre performance is currently underway.

Application of the method to text analysis: possibility of developing a system of notation

This method also allows a psychophysiological analysis of a play in terms of "bits of acting behavior," giving the proper emotional sequences involved in each line of the text. In fact, there is practically nothing written for the theatre and therefore nothing occurring on the stage which is devoid of some degree of emotional tone. An emotional baseline can be outlined for each scene, on top of which an emotional "melody" of particular emotional reactions stands out. This is done by a rigorous dissection of the play, leading to a system of notation by which not only the movement plan is outlined but also the psychophysiological "emotional" plan is represented. In this way, a sort of emotional "partitura" can be noted in a clear and reproducible way.

This method also helps the actor and director to recognize and identify more clearly the emotional behaviors to be performed. It often occurs that the psychological language used in the theatre to denote emotions is too imprecise, and it certainly helps both actor and director to standardize their language using an up-to-date terminology.

Thus, with the collaborative effort of director, actors and psychophysiologists, not only can the proposed effector patterns be successfully applied to theatre performance but also a system of semantic reference which unifies terminology can be developed for theatrical purposes.

CONCLUSIONS

The method described here (BOS method) results from considering acting as a particular form of behavior: acting behavior. As such, it implies the application of psychophysiological findings. This kind of approach brings the study of acting – up to now an almost exclusive domain of the arts – into the field of neuroscience.

The application of the method to the training of actors reveals that the correct performance of the effector patterns of emotions is sufficient to evoke the corresponding emotion in the observers (public). At the same time, the reports of the actors show that the correct execution of the effector patterns may trigger in themselves the corresponding subjective feeling. However, the results of the training also show that by a very precise technique of step-in and step-out of the effector pattern, the actor may retain the ability to perform the expressive components that evoke the corresponding emotion in the audience, without his/her subjective involvement. Finally, as a byproduct, the method helps to control the stress generated during work on the stage and by the same token may have a psychotherapeutic action.

In a recent experiment, Ekman *et al.* (1983) have shown that if an actor is instructed to produce just the facial prototype of a basic emotion, physiological changes occur which can distinguish among different emotions. What is particularly striking about their results is that the physiological indices were more marked when the facial prototype was performed than during the period in which the emotion was recalled. Such a result is in direct accordance with our findings and supports our contention that the execution of the effector pattern of an emotion actually triggers the corresponding emotional state. In our experimental protocol, the effector pattern is more complete and therefore more organic, as it involves not only the facial effectors but also the body posture and, most importantly, the breathing pattern. While Ekman and his colleagues propose that it is the contraction of facial muscles to produce universal emotion signals that brings forth an emotion-specific autonomic activity, we go one step further by saying that it is the performance of the respiratory–postural–facial pattern of an emotion that evokes the corresponding subjective activation or feeling in the performer as well as in the observer.

The experience that we have accumulated so far from using this method for training actors, for analyzing theatre plays and for assisting theatre direction allows us to formulate the following advantages for its use in acting and directing.

1 It defines the expression of an emotion in a concrete and precise way.

2 It standardizes the language, thus facilitating the communication between actor and director.

3 It helps the actor to regulate with more precision the different degrees of intensity of the required emotion.

4 It makes it possible for the actor to employ a technique to work with "mixed" emotions.

5 It contributes towards protecting the psychological balance of actors by providing them with a technique that makes it possible to bypass the subjective involvement.

6 It provides the actor with a quick and efficient technique to "step out" of an emotion, which further contributes to his/her psychological balance and at the same time allows a more controlled flow of the emotions during the performance.

7 It helps to eliminate undesirable "clichés" by allowing the actor to present physiological parameters which are close to the genuine emotion.

8 It proves to be useful for text analysis and saves rehearsal time when compared with the classical Stanislavski method of "affective memory."

9 It proposes a system of notation for the "emotional" plan of a play.

Actors trained with this method can use the patterns as a tool, that is, as a technical support for their acting behavior so as not to depend almost exclusively on their own personal experience and/or limitations. By no means does such a method pretend to replace the actor's intuition, creativity and imagination.

Over the last decade, there has been growing interest in the study of emotions involving a number of different disciplines. We believe that our work connecting the scientific study of emotions to actors' training and to theatre performance is an opening for interdisciplinary research between neuroscience and dramatic art.

PART  III

(Re)Considering the actor
in performance

16

INTRODUCTION

Phillip B. Zarrilli

The essays included here explicitly address the strategies, techniques, theories, ideas, and approaches that particular actors or groups of actors have developed for performance.

ACTING AS A REVOLT AGAINST ...

As should by now be evident, paradigms and techniques of acting have often defined themselves as a revolt against another paradigm, style, or set of techniques. For example, the Group Theatre and Lee Strasberg at the Actors' Studio in their formative years engaged in radical experimentation, especially concerning how improvisation and sense memory exercises were used to develop kinetic recall central to the American method's construction of theatrical characters. Some of the Group's productions and exercises experimented with non-realistic modes of performance.

The experimentation and creative fervor which were part of the early work of the Group Theatre and Strasberg belie the systematization of the method during the 1950s and 1960s when the method became *the* way to train American actors. During this period it was often assumed that the American method had been directly derived from Stanislavsky. Many believed that actor training in Russia was similar to the techniques used in teaching the method in America. However, when director Jack Poggi traveled to Moscow in 1969 to observe actor training, he experienced the historical disjuncture between American versions of Stanislavsky and the Stanislavsky system as it had evolved in Russia: "it soon became apparent that my conception of the Stanislavsky System (based on books and on the work in some New York studios) had little bearing on what I was actually seeing" (1973: 124). The training Poggi observed involved "meticulous line-by-line coaching to clarify the meaning of the text. I saw no improvisations, heard no discussion of 'objectives' or 'actions'" (1973:

125). P.V. Massalsky, a leading actor at the Moscow Art Theatre and teacher, explained to Poggi that what he was seeing was "the most important phase [of the acting process in which] they find each action, however small. In 'the System' the essential thing is to be precise at every moment" (1973: 125). Poggi found that "the whole theory of 'subtext' boils down to a statement that the actor must know what he is talking about" (1973: 128). Poggi finally concluded that

> The elaborate system that Stanislavsky worked out and set down in his books is a very different thing from the tradition that he handed down to the people I saw working at the Nemirovock–Danchenko School–Studio. In practice there is no "System" at all. Teachers coach students – that is all there is to it. Everything depends on the perception of the individual teacher, on how well he can see into the life of the text and communicate that life to his students.
>
> The qualities I most admired in Russian actors, and the ones that seem to derive most directly from their training, are clarity and intelligence. They almost always seem to know exactly what they are doing – though of course I sometimes disagree with their choices. Because they tend to play each moment for what it is, their stage life is full of splendid surprises.
>
> (Poggi 1973: 128, 131)

Reports like Poggi's prompted some actors and teachers of acting to (re)consider the relationship between Stanislavsky's own system as it evolved in Russia, and the quite different socio-historical, and political circumstances which helped to shape American method acting in the United States.

Although versions of the method have continued to dominate the training of the American actor, by 1972 Michael Kirby in his essay "On Acting and Not-Acting" (Chapter 4) announced that "the 'method' no longer has the absolute dominance it once did in this country, and certain alternative approaches are attracting great interest." Indeed, it could be said that American acting has been undergoing a lengthy period during which method techniques themselves and their role in the total training of the actor have been seriously reconsidered (see Mekler 1988) – a period that has been marked by the publication of a variety of new acting texts and books on acting.[1]

Among recent books Richard Hornby's *The End of Acting: A Radical View* (1992) is an intentionally polemical, and "unashamed attack on the American acting establishment" (1992: 1). His target is the Strasbergian method which Hornby asserts has bound American acting for the past sixty years:

> [I]t is a mimetic theory, reflecting the influence of realism that prevailed in

the theatre during Stanislavsky's early years, but has been adapted to suit the needs of a highly individualist, capitalist society.

The result generally ignores Stanislavsky's later work, specifically his "Method of Physical Action," which is why I prefer to call it Strasbergian rather than Stanislavskian; it is never tested and rarely challenged. In sum, it is more ideology than theory, and like other ideologies it is mindlessly and passionately espoused, and faithfully defended against earlier theories, long after all the adherents of those theories are dead. It shackles American acting.

(Hornby 1992: 5)

Speaking directly to American actors and teachers of acting, Hornby calls for the overthrow of a Strasbergian-based self-absorbed, classroom-based method of training, and concludes that it should be used only as a special technique for film acting.

Hornby goes on to challenge many of the problematic assumptions which cropped up among teachers of American method acting and which have confused American students of acting for years – its Cartesian mind–body dualism, the assumed polarity between internal and external and between realism and style (alternative disguises of Cartesian dualism), and the difference between "real" (everyday) and "imaginary" (theatrical) emotion. By historicizing both Stanislavsky and American versions of Stanislavskian realism, Hornby challenges the ahistorical manner in which American method acting has often been taught, calling realism "one acting style among many" (1992: 214).

Hornby's call for an *End of Acting* would not end *all* acting, but would displace a Strasbergian method with a revised Stanislavskian based approach to character acting, emphasizing a return to the primacy of the dramatic text. Whether one considers Hornby's view "radical" or not depends on how one positions oneself, not only in relation to Strasberg's approach but also in relation to whether one considers playtext-based acting as radical or not. Hornby proposes an integrated model of acting "that sees it as a skilled, felt activity" (1992: 115), and gives primacy of place in "finding the character" to the later Stanislavsky's Method of Physical Action as read through Stanislavsky's disciple, Michael Chekhov.[2]

In addition to Hornby, a second recent (re)consideration of acting is John Harrop's *Acting* (1992). Like Hornby and many others among a new generation of acting teachers and commentators, Harrop uses as his primary metaphor the dynamic, active, and energetic image of the actor as skillful athlete. For Harrop the skill of the actor-as-athlete is built through a process which uses Stanislavsky's system as "a template of acting process' – a template for textually-based character acting expanded from the *later* Stanislavsky's Method of Physical Action.

PLAYING POLITICS: (RE)CONSIDERING BRECHT, THE ACTOR, AND HIS LEGACY

John Rouse's "Brecht and the Contradictory Actor" (Chapter 17) helps us to understand why Bert States included the Brechtian actor–audience relationship as an example of the "collaborative mode" of acting in which the actor actively seeks to establish an open and immediate rapport and collaboration with the audience. Through this sketch of what Brecht expected of his actors during his post-war years at the Berliner Ensemble, it becomes clear that Brecht "not only encouraged the use of a wide variety of performance techniques, [but] structured his rehearsal process in a way that allowed these techniques to be subsumed in the service of his interpretational ends."[3]

As Ron Jenkins shows us (Chapter 18), Dario Fo combines a Brechtian politics with the "classic" audience/performer collaboration implicit in *commedia dell'arte* and town jesting to create his virtuosic "Brechtian clown." Most evident in his solo performances, Fo's acting foregrounds physical techniques through which he plays "all parts of himself to rhythmically orchestrate his entire body," and thereby create an immediate relationship with his audiences.[4]

Although Augusto Boal directs "straight" plays, and even began his own theatre work in Brazil making extensive use of Stanislavskian-based acting techniques (Boal 1992: 40–59), when he eventually developed his Theatre of the Oppressed he took Brecht's notion of spectatorial collaboration with actors a step beyond both Brecht and Fo. As Richard Schechner says of Boal, "You have achieved what Brecht only dreamt of and wrote about: making a *useful* theatre that is entertaining, fun, and instructive. It is a different kind of theatre – a kind of social therapy . . . it focuses the mind, relaxes the spirit, and gives people a new handle on their situations" (Boal 1992: back cover).

Whether in Boal's Image Theatre exercises, in his Invisible Theatre pieces staged in "real life" settings such as restaurants or subways, in his "cop in the head" exercises (Boal 1990), or in his Forum Theatre interactions (Chapter 19), the "real" actors are not the actors/instigators who initiate a "performance," but rather the "spect-actors," that is, the spectators who are transformed into active "spect-actors." For Boal,

> Theatre is a form of knowledge; it should and can also be a means of transforming society. Theatre can help us build our future, rather than just waiting for it . . . Theatre of the Oppressed is *theatre* in this most archaic application of the word. In this usage, all human beings are Actors (they act!) and Spectators (they observe!). They are Spect-Actors.
>
> (Boal 1992: xxx–xxxi)

In Boal's theatre we move further and further away from theatre as a fiction to theatre as a force which is intended to actualize a change of conditions in the "real" world, whether social, political, ideological, and/or personal.

The theories of acting/paradigms of theatre examined thus far assume that the actor is a specialist who trains toward virtuosity in those "extra-daily" techniques and skills that are needed to perform. Boal's actors, when preparing an Invisible Theatre action or a Forum Theatre scenario or play, train like other actors toward virtuosity; however, they also must learn to be *enablers* by developing social, critical, and pedagogical skills. Boal's actors also guide a process of critical inquiry around an issue to achieve what Boal "calls *metaxis*, the state of being critically aware of yourself on two levels – as *actor or doer* and as *analyzer or critical observer*" (Grady 1992: 18). Boal's theatre "does not seek to manipulate people. At best, it liberates the spect-actors. At best, it stimulates them. At best, it transforms them into actors. Actor-he or she who acts" (1992: 39).[5]

NEGOTIATING NEW PATHS: ACTING BETWEEN BRECHT, STANISLAVSKY, AND FEMINISMS

As Rouse points out, Brecht's theoretical statements about acting have often been both absolutized into an "inviolate theory of so-called Epic performance," and compared to Stanislavsky's system. There have been practical and political reasons to do so. The later essays by Duane Krause (Chapter 20) and Lauren Love (Chapter 21) are two specific examples of the struggle that contemporary American actors are having to understand and make use of sources *beyond* Stanislavsky and the American method counterparts, that is, in this period of (re)consideration they are negotiating their own performance process out of the spaces between feminism(s), Brecht, Stanislavskian, and American method(s) of acting. Both essays culminate in specific examples of roles they have played in which they have attempted to bring theory into acting practice – for Love when cast in the role of Gwendolyn Fairfax in a production of Oscar Wilde's *The Importance of Being Earnest*, and Krause when he played Madame in a production/adaptation of Genet's *(Playing) The Maids*.

Krause attempts to build a practical synthesis between those elements of his Stanislavskian method-based training that he has found useful, and his own understanding of a psychophysiological realization of Brecht's notion of *gestus*. Krause's synthesis clearly reflects Brecht's own synthetic and pragmatic approach to acting, at least as reported by Rouse in Chapter 17, that is, that there was no single dominant all-encompassing Brechtian acting technique, but rather an expectation that his actors would apply "virtually the full range of customary actor technique from vocal and physical flexibility to precise emotional control" to achieve the desired stage effect. What matters is *how* these skills are used in the production context to fulfill the goal of critical awareness in the spectator.

Love's approach to feminist performance is informed by many recent developments in feminist theory and practice, and is marked by her own struggles with her past training in method acting and with a number of the assumptions in that training which as a feminist she finds problematic, and with the limitations imposed by her working conditions in a male dominant theatre. In negotiating her way toward a feminist approach to acting, Love draws upon a materialist feminist critique of the ideology of representation (Dolan 1988), and the constraints on identity that the apparatus of psychologically realistic acting places on the actress. Her concerns are similar to those voiced earlier by Jenkins and Ogden-Malouf:

> "Method" acting, as it is traditionally taught, asks the performer to align with a part, to search for those self-revelations that are appropriate to a role. The acting coach or director frequently serves as an all-knowing guru for whom the performer must be absolutely vulnerable (opening the way to both psychological and sexual exploitation) ... If an actress really knows the negative effects of what she is doing, she can only act if she effaces herself, if she becomes disembodied, if the belief she suspends is, in fact, a positive belief (1985: 66).[6]

Love also draws on recent feminist (re)considerations of Brecht (Diamond 1988; Laughlin 1990; Reinelt 1990). Just as feminist theorist Elin Diamond conducts an intertextual reading of "key topoi" of feminist theory and Brechtian theory in order to recover "the radical potential of the Brechtian critique and a discovery, for feminist theory, of the specificity of theatre" (1988: 82), so Love in her approach to acting appropriates and exploits several "key topoi" of theory translated into practice, especially the Brechtian "not, but".[7] At the time Love authored this essay, she clearly marked her position as provisional – a place on the way to a more complete realization of a feminist approach to acting which might only find a fuller expressivity when she begins to work with feminist directors, actors and designers – a goal she has recently begun to pursue by co-founding her own feminist theatre company in Chicago.

As noted in the general introduction, Rachel Rosenthal's life was radically altered after she "began to see that I could be an artist and be a woman." Influenced by both orthodox Western theatre and happenings, and having trained in everything from American method acting to Asian martial arts, Rosenthal's performances are, like Dario Fo's, a montage. Eelke Lampe, in her essay (Chapter 22), describes Rosenthal as making use of an "indirectly codified" performance vocabulary which she utilizes in her solo performances to move through a variety of transformations in which she constantly shifts roles, identities, and personae. Rosenthal's performance of personae frees her from the constraints of the single character, and allows her to play her multiply dynamic "selves" without being forced to conform to either socially or representationally inscribed limits of the "female" or "woman."

DEVELOPING AND PERFORMING A PERFORMANCE SCORE

In Chapter 23, Philip Auslander describes the personae that Willem Dafoe of the Wooster Group plays. Never creating discrete, psychologically three-dimensional, realistic characters, Dafoe's performances are "essentially a task, an activity: the persona he creates is the product of his own relation to the 'paces' he puts himself through in the course of an evening." Wooster Group actors each play a complex physical and vocal performance score. Auslander describes Dafoe's process, not as an interpretation of a role but as a re-enactment of decisions – an approach which leaves the performer free "to explore his own relationship to the task he is carrying out."

David Warrilow, in his search for alternative performance venues, joined Mabou Mines in its formative years to create opportunities to realize his own work as an actor. In Chapter 24 Laurie Lassiter allows us to see Warrilow's careful process of creating physically-based scores for his performances which, through his attention to his breath, allows him to refine his scores. For Warrilow "breathing [is] the one constant" in his performances. Especially noted for some of his Beckett roles, he came to "use the body as a way of creating symbol and cypher and of depicting energy in action and in space" to the point where he could play his performances/bodymind as a musical score. His art, therefore, has become concerned with "self-mastery."[8]

17

BRECHT AND THE CONTRADICTORY ACTOR

John Rouse

Much scholarly material has been written on the subject of Brecht and the actor. The vast majority of this material, however, has focused on Brecht's various theoretical statements about acting, absolutizing them into an inviolate theory of so-called Epic performance and getting caught up in vaguely generalized comparisons between Brecht's "system" of acting and Stanislavsky's.[1] I would not want to deny the partial validity of these discussions or impugn the assistance they have given several generations of theatre people in understanding and making use of Brecht's accomplishments. Such discussions tend, however, to undervalue the fact that Brecht was not primarily a theoretician who sometimes directed in order to exemplify his principles, but rather a director who continually modified or reconstituted his theories on the basis of what he learned from his practice; as Brecht told a group of students in 1954, "one mustn't think of it as if there were someone with a specific conception of theatre that he wants to impose at all costs."[2] The *Short Organon* (1948), for example, is not Brecht's ultimate statement either about theatre in general or acting in particular. Rather, it is a position paper summarizing Brecht's thinking about his theatre work up to around 1947. During the remaining nine years of his life, Brecht constantly modified this thinking on the basis of his directorial and dramaturgical work at his Berliner Ensemble – as the many and varied amendments, clarifications, and counter-statements to the *Organon* collected in Volume 16 of the *Gesammelte Werke* make perfectly clear.

I am not attempting to insinuate that we should replace an absolutized characterization labeled "Brecht the theoretician" with an equally absolutized characterization that could be labeled "Brecht the director." Rather, I am suggesting that we cannot adequately understand Brecht's thinking about the theatre in general, and certainly not his thinking about acting, until we complement consideration of his theoretical perspectives with consideration of his practical work. This is hardly a task that can be accomplished in a single essay. Consequently, I should like here to sketch an overview of Brecht's work with his actors, or, more precisely, an overview of what Brecht expected the actor to contribute to the total complex of a theatrical production and how he worked with the actor to fulfill this requirement. I should point out that this discussion will itself be fairly theoretical; only a pure description of Brecht's day-to-day work with his actors could hope to be anything else.[3] I shall hope at least, however, to indicate the value of reconsidering the theoretical concepts Brecht develops in the *Organon* and the *Messingkauf Dialogues* in the light of his theatre practice.

My discussion will concentrate on only one phase of Brecht's practical work. Since Brecht was able to work concretely for an extended period of time with a carefully selected ensemble only during his postwar years at the Berliner Ensemble, this period can rightly be given priority for our discussion. Besides, it was the results of this work, as exemplified in the Ensemble's guest performances in Paris and London, that influenced practical theatre men like Giorgio Strehler, Roger Planchon, William Gaskill, and Peter Brook – and through them the entire European theatre of the mid-twentieth century.[4]

Even more significantly for our purposes, an overview of Brecht's work with his actors at the Ensemble underlines with particular clarity both the shift of emphasis that results when we consider Brecht's theory in light of his practice and some of the consequences of that shift. Brecht's theoretical writings abound with references to acting methods, both particular and general. As we shall see, however, Brecht was far less concerned with acting method than he was with the interpretive basis of the actor's work. In fact, as Brecht once told Peter Palitzsch during a discussion on Stanislavsky, his theatrical activity was not centered around the actor

> as a point of departure. Stanislavsky directs primarily as an actor, I direct primarily as a playwright.... He begins with the actor....[You] can also hear me say that everything depends on the actor, but I nevertheless begin completely with the play, its requirements and demands.
>
> (Brecht 1967a: vol. 16, p. 865)

This begins as a statement defining the relationship between director and actor and ends up as a statement defining the relationship between director and text. The abrupt transition is instructive: Brecht reveals himself as a director who gives the text (or rather, as we shall see, his interpretation of the text) absolute priority. The actor's work, and the director's work with the actor, may be critically important, but they are important only in so far as they serve to realize the director's interpretational ends.[5] If we are to understand what is unique about Brecht's work with the actor, therefore, we must first examine his directorial goals in terms of his work on the text.

Only then can we adequately discuss the actor's particular contribution to the fulfillment of these goals and the particular kind of rehearsal process through which the actor develops this contribution.

The Brechtian theatre's most fundamental principle is its commitment to social change. The dramaturgical principle most basic to fulfilling this commitment is, in turn, that the theatre must attempt to present society and human nature as changeable. Theatre does not, however, depict either society or human nature directly, but rather through interpretive examples. As Brecht defines it, theatre "consists of the production of living illustrations of historical or imagined occurrences between people" (1967a: vol. 16, p. 663). This definition serves as the foundation both for Brecht's general theatre theory and for his directorial work on individual dramatic texts. Using Brecht's general perspective, the core of any text may be examined as a total composition, a structuring together in time of all the individual occurrences that take place between the play's characters (see 1967a: vol. 16, p. 693). The original author's interpretation of his historical experience becomes visible in the character of the occurrences he chooses to illustrate and in the way in which he structures these occurrences together. Directorial interpretation, in turn, proceeds through the reworking of the occurrences illustrated and the restructuring of their relationship to each other. Brecht uses a special term to describe both the original composition of incidents and its interpretational re-composition, calling both "fables." He also emphasizes the predominant role of the interpretational fable in production work: "Everything depends on the fable; it is the heart of the theatrical production" (1967a: vol. 16, p. 693).

The first question such an interpretive approach must answer is whether one stresses the occurrences between characters or the characters themselves. Brecht is quite specific in his demand that production must shift focus away from the characters themselves to what happens between them. As he puts it, "from what happens *between* them, people get everything that can be discussed, criticized, changed" (1967a: vol. 16, p. 693).

This shift already carries with it a shift from the individual to the group and from the psychological to the sociological. In themselves, however, these shifts are not sufficient. Brecht sets two further requirements that clarify the ideological framework within which interpretation must take place. First, both the fable's occurrences and the relationship between them must be examined dialectically. As Brecht notes, the dialectical approach treats

> social conditions as processes and pursues these in their contradictions. Everything exists to this perspective only inasmuch as it transforms itself.... This is also true for the feelings, opinions, and behavior of men, through which the contemporary mode of their social life together expresses itself.
>
> (Brecht 1967a: vol. 16, p. 682)

Brecht's theatre, then, concentrates on "the contradictions in people and their relationships." At the same time, however, a dialectical theatre must also reveal the "determinants under which [these contradictions] develop" (1967a: vol. 19, p. 547); further, it must reveal these determinants critically. Both these requirements are essentially part of the same concern – the depiction of the contradictory process through which men structure and restructure their lives and the critical examination of the ways in which these structures are used by men to repress other men. Historical determinants – the economic, political, and social factors that influence the social conditions of any historical period – must not simply be made recognizable. They must be made recognizable as constitutive elements in the individual occurrences between human beings:

> One clearly must not think of *historical determinants* as dark powers (backgrounds); rather, they are made and maintained by men (and will be changed by them): they are constituted by what is being done right now.
>
> (Brecht 1967a: vol. 16, p. 679)

Brecht is speaking here not about reality but about the theatrical illustration of reality. The theatre is for him precisely the place best suited to examine the social conditions in any historical period as constitutive elements in human relationships. This examination is what the director undertakes together with the actors as they structure out the fable's examples of the moment-by-moment occurrences between people.

The first step in applying this general interpretational framework to a specific text involves the pre-rehearsal work of the director and dramaturgical colleagues. The text is treated as an historical document. The background of the text and its author are painstakingly researched in order to identify both the historical character of the social life being illustrated and the determinants that influence it. The text is then subjected to a dialectical analysis that reads its structures back into the historical experiences they mediate. Finally, the text's fable is recomposed in brief sentences that describe the fundamental action of each individual occurrence. Or rather, the sentences describe each occurrence as the production will elaborate it; Brecht's theatre is true to its interpretation of the text, not necessarily to the text itself, which may be left relatively untouched or drastically restructured.

The precision with which this dramaturgical approach focuses on each separate interaction between the play's characters is well illustrated by Brecht's directorial breakdown of the first scene of his own *Mother Courage*:

—Recruiters roam the country looking for cannon-fodder.

— Courage presents her family, acquired in various theatres of war, to a sergeant.

— The market woman defends her sons with a knife against the recruiters.

— She discovers that her sons are succumbing to the recruiters, and prophesies an early soldier's death for the sergeant.

— In order to scare them away from the war, she also lets her children draw the black mark.

— As a result of a small bit of bargaining, she ends up losing her brave son anyway.

— The sergeant prophesies something for Courage: he who would live off the war must also give it something.[6]

As in the Stanislavsky approach, this scene is broken down into its "beats;" indeed, the American-Stanislavskian term is an excellent equivalent to Brecht's "individual occurrence" (*Einzelgeschehnis*). From a Stanislavskian perspective, however, Brecht's breakdown remains a director's description of the fable rather than an actor's. The basic actions and relationships between all the characters in each beat have been sketched in, but the description does not center on any individual character's objectives, nor has a through-line of motivation been developed to link the various beats together. The concentration of effort at the level of the beat allows an assimilation of Stanislavsky's acting methods to Brechtian interpretational ends.

Brecht's actors were not encouraged to structure the separate beats smoothly together. On the contrary, Brecht considered the transitions between beats as significant as the beats themselves, and he demanded that these transitions occur dialectically. Each beat can be examined as a self-contained entity in which a particular interaction takes place or a particular situation arises. As Manfred Wekwerth points out, the personal and social forces that determine these relationships can change in respect to each other, bringing about an alteration in the situation; this change is marked by the evolving of one beat into another. On the other hand, each determining factor can suddenly pass over into its opposite, bringing about a completely new situation, marked by a sudden leap from one beat to the next (Wekwerth 1975: 119).[7] There need be no more unity either of character or of action between the beats than there is between the self-contained scenes around which Brecht's dramaturgy is structured on a larger scale. Indeed, Brecht made extensive use of all the possibilities inherent in a disunity of action in order to present the "development of characters, conditions, and events as discontinuous (in leaps)" (Brecht 1967a: vol. 16, p. 724).

The director's paramount task in rehearsals is to structure out the dialectical transitions between beats and the historically determined interactions between characters in the beats themselves. The descriptive reconstitution of the fable is already a first step in the development of a theatrical interpretation, but the fable still needs, of course, to be elaborated using all the means of the theatre. Most importantly, the fable depends on the actors, since they physically enact the events out of which the fable is composed. Consequently, their activities need themselves to be structured to achieve what appear, at first glance anyway, to be fundamentally directorial results. We shall, therefore, move from our consideration of Brecht's pre-rehearsal work to a consideration of the actor's contribution to his finished theatrical interpretation, putting aside for a moment the rather surprising process through which the actor perfected this contribution.

As Brecht states, the most important procedure by which the fable is presented to the audience is "the blocking, that is, the placing of the characters, the determination of their position regarding each other [there is a pun here in the German: '*Stellung*' refers both to physical and attitudinal position], changes in this position, entrances and exits. The blocking must tell the story intelligently" (1967a: vol. 16, p. 755).

The pun in the midst of what seems otherwise a fairly straightforward description of blocking should alert us that Brecht is talking here about something quite different from traffic directing. The German term for "*Arrangement*" perhaps comes closer to what Brecht is aiming for – an absolutely transparent physical elucidation of the fable. As Peter Palitzsch puts it, "the blocking and the *gestus* of the actors tell the fable in such a way that one could discover what is happening even if one couldn't hear anything. Transformations in the dialectic are marked on stage through transformations in the blocking."[8]

The importance of this kind of physical elaboration of the fable is reflected in the term "*gestus*," a word Brecht made up based on the German for "gesture" (*geste*) and which he somewhat confusingly defined in several different ways. Each of the fable's individual occurrences has what Brecht calls a "*grundgestus*" (1967a: vol. 16, p. 693). On one level, this *grundgestus* is simply the production staff's interpretation of each textual beat. Underlying this *grundgestus*, however, is the "*gesellschaftliche*" or "social" *gestus*: "the mimetic and gestural expression of the social relationships in which the people of a particular epoch stand to each other" (1967a: vol. 15, p. 346). The notion of *gestus* is thus, as Giorgio Strehler has pointed out, at bottom not an esthetic but a sociological one – sociological in that it allows historical determinants to be concretely manifested in the physical elaboration of the motivated actions that move the characters from beat to beat (Strehler 1977: 87–8).

This notion of the physical manifestation of historical determinants goes beyond the use of blocking to include the actor's smallest physical gesture.

As Hans Curjel noted while observing Brecht rehearsing his 1948 *Antigone*, "The directorial method was based on investigation and varied experimentation that could extend to the smallest gestures – eyes, fingers.... Brecht worked like a sculptor on and with the actor" (1967: 137–8). Curjel was also impressed by the ability of this approach to clarify and enliven the transitions between beats: "Certain pregnant behavioral motifs were extended over long passages of text and situation, to then be transformed into new gestures, basic behavior, or movement structures as if on hinges" (138).

The second beat in the first scene of Brecht's 1950 adaptation of Lenz's *Der Hofmeister (The Private Tutor)* provides an excellent example of this kind of detailed physical interpretive work. Läuffer, having just told the audience in the Prologue that he intends to sell himself as a private tutor, approaches and bows to the Major (his prospective employer) and to his brother the Privy Councilor, who are discussing the terrible state of the economy. The two ignore Läuffer, even when he repeats his bow three more times. In the middle of the fourth bow, he curses them under his breath. He then exits.

The beat is a brief one, but as staged it provided its audiences with some essential interpretive information about the relationship between the play's characters. In the first place, the "bow" that the actor Hans Gaugler developed for his character was a highly stylized, highly exaggerated, very funny bit of actor technique. It was also far more elaborate than the "natural" bows of the period (Lenz's play takes place around 1774), and it went lower to the ground – or to the feet of the Major, as the case may be. First established in this beat, it was used as a "quotable" gestural leitmotiv for Läuffer throughout the production.[9]

As performed by Gaugler, Läuffer's bow also became a fine example of Brecht's concept of "*Verfremdung*." Despite all the critical blood that has been spilled over it, the term's basic definition is quite simple: "A defamiliarized illustration is one that, while allowing the object to be recognized, at the same time makes it appear unfamiliar" (Brecht 1967a: vol. 16, p. 680). Brecht's definition will, I hope, clarify why I have rejected either "alienation" or "distancing" in favor of "defamiliarization" as a translation of the term; Brecht's ultimate point is that a spectator will not think about anything happening on stage if clichéd conventions or a mistaken naturalism make what is happening appear familiar. Everyone knows, for example, that people bowed to each other in the eighteenth century, so why should a bow be the stimulus for a critical social examination of an interpretation of occurrences between people? As Gaugler executed it, Läuffer's bow became a *gestus* that defamiliarized itself, forestalling any possibility of its being accepted as simply a customary greeting rather than the conscious action of a man who wants something from another man with more economic power.

This meaning is not, of course, explicit in the bow itself. Rather, it is a significance the audience could be led to recognize within the context both of Läuffer's expressed intentions in the Prologue (written by Brecht, not Lenz), and of the discussion on economic matters which the bow interrupts (by directorial design). The audience could, however, work through to this recognition only if instructed to examine the bow as an object of analysis.

Partly for this reason, the bow was emphasized twice over in performance. First, it was repeated four times, each bow more aggressively fawning than the last. The repeated ignoring by the Major and Privy Councilor of Läuffer's greeting thus became clearly the result of a conscious choice. Second, the bow was defamiliarized by the text itself.[10] As Laüffer executes his last, most fawning bow, he curses his two "betters" under his breath: "Der Teufel hol Euch, Flegel [Go to the devil, louts]" (Brecht 1967a: vol. 6, p. 2335). Läuffer's language here (especially the choice of "*Flegel*") recalls the way in which during this period people such as the Major talked to their servants, and not vice versa.

Läuffer's bow, its conscious rejection by the Major and the Privy Councilor, and Läuffer's response to this rejection all provide the audience not simply with information about Läuffer but about the character of the play's social relationships. Even as he grovels before them, Läuffer holds his interlocutors in contempt; and they return the favor. The dialog in the beat following Läuffer's exit underlines this: the Major discusses his intention to hire this "lickspittle," as the Privy Councilor calls him (1967a: vol. 6, p. 2335), because he comes cheap. Established in the bow and the reaction to it, the scene's underlying social *gestus* is developed after Läuffer's exit.

Läuffer's bow illustrates the degree to which the dramaturgical and directorial interpretation of the script depends not only on the actor's gestural work on his characterization but also on his gestural work in interaction with his fellow actors. Gaugler's exaggeration of his character's "natural" behavior is also as good a practical example as we are likely to get of Brecht's concept of the actor standing beside the role in performance, at once demonstrating and commenting on the character's behavior.

Our example from the *Hofmeister* is particularly clear in part because the beat's *grundgestus* is focused in a single character *gestus*, in part because this *gestus* is so highly exaggerated. Such exaggerations are, however, better suited to comic texts than to straight dramatic ones. Indeed, Brecht once mentioned to Giorgio Strehler that his defamiliarizing acting style was much easier to achieve in comedies, since the comic form tends itself to defamiliarize its characters and events.[11] This is one reason why the Ensemble tended to use a much less gesturally over-elaborated style in its productions of serious texts, including such Brecht texts as *Mother Courage*.

This difference was, however, primarily one of degree. Brecht and his actors used stylization and exaggeration of gesture, intonation, or tempo in some of their most serious productions, although with a different emotional emphasis and a different balance between playing the role and demonstrating it. One of the best known "emotional" moments in Brecht's theatre work, for example, is Helene Weigel's silent scream in the 1951 *Courage* (an Ensemble revival of a production originally staged in 1949). As she hears the salvo that signals the execution of her son Swiss Cheese, Weigel's Courage is seated on a low stool with her hands in her lap. She clenches her rough skirt, leaning forward with a straight, tense back as if shot in the stomach. At the same time, she thrusts her head straight back against her shoulders; her mouth tears open until it seems that her jaw will break, but no sound comes forth. For a moment, her whole physicality has the impossible, angular contortion of one of Picasso's screaming horses in *Guernica*. Then she snaps her mouth shut, brings her torso and head back into alignment, and collapses the tension in her torso, slumping in on herself.

The moment is justifiably famous, both as an example of Weigel's unmatched skill as an actress and as an example of the type of carefully elaborated physicality that the Ensemble's actors were expected to develop in fulfilling their responsibility to the production interpretation. It is also an unabashedly emotional moment – an emotionality, however, carefully controlled and used both by Weigel and by the production developing around her. In the first place, the very physicality of the moment moves it beyond the level of naturalistic grief with which an audience can empathize. We are shocked, stunned, shaken by Courage's grief, but we are not allowed to share it on the plane of petty emotional titilation. The technically accomplished extremity of Weigel's acting, in short, defamiliarizes Courage's grief through the very demonstration of that grief.

Moreover, both Brecht's play and his production allow Courage this intensely human moment in order to illustrate for the audience the basic social contradiction out of which the character is built. Courage is both businesswoman and mother. Or rather, she tries to be both; the social realities of the total war from which she tries to profit as businesswoman prevent her from fulfilling her responsibilities as mother. She has been confronted with a nearly impossible economic choice – either she lose her son or she pay a sum that will cost her the wagon, her only means of supporting herself and her daughter. But she has tried to avoid making this choice in attempting to deal her way out. Just prior to the execution, Courage has sent the prostitute Yvette offstage to bribe the soldiers holding Swiss Cheese. She is unwilling, however, to pay the ruinous sum demanded, and sends Yvette back again and again to bargain. Just before the salvo, she turns to the army chaplain whom she is hiding from his so-called religious enemies and comments haltingly that perhaps she has haggled too long. Sounds of gunfire teach both her and the audience that her delay is indeed costly. Courage bears responsibility for her own extreme moment of grief – a lesson underlined in performance by the simple expedient of having the chaplain, who is seated on a stool next to Courage, get up and walk away from her in the middle of her scream. Brecht allows Courage her grief, but he also uses it to provide his audience with the necessary data for a dialectical analysis of his play's social relationships.

Weigel's scream, although unusual in its degree of technical accomplishment, illustrates the way in which Brecht combined the actor's gestural elaboration of role with the careful elaboration of emotive and textual contexts. The characters' reactions to the scream provide Brecht's audiences with insight into the social contradictions affecting even the most seemingly personal, emotional behavior. As with Läuffer's bow, this gestural elaboration could extend to the development of a basic physical *gestus*, centered on one or a series of quoted gestures, even for a straight dramatic character. *Courage* provides several examples of such a *gestus*, modified to suit the development of a dramatic character. One of the better known is Weigel's treatment of money. Every time she received payment in the course of her play's performance, Weigel's Courage would "mistrustfully" bite the coin to make sure it was real (Berlau, Brecht *et al.* 1952: 264). Now, this kind of gesture is certainly something any creative director or actor might invent while working on the play – assuming they understand the play's dialectics properly.

Still, Brecht's productions developed their fables so clearly, not because of any special magic, but because Brecht and his actors went to the trouble to understand and outline in performance vocabulary the story they were telling. Without the aid of Brecht's *Modellbuch* (a photographic and descriptive record of an Ensemble production intended to guide interpretation elsewhere), for example, it is doubtful that a director working within the conventions of the German theater of 1949 would have thought through to the telling variation of Courage's treatment of money that Brecht and Weigel used at the very end of the play. Courage's daughter Kattrin has been shot trying to alert the city of Halle to an impending enemy attack. Courage is now alone. She must drag her wagon herself back into the war, back into the train of the army that feeds her. She cannot afford to wait to bury Kattrin herself, so she pays a peasant family to bury her daughter for her. She fishes a handful of coins from the leather purse at her waist, starts to hand them to the peasants, looks at the coins, hesitates, slowly puts one coin back in her purse, then gives the rest over in payment. Even as she displays her character's total personal collapse, Weigel demonstrates once again the basic contradiction between business-woman and mother that has led to that collapse.[12]

This last example, like the others we have examined, illustrates both the degree to which Brecht expected his actors to serve directorial inter-pretation and, at the same time, the degree to which this interpretation depended on the actor's contributions. On the other hand, the examples do not reveal the dominance of any single all-powerful acting technique, let alone the dominance of a global acting methodology, over either the actor's work or the director's demands. On the contrary, the examples reveal the application of virtually the full range of customary actor technique, from vocal and physical flexibility to precise emotional control. This fact, in turn, has a significant corollary: "There is *no* technique that *cannot* be used in the Brecht-theater, so long as it serves to expose the contradictions in processes in such a way that they can be pleasurably recognized by the spectator and lead to his own transformation" (Wekwerth 1980: 108). In fact, Brecht not only encouraged the use of a wide variety of performance techniques but also structured his rehearsal process in a way that allowed these techniques to be subsumed in the service of his interpretational ends. Since the nature of this process has a great deal to do with the strengths of performances such as Hans Gaugler's or Helene Weigel's, we will profit by turning back to it here.

Our examples from the *Hofmeister* and *Mother Courage* have under-lined the degree to which the detailed "*Fabelbau*" – the building up of the fable – is the principal goal not simply of pre-rehearsal analysis but of rehearsal itself. The kind of detailed analysis of beats we saw in Brecht's *Courage* breakdown provides an anchor-point in rehearsals; when prob-lems arise, one can check to see whether the fable is being told in the most effective way, or whether the right fable is being told. At the same time, the concrete discoveries made by the actors, director, and dramaturgs during rehearsals are used to tighten and fine-tune the analysis of the fable as its concrete theatrical elaboration is developed. The precise choreo-graphic effect of Läuffer's repeated bows, for example, is not something a directorial team can plan beforehand.

Or, at least, this effect is not something Brecht and his co-workers planned beforehand. Although Brecht went into rehearsals with a detailed description of the text and concrete plans for initial blocking to provide a structure for the exploration of character relationships, he did not begin rehearsals with a specific scheme of the final physical production. He knew what his goals were, but not the concrete measures necessary to achieve them. Consequently, he could maintain that "we develop pretty much from nothing, exploring the most varied possibilities. We speak the text, move around within the situations. Slowly we try to find out what is interesting.

That is then kept, other things are let fall. We then develop the characterizations, and also the blocking" (1975: 125).

This kind of leisurely approach to the building up of the concrete production is clearly an essential safeguard against the impatient tendency to impose directorial decisions on the actor from outside – to treat the actor like a puppet. Consequently, Brecht took this approach seriously. Carl Weber remembers the first time he watched the Ensemble at work: Brecht, his assistants, and the actors stood around, smoked, talked, laughed. Every so often an actor would go up on stage and try one of thirty ways of falling off a table. Weber thought everyone was taking a break, until the horseplay went on long enough to make him realize he was watching the rehearsal (1967: 102–3) – a rehearsal, one suspects, devoted to the serious business of discovering the one way of falling off a table that will illuminate concretely its historical determinants.

Brecht's actors were encouraged to make their own discoveries – subject only to Brecht's dramaturgic principle that the fable retain dominance over its characters. Brecht suggested that this process of discovery and elaboration takes place in three broad and overlapping phases. The first of these extends through reading rehearsals and the early blocking rehearsals. It involves making a first acquaintance with the character by continually asking why that character does what it does: "you look assiduously for contradictions, for deviations from type, for the ugly in the beautiful and the beautiful in the ugly" (1967a: vol. 16, p. 843). This is also the phase during which the actor most intensely fulfills a specifically dramaturgical responsibility, studying the fable and familiarizing herself with the results of the production staff's background work: "The study of the role is at the same time a study of the fable; more precisely, it should at first be a [study] of the fable. . . . For this, the actor must mobilize his knowledge of the world and of people, and he must ask his questions as a dialectician" (1967a: vol. 16, p. 704).[13] An actress playing Mother Courage, for example, would be expected to note that in one beat she attempts to protect her children by rigging the business of drawing for the black spot, while in the very next beat she ignores her children completely in order to swing a deal over a belt buckle, thereby letting Eilif get stolen out from under her nose. She would not, however, be asked to bridge this contradiction by developing a complex character conception; rather, this contradiction is the element to be explored in rehearsal. Clearly, this first phase is crucial – if the actor is not able to think along the same lines as the directorial staff, he will not be able later to teach his directors what they need to learn.

The second phase continues the work already done, but in an antithetical direction – one in which more than a few theoretical purists have assumed Brecht was not interested. As Brecht describes it, "the second phase is that of identification with the character [*Einfühlung*], the search for the character's truth in a subjective sense; you let it do what *it* wants to do, to hell with criticism as long as society provides what you need" (1967a: vol. 16, p. 843). The actor must explore her character in all the detail demanded by the most naturalistic director, but the criterion for selection among her discoveries remains the character's social behavior. Brecht never denied that there were character elements outside the realm of social determination, but he frequently pointed out that such aspects "hardly belong to the constitutive elements of the illustration of reality" (1967a: vol. 15, p. 282). Indeed, as Werner Hecht puts it, "we don't want 'characters' in the literal sense of the word on our stage, that is, people with engraved, unchangeable peculiarities that at best unfold themselves monadically. What interests us about people is their way of behaving, the historically conditioned reactions" (Hecht 1972: 151). With this orientation, it is hardly surprising that "Brecht in fact almost never spoke about the character of the stage figure during rehearsals, but rather about his way of behaving; he said virtually nothing about what a man *is*, but rather what he *does*. And when he did say anything about character, he related it not to the psychological but the sociological."[14]

In fact, Brecht rarely spoke about individual characters in isolation. Rather, he exhorted his actors to create their characters dialectically with each other, to react rather than act: "The smallest social unit is not the individual; but two people. We create each other in life, too" (1967a: vol. 16, p. 688). Hence, Brecht could describe his second phase as one in which the actor lets the character react to the other characters, to the milieu, to the fable. As Brecht rather un-epically puts it, "this collecting process proceeds slowly until it then nevertheless takes a leap – until you leap into the final character, unite yourself with it" (1967a: vol. 16, p. 843).

Only when the work of this "naturalistic" or "Stanislavskian" phase has been completed can the third, antithetical, more properly "Brechtian" phase begin.[15] During this phase the actor, having come to identify with the character, to know it from the inside, examines it once again "from outside, from the point of view of society," and attempts to recapture the "mistrust and astonishment of the first phase" (1967a: vol. 16, pp. 843–4). It is primarily during this phase that the actors and director, using the insights won from a critical reexamination of the social behavior of the characters they have come to know intimately, structure out the final composition of gestures and positions that will elaborate the fable concretely in performance. The actor's goal during this phase is not, however, to reject everything she has learned during the second phase lest the audience be contaminated by un-epic playing. Rather, as Brecht points out clearly in one of his 1954 appendixes to the *Organon*, the actor's ultimate goal in performance is to achieve a dialectical unity between the gestural presentation of the character in his social relationships and a realistic emotional foundation won through identification:

> Ignorant heads interpret the contradiction between playing (demonstration) and experiencing (identification) as if only the one or the other appeared in the actor's work (or as if according to the *Short Organon* one only plays, according to the old technique one only experiences). In reality it is, of course, a matter of two competing processes that unite in the work of the actor.... Out of the struggle and the tension between the two antipodes ... the actor draws his real impact.
>
> (Brecht 1967a: vol. 16, p. 703)

Brecht, of course, did develop and discuss a number of his own techniques intended to enforce the dialectic between "playing" and "experiencing." Most of these techniques were, strictly speaking, rehearsal exercises, such as having the actor speak the character's lines in the third person or speak the stage directions along with her lines. Many of these exercises were, in fact, used at the Ensemble, particularly during the early productions, most notably the *Hofmeister*. They were, however, included when useful during the second and third stages of the actor's work and without theoretical discussion about their epic purpose. Brecht knew that the practical workshop is not the place for theoretical discourse.[16]

Indeed, Herbert Blau is quite correct when he maintains that Brecht's approach to acting is "more a matter of the environment created around the actor than a methodology of acting itself" (Blau 1961: 121). The concentration of communal effort on the interpretation of dramatic texts may be seen as one element of this environment, the use of a leisurely approach to building up a production is another, the time committed to this approach a third. Underlying all of these, however, is the creation of true ensemble working methods. Only when directors, designers, dramaturgs, and actors work continuously together, using a shared dramaturgical approach and developing group methods to explore a number of productions treating texts from different historical periods and different genres, can they create the common vocabulary necessary to allow the ensemble members to use their particular training, experience, and techniques towards the creation of a production that bears the stamp not just of individuals but of a recognizable whole. That is something we should keep in mind when we try to characterize the distinctive quality of Brecht's work with the actor, and certainly if we try to make practical use of it.

18

DARIO FO

The roar of the clown

Ron Jenkins

The intellectual complexity and bacchanalian passions of Dario Fo's epic comedy are usually reduced in translation to the flatness of a political cartoon. Even successful productions such as Rennie Davis' version of *We Won't Pay, We Won't Pay* leave the audience with the impression of Fo as a clever satirist whose work can be comfortably categorized as political theatre. This limited view ignores the subtler dimensions of Fo's talents. In their original versions Fo's plays are dense with poetic wordplay, visual references to medieval paintings, and sophisticated rhythmic structures that are lost by translators and directors who focus singlemindedly on Fo as a political clown.[1]

Of course, there is a fundamentally political dimension to all of Fo's work, which includes mocking references to police brutality, government fraud, and social injustice. His recurring theatrical allusions to current events reflect Fo's commitment to a theatre that is politically relevant, but during the three months that I traveled with him and his company, he rarely spoke explicitly about politics. Rehearsals, seminars, and casual mealtime conversations revolved around topics such as the theatricality of regional dialects and the actor/audience relationship. Artistic concerns such as these are linked to political issues, but Fo manages to make the connections without waving flags as blatantly as do some of his adaptors abroad. An actress in the New York production of *We Won't Pay* referred to it as a "spoon waving" version of the play, because she was directed to play the role of a housewife by standing on the edge of the stage and waving a spoon at the audience as she lectured them on the evils of capitalism.

Fo's outrage against political and social injustice emerges more obliquely, as in the moment at the dinner table when the company's electrical technician asked him if he believed that people spoke regional dialects because they were too ignorant to speak "proper Italian." Fo responded with a spirited defense of the inherent beauty of the dialects and an attack on the Italian school system's policy of branding the variations as inferior. In his plays Fo uses a poetic blend of regional dialects, and it is clear that the choice reflects his commitment to the celebration of working class popular culture. What Fo's audiences hear onstage, however, is not a didactic manifesto about the "language of the people," but a magnificent cascade of coarse poetry that is an indirect tribute to the lyricism of the dialects spoken in Italy's village markets.

Fo's fusion of subversive politics and poetic slapstick is exemplified in his portrayal of Harlequin. Having been sent by his master to fetch a love potion, Harlequin uses it himself in a visit to a prostitute. When he returns home, Harlequin's disobedience is betrayed by the fantastic and uncontrollable growth of his penis. Using his mimetic talents, Fo creates the illusion that his organ has become almost as big as Harlequin himself. To avoid detection he wraps it in a blanket and pretends it is a baby. All the women in the neighborhood coo and stroke it, resulting in a great comic situation. The focus of the comedy is ostensibly erotic, but at the heart of the piece is the servant's revolt against his patron, the refusal of the impoverished Harlequin to submit to the master's repressive rules. The humor is generated by the tension between Harlequin's fear of his tyrannical master and his pleasure over his enhanced potency. Fo's performance is an allegory of rebellion camouflaged behind a mask of crude buffoonery. The politics are clear, but they never overwhelm the piece's exquisite slapstick poetics.

Fo blends politics and art with an effortless eloquence that makes him a Brechtian clown. Frequently describing the style of his theater as "epic," Fo borrows Brecht's terminology, but his points of reference go back to the medieval town jesters (*giullari*) and the *commedia dell'arte* players who were the originators of Italy's epic comedy tradition. Looking to these models for inspiration, Fo has developed a modern style of epic performance that speaks to his audience with the immediacy of a newspaper editorial, shifts perspectives with the fluidity of cinematic montage, and pulsates with the rhythmic drive of a jazz improvisation.

A good example of Fo's epic clowning can be found in his play about the relationship between Shakespeare and Queen Elizabeth, *Elisabetta: Quasi per Caso una Donna*. Shakespeare never appears on stage, but Fo, playing a maidservant, acts out the entire plot of *Hamlet* for the head of Elizabeth's secret police as he explains that it is a veiled satire of the Queen's regime (Figure 18.1). Playing all the parts himself, Fo uses gestures and gibberish to re-enact the high points of Shakespeare's tragedy in less than two minutes, as if the action were unfolding on high-speed film. The police captain is totally bewildered, and Fo has structured the episode so that the audience identifies the official's dullness with the thickheadedness of modern Italian police investigators. Angered by the abusive mockery of her policies, Elizabeth tries to prevent Fo from recounting his second-hand Hamlet, but the clown is unstoppable. When she grabs his left hand, he continues miming the story behind his back with his right hand, and when she manages to tie up both his arms, he continues gesturing with his feet. The comedy of the scene is rooted in the muscular rhythms of Fo's performance. The Queen's clumsy attempts at physical censorship are no match for the irrepressible satiric impulses of the clown.

This style of densely-layered comedy appears frequently in the plays that Fo writes for his theatre ensemble, but the simplest way to isolate the essential techniques of Fo's epic clowning is to look at examples drawn from his solo comic performances (Figure 18.2). In one-man plays such as *Mistero Buffo*, *Fabulazzo Osceno*, and *Storia della Tigre* Fo demonstrates most clearly his genius for creating theatre that unites art and politics in a seamless comic blend. Among the key elements that give Fo's performances their distinctive power are his musically orchestrated rhythms, his montage-like use of multiple perspectives, and the intimately immediate quality of his relationship with his public.

RHYTHM

When Fo directs rehearsals of his plays or critiques the work of his students, he always stresses the importance of rhythm. Fo is a musician as well as a playwright, and his theatre flows with a dynamic musicality that is generated by the basic emotional impulses of the situations he enacts. For example, his portrayal of a starving man in *The Grammelot of the Zanni* is structured around the rhythms of hunger as experienced by a fourteenth-century peasant.

The hungry Zanni is so famished that he begins to eat his own body, popping his eyeballs into his mouth and slurping up his disemboweled intestines as if they were pasta in a bowl. The action could easily become mired in infantile grotesquerie, but Fo makes it comic by cannibalizing himself with the rhythmic joy of a big band leader in full swing. The body parts are devoured with tempos of building excitement that culminate in percussive burps or climatic sighs of contentment. Although the piece is extremely funny, there is nothing frivolous about the mood Fo's rhythms evoke. There is never any doubt that the man is in pain, that he suffers not only a hunger for food but also a hunger for dignity and justice.

After consuming himself, the peasant challenges the complacency of God and the audience by threatening to eat them next, but he gets sidetracked by the dream of cooking a feast in an overstocked kitchen. His delirious fantasies are accompanied by the syncopated sounds of gurgling stews and sizzling oils. Fo creates all the effects himself with musical vocalizations that resemble a jazz singer scatting his way through a song.

Figure 18.1 In *Elisabetta: Quasi per Caso Una Donna* (1984), Fo performs a two-minute version of Hamlet in drag as the maidservant to Queen Elizabeth. (Photo by Corrado M. Falsini.)

Figure 18.2 Fo uses his face and hands to turn his one-man show into an epic spectacle. (Photo by Eugenio Bersani.)

The piece concludes when the famished man wakes up from his dream and satisfies his cravings by eating a fly. He sucks the juice off the wings and savors each morsel of the insect with a primal howl of delight. Fo's performance is comparable to Chaplin's classic routine of eating a boiled shoe in *The Gold Rush*.

Fo's rhythmic pantomime is antithetical to the style of a performer such as Marcel Marceau. There is nothing refined, delicate or quiet about a performance by Dario Fo. It is full of crude sounds and coarse gestures expressing human desires and needs. Marceau's technique of pure mime calls attention to itself as something apart from everyday gesture. Fo submerges his technique in a flurry of sounds and movements. He seems to have just come off the subway and invented it all on the spot. Fo is full of passions, obscenities, odors, growls, and desires that could not exist in the rarified world of classical mime. These irrepressible urges give Fo's performances their inner pulse. The comic cadences of the hungry Zanni's actions are inseparable from his struggle to survive.

MONTAGE

The earthy rhythms of Fo's style are complemented by his ability to present a story from several perspectives successively rather than from a single point of view. In the enactment of Zanni's hunger, for instance, Fo first offers the grotesque fantasy of the man eating himself, then shifts to the pleasurable dream of a giant kitchen, and concludes with the stark portrait of a starving man eating a fly. All of this is presented in the context of a political/historical explanation for the man's hunger presented by Fo in his introductory prolog.

The shifts of perspective are intentional. Like Brecht, he wants his audience to see a situation from a variety of viewpoints so they can reflect on its multiple aspects, instead of simply losing themselves in empathy for a single point of view. In describing the way his epic style of character-ization differs from traditional acting, Fo uses the analogy of a sculptor carving a statue. As a performer he circles a situation the way a sculptor circles an unfinished statue, examining the way the lights and shadows are formed when viewed from different directions.

Fo's technique of shifting perspectives is equivalent to cinematic montage. One of the most vivid examples of Fo's multiple-perspective storytelling is his satire of the attempted assassination of the Pope. Alone on the stage without props, Fo recreates the scene of the Pope's arrival in Spain. Fo becomes the people shouting their greetings in the welcoming crowd. Fo becomes the Pope's airplane, advertising its sacred passenger with a giant papal cap on top of its wings. Fo becomes one of the peasants explaining to another that the magnificently attired plane is not the Pope, but that the Pope is inside the plane. Images and characters appear and dissolve with a rapidity that gives the audience the impression of watching a televized news report of the event, with the camera angles changing every few seconds.

The Pope emerges from the door of the plane. Fo both portrays and describes him, presenting the scene in first and third person simultaneously. After showing the Pope in all the splendor of his jewels and colored robes, Fo slips out of the story completely to recount a newspaper article he had read recently that criticized the Pope's taste for opulence as the opposite of Christ's renouncement of material pleasures. Fo then quotes the Bible story in which Jesus was tempted by the devil with the power to fly all over the world. "Jesus said no to the devil," quips Fo, "but the Pope says 'yes'." Continuing to mock the pope's incessant world travels, Fo jokes that "God is everywhere, but the Pope's already been there."

Moving back to the newsreel images of the Pope, Fo portrays the gunman, the Bulgarian agents with walkie-talkies directing the gunman, the police asking the gunman what he is doing with the bullets, and the gunman replying that they are a new kind of rosary bead. He says a prayer as he loads each one into the chamber, and the guards leave him alone. Fo then resumes the role of narrator to wonder aloud why no one was able to stop the gunman, given that so many photographs were taken of him in varying phases of preparation for the assassination. Fo becomes a series of still photographs leading up to the gunshots, and he then acts out the fall of the wounded Pope, the television commentators announcing that the Pope has been shot in the sphincter, and the outraged Vatican spokesman who refuses to acknowledge that the Pope has a sphincter, insisting instead that the Pope's bowels should be referred to as a divine conduit.

Fo's looney tune version of the shooting leads to another quick change of perspective, this one more drastic, taking the audience to the twelfth century and the Papacy of Pope Boniface VIII. Fo's story is a twelfth-century illustration of the twentieth-century newspaper column describing the Pope as the opposite of Christ. Boniface is presented as he prepares himself for a public appearance, adorning himself in fine clothes, expensive rings, and elegant robes. When the Pope's procession meets the humbler procession of Jesus, Fo portrays Boniface's hypocrisy by showing him unrobing and covering himself with mud in feigned humility before Christ.

Up until the meeting with Jesus, Boniface has been satirized for his vanity and arrogance. When altar boys wrinkle his clothes he threatens to hang them by their tongues, a punishment, Fo explains, actually used by Boniface to deal with religious dissidents. Fo uses this graphic image as a recurring bit of black comedy. Each time the altar boys displease him, Boniface mimes hanging them by their tongues. Fo mimes hammering the tongue into the wall, then his hands become the tongue swinging in the wind. Next he transforms himself into a boy as he would appear if his body were hanging suspended from the tongue.

By shifting from the subject to the object of the threat and from the close-up of the tongue to a long shot of the hanging victim, Fo tells the story as if he were a camera shooting the scenes. The sequence is repeated several times throughout the piece from different angles and for shorter durations, as if miniature flashbacks of the original threat were inserted into a corner of the stage. With such montage techniques Fo insures that the audience never gets lost in the characterization of the Pope and is continually reminded of the contextual frame of religious tyranny within which the action takes place.

IMMEDIACY AND AUDIENCE INVOLVEMENT

Fo talks to the public directly through prologs, intentional narrative interruptions, and improvised responses to spontaneous situations that arise onstage. Fo's intimate rapport with large crowds gives his performances an immediacy that elicits the public's active involvement in an ongoing dialog of ideas. Fo challenges the audience with a phrase or gestures, and they respond with laughter or applause. Using his public as a collaborator, Fo structures his monologs with the rhythms of their responses in mind. During his performances the integration of the audience seems unplanned, but when Fo advises other actors of his material in rehearsals, he explicitly directs them to anticipate the public's response at specific moments. Rehearsing monologs with student actors, Fo will play the role of the audience responding to each line, so that the student learns to transform the monolog into a dialog with the public.

The immediacy of the audience is central to Fo's retelling of the miracle when Jesus turns water into wine. Fo initially presents two competing storytellers. One is an angel who tells the official version of the story in a detached style that does not take into account the public's desires. The other story teller is a drunk who claims to have been present at the miracle and offers an earthy account of the celebration that speaks more directly to the audience's spirit of revelry. The drunk plucks the angel's feathers, chases him away, and proceeds to tell his Dionysian version of the miracle, emphasizing the pleasures of drinking wine with an inebriated ecstasy that serves as a direct call to the senses of his audience. He invites them to feel, smell, and taste the wine with him as he relives the pleasures of Jesus' miracle. In one sequence he drinks wine as if bathing in it, mimes the passage of the red liquid as it seeps through his veins, and expresses the depth of his pleasure with a gigantic burp that sends the aroma of the wine across the countryside. In a cinematic transition the expansive burp opens up the landscape of the action, and Fo presents the trail of the wine's aroma leading to a man on horseback who smells it and shouts out with gratitude, "Jesus sei di/vino" ("Jesus you are divine/of wine"). Fo's vocal and visual shifts have been building up to this climactic shout, which inevitably results in applause from the audience appreciating the pun. The sequence is structured in a way that would render its rhythms incomplete without the culminating punctuation of the audience's gleeful response.

Arguing that drinking wine could never be a sin if Jesus offered it to his mother, the drunk is implicitly urging the public to challenge the angel's pious attitudes and celebrate the liberating effects of wine. To strengthen his argument, the drunk reasons that Adam and Eve would never have been tempted by the snake to eat the apple if there had been wine in the garden for them to drink. The performance is a masterpiece of comic rhetoric designed to persuade the audience to abandon the angel's puritan point of view and accept a more joyous vision of religion. As the story progresses, the drunk's argument becomes funnier and more reasonable at the same time. The public is swayed by his comic logic about Adam in the garden of Eden: if Adam had been like the drunk, the human race would still be living in Paradise. Fo's success in persuading the audience can be measured in their roars of laughter and applause at moments such as the horseman's yell.

A TAPESTRY OF POLITICS AND POETRY

Fo weaves the technical elements of his epic clowning into a dense theatrical tapestry in which politics and poetry are inseparable. His comic rhythms grow out of the dialectic between freedom and oppression that is at the core of the stories he tells. Each slapstick crescendo is orchestrated around a liberating triumph over injustice. Generated by the conflict between the powerful and the powerless, the frantic tempo of Fo's farces is an implicit tribute to his characters' abilities to outwit their oppressors and survive.

Fo's montage-like use of shifting perspectives is linked to his political beliefs. Presenting a situation from multiple points of view enables him to emphasize the relationship between individual behavior and its cultural context. The theatrical jump-cuts in Fo's performances suggest a complex interaction between history, economics, religion, morality, and mundane current events. Fo's comedy exists at the overlap between the private and the public domains.

The relationship between Fo and his audiences reveals another aspect of this overlap. The public is included in the performance because Fo believes in their intelligence. He speaks to them with a direct and candid simplicity that transforms spectators into Fo's co-conspirators against injustice.

All of Fo's techniques coalesce in the powerful conclusion to his story of Jesus and the wine. Having just presented Adam's rejection of the Serpent in favor of a glass of wine, the drunk offers a toast to God, the audience, and the earth beneath his feet. Tilting the glass to the public, Fo is graciously thanking them for their involvement. Pouring a few drops on the ground he is paying homage to the earthy impulses that stand in opposition to the repressive censorship of the angel he battled at the beginning of the piece. And raising the glass toward heaven he shifts the focus from the mundane to the spiritual world. This simple, skyward motion is the last gesture of the story, and it is charged with startling eloquence. Having defied the authority of heaven, the buffoon strikes a pose that momentarily transforms him into an angel in spite of himself. The closing sequence epitomizes the spirit of Fo's epic clown in the breadth of its vision, the depth of its feeling, and the generosity with which it embraces the world beyond the stage.

19

FORUM THEATRE

Augusto Boal

Before coming to Europe, I had done a lot of Forum Theatre, in a number of Latin American countries, but always in "workshop" situations, never as a "performance." Here in Europe, at the time of writing, I have already done several Forum Theatre sessions as performances.[1] In Latin America, the audience was generally small and homogeneous, the spect-actors almost always being the workers from one factory, the residents of a particular neighborhood, the congregation of a church, the students of a university, etc. Here, besides that kind of "workshop" forum, I have also done shows for hundreds of people who did not know each other at all. This is a new type of Forum Theatre, which I began to develop here, with some very positive results.

Also, most of the Forum Theatre pieces I did in Latin America had a "realistic" style. Here in Europe I have also done "symbolist" scenes, as was the case in Portugal for a work about agrarian reform.

THE RULES OF THE GAME

Forum Theatre is a sort of fight or game, and like all forms of game or fight there are rules. They can be modified, but they still exist, to ensure that all the players are involved in the same enterprise, and to facilitate the generation of serious and fruitful discussion.

DRAMATURGY

1 The text must clearly delineate the nature of each character, it must identify them precisely, so that the spect-actors can easily recognize each one's ideology.
2 The original solutions proposed by the protagonist must contain at the very least one political or social error, which will be analyzed during the forum session. These errors must be clearly expressed and carefully

rehearsed, in well-defined situations. This is because Forum Theatre is not propaganda theatre, it is not the old didactic theatre. It is pedagogical in the sense that we all learn together, actors and audience. The play – or "model" – must present a mistake, a failure, so that the spect-actors will be spurred into finding solutions and inventing new ways of confronting oppression. We pose good questions, but the audience must supply good answers.

3 The piece can be of any genre (realism, symbolism, expressionism, etc.) except "surrealism" or the irrational; the style does not matter, as long as the objective is to discuss concrete situations (through the medium of theatre).

STAGING

1 The actors must have physical styles of playing which successfully articulate their characters' ideology, work, social function, profession, etc. It is important that there is a logic to the characters' evolution, and that they *do things*, or else the audience will be inclined to take their seats and do the "forum" without the theatre – by speech alone (without action) like a radio forum.

2 Every show must find the most suitable means of "expression" for its particular subject-matter; preferably this should be found by common consent with the public, either in the course of the presentation or by prior research.

3 Each character must be presented "visually," in such a way as to be recognizable independently of their spoken script; also the costumes must be easy for the spect-actors to get in and out of, with the minimum of fuss.

THE PERFORMANCE GAME

The performance is an artistic and intellectual game played between actor and spect-actor.

1 To start off with, the show is performed as if it were a conventional play. A certain image of the world is presented.

2 The spect-actors are asked if they agree with the solutions advanced by the protagonist; they will probably say no. The audience is then told that the play is going to be done a second time, exactly as it was done the first time. The actors will try to bring the piece to the same end as before, and the spect-actors are to try to change it, showing that new solutions are possible and valid. In other words, the actors stand for a

particular *vision of the world* and consequently will try to maintain that world as it is and ensure that things go exactly the same way . . . at least until a spect-actor intervenes and changes the vision of the world *as it is* into a world *as it could be*. It is vital to generate a degree of tension among the spect-actors – if no one changes the world it will stay as it is, if no one changes the play it will come to the same end as before.

3 The audience is informed that the first step is to take the protagonist's place whenever he or she is making a mistake, in order to try to bring about a better solution. All they have to do is approach the playing area and shout "Stop!" Then, immediately, the actors must stop where they are without changing position. With the minimum delay, the spect-actor must say where he or she wants the scene taken from, indicating the relevant phrase, moment, or movement (whichever is easiest). The actors then start the scene again from the prescribed point, with the spect-actor as protagonist.

4 The actor who has been replaced does not immediately retire from the game; he or she stays on the sidelines as a sort of coach or supporter, to encourage the spect-actors and correct them if they start to go wrong. For example, in Portugal a peasant who was replacing the actor playing the part of the Boss started shouting "Long live socialism!" The replaced actor had to explain to her that, generally speaking, bosses are not great fans of socialism . . .

5 From the moment at which the spect-actor replaces the protagonist and begins to put forward a new solution, all the other actors transform themselves into agents of oppression, or, if they already were agents of oppression, they intensify their oppression, to show the spect-actor how difficult it is to change reality. The game is spect-actors – trying to find a new solution, trying to change the world – against actors – trying to hold them back, to force them to accept the world as it is. But of course the aim of the forum is not to win, but to learn and to train. The spect-actors, by acting out their ideas, train for "real life" action; and actors and audience alike, by playing, learn the possible consequences of their actions. They learn the arsenal of the oppressors and the possible tactics and strategies of the oppressed.

6 If the spect-actor gives in, he or she drops out of the game, the actor takes up the role again, and the piece rapidly heads back towards the already known ending. Another spect-actor can then approach the stage, shout "Stop!" and say where he or she wants the play taken from, and the play will start again from that point. A new solution will be tried out.

7 At some point the spect-actor may eventually manage to break the oppression imposed by the actors. The actors must give in – one after another or all together. From this moment on, the spect-actors are

invited to replace anyone they like, to show new forms of oppression which perhaps the actors are unaware of. This then becomes the game of spect-actor/protagonist against spect-actor/oppressor. Thus the oppression is subjected to the scrutiny of the spect-actors, who discuss (through their actions) ways of fighting it. All the actors, from off stage, carry on their work as coaches and supporters, each actor continuing to help and urge on his or her spect-actor.

8 One of the actors must also exercise the auxiliary function of joker, the wild card, leader of the game. It is up to him or her to explain the rules of the game, to correct errors made, and to encourage both parties not to stop playing. Indeed, the effect of the forum is all the more powerful if it is made entirely clear to the audience that if they do not change the world, no one will change it for them, and everything will inevitably turn out exactly the same – which is the last thing we would want to happen.

9 The knowledge which results from this investigation will, of necessity, be the best that that particular human social group can attain at that particular moment in time. The joker is not the president of a conference, he or she is not the custodian of the truth; the joker's job is simply to try to ensure that those who know a little more get the chance to explain it, and that those who dare a little, dare a little more, and show what they are capable of.

10 The "forum" over, it is proposed that a "model of action for the future" be constructed, this model first to be played out by the spect-actors.

EXAMPLES OF FORUM THEATRE

1 Agrarian reform seen from a public bench

In Portugal, just after 25 April 1974, the people took agrarian reform into their own hands. They did not wait for a law to be passed, they simply occupied the unproductive land and made it productive. At the time of writing, the government intends to institute an agrarian law which will challenge the popular conquests on that front, returning areas of land to their former owners (who made no use of them).

First action

The scene takes place on two benches in a garden. A man, the Landowner, is lying stretched out across both benches, taking his ease. Enter seven men and women singing "Grandula Vila Morena" by José Afonso, the Eurovision Song Contest tune used as the signal for the start of the military action which ousted the 50-year-old fascist Salazar–Caetano dictatorship.

The seven men and women evict the great Landowner from one of the two benches in which he is ensconced; in spite of his removal, they are none the less cramped on their one bench, because there are many of them.

Second action

They get down to work, miming the tasks of cultivation, while singing other popular songs. They start to discuss the need to push their conquest of public benches further. They take exception to the unproductiveness of the Landowner who has stayed put, with one bench all to himself, but opinions are divided: some want to turf him out, while others think that they have done enough already, that enough ground has been gained.

Third action

A Policeman comes along, bearing an order that they vacate 20cm of the collective bench ("the law of return"). They break into factions: some are for giving way, others are not, since to make a concession now would signify a victory for the forces of reaction, which would then gradually try to regain more ground. Eventually they give in.

Fourth action

The Landowner, protected by the Policeman, sits himself down on the vacated end of the bench. The seven others crowd in on the remaining section. The Landowner opens up a big umbrella, obscuring the light from the others. The seven protest. The Policeman declares that the Landowner is entitled to do what he is doing, since though the ground may be taken, the air is not. The seven are divided: some want to fight, others are happy with the little that they have obtained and want peace at any price.

Fifth action

The Policeman insists on the need to erect a wall dividing the collective bench into two parts, this wall to be built on "land" which does not belong to anyone; evidently the intention is that it will be built on the part of the bench occupied by the seven, not on the former owner's side. More discussions, more divisions, more concessions. One of the seven abandons the struggle, a second also goes, then a third and a fourth.

Sixth action

The Policeman announces that the occupation is pointless since the majority of the occupants have abandoned the occupied land. Consequently, the last three are thrown out and the former owner reassumes his rights over both public benches.

The forum

This scene was performed at Porto and at Vila Nova de Gaia. On the day of the first performance, there were more than a thousand people on the square in the open air. The "model" was performed, then the "forum"

began. On the second showing, a number of spect-actors enacted their
vision of how to resist the Landowner's counter-attack. But the best
moment was when a woman in the audience protested. On the simple stage,
there were some male spect-actors arguing among themselves – in role –
about the best tactics to use; finally they decided that they were all of one
mind and that the forum had been useful. At this point the woman in the
audience said:

> There you go, talking about oppression – that's all very well; the only people
> on the stage are men from the audience, who don't seem in the slightest
> oppressed by the actors, who were their deadly enemies a moment ago. And
> meanwhile, here in the audience, it's us women who continue to be
> oppressed since we are just as inactive as before, sitting here, watching the
> men act!

One of the male spectators then invited several women to give vent to their
feelings in the different roles. They agreed to do so, allowing only one man
to remain on stage, the man who played the Policeman. As the woman
said:

> Since the Policeman is the number one oppressor, that part can certainly be
> played by a man.

2 The nuclear power station

In Sweden, the controversy over nuclear energy and the construction of
power stations was very much a live issue. Some even said that the main
reason for the gunning down of Prime Minister Olof Palme was his having
affirmed that he would pursue a policy of nuclear gearing-up. His
opponents said the opposite – and afterwards, they did it anyway.

First action
Eva is in her office, at work. The scene shows friends, the Boss, day-to-day
problems, the process of finding new projects to work on, the daily grind
of a hard life.

Second action
Eva is at home; her husband is out of work, their daughters are spendthrifts,
they need money. A Female Friend drops round, they go out. They go
straight to a demonstration against the construction of atomic power
stations.

Third action
Back at the office. The Boss comes in whooping with joy: a new project
has been accepted! Everyone celebrates the news! Champagne is con-
sumed! Joy unbounded ... till the Boss explains what this new project is
about – the development of a refrigeration system for a nuclear power

station. Eva is torn; she needs work, she wants to support her fellow workers, but this situation poses a moral problem for her. She gives all the reasons she can for not accepting this new project, and her colleagues give their opposing reasons. Finally Eva gives in and accepts the job!

The forum

In this piece it was clear that the protagonist was going to have to commit an error and not be heroic. The audience almost cried when Eva gave in. And the effect of this was an extraordinary intensification of the fight – the game of actors/oppressors against spect-actors/oppressed – when it came to finding reasons for Eva to say no. Each time a spect-actor gave in and saw that she was beaten, the piece rapidly retraced its path towards Eva's "Yes." Passions in the audience ran high again till someone shouted "Stop!;" then the scene stopped and the new spect-actor tried a new solution starting from the first action, or the second, or even the third. Everything was analyzed: the husband's unemployment, the daughters' mania for consumption, Eva's indecision. Sometimes the analysis was purely "psychological," then another actor would come in and try to show the political side of the problem.

Should we be for or against nuclear power stations? Can one be against scientific progress? Can the word "progress" be applied to science when it leads us to the discovery of nuclear weapons?

And on the question of the disposal of "nuclear waste:" surely it could be satisfactorily disposed of in a social system whose central value was the human being rather than the profit motive?

I have already twice had the opportunity to take part in pieces of this kind. The first time was in the USA, where an analogous piece had been written about the inhabitants of a town which was producing the napalm used in Vietnam. In the end, in the American example, the inhabitants accepted the factory, reaching the conclusion that it would be economically ruinous to close. . . . Ruinous for whom? The second time was in Lisbon, again with a similar model: there is a refinery there which is causing a noticeable increase in the occurrence of lung cancer . . . but it is important for the economy. Here again, the residents gave way and resigned themselves to living with pollution, rather than living without jobs.

In this example, the function of Forum Theatre is quite clear: it is the other side of Ibsen's *An Enemy of the People*, whose leading character, Stockman, faced with an identical situation, takes an heroic stance.

Who exactly is taking an heroic stance? The character, the fiction. What I want is for the spect-actor to take an heroic stance, not the character. I think it is perfectly clear: if Stockman is a hero and prefers to stand alone, not compromising his moral principles, that can serve as an example. But this is cathartic – Stockman has an heroic attitude and demands of me that I sympathize with his heroic attitude. He drains me of my desire to behave like a hero myself.

In Forum Theatre, the reverse mechanism is at work. The character gives in and I am called upon to correct him, to show him a possible right, to rectify his action. And in so doing within the fiction of the play, I am preparing myself to do it in reality as well. I come face to face with reality (fictitiously). I become acquainted with the difficulties which I will meet later – fear of unemployment, my fellow workers' arguments, etc. – and if I manage to overcome all these things in Forum Theatre, I will be better qualified to overcome them in reality when the situation arises. Forum Theatre does not produce catharsis: it produces a stimulant for our desire to change the world.

These forms of Theatre of the Oppressed have developed in response to concrete and particular political situations. When in 1971 the dictatorship in Brazil made it impossible for the people to present popular theatre, we started to work on Newspaper Theatre techniques,[2] which were forms of theatre easily realizable by the people, so that they would be able to produce their own theatre. In Argentina before the last elections (1973), when the level of repression eased (without completely disappearing), we started doing Invisible Theatre in trains and restaurants, in queues for shops, in markets. When certain conditions arose in Peru, we began to work on various forms of Forum Theatre so that the spect-actors would fully assume their function of protagonist, which is what they were at the time; we thought that the people would have a role to play in the near future. That was in 1973.

In fact, all of these forms of theatre emerged when we were barred from traditional and institutional theatre. An experiment I would love to try would be doing Forum Theatre in the theatre, in a conventional theatre building, with an advertised starting time for the show, with sets and costumes, with extant scripts, by single writers or written collectively.[3]

Would it not be wonderful to see a dance piece where the dancers danced in the first act, and in the second showed the audience how to dance? Would it not be wonderful to see a musical where in the first act the actors sang and in the second we all sang together?

What would also be wonderful would be a theatre show where we, the artists, would present our world-view in the first act and where in the second act, they, the audience, could create a new world.

Let them create it first in the theatre, in fiction, to be better prepared to create it outside afterwards, for real.

I think that this is how magicians should be: first they should do their magic to enchant us, then they should teach us their tricks. This is also how artists should be – we should be creators and also teach the public how to be creators, how to make art, so that we may all use that art together.

FORUM THEATRE: DOUBTS AND CERTAINTIES

Forum Theatre is still in its infancy, and much research and experimentation will be required before this new form reaches its full maturity; at present we are still at the stage of exploration, of finding and opening up new ways of working.

This particularly applies to the Forum Theatre "show." In Latin America, I never took part in a "show;" all the Forum Theatre sessions were organized by a core group of people of homogeneous social origin, whose common interest was the resolution of relatively immediate problems. The Latin American experience had led me to construct a model ideal for Latin America, or at least for the particular experiments I had taken part in. The development of Forum Theatre in numerous directions in Europe inevitably entails a reconsideration of all the forms, structures, techniques, methods and processes of this kind of theatre. Everything is once again open to question.

THE FUNCTION OF THE WARM-UP

In all of the forum shows I have taken part in, there has always been an element of "warming-up" of spect-actors. Generally this is done in one of two possible ways.

1 Over ten or fifteen minutes, the joker explains Theatre of the Oppressed, recounts some experiences of forum shows or Invisible Theatre, and fixes the rules of the game which is to follow.

Then he proposes some exercises, starting with the simplest, the least off-putting, those that arouse the least resistance. For example, in Egypt, touching exercises provoked a very powerful resistance; which, by contrast, was far from the case with magistrates in Paris! It all depends on the culture, the country, the region, the moment.

After the exercises, we move on to Image Theatre. Here the spect-actors begin to work esthetically, and to suggest subject-matter for images themselves.

Then finally the group presents the anti-model, and from that starting point comes the forum.

2 I have in the past used, and seen others use, other less effective processes – starting immediately with exercises, with an explanation a posteriori. In these cases, I have noticed that a portion of the audience feels manipulated and reacts negatively. By contrast, when the

explanation comes first, the joker almost always ends up winning over the audience, and gaining their acquiescence and their confidence.

This does not mean that the warm-up is absolutely indispensable. I believe it prepares the spect-actors for action. In any case, the thing which will best prepare them is really the subject-matter and the play itself. The case of Het Trojaan Paard, a Belgian group from Antwerp, is significant; they have performed the same show, about the woman who is "a leader at work, a slave in the home," in a hundred towns in Belgium and Holland (the group speak Flemish), without ever doing the slightest preliminary warm-up. They just explain what is going to happen. And the show is so evocative and so galvanizing that all the spect-actors always want to take part.

THE FUNCTION OF THE ACTOR

Forum Theatre demands a different style of acting. In certain African countries the people measure the talents of singers by the extent to which they can seduce their audiences into singing along with them. That is what should happen with good Forum Theatre actors. In their performances there must not be the slightest trace of the narcissism so commonly found in *closed* theatre shows, because the presentation of the anti-model should, by contrast, principally express doubt; each action should contain its own negation; each phrase should leave open the possibility of saying the opposite of what is being said; each *yes* allows for an imagined *no*, or a *perhaps*.

During the forum proper, actors must be extremely dialectical. When they take up a counter-stance against a spect-actor/protagonist who wants to break the oppression, they must be honest and show that the oppression is not so easily defeated. They must show the difficulties which will appear, while retaining a manner which encourages the spect-actor to break the oppression. This means that, while still countering every phrase and action, they should awaken in the spect-actor other stances, other approaches. While impeding the attempt to break the oppression, they should rouse the spect-actor to achieve it.

If the actor is too firm, it can discourage or, worse still, frighten the spect-actor. If the actor is too soft and vulnerable, with no counter-arguments or counter-actions, it can mislead the spect-actor into believing that the problem posed by the play is easier to resolve than he or she thought.

In Berlin, at the Hochschüle der Kunst, a forum showed a young man trying to convince his family to give him a certain sum of money per month. In order to achieve this, he had to undergo endless rituals, family conversations and reunions, discussions about the war, about the past, about members of the family who had disappeared, etc. The actors were so enthusiastic that every spect-actor who came forward was subjected to an avalanche of arguments, to such an extent that very soon the whole audience was up in arms and shouted in unison "Stop – that's magic!," concluding that no family could be as fearsomely exasperating as that.

I repeat, the actors must be dialectical, must know how to give and take, how to hold back and lead on, how to be creative. They must feel no fear (which is common with professional actors) of losing their place, of standing aside. A great magician is someone who knows not only how to do magic but also how to teach tricks to others. A great footballer loses no status by teaching someone else how to shoot with both feet.

One learns by teaching others. Pedagogy is transitive. Or it is not pedagogy.

[Editor's note: This brief essay, translated by Adrian Jackson is excerpted from Augusto Boal's *Games for Actors and Non-Actors* (London: Routledge, 1992) and is published by permission of Routledge, the author, and translator.]

20

AN EPIC SYSTEM

Duane Krause

It has been my experience that there is a general perception among many actors that a Brechtian-based "epic" approach to acting is antithetical to what is commonly called "method" acting.[1] I believe that this perceived antithesis is precisely just that – perceived; that, while the differences between these two approaches to acting must be acknowledged, these differences are not as great as widely imagined and are a result of a misunderstanding of epic theatre and a misapplication of the method, based on Stanislavsky's system. I would like to suggest that my own process, one that might be termed an "epic system,"[2] is eminently practicable. I want to assert that the perceived antithesis of epic and method acting styles is rooted in and informed by ideological attitudes; not in practical technique, but in the use of that technique. I will begin by examining the ideological attitudes that affect that use.

EPIC THEATRE/CLASSIC REALISM

"The theatre as we know it shows the structure of society (represented on the stage) as incapable of being influenced by society (in the auditorium)" (Brecht 1964b: 189). This is how Bertolt Brecht, writing in 1948, characterized the illusionist theatre of his time, in response to which he formulated his theories of the epic theatre. In contrast to the immutability of society shown by this illusionist theatre, Brecht wrote:

> The concern of the epic theatre is [that] human behavior is shown as alterable; man himself [sic] as dependent on certain political and economic factors and at the same time as capable of altering them.
>
> (Brecht 1964b: 86)

The illusionist theatre to which Brecht refers bears a remarkable resemblance to what Catherine Belsey calls "classic realism" or "literature which creates an effect of illusion of reality" (1980: 51). This illusion is created by assembling the structure of classic realism "out of what we already know, and it is for this reason that we experience it as realistic" (51).

In other words, classic realism, by entrenching itself in the dominant discourse, presents its content as the truth, "common sense" (Belsey 1980: 2), or obvious. To this Brecht countered, "When something seems 'the most obvious thing in the world,' it means that any attempt to understand the world has been given up" (1964b: 71). By presenting its content as obvious, then, classic realism purports to be free of any specific ideology, thereby masking its ideology.

There is a double irony here. First, that the very construction of classic realism's illusion creates "a seamless whole which conceals the fact that it is *constructed*" (Eagleton 1976: 64), and, second, that this concealment itself, this "seeming transparency," most likely accounts for much of classic realism's staying power (Patraka 1989: 129). Belsey notes that "Despite the recognition Brecht has received ... the spectator ... as consumer remains the norm in our society" (1980: 125). This image of the consumer is consistent with Brecht's views on illusionist theatre and coincides with his depiction of it as presenting the world as fixed.

This, then, is the basic ideological difference between illusionist, or classic realist, theatre and epic theatre: the view of an unalterable world/ society versus a constantly changing and therefore alterable one. In order to uphold this view of a fixed world the illusionist theatre, Brecht noted, had developed a

> habit of taking the different social structures of past periods, then stripping them of everything that makes them different; so that they all look more or less like our own, which then acquires ... a certain air of having been there all along, in other words of permanence pure and simple.
>
> (Brecht 1964b: 190)

This idea is echoed in Jill Dolan's charge that the ideology of realism is "determined to validate dominant culture" and "makes difference accept-able only as sameness" (1990: 3). The need to construct "sameness" leads the practitioner of classic realism to adopt an attitude of universality, a belief that human behavior is basically consistent across differences of time, culture, race, and gender. Brecht responded to the elision of time and culture with "a crucial technical device: historicization" (1964b: 140).

Within the theory of historicization events on stage are presented "as historical ones. Historical incidents are unique transitory incidents asso-ciated with particular periods. The conduct of the persons involved ... is not fixed and 'universally human'" (Brecht 1964b: 140). Through the use of this device Brecht states that "the spectator is given the chance to criticize human behavior from a social point of view" (1964b: 86). "The crux of 'historicization,'" as Elin Diamond puts it, "is change: ... spectators observe the potential movement in class relations, discover the limitations and strengths of their own perceptions, and begin to change their lives" (1988: 86–7). She concludes that "Brechtian historicization challenges the presumed ideological neutrality of any historical reflection" (87).

The "presumed ideological neutrality" characteristic of classic realism is a result of, according to Belsey, "narrative which leads to *closure*, and a *hierarchy of discourses* which establishes the 'truth' of the story" (1980: 70). The term "hierarchy of discourses" refers to the relation of the plot by means of an authorial, authoritative voice "which effaces its own status as discourse" (72). The spectator is given the illusion that she or he is involved in the creation of "shared meanings" (72) by the observation of "reality."

"Narrative closure" is the resolution of whatever conflicts or contra-dictions have evolved in the plot presented on stage. By moving inevitably to this figurative "tying up of loose ends" classic realism "ensures the reinstatement of order, sometimes a new order, sometimes the old restored, but always intelligible because *familiar*" (Belsey 1980: 75; my emphasis). This is what Dolan calls the "authority of narrative closure" which "offers the relief of catharsis" (1988: 106) but at the price of being subjected to that authority. The alternative, "the possibility of leaving the [spectator] simply to confront the contradictions" is precluded by "The logic of [classic realism's] structure – the movement towards closure" (Belsey 1980: 82).

Brecht, however, wanted the spectators of the epic theatre to confront the contradictions presented there and so refused to offer them the closure they had come to expect, leaving the conflicts and contradictions to be resolved, not by a twist of plot, but by their individual minds. This is facilitated by "foregrounding contradiction rather than effacing it" (Belsey 1980: 128).

This foregrounding, and, through it, historicization, was achieved by Brecht through the use of what he termed "the alienation effect" or "A-effect" (Brecht 1964b: 136). The first step towards the realization of this effect is that the "stage and auditorium must be purged of everything 'magical'" (1964b: 136) so that "the audience can no longer have the illusion of being the unseen spectator at an event which is really taking place" (1964b: 92). Production elements are chosen with the intent of reminding the audience that they are witnessing a *theatrical* presentation. The purpose of the alienation effect, as Terry Eagleton states it, is "to prevent [the audience] from emotionally identifying with the play in a way which paralyses its powers of critical judgement" (1976: 66).

In order to prevent the spectators from "emotionally identifying with the play" perhaps the most important step was to prevent them from emotionally identifying with the characters. Towards this end Brecht proposed a way of acting in which, contrary to the goals of classic realism, the actor "does not allow himself [*sic*] to become completely transformed on the stage to the character he is portraying ... he shows [the character]" (1964b: 137). The goal was "to make the incidents presented appear strange" (1964b: 91) so as not to interfere with the critical reflection of the spectator.

Even with the emphasis on showing rather than becoming, Brecht realized that any showing done by an actor would be an individual interpretation of a given character in a given situation. To counteract this, the concept of implying alternatives, or the "not ... but" (1964b: 137) was formulated. By this, Brecht meant that the actors should

> act in such a way that the alternatives emerge as clearly as possible, that [her/]his acting allows the other possibilities to be inferred ... every gesture signifies a decision which "remains under observation and is tested."
>
> (Brecht 1964b: 137)

Brecht's technique of *gestus* is directly applicable to the concept "not ... but." *Gestus* includes "physical attitude, tone of voice and facial expression" in order to show "the attitudes which people adopt toward one another" (Brecht 1964b: 189). Through the use of *gestus* the epic actor is consciously commenting on the character's social relations with others, not simply, as with classic realism, embodying whatever expressions or actions seem "natural."

Diamond brings up an important point when she notes that since the *gestus* "is effected by a historical actor/subject, what the spectator sees is not a mere miming of social relationship, but a *reading* of it" (1988: 90). She also addresses an integral difference between the epic and classic realist theatres when she states that although

> Looking at the character, the spectator is constantly intercepted by the actor/ subject ... the difference ... between this triangle and the familiar oedipal one is that no one side signifies authority, knowledge, or the law.
>
> (Diamond 1988: 90)

Indeed this is the fundamental difference between the two forms. Belsey might well be speaking for Brecht when she writes that

> while it is impossible to break with ideology in the general sense, nonetheless it is possible to constitute a discourse which breaks with the specific ideology (or ideologies) of the contemporary social formation.
>
> (Belsey 1980: 62–3)

While Brecht himself may not have seen the applicability of epic theatre to social formations other than economic class, such as the constitution of race or gender, it is worthwhile to note that his theories provide one way of making them visible.

STANISLAVSKY MADE EASY

Whether social formations are presented as fixed or alterable is, then, the point. To simplify matters, in order, as an actor, to present social formations as alterable, one needs to "show" the character (epic acting). By "becoming" the character the actor represents social formations as fixed. This "becoming" the character is the crux of method acting as it is commonly understood and this understanding, while it has a basis in fact, is by no means complete.

The method itself is understood to have been derived from the teachings and writings of Constantin Stanislavsky. This understanding is also based on fact but, again, incomplete.

In "From Russia to America: A Critical Chronology," Paul Gray (1966) outlines the means by which Stanislavsky's ideas were disseminated in this country [USA]. In 1911 Stanislavsky formed the First Studio to function as an after-hours laboratory for younger actors of the Moscow Art Theatre company. The training at the First Studio in these early stages centered on "emotional memory" and an "inner technique."

Eight years later, when a portion of the MAT touring company was in southern Russia, they were prevented from returning to Moscow for a period because of the advance of the White Army. Some, including Richard Boleslavsky, defected and established a "Moscow Art Theatre" in Prague. In 1923 Boleslavsky began an acting school in New York; the next year he was joined at the school by Maria Ouspenskaya. According to Gray, "the course of study offered by Boleslavsky and Ouspenskaya was close to the teachings of Stanislavsky at the First Studio" (1966: 146). These actors, and others trained in the early days of the Studio, were the first to bring Stanislavsky's system to the United States in a tangible form.

In 1929 Boleslavsky published "Memory of Emotion" which had as its intended audience beginning actors. He concentrated on classroom exercises and, according to Gray,

> codified the System into an instrument attractive to the young American Stanislavsky admirers who lacked the full experience of acting themselves. Personal and natural emotion became the key to both American training and acting.
>
> (Gray 1966: 147–8)

Two years later The Group Theatre was founded by Lee Strasberg, Harold Clurman, and Cheryl Crawford. Strasberg and Clurman, as well as Stella Adler, one of the company's leading actors, had been students of Boleslavsky and/or Ouspenskaya. Strasberg functioned as the director of The Group and "put extraordinary emphasis on the creation of 'true emotion'" (Gray 1966: 148).

So by this time Stanislavsky's "system," as he called it, had set its roots in the United States and was well on its way to evolving into the "method," by way of students of Stanislavsky's early teachings who in turn taught young Americans who would go on to teach still others. But, as Richard Schechner sums up, "Stanislavsky's ideas evolved, while the American theatre took its shape from what Stanislavsky was doing in the First Studio" (1966: 20).

The situation is important to see clearly because Stanislavsky's first teachings were focused on "inner technique" as a direct response to what he saw to be a *purely* external technique which stemmed from a kind of "showing off" for the audience by many actors. In *Building a Character*, Stanislavsky wrote

> Anything that might screen their own human, native individualities from their audience seems to alarm such actors.... You can *show* not only yourself but a role created by you.

> (Stanislavsky 1968: 22; my emphasis)

His reaction to actors who were "obsessed by their audience" (Gray 1966: 138) was an overreaction to the point of focusing only on the inner aspects of the character and Brecht himself was certainly aware of this when he said: "The false impressions of Stanislavsky arose because he lighted on an art which after great high-points had sunk to stereotype. He therefore had to underscore everything" (Gray 1966: 134). This underscoring was the aspect of his work that made the first impression in the United States. It has also been the strongest and longest lasting impression of his work.

In 1934 Stella Adler went to Paris and met Stanislavsky who was there convalescing after an illness. She confided to him that she was displeased with his system and "became the only Group actor to work directly with Stanislavsky" (Gray 1966: 150). When she returned to New York she "told the company they had been misusing emotional memory ... by over-emphasizing personal circumstances" (Gray 1966: 150) in their work. Stanislavsky had grown away from that technique. But Strasberg, who was to become the most influential Group member in terms of the dissemination of his ideas, insisted that his "method" was preferable to Stanislavsky's "system" because it had been developed in America for Americans.

In 1941 Strasberg published an article concerning actor training in John Gassner's *Producing the Play*, lauding the "achievement of Stanislavsky and his actors" (Strasberg 1941: 136), stating that "Stanislavsky laid the foundations of our modern technique" (137), and citing Boleslavsky and Ouspenskaya as his mentors. In the article "he concentrated on the inner approach to the exclusion of external theatrics" (Gray 1966: 156).

In 1951 Strasberg became the head of the Actors Studio in New York.

In an interview with Gray, Robert Lewis, another original member of The Group, stated:

> The Adler affair proved that Strasberg was mistaken. And now that the Actors Studio has re-empowered him he has found a whole new generation and is doing the same thing – making the same mistakes over again.
>
> (Gray 1966: 161)

These "mistakes," which one imagines have had a profound effect on the conception of the method could only have become more deeply ingrained with the development, in the 1950s, of an American drama which privileged "individual tribulations" (Love 1989: 42) over a representation of the workings of social formations. As Gray states it, "a voyeurist theatre asked for and got exhibitionist actors" (Gray 1966: 164). Ironically, exhibitionism was the very practice Stanislavsky had sought to eradicate when he began the training of his young actors.

If, then, the "American Method" as it is widely perceived is a bastard simplification of Stanislavsky's theories, what more is there to the system that is not commonly understood; what is it that makes me believe it is not necessarily antithetical to Brecht's theories about epic acting? Let us review some of Brecht's ideas and compare them directly to parallels in both the method and in Stanislavsky's system.

EPIC ACTING/METHOD ACTING

Let us begin with the most basic element of the epic style of acting, the *gestus*. This can be realized not only in terms of gestures of the hands and arms, as is commonly understood, but, as Diamond points out, also in terms of "a word, an action, a tableau" (1988: 89). At the risk of simplifying I will, however, focus on the gestural element to compare this concept to that of the "psychological gesture," the phrase in the method lexicon most often paralleled with *gestus*.

It is essential to keep in mind here that *gestus* is the means "by which ... social attitudes ... become visible to the spectator" (Diamond 1988: 89). This visibility is often construed by actors to mean simply that gestures are to be expansive in the epic context, and if they are to be expansive, their reason tells them, the gestures cannot be connected psychologically to a character. Many American actors have this notion because they are trained to work purely "from the inside out," waiting for any physical movement to be inspired by a psychological impetus, thereby ensuring a lifelike [read "small"] result.

It is fascinating to note that Michael Chekhov, through whose writings the term "psychological gesture" became popular, developed the psychological gesture as a rehearsal technique by which an actor could come to fuller realization and understanding of psychological impulses precisely by making gesture and movement expansive. His idea was that any psychological moment could be embodied, displayed in a full, expansive, non-realistic gesture. In *Lessons for the Professional Actor* Chekhov writes:

> If there is a gesture to draw ... imagine a character ... who draws a conclusion. We can rehearse the process of drawing a conclusion by choosing the gesture – let us say the gesture is like that and the quality is "thoughtfully." Or we can draw a conclusion "slyly." The gesture will tell me much more about the psychology of the character, than if I were to sit and *think* about how a character draws his [*sic*] conclusion.
>
> (Chekhov 1985: 108)

The goal, then, is to discover "a gesture with qualities" (Chekhov 1985: 107), the discovered "qualities" being able to inform and fill the acting of a particular moment even when the overt gesture is removed. This use of expansive movement to realize psychology, by a student and colleague of Stanislavsky, echoes, on one level, Brecht's assertion "that everything to do with the emotions has to be externalized; that is to say, it must be developed into a gesture" (1964b: 139). It also certainly flies in the face of the notion that overt use of gesture, which many see *gestus* as being, need be mechanical or only illustrative. Helene Weigel, the leading actress of Brecht's company for many years, even stated, "One must make a determined effort to avoid working mechanically or in a bored way" (Cole and Chinoy 1970 [1949]: 316).

While Chekhov does allow that his fully acted out gesture will probably not be used in performance, he also concedes that "Your taste will tell you how much you should use this ability. The ability must be there, but how to apply it is a question which you, as an individual artist, must find out" (1985: 84).

It is this element of taste, I would suggest, which is the distinguishing factor between *gestus* and psychological gesture. Chekhov's taste obviously tended toward the elimination of overt gesture as he was working in an illusionistic theatre but it can be seen that this "method" technique is not necessarily at odds with an epic style wherein the focus is on choosing the *gestus* for the purpose of making social formations visible.

This focus is what Brecht was referring to when he wrote that the

> expressions of a gest are usually highly complicated and contradictory ... and the actor must take care that in giving his[/her] image the necessary emphasis [s/]he does not lose anything, but emphasizes the entire complex.
>
> (Brecht 1964b: 198)

While most actors who work purely from the method would agree that the characters they play and the actions of those characters are highly complex and complicated, I find it curious that in performance they downplay those complexities and complications. Certainly inherent in such circumstances are a plethora of contradictions which are glossed over, minimized, or even outright denied. The opportunity to focus on contradictions, which should be embraced, is regarded with horror. "My character just wouldn't *do* that" is a cry I have heard uttered countless times by an actor schooled in making sure that her/his character develops "logically" in the same way that a classic realist text must develop "logically" to closure. What is embraced on one level of theory but denied in practice is the epic notion of "not ... but;" the foregrounding of contradictions and, thereby, the displaying of alternatives.

The display of these alternatives, I would argue, is the only thing deterring an actor from making choices that might seem strange for the simple reason that this "jarring element" (Brecht 1964b: 28) could possibly call into question the dominant socio-economic ideology which may or may not empower them but in which they feel secure because their roles are defined and "unalterable."

Brecht's comment that "the artist's object is to appear strange and even surprising to the audience" (1964b: 92) sums up the goal of his alienation effect which is probably the single element of epic acting most vehemently decried by Brecht's method detractors. Acting in which a character is "shown" or "demonstrated" rather than identified with has been called "acting dishonestly" by Uta Hagen in *Respect For Acting* (1973: 218), a book which has enjoyed wide popularity as a text for student actors.[3] A respected teacher of the method, Hagen goes so far as to warn actors: "Above all, in both rehearsals and in performance avoid *commenting* on the play, or the character, or the circumstances, or the symbols, or the message" (219).

For Hagen, as for many other method purists, good acting means identifying psychologically and emotionally with a character to the extent that the identities of actor and character are blurred and the actor "becomes" the character. This identification process has become so pervasive as to cause numerous actors I have worked with emotional discomfort with the idea that audiences may dislike their characters. For example, one MFA graduate of the University of Wisconsin wrote that a certain line he was called on to deliver was

> particularly troublesome because I could not imagine how any human being would like my character in the least after such a comment ... I've found when I'm playing a character who is not "nice[,"] I must find ways to like and support him no matter what he does, in order to avoid commenting on my character's negative traits.

(Williams 1988: 44)

But Stanislavsky himself (in whose name this rubbish is perpetrated), at least in his later writing, was well aware of the fallacy of the actor "becoming" a character. He wrote

> I recalled the fact that while I was playing the part of the Critic I still did not lose the sense of being myself . . . while I was acting I felt exceptionally pleased as I followed my own transformation. Actually I was my own observer . . . I divided myself . . . into two personalities. One continued as an actor, the other was an observer.
>
> (Stanislavsky 1968: 21)

It is notable that Stanislavsky marks this split focus not between actor and character or observer and character but between actor and observer. The character does not even enter into the dual consciousness equation.

I believe this is important because, while "methodists" will acknowledge a sort of dual consciousness, one half of this split is still often seen as "the character," referred to as though it were an independent entity with a will of its own. And yet I have never spoken to and seldom heard of an actor who actually believed s/he did not have control over his/her character's actions on stage.

The idea that an actor might, by reaching an empathic understanding, "become" a character implies that once that state of empathy is achieved the character makes choices which are completely natural and unavoidable. This concept ignores the fact that the actions of a character are *formed* by the actor, the director, and (when a written script is involved) the author. Even when a characterization is based on "observation of reality" it must be remembered that the individual actor, director, or author will necessarily notice and, therefore, privilege certain aspects of that reality and not others. To suggest that a character might develop independently of the actor embodying it is to deny the responsibility of the actor in making acting choices.

This is not to say that the epic actor does not identify with a character at all. This is a common misunderstanding which often leads to the charge that epic acting does not allow for the portrayal of real people on stage but only caricatures.[4] But Brecht actually did call for his actors to use the "psychological operation" (1964b: 137) of identification to

> feel their way into their characters' skins with a view to acquiring their characteristics . . . But whereas the usual practice in acting is to execute it during the actual performance, in the hope of stimulating the spectator into a similar operation, he [sic] will achieve it only at an earlier stage, at some time during rehearsals.
>
> (Brecht 1964b: 137)

Brecht acknowledged that "We shall get empty, superficial, formalistic, mechanical acting if in our technical training we forget for a moment that it is the actor's duty to portray living people" (1964b: 234). I believe the key word in this statement is "portray." It seems to me that "demonstrate" is a much more apt synonym for "portray" than "become."

Brecht's approach to using psychological identification within a rehearsal process is identical to his use of empathy; it is to be used in rehearsal, but not in performance. An important distinction must be made between empathy and emotion. The use of emotion in acting need not include empathy.

Encouraging audiences to empathize with a character in a particular situation frustrates their ability "to reflect critically ... and so to recognize how it might all have happened differently" (Eagleton 1983: 170), which is the aim of epic theatre. But epic theatre

> by no means renounces emotion, least of all the sense of justice, the urge to freedom, and righteous anger; it is so far from renouncing these that it does not even assume their presence, but tries to arouse or to reinforce them. The "attitude of criticism" which it tries to awaken in its audience cannot be passionate enough for it.
>
> (Brecht 1964b: 227)

The emphasis which Brecht placed on the effect of an actor's efforts on the audience is commonly viewed as a hallmark of epic theatre but Stanislavsky, while admittedly owning a different ideal of the actor/audience relationship, was also intensely aware of the fact that acting is not meant to be a private exercise. He wrote, "Have you any idea what tremendous power an actor wields and how great his [sic] sense of responsibility must be?" (Stanislavsky 1961: 225).

Given this, the adamance with which many method actors seek to avoid contact with, or even awareness of, the audience by imagining a "fourth wall" is a source of fascination to me. I sometimes wonder when sitting in the third row of an acoustically sound theatre, straining to hear what an actor less than twenty feet from me is saying, whether that actor is regrettably proficient in the use of this device. Erwin Piscator, a collaborator of Brecht's, made clear the idiocy of such a convention:

> Are we ever completely natural on the stage? Don't you begin immediately to speak much louder than in real life, even if you are alone in one room on the stage? ... Think of all the queer positions you assume. Don't you always strive to prevent yourself from being hidden and not to hide your partner? ... Why this make-believe, if you really think that you are all alone on the stage, shut up between four walls, and that there is no audience to be convinced? ... Since you are playing for an audience the center of our attention must be expanded forward to the center of that audience. *You* know

that and the *audience* knows it too. Recognizing this we can proceed to the next point.

(Cole and Chinoy 1970 [1949]: 303)

Considering the many misunderstandings of epic acting (that it is devoid of emotion, declamatory, rooted in broad physical caricatures with no basis in reality), it is not surprising that many method adherents suspect that it is boring, lacking in entertainment value. Indeed a practical application of what epic acting is commonly misconstrued to be would probably be boring and unentertaining. Another aspect of epic theatre which contributes to this image is its didactic quality; but Brecht rightly points out that "the contrast between learning and amusing oneself is not laid down by divine rule; it is not one that has been and must continue to be" (1964b: 72).

All theatre is, to an extent, political. I mention this because one of the most common objections to epic theatre I have heard is made by actors who claim that they just want to entertain their spectators and avoid political art. To this Stanislavsky replied, "If the whole object of theatre had been ... entertainment, it would perhaps not have been worth ... so much labour" (1961: 92) and Brecht realized that "for art to be 'unpolitical' means only to ally itself with the 'ruling' group" (1964b: 196).

I hope to have made clear that there are a variety of acting techniques that are common to Stanislavsky's system and Brecht's epic system, all of which involve making choices concerning how a character is to be presented to an audience. The difference, as I see it, between what is called "the method" and epic acting is that in the former the actor masks those choices, disguises them and makes them appear to the audience as inevitable. In an epic approach the actor attempts to reveal those choices clearly *as* choices so that other alternatives are more easily recognized by the spectator.

Let me conclude with a brief description of one role I played in which what I have described here as "an epic system" was, from my perspective as an actor, fully realized. In 1988 I was cast in the role of Madame in Genet's *The Maids* (see Figure 14.2). In this fractured, postmodern production of Genet's play, directed by Phillip Zarrilli, I was one of four Madames – all the roles had been quadruple cast. Throughout the performance the action circulated between and among, or was simultaneously played between, a high style Baroque cast whose heads were topped with mannequin-like white bald-caps; a chic, leather-bound, constantly posturing, MTV-viewing postmodern cast; a Japanese *kabuki*-style cast complete with overstated *kabuki*-style costumes and wigs; and an unlocatable, marauding band of rod puppets which, like naughty children, could be dressed up by their handlers in clothes matching and mimetically ridiculing any of the other stages. Cast as the *kabuki*-style Madame and coached in *kabuki* technique by Richard Nye, I constructed the entire role as a grand (psychological) gesture – the epitome of Brecht's *gestus* combined with Chekhov's psychological gesture – which, through the embodiment of *kabuki*-style vocal patterns and physicalization allowed me to display openly the "attitudes" which Madame adopted toward Claire, Solange, and her lover on Devil's Island (Brecht 1964b: 189). It allowed me to inhabit an epic *gestus* far from realism, to "drop" completely this constructed façade at several points when I assumed my "natural" male voice and posture to address the audience directly, and simultaneously to develop a clarity and connection to each moment in my score which was far from Hagen's derogatory "dishonesty" which she might have applied to a role which so openly displayed its construction as this. From my perspective onstage, "inside" this role, I would definitely say that this production allowed me to utilize an "epic/system" which was no doubt "strange" as well as "surprising" for at least some of the audience.

21

RESISTING THE "ORGANIC"

A feminist actor's approach

Lauren Love

As a feminist actor, my performance experiences in conventional theatre grow increasingly frustrating, because my corporeal presence within its representational frames demands my complicity with an ideology I seek to resist. The very fact of my biology on stage commodifies my presence – I become an object to be traded between the male characters and the male spectators. In *The Feminist Spectator as Critic*, Jill Dolan states that: "placing women in a representation always connotes an underlying ideology and presents a narrative driven by male desire that effectively denies women's subjectivity" (1988: 57). Given this, how do I reconcile my politics with my work as an actor in conventional theatre? What is my potential to resist objectification from a position within representation?

Materialist feminist theories, which borrow from the discourses of Marxism, semiotics and post-structuralism, and other discourses that seek to destabilize naturalized dominant ideology, seem to offer the most viable positions of resistance.

Materialist feminists point to the construction of gender, class and race by white middle-class males seeking to ensure the hegemony of their class. "In materialist discourse gender is not innate. Rather it is dictated through enculturation, as gender divisions are placed at the service of the dominant culture's ideology" (Dolan 1988: 19). Constructing the female gender as passive and the male as active places women as objects and men as subjects within conventional representation.

The male spectator of conventional representation is invited to identify with the male subjects of a narrative and to take the female characters as the objects of his desire just as the male characters have done. The female spectator, then, is left in a highly uncomfortable position: "If she identifies with the narrative's objectified, passive woman, she becomes complicit in her own indirect objectification. If, ... she admires the represented female body as a consumable object, she participates in her own commodification" (Dolan 1988: 13). The female performer is also implicated, possibly to an even greater degree, because she becomes the objectified body.

While the materialist feminist perspective confirms that representation is inextricably embedded in dominant ideology, it also theorizes positions of resistance. Dolan suggests that "the materialist feminist project then becomes to disrupt the narrative of gender ideology, to denaturalize gender as representation and to demystify the workings of the genderized representational apparatus itself ... if actually leaving the frame seems a utopian ideal, the project is to reveal the complicity of the representational apparatus in maintaining sexual difference" (10). From my perspective, the prospect of leaving the frame altogether is hardly utopian, hence I would propose undertaking the task of developing feminist acting approaches based on Dolan's latter suggestion.

A performance technique which allows the actor to point to the construction of her gender needs to be developed as a bridge between theory and practice. I am eager for a feminist approach to acting which will empower me to deconstruct a performance just as feminist theorists have begun to deconstruct play texts. I wonder whether I can apply the skills I have already learned to a feminist agenda, or whether they are too mired in oppressive ideology to use successfully.

Much of my actor training was rooted in the method systematized by Constantin Stanislavsky.[1] "Truth" was his aim for art, and the approach he developed for the actor was based in psychological realism and its search for universal human values. Materialist feminist discourse problematizes this essentialism, noting that it assumes a plane which is untouched by ideology. Psychological realism as a genre in theatre and the method acting approach which is designed to serve its principles, are liberal humanist discourses that privilege white, middle-class male ideology as "natural." The "truth" to which Stanislavsky's acting student aspires is embedded in dominant ideology.

The method approach has been taught to American actors as a tool for "truthful" acting, which masks its basis in psychological realism and liberal humanist discourses. Uta Hagen, a renowned American acting teacher whose text *Respect for Acting* served as my basic primer, claims that the method's techniques are appropriate for any theatrical style. According to Hagen, psychology exists outside of ideology and, therefore, can be applied to any theatrical genre. While various genres are recognized as constructions, psychology is promoted as a tool through which the actor can reveal each genre's essential meanings.

The illusion that the actor is creating "real people" on stage denies the fact that her/his personal identity and her/his acting methods are themselves constructed by dominant discourses. It is now in vogue, in fact, to refer to Stanislavsky's system not as "the method" but as the "organic approach." While the American acting technique is, admittedly, an incomplete translation of Stanislavsky and has undoubtedly evolved in the last 50 years, its permutations remain rooted in psychological processes for creating a character. To refer to this technique as "organic" solidifies its naturalization.

Challenging these principles becomes more difficult because they rely on the "truth of the actor's experience." Describing a technique in this way, as an organic process, helps to secure the actor's complicity with its principles and by extension with dominant culture. Whose experiences can reflect any truths other than those of the culture in which they were raised?

The organic approach is imposed on conventional theatrical productions of any style. It is viewed as an objective tool, and the layers of meaning it produces are ignored. The differences between the dominant culture's beliefs at the time of production and those held by other cultures or at other times in history are erased by organic acting. Hagen supports this masking of difference as an approach to acting:

> Historic distances fade, seemingly fictional facts become a reality if one is as lucky as I was at the age of nine to spend a summer in a medieval castle on the Rhine. The fantasies I experienced ... allowed me to believe that I had lived for a short while in the Middle Ages. If you can't go abroad ... you can still read biographies and histories. Read them until you know you've lived in those rooms with those people, eaten that particular food, slept in that strange bed behind those curtains; danced, jousted and tilted with the best of them. (Read *Walden* and you'll understand pollution.)
>
> (Hagen 1973: 30)

Hagen's privileging of the actor's imaginary experiences in creating a character denies the actor's inability to escape ideology. Her remarks about the usefulness of histories and biographies fail to recognize the ideological markings of these texts, and her assumptions of the reader's class status are insulting.

Because the white, middle-class male's perspective is privileged in liberal humanism, women, ethnic and racial minorities, lesbians and gay men and members of the lower classes are relegated to the margins of representation, whether they are moving relative to its frames as actors, directors, designers or spectators. The experiences of the disenfranchised are rendered invisible when the privileged class's experiences are represented as "universal" and "true." In protest, "materialist feminism ... acknowledges the varied responses of spectators mixed across ideologies of gender, sexuality, race and class" (Dolan 1988: 121). I would extend materialist feminist acknowledgment to encompass theatre practitioners' responses as well.

One of the problems a feminist actor trained in the organic approach must confront is that psychological identification with a character, in privileging the myth of the actor's free will, perpetuates the masking of tension between the privileged class and marginalized peoples. The fact that dominant ideology constructs its images of race, gender, class and sexuality to preserve its position of authority is hidden in the essentialism of the method. The method serves dominant ideology through its appropriation of Freudian discourse. In *Feminism and Theatre*, Sue-Ellen Case explains that

> The psychological construction of a character using techniques adapted from Stanislavsky places the female actor within the range of systems that have oppressed her very representation on stage. The techniques for the inner construction of a character rely on Freudian principles, leading the female actor into the misogynist view of female sexuality.
>
> (Case 1988: 122)

Should the actor be identified with any number of these marginalized groups, s/he must not reveal it on stage. Instead the actor in realism must swim into the center of the mainstream, never hinting that s/he generally occupies a position on the banks. Even when the character is represented as a person on the fringe, that character will always be constructed and viewed from a point within the stream. The actor may know better, but the character will never tell.

Using the method approach, which is based in psychological paradigms, actors are required to justify a character's choices by defining their psychological objectives from moment to moment within a given scene. The objective is usually required to be connected to the scene partner and is phrased by the actor as the need for a response from the "other." As a student employing this particular technique, I recognized a pattern in my objectives. In heterosexual relationships – the mainstay of conventional theatre regardless of genre – my female character's needs were dependent upon my male partner taking action. My character's desire, then, was to be desired by the male subject of the narrative. Case points to the trap that I stumbled into:

> Female characters, when they do have a complex psychological base, are usually frustrated and unfulfilled – like the Electra on whom their complex is based, they wait for the male to take the subject position of the action. Their desire is for him to act for their own fulfillment.
>
> (Case 1988: 122)

In choosing objectives for my character, I privilege the author's intent. The secret is that, predominantly, authors are white, middle-class men and their intentions support their own hegemonic position. Stanislavsky's devotion to the text is held up as a model for students and supported in the following excerpt from *Stanislavsky on the Art of the Stage*:

> It is, therefore, the duty of the actor to grasp the meaning of the ruling idea

for the sake of which the author wrote his play. In addition he must make sure that the ruling idea appeals to him – both intellectually and emotionally. For the playwright's intentions will never be fully expressed by the actor if the ruling idea does not strike a chord in the heart of the actor himself.

(Stanislavsky 1961: 70)

I can take no "feminine" position within conventional theatre that strikes a chord in me except a resistive one. As a feminist seeking to deconstruct gender, my heart is not fully in my work, because any white, male heterosexual author's ruling idea is only one expression of an oppressive ideology. "Feminine positions are produced as responses to the pleasures offered to us; our subjectivity and identity are formed in the definitions of desire which encircle us . . . female desire is constantly lived by discourses which sustain male privileges" (Coward in Weedon 1987: 151).

Though the organic technique seeks to indoctrinate me into the discourses of the patriarchy, I may be able to exploit it by clearly acknowledging its constructedness and revealing myself in opposition to it. Instead of completely subverting my identity to the character's, thereby privileging the authority of the text, I can "stand beside my character," at one moment acting for her and at another commenting on her actions in a kind of hybrid Brechtian/Method technique.

As an "organic" actor, my emotional/psychological focus has prevented me from conceiving a given production's layers of meaning, because I am narrowly involved in only the meaning that I am producing. I cannot step outside to observe the apparatus if I become the character, involving myself completely in her psychological needs. Contrary to Brecht, Hagen warns the actor to "avoid commenting on the play or the character, or the circumstances or the symbols, or the message" (1973: 219). For Hagen, commenting is "bad acting" because complete psychological identification with the character is naturalized as "good acting" – believability is all. "If, as the character, he [the actor] shows the audience how he wisecracks instead of proving his humor to the other character on stage, he is acting dishonestly" (218).

My task, then, as a "Methodite," is to transform into the character – to live her moment to moment reality on stage. I am not in a position of reflection during performance – I am reacting to my environment. Hagen explains:

I can accept deliberate thinking only from a philosopher who organizes and arranges the otherwise chaotic and subjective processes of human thought into an objective viewpoint of life. He is taking himself out of the action – we actors are involved in it. To act is to do, not to think.

(Hagen 1973: 66–7)

Such an obedience would indeed be a blind one. There is perhaps no sharper feminist criticism of this traditional approach to acting than Hagen's own directive to the acting student to shut off her/his mind.

The fact that "the lighting, setting, costumes, blocking, text – all the material aspects of theatre – are manipulated so that the performance's meanings are intelligible to a particular spectator, constructed in a particular way by the terms of its address," (Dolan 1988: 1) is not encompassed by my awareness as I "live my character's life" on stage. In other words, I must mask my own awareness of the theatrical apparatus that frames me.

This narrow focus, in which an emotional response is privileged over a critical one, allows me to relinquish responsibility for any meaning I am creating. My entire process is mystified as a "spiritual" experience. Hagen tells me to empty myself like a vessel so that I can fill myself with the character. My organic process allows no room for social/political criticism. I must accept an ideology that oppresses me and become its spokesperson.

A Brechtian acting technique, on the other hand, would demand my presence as a performer alongside my character's presence. I would be required to think about what my character was doing and to communicate those thoughts to the spectators.

In the remainder of this essay, I will describe one example of my process as a feminist performer attempting to challenge the boundaries of conventional theatre by using the psychological techniques from my training to manipulate my emotional responses, along with Brechtian techniques that allowed me to maintain a critical distance from my character and to become a "thinking actor" – a 1989 production of Oscar Wilde's *The Importance of Being Earnest* in which I played the role of Gwendolyn.

When I was asked to play Gwendolyn Fairfax I tried to imagine a performance that would not compromise my political or artistic integrity. My *Earnest* task, then, was to find a non-organic approach, a way of stepping outside of character and resisting the representational frame without completely disrupting the production.

Wilde's most famous play is not a realistic text. Its full, original title, *The Importance of Being Earnest: A Trivial Comedy for Serious People*, implies Wilde's critique of Victorian society and undercuts his own authority as a "serious artiste." In order to mock the oppressive mores of his time, Wilde constructed a parody, and parody demands a flamboyant acting style that need not be rooted in psychological paradigms. Wilde's most recent biographer, Richard Ellman, states

> In "The Soul of Man Under Socialism," Wilde had repudiated marriage, the
> family, and private property; in his play, he repudiated them by pretending

to care ineradicably, urging their enforcement with a mad insistence which shows how preposterous they are ... Wilde made art into a new kind of ethic, replacing worn-out conventions with new generosity, freedom and individuality.

(Ellman 1988: 422)

As a feminist, I find Wilde's particular brand of satire politically incisive. The issues he raises for examination often fall under a feminist agenda, "marriage, family, private property," especially as they relate to one another and affect women's lives. And the way Wilde manipulates language, overturning sternly held assumptions with the clever turn of a clichéd phrase such as Gwendolyn's "If you are not too long, I will wait here for you all my life," catches the spectator off guard, forcing him/her to examine cultural practices and beliefs.

The characters in *Earnest* represent types in Victorian English society. Wilde draws them broadly to call attention to their ridiculous posturings in the name of "Propriety." I chose to play Gwendolyn as a larger-than-life, two dimensional figure to reinforce Wilde's intentions as well as my own political ones. In this case, the author and I seemed to walk some common philosophical ground, and I felt comfortable in my interpretation of his words, without being compelled to resist his authority through them. However, the production style was, in my opinion, resisting Wilde's intentions by allowing "organic," psychologically-based principles to inform its meanings.

An "organic approach" was privileged, not because the director asked for analyses of the characters' psyches, rather it is so deeply embedded in our training as actors that it stifles most of our attempts to execute broad acting choices or to camp things up. Our organic training tells us that we should develop all characters by relying on our essential humanity, emphasizing that we can be stylized without being "unreal." Again, believability is all. We are taught to search for the psychological justification of our character's choices so that the spectator can identify with our emotions and actions. This drive toward "universal truths" diminishes heightened forms because actors are trained away from the manipulation of signs that point to their own artifice.

The organic approach is much less suitable for playing Wilde than the esthetic of camp, most markedly visible in contemporary male homosexual drag shows. In her article, "Toward a Butch–Femme Aesthetic," Sue-Ellen Case proposes camp as a feminist strategy and recognizes Oscar Wilde as one of its pioneers:

> Michael Bronski describes the work of late nineteenth-century authors such as Oscar Wilde in creating the homosexual camp liberation from the rule of naturalism, or realism. Within his argument, Bronski describes naturalism

> and realism as strategies that tried to save fiction from the accusation of
> daydream, imagination, or masturbation and to affix a utilitarian goal to
> literary production – that of teaching morals ... Oscar Wilde brought ...
> artifice, wit, irony and the distancing of straight [heterosexual, conventional]
> reality and its conventions to the stage.
>
> (Case 1990: 287)

Wilde's use of "artifice, wit and irony" allowed him to critique the Victorianism that oppressed him. The exaggeration of these values makes their constructedness visible. No longer are they absolute beliefs that we must all adhere to without question; now they become outrageous examples of rigid intolerance.

Using the organic approach, the actor would become the character existing within the social restrictions of his/her day, thereby evoking the style of production. In camp performance, the character and the performer are both present, which creates a unique tension that opens space for critique. Homosexual drag shows put gender on display and assumptions about "natural" behavior for men and women are thrown into relief. I played Gwendolyn as a drag role, wearing her gender as I wore her oversized hats, as something exaggerated that garnered attention. As I traveled through the performance text I attempted to play against conventional interpretations of Gwendolyn and to reveal the construction of her gender. I felt that a conventional reading would trap Gwendolyn in misogynist ideologies, representing her as the object of John Worthing's desire. But by playing Gwendolyn as my image of a stereotypical romantic heroine, her gender could be magnified and revealed as artifice. As Dolan asserts in *The Feminist Spectator as Critic*, "the drag role requires the performer to quote the accepted conventions of gender behavior. A woman playing ... the traditional representation of woman is quoting gender ideology, holding it up for critique, the performer makes gender available for discussion" (1988: 116).

I had to work to resist a conventional reading through a method of acting that naturalizes dominant discourses, especially psychology. As I mentioned earlier, psychology is presented to actors as a neutral tool for characterization. But psychological paradigms are not neutral; they are fathered by men such as Freud and Jung and Lacan whose male biases have been effectively deconstructed by many feminist theorists. For the feminist actor to employ these paradigms is problematic. Was there some way for me to use these potentially oppressive tools, which were the core of my training, against themselves? I tried to find one through my manipulation of subtext.

"Subtext" literally refers to the meanings below the text. Through shadings in inflection and gesture, an actor can impose almost any meaning on a given line. For instance, the line "I love you," can be delivered sincerely, or sarcastically to imply its opposite: "I hate you."

Many factors inform an actor's choice of "reading" for a line: author's intent and director's interpretation are generally privileged. The author's intentions are referred to as the given circumstances of the play to make them more practical for the actor. They encompass factors ranging from the time of day at which the action takes place, to a character's age, to the "fact" that certain characters are in love. Anything the author gives the actor as the character's "circumstances" must be accepted at the outset according to the organic approach. However, even though Wilde might intend his characters to be played artificially, the organic approach would demand believability. This effort to make a character "real" on stage forces the actor to conform to dominant notions of real behavior. Hence, what is believable is "natural" human behavior and appropriate for the sustenance of hegemonic discourse. In 1989 at the University of Wisconsin–Madison, we might have felt that we had the historic, geographic and cultural distance to critique Wilde's Victorian England, but our own assumptions about what a woman is remained unexamined and Wilde's own critique was diffused.

When an actor manipulates subtext s/he gives the audience clues about the character's intentions which are not completely revealed by the text on the page. Those moments in *Earnest* when the greatest tension existed between conventional notions of "womanhood" and my subtextual choices were perhaps most clearly resistant to conventional readings. Whenever Gwendolyn proclaimed her love for John, she did so under the guise of "The Romantic Heroine," which stood in contrast to John's more genuine and rather desperate platitudes. I made no attempts to make Gwendolyn's love for John believable, for her investment was in playing the game of love, not in sincere emotion.

While I was able to manipulate some specific subtextual choices, other aspects of the production were producing meaning around me. I tried to be aware of these competing strategies during my performance so that I might disrupt their intentions. As Case warns:

> Social conventions about the female gender will be encoded in all signs for women. Inscribed in body language, signs of gender can determine the blocking of a scene, by assigning bolder movements to the men and more restricted movements to the women, or by creating poses and positions that exploit the role of women as sexual objects. Stage movement replicates the proxemics of the social order, capitalizing upon the spatial relationships in the culture at large between women and the sites of power.

(Case 1988: 117–18)

My blocking in Act 1 was a good illustration of Case's argument. In this act, Gwendolyn and her mother, Lady Bracknell, visit her cousin, Algernon. There, Gwendolyn discovers John Worthing, the object of her desire. As I played her, Gwendolyn's attraction to John (using Ernest as a pseudonym) is devoid of emotional consequence. Wilde implies this reading in Gwendolyn's opening speech, but our conventional ideas about women and their appropriate behavior pressure contemporary female actors to make Gwendolyn sound sincere. The text reads as follows:

> We live, as I hope you know, Mr Worthing, in an age of ideals. The fact is constantly mentioned in the more expensive monthly magazines and has reached the provincial pulpits, I am told – and my ideal has always been to love someone of the name of Ernest. There is something in that name that inspires absolute confidence. The moment Algernon first mentioned to me that he had a friend called Ernest, I knew I was destined to love you.
>
> (Wilde 1979: 263)

If an actor were to justify this text, privileging sincere love as Gwendolyn's motivation, she might easily be read as "dizzy."

A conventional portrayal of Gwendolyn demands that she be perceived as the willing object of John's desire. Acting students are reminded that to make comic characters believable, the character must not be aware that they are funny. But the Gwendolyn that I played was not in love with John, nor was she "empty-headed," and she was fully aware of her own outrageous manipulation of language, thereby thwarting conventional expectations of "natural" gender behavior. Her fascination was with an artificial idea of love, not with Mr Worthing.

As an example of how women in representation are presented as objects, in this scene I was blocked by the director to stand very near the audience during the monolog I mentioned earlier. The actor playing John was placed behind me on the opposite end of the stage. From the spectator's viewpoint, the male character took possession of the female character through his gaze.

To play the scene "believably," I would have to turn my body to face John, with my back to the audience. This would reinforce the illusion that the stage representations were real life events, and would also reinforce John's position as subject and Gwendolyn's as object. Of course, I had other readings in mind. It seemed to me that if Gwendolyn turned to address the audience, she could resist objectification by breaking the exchange of gazes between the male protagonist and the spectator. And so I presented the text to the audience, showing them Gwendolyn reveling in her masquerade as the Romantic Heroine (Figure 21.1).

Knowing that a series of impressions strung together in a performance must be read very quickly by the spectator, I understand that the visual impact of any given moment is extremely potent. As an actor, while I can

Figure 21.1
Lauren Love as Gwendolyn
Fairfax in Oscar Wilde's *The
Importance of Being Earnest*,
University of Wisconsin–
Madison Theatre 1989.

infiltrate the overall image, I cannot claim complete control over meanings being sent to the audience.[2] Through manipulation of the focal point in composition, directors – and to some extent designers – determine subject/ object relationships between characters. When placed in the point of visual focus, a character is granted authority by the director. Because they are most often the subjects of representation, men usually occupy this position on stage.

Since I was often unable to claim authority as Gwendolyn because of my subservient position on stage as I was directed, I tried to undermine John's authority by trivializing his sincere desire for Gwendolyn. I chose to disengage Gwendolyn's emotional response from her relationship with John; his declaration of romantic love had no power to possess her. Gwendolyn was prepared to pursue her own agenda regardless of John's feelings.

I maintain that my acting choices, while they were designed to thwart conventional expectations, could be legitimized through Wilde's text, given his own intention to disrupt discourses of social convention. Wilde told a friend that the philosophy of his play was that "we should treat all trivial things very seriously, and all the serious things of life with sincere and studied triviality" (Ellman 1988: 422). As I interpreted her, Gwendolyn was in full agreement.

I had learned to manipulate my emotional responses through my training in realistic technique. It followed that if I could turn various emotions "on," I could also turn them off. For example, when Gwendolyn returns to the scene in Act 1 just after her mother has rejected her engagement with John, she says:

> Ernest, we may never be married. From the expression on Mamma's face I fear we never shall . . . But although she may prevent us from becoming man and wife, and I may marry someone else, and marry often, nothing that she can possibly do can alter my eternal devotion to you.

For Gwendolyn's "super" or overall objective, I chose a desire for sexual experimentation, rather than the more conventional desire to be provided for by a man through marriage. This idea colored my interpretation of the above speech, and I employed it to help me to make interpretive choices throughout the production. The concept of the "superobjective" is based in realistic acting technique, and by choosing an unconventional one for Gwendolyn I could raid what was most useful in my training for a feminist deconstruction of gender in performance. Her sexual appetite, then, became Gwendolyn's driving force – all of her actions were based on this desire.

By playing the aforementioned scene with John as Gwendolyn's idea of the Romantic Heroine, I was also able to justify the distancing of believability through realistic technique. For it was Gwendolyn, the character, who chose to achieve her objectives by playing a role herself. Neither Gwendolyn nor I as the actor playing her identified with the Romantic Heroine; rather, the image was displayed to the other people on stage and, when possible, to the audience. So Gwendolyn's emotions were put on for effect; her needs were not dependent upon John's desire. She was only playing at love, but John was seriously smitten. Gwendolyn's ideas about "eternal devotion" were tied to her role playing, but her deeper needs were much more carnal – she was very serious about multiple marriages.

I used Gwendolyn's inflated sense of her own presence to justify psychologically an exaggerated acting style throughout the production. In the famous tea scene in Act 2 between Gwendolyn and Cecily, the two ingenues, I exaggerated my facial expressions and vocal and gestural inflections to resist a realistic reading of Gwendolyn. I did exactly what Uta Hagen warns actors not to do – I commented on the circumstances and showed the audience the character's reactions.

Gwendolyn has come to see John at his country estate. When she discovers his absence, she confronts his young ward, Cecily Cardew. Both women believe they are engaged to the same man because John and Algernon have each used "Ernest" as an alias, and a typical heterosexual rivalry is born.

When the women have tea, I chose to privilege Gwendolyn's fear of losing face socially over "winning the man" as my objective. Again, I attempted to root my choice to parody notions of femininity in the character's psychological need to present herself as a popular cultural type – the romantic heroine made so familiar to her in pulp novels etc. The more conventional motivation for Gwendolyn's growing discomfort in this scene would emerge from her emotional attachment to John, but my choice was rooted in maintaining the composure of the heroine within the tenuous decorum of this environment. Whenever Cecily challenged Gwendolyn's false superiority, her mask of social pretension set more rigidly.

In the tea scene, Wilde has written an aside for Gwendolyn which can be delivered directly to the audience. While Cecily is serving her, Gwendolyn turns and breaks the fourth wall by saying, "Detestable girl! But I require tea!" (Wilde 1979: 293). I followed this moment of Gwendolyn's confidence with the audience with one of my own as a performer, communicating through facial expression my disapproval of my character's behavior. By raising my eyebrows and tilting my head as I turned back into the scene, I tried to convey my distaste for the entire masquerade. My approach to this moment, among others, can be described as somewhat Brechtian because, "rather than being psychologically enmeshed with the character, as the performer is in Stanislavsky's technique, ... the [Brechtian] performer continually stands beside the character, illustrating its behavior for the spectator's inspection" (Dolan 1988: 114).

By broadening the field of my awareness on stage to include the audience as another character, I tried to create many moments which could be read as direct communication with the spectators. For example, in the third and final act, Lady Bracknell has once more refused to consent to Gwendolyn's engagement to John. John has suggested that if Lady Bracknell grants her consent to his marriage to Gwendolyn, he will allow his ward, Cecily, to marry Lady Bracknell's nephew, Algernon. Lady Bracknell flatly refuses the deal, to which John responds, "Then a passionate celibacy is all that any of us can look forward to" (Wilde 1979: 308). Gwendolyn's reaction was one of shock and dismay – the prospect of a life of celibacy is unbearable to her; I tried to show the audience her reaction by making it bigger than organic, believable acting would allow by literally gaping at the idea and turning to share that moment with the audience.

These are some examples of the ways in which I tried to add to and mix up the bag of meanings being presented to the audience. Whether or not the spectators questioned their assumptions about gender or representation is unknown to me and highly doubtful. Perhaps, within the frame of conventional theatre, all the feminist performer can offer is a place of resistance which puzzles the spectators by thwarting their expectations.

A more complete feminist performance technique could clearly reveal the state of tension created between the actor's and character's identities, rather than allowing their conflation, as in realism. One could call attention to the codification of gestures and gender in conventional theatre as they have been constructed through culture. Perhaps the feminist actor, to be fully expressive, must work together with feminist directors, actors and designers. Until such a collaboration occurs, however, by stepping in and out of character, behind and through the fourth wall, and against constructions of gender, the feminist performer within conventional theatre might begin to name and resist her oppressor, thereby beginning to develop a feminist acting technique.

22

RACHEL ROSENTHAL CREATING HER SELVES

Eelka Lampe

In theatre you mostly work from or with a text, in performance you squeeze out yourself, you dredge it up from your unconscious. It is a process of giving it a form from the inner to the outer. The process cannot be frivolous, but must be deep, a deep commitment to yourself. It can be really transformational. Start from scratch. [. . .] Take risks, psychologically and physically. Generate your own stuff. Think of everything you do as if it is the only chance in life that you have to do it: now, here, in a particular way. You will never have the chance again.

(Rachel Rosenthal 1985c)

A bald woman with long, black gloves, wearing a fluttery gray–green silk tunic, raps, chants, sings, and screams to the sound of an amplified violin. The diversified audience at the Central Park band shell in New York City is transfixed as she rages about loneliness, eating habits, damaged knees, her mother haunting her, and growing up forced to perform in the high-class Paris environment of the 1930s. But gradually she transcends her personal pain and moves on to global concerns. She speaks up for human and animal rights and takes full responsibility for the damage civilization has done to the world. "I am guilty of being alive. Through being alive I have tacitly agreed to [. . .] the obscenity of the food chain, of the carnage of the earth, of the malicious plays of survival, of the obscene exploitation of the weak, of the obscenity of agriculture, of husbandry, of butchery, of marketing, of fascism, of medicine, of laboratory animals, of obscene experimentation" (Rosenthal 1981).

I am witness to the performing power of Rachel Rosenthal, who wants to reach out with her work beyond the narrow boundaries of the art community. After the performance on 31 July 1987 I hear a young man, who was obviously strongly affected by her performance, asking her, "Where does this come from?" Rosenthal laughs: "Where does it come from? . . . from 60 years of life."

A LIFE HISTORY

In interviews, Rosenthal gave me a more complete picture of her artistic background. Rachel Rosenthal became a performance artist in 1975. Before that, her varied career spanned theatre, dance, and the visual arts. Born in 1926, she was raised in Paris until her family fled the Nazis to Brazil in 1940. One year later they moved to New York City where she attended the High School of Music and Art.

After the war, from 1947 to 1955, Rosenthal went back and forth between Paris and New York. During these years she studied acting at the Jean-Louis Barrault School of Theatre and with Herbert Berghoff. She apprenticed with director Erwin Piscator and then directed several off-Broadway productions on her own. She served as assistant designer to Heinz Condell at the New York City Opera, and worked as a painter, sculptor, and engraver.

In addition, Rosenthal danced in Merce Cunningham's young company and became close friends with John Cage, Remy Charlip, Robert Rauschenberg, and Jasper Johns. Cage introduced her to Zen Buddhism and Asian philosophy and she started training in various Asian martial arts (karate, kung fu, *t'ai chi ch'uan*) which she continued practicing until the mid-1960s. In 1955 she was asked to teach acting for the Living Theatre, then located in the living room of Judith Malina and Julian Beck. She refused because she was just beginning to find her "own way" (Rosenthal 1985a). Instead she moved to Los Angeles where she taught acting and dance at the Pasadena Playhouse. In 1956 Rosenthal founded Instant Theatre, an improvisational group influenced by the esthetics of Antonin Artaud and Cage. She married King Moody, an actor in the group who later became the clown Ronald McDonald. Instant Theatre disbanded in 1966 and Rosenthal went back to painting and sculpting while living a "housewife's life" in an affluent suburb of Los Angeles. Her marriage was childless and ended in divorce in the late 1970s.

In 1971 Rosenthal's life was radically altered when she was introduced to feminism and feminist art at a conference of women artists at the California Institute of the Arts. Because she had been taught a history of art that considered only the contribution of male artists, and because she thought of herself as an artist, she identified with men. "Then I came to this conference, and I saw slides of extraordinary work.[...] And for the first time in my life, I began to shift my identification, and began to see that I could be an artist and be a woman" (Rosenthal 1985a).

Two years later, Rosenthal became involved with Womanspace, a Los Angeles based group that established and ran feminist art galleries. She then started to experiment with performance. The feminist credo guiding her work was, "the personal is the political." Between 1975 and 1981, she "exorcised" personal obsessions and disturbances. According to Rosenthal: she overcame a chronic knee condition in the healing ceremony of *Replays* (1975); in *Charm* (1977), she worked out traumatic memories of her elite but repressed Parisian childhood; she reflected on her relationship with her half-sister in *The Head of O.K.* (1977); and, in *Bonsoir, Dr Schon!* (1980), she displayed three different aspects of herself – vulnerable, powerful, beloved – and integrated them into one "powerflowing" life (Rosenthal 1980: 90). The theme of each work was Rosenthal's own death and rebirth. This approach reached its apex in *The Death Show* (1978) and *Leave Her in Naxos* (1981). In *The Death Show*, she sought to overcome her fear of letting past phases of her life "die" (Rosenthal 1979: 45). *Leave Her in Naxos* revealed intimate details of Rosenthal's love life in interview form and, close to the end of the piece, a performer shaved off all of Rosenthal's hair. This action was an offering of "her femininity, her beautiful red hair, in a 'ritual of dying to allow for rebirth'" (Christensen 1983: 10).

With *Soldier of Fortune* (1981) and *Taboo Subjects* (1981), Rosenthal went through a transitional phase, reflecting on the genre of performance art and her own work in relation to it. *Traps* (1982) was the first performance in which she moved clearly toward an integration of personal and social concerns. By this time Rosenthal was afraid that she had "used up my material, my life. [...] I would have to move forward or die" (Apple 1983: 13). By 1983 her interest had shifted toward making "a passionate plea for the fate of the Earth and a new consciousness" (Apple 1983: 13). *Gaia, Mon Amour* (1983), *KabbaLAmobile* (1984, on the car as cultural icon), *The Others* (1985, on animal rights), *Was Black* (1986, on Chernobyl), *L.O.W. in Gaia* (1986), and *Rachel's Brain* (1987), all focus on social and political issues.

But even these recent pieces refer societal issues to personal experience.

> My concern about broader issues, the state of the world, starts, of course, from my very personal self. Who are you and what you make cannot be separated. There is a continuum between life and art. We make up artificial borderlines trying to imprison phenomena into certain categories.
>
> (Rosenthal 1984a)

For the sake of analysis I divide Rosenthal's performance work into three constituents: (1) the performance sequence of training, workshop, rehearsal, warm-up, performance, cool-down, and aftermath (Schechner 1985: 16–21); (2) the macrostructure of the overall organization of a piece; and (3) the microstructure of her performance technique.

PERFORMANCE SEQUENCE

For a performance artist, Rosenthal is unusually equipped with a solid background in theatrical training. Her work is rooted in the Western theatrical tradition which holds that actors can draw on different performing techniques according to circumstance and individual need. Over the years, Rosenthal's own training has ranged from Stanislavskian techniques to Zen meditation. However, because of her personal preference for stylization – heavily influenced by Barrault – she modifies these techniques by informing her body movement with the underlying principles of Asian martial arts. The result is a performance vocabulary that can be described as "indirectly codified."

The longest and most intense segment of her creation process is the workshop phase. She describes workshop as a time of gathering and exploring material before deciding upon the final shape of the piece.

> When I work on something, it's a little bit like gardening: you prepare the soil and feed it and you turn it over, and this all takes a long time. Then you put down the seed and wait and see what happens. I do a lot of research, I do a lot of reading, and I do a lot of fooling around in the areas that I think the piece will be about. Then I leave it alone and go into a kind of semi-unconscious state and it begins to happen.
>
> (Rosenthal 1985a)

The more a performance explores the self – as in Rosenthal's autobiographical phase, which often resulted in a once-only performance – the less she rehearses. Accordingly, more of the raw "workshop" quality gets carried into the actual performance, a very typical feature of the original conception of performance art. The less "exorcising of the self" there is, the more rehearsing is needed, for what is being prepared is a repeatable theatrical production.

> Since *Gaia* I have been rehearsing a little bit more, because it involves other people. I have been obliged to rehearse. [But] I still come pretty unformed to the performance and the performance kind of jells it. But, I find that since I'm doing pieces that I'm repeating a lot, I probably have to rehearse them more. The more I do them the better I do them and I don't want to wait until I have done them many times to get a real handle on them. So I may have to change and start thinking about rehearsing.
>
> (Rosenthal 1985a)

For Rosenthal, each performance serves as a rehearsal for the next, merging these two phases of the performance sequence. This way of working is not solely due to the performance art context:

It was influenced by my [work with] Instant Theatre, by my need for improvisation, by my trust that it would happen in front of the audience. A lot of it had to do with my trust that I can come on and do my "song and dance."

(Rosenthal 1985a)

Despite moving closer to ordinary theatre practices, she still retains a feature typical of performance art, particularly women's performance art: the use of ritual. Rosenthal is ritualistic in her handling of the warm-up, the phase immediately before the performance. Usually Rosenthal paces while enacting her own rituals: lighting incense, rattling a gourd, "sending energy through the gourd or sometimes even with my drum into my performance space, the space used by my musicians, if any, and also the audience's space. I usually have a candle lit in the center of the stage. And then I do some breathing and vocalizing, and sometimes when I have problems with a difficult text I quickly go over the beginning" (Rosenthal 1985a).

After the performance, Rosenthal frequently engages in an audience response session. She has dinner with friends and then goes home.

The aftermath, which can extend for weeks or even years after a performance, is the final phase of the performance sequence. Rosenthal acknowledges that she cannot be sure what will develop as an aftermath. She reports that it is not uncommon for spectators to approach her a long time after a performance and tell her how they were affected by it (Rosenthal 1985b).

MACROSTRUCTURE

The term "macrostructure" refers to the large network within which the performance takes place, the frame that shapes the content of a piece, and within which the performance techniques are nourished and/or restricted. Shaped by two main influences – orthodox Western theatre and Happenings, particularly John Cage – Rosenthal's performances are multifaceted structures within which many sources simultaneously converge.

MICROSTRUCTURE

When asked to distinguish between acting and other forms of performing, Rosenthal responded: "I don't see a difference between performing myself, or a character, or a ritual" (1984a). This concisely expresses a shift of consciousness in the performance world of the United States and Europe since the 1960s. The artistic rebellion against traditional Euro-American acting techniques led performance theorist Michael Kirby to develop his acting/not-acting model (Chapter 4). Kirby defines acting as pretense or

Figure 22.1   Rachel Rosenthal as the warrior in *Traps* (1982). (Photo by Daniel J. Martinez.)

mimesis, an idea traceable to Aristotle and spanning 2,500 years of Western culture. Kirby's model helps theorists to determine if a performer is playing a character, or is "just" her/himself. It is a device for measuring the degree of imitation used in performing. Although intended to analyze performance forms that do not use "acting," Kirby's model does not question the premise of mimesis which continues to be the base line.

Rosenthal goes beyond mimesis. She performs a "total act" (see Grotowski 1968: 125). Although her pieces are multimedia events, it is her commitment of body, voice, and soul that makes her work succeed. Describing her performing, Rosenthal says, "With skill I do not mean to simulate but to heighten" (1984a). In Eugenio Barba's words, she strives for an "extra-daily technique" of performing parallel to an Asian performer's manifestation of presence and energy. Barba believes that actors in noncodified Occidental genres are "prisoner[s] of arbitrariness and an absence of rules" (1986b: 136). But Rosenthal is one of those who has bridged the gap between Asian (codified) and Euro-American (uncodified) theatres. Her performing style is an individualistic, psychological approach informed by Asian martial arts and performing traditions (Rosenthal 1984b).

I was not trained in Asian theatre forms, but I had the chance to observe and learn from them (*kathakaḷi, nō, kabuki*). I feel and have always felt very close to the Japanese culture; it is like being at home with it.

(Rosenthal 1984a)

Whenever she enters the extra-daily mode, Asian principles of performing govern her work. Those are: centering her energy below the navel; playing

Figure 22.2 Rachel Rosenthal as Marie-Antoinette in *Rachel's Brain* (1987) at the L.A. Festival, Bradley Theatre (LTC), Los Angeles. (Photo by Jan Deen.)

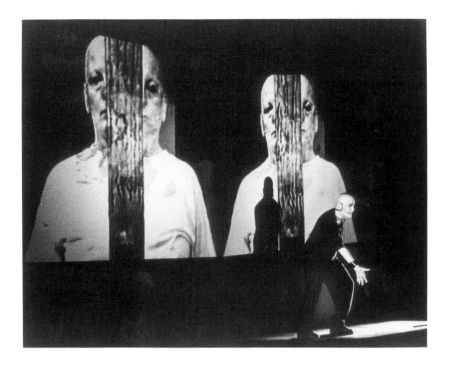

Figure 22.3 Rachel Rosenthal explores her many-fold selves in *Pangaean Dreams*. (Photo by Jan Deen.)

with the alteration of balance; opposing physical forces inside her body; and isolating, simplifying, and enlarging movements (see Barba 1986b: 153). In *Traps*, these techniques were evident in her performance of the monk and the warrior, the tranquil and aggressive versions of herself (Figure 22.1).

Most strikingly, she uses these extra-daily techniques to deconstruct Western representations of gender. She appropriates non-Western codified performance languages to create personae that, for Western audiences, come across as androgynous. The monk and the warrior personae are beings that exist outside the Western binary gender system. Rosenthal's "persistent defiance of categorization, or role-playing as it has been genderized by our culture" (Forte 1985: 34) exemplifies her particular commitment to feminism.

Whenever Rosenthal uses gender clichés, she foregrounds them as cultural fabrications. In *Rachel's Brain* her highly stylized version of Marie-Antoinette is a metaphor of Enlightenment (Figure 22.2). But Marie-Antoinette is also "woman," a fashion object who in her body objectifies and represents "man's" view of the world. In her parodistically exaggerated costume Rosenthal moves with utter control across the stage, fighting back the "natural instincts" surging up from Marie-Antoinette's lower body. She sings, chants, and screams an eclectic text proclaiming the supremacy of thought over emotion.

But Rosenthal also has instances in her performances that are closer to psychological "acting." When I asked her if she considered herself to be "acting" when she was stripped naked by other performers in *Bonsoir Dr Schon!*, and how this compared to the next moment of impersonating the character of Dr Schon, she responded: "It's all me. I showed three fragments of myself: the nude me, easy to get hurt; the Dr Schon one, male and presentable; and the Rachel Rosenthal as I am socially received" (1984a). This is a skillful deployment of "performed selves," each at a specific distance from her daily self; she plays with Rosenthal personae not usually visible in a daily context (Figure 22.3). These represent psychological qualities but cannot depict the full "message" or "narrative" of a Rosenthal piece. Others function as living metaphors, esthetic constructs presenting non-psychological beings, such as the monk in *Traps*, a post-nuclear holocaust creature in *L.O.W. in Gaia*, or Marie-Antoinette in *Rachel's Brain*.

Rosenthal distinguishes between the creation of "character" and "persona" in relation to her own psyche:

> In acting, or playing a character, you want to impersonate the personality of a person that is not yourself. A persona, however, is an artifact, a fabrication, that corresponds to what you want to project from yourself, from within. It is like taking a facet, a fragment, and using that as a seed to elaborate on. It is you and yet not you – a part of you but not the whole. It is not a lie but neither the full truth. In *Traps*, for example, those were all personae. For instance, the warrior. I see myself as a warrior, a frustrated warrior. I am bellicose: somebody who wants to fight but has to sublimate that. A performance is the only place and time that I can be a fighter, can be aggressive.
>
> (Rosenthal 1984b)

"Performing" encompasses more modes of social and esthetic behavior than "acting" ever could. "Acting" and "character" are linked to the Western notion of "narrative" and all three together are major building blocks of the apparatus of Western theatrical representation which inscribes the binary and hierarchical gender distinction of male and female. In contrast, "performing" and "persona" disrupt the working of conventional Western narrative and, as exemplified in *Traps*, allow for the cological expression of multiple selves. Through personae a woman can speak as a subject from the perspective of multiple selves, moving beyond the limiting object position of the female gender in theatrical representation.

The construction of character in the Western theatrical tradition can be explicated by an aspect of Richard Schechner's "restoration of behavior" model (1985: 35–116). Schechner integrated D. W. Winnicott's and Gregory Bateson's ontogenesis of individuals, with Victor Turner's social action of ritual, in order to develop a model of the "symbolic, even fictive, action of art" (1985: 113). Whether it is a child's process of learning to distinguish between a "me" and a "not me," or a person undergoing an initiation rite that transports her or him from one cultural status to another, or an actor rehearsing to become a "character," the process employs a transitional phase during which a person suspends the security of just being "me" while not yet reaching a new state of the "not me." Schechner defines the act of performing as a "double negative:"

> While performing, he [the performer] no longer has a "me" but a "not me," and this double negative relationship also shows how restored behavior is simultaneously private and social. A person performing recovers his own self only by going out of himself and meeting the others – by entering a social field. The way in which "me" and "not me," the performer and the thing to be performed, are transformed into "not me … not not me" is through the workshop-rehearsal/ritual process.
>
> (Schechner 1985: 112)

In performance, artistic quality depends on how successfully performers maintain the tension or the dialectical balance between the actual and the fictive, the "me" and the "not me." This concept of "restored behavior" is similar to Rosenthal's explication of performing a persona: "It is you and yet not you – a part of you but not the whole" (1984b). But in Schechner's model there is no difference between a performer who performs only an aspect of her/his self (persona) and the one who performs a complex being other than her/himself (character).

> Put in personal terms, restored behavior is "me behaving as if I am someone else" or "as if I am 'beside myself,' or 'not myself,'" as when in trance. But this "someone else" may also be "me in another state of feeling/being," as if there were multiple "me's" in each person.
>
> (Schechner 1985: 37)

According to Schechner all these examples fall under the same principle of restored behavior, no matter how gradual the move away from the construction of "me." Schechner has created a complex alternative to the traditional Aristotelian concept of mimesis and, in doing so, restoration of behavior is closer to Kirby's ideas of "acting" and "not-acting" than to Barba's ideas of extra-daily performing. However, Schechner goes far beyond the traditional realm of acting. Restoration of behavior draws from and expands into the social and ritual realms of performative behavior. In contrast to Schechner, I want to specify what distinguishes "acting" from various other types of performing.

Erving Goffman's definition of performance in *Frame Analysis* is very useful here: "A performance [. . .] is that arrangement which transforms an individual into a stage performer, the latter, in turn, being an object that can be looked at in the round and at length without offense and looked to for engaging behavior, by persons in an 'audience' role" (1974: 124). The more exclusively an "audience" pays attention to a "performance," the "purer" the performance in Goffman's definition. Goffman created a continuum from the most to the least pure performances, that is, from staged ones like theatre or concerts, to sports events and personal ceremonies, to performing occupational roles in social contexts. Goffman employed the theatrical concept of performance as a model for the social realm; for both on stage and off, he distinguished between a person as an individual complex identity and the specialized function of a person in a social role. Performances can have layers of appearances and intentions which possibly contradict each other (see Goffman 1974: 125–8). In Rosenthal's performances, not only the switching between performance modes, but also the layering of modes is important.

A MODEL OF PERFORMING/NOT-PERFORMING

I have combined the theories of Goffman, Schechner, Barba, and Kirby with my own findings about Rosenthal's work to develop a performing/not-performing scale (Figure 22.4). As a continuum my model features, from left to right, an increase in control over performative display. But this linear aspect is secondary to the model's major function: to illustrate a network of performance modes. In my model, I separate the social from the esthetic while in fact the two are mutually permeable. In orthodox Western acting a performer constructing a character might draw on aspects of her/his own self, personality, or various social personae. The reverse can also be true: a personality can be a fictional character of one's own construction. The same holds for the fabrication of a person's social personae. Both the social and the esthetic personae can be built from very private aspects of the self. And, conversely, a person's social persona might be displayed while s/he is playing a self-absorbed game. Performing is a mixture and/or a layering of several of the model's "pure" stages. My categories "self in ritual" and "techniques of virtuosity" (Barba 1986b: 139) are separated from the main body of the performing network because they transform the person beyond the reach of both daily and extra-daily practices.

During her Spring 1985 NYU workshop, which I attended, Rosenthal performed an excerpt from *Gaia, Mon Amour*. As she prepared herself by walking through the space and reciting lines to herself, she seemed

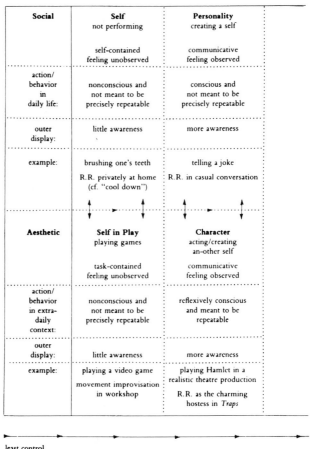

Social	Self not performing	Personality creating a self
	self-contained feeling unobserved	communicative feeling observed
action/ behavior in daily life:	nonconscious and not meant to be precisely repeatable	conscious and not meant to be precisely repeatable
outer display:	little awareness	more awareness
example:	brushing one's teeth R.R. privately at home (cf. "cool down")	telling a joke R.R. in casual conversation
Aesthetic	Self in Play playing games	Character acting/creating an-other self
	task-contained feeling unobserved	communicative feeling observed
action/ behavior in extra- daily context:	nonconscious and not meant to be precisely repeatable	reflexively conscious and meant to be repeatable
outer display:	little awareness	more awareness
example:	playing a video game movement improvisation in workshop	playing Hamlet in a realistic theatre production R.R. as the charming hostess in *Traps*

least control
over performative
display

Figure 22.4   A performing/not performing scale.

unaware of the onlookers. Appearing nonconscious of her behavior during this time, she was "not performing." Twice she broke her concentration to address the workshop participants. The first time she suggested that we read particular books. The second time she explained *Gaia's* sound score. Both times she undertook a conscious act of communication. Yet, these were not to be repeated; talking to the participants was a spontaneous expression of her personality. Rosenthal was aware of being observed, so she "created her self" in front of us. But since the context of her interaction with us was not private but framed by the workshop, her manner of talking

Social Persona performing a part of oneself	SOCIAL + AESTHETIC	**Self in Ritual** transcending the self
communicative feeling observed		self-contained unobserved/observed
consciously trained precisely repeatable		consciously or nonconsciously trained repeatable
reflexive awareness		awareness/no awareness
working as an airline hostess R.R. as teacher	aesthetic modification:	trance dancing R.R. drumming in *Gaia, Mon Amour*
Aesthetic Persona performing a part of oneself	AESTHETIC + UN- SOCIAL	**Techniques of Virtuosity** transforming the self
communicative feeling observed		task-contained feeling observed
reflexively and consciously trained to be precisely repeatable		reflexively and consciously trained to be precisely repeatable
reflexive awareness		reflexive awareness
Asian stage attendants R.R. playing the warrior, the monk, or Gaia		acrobats

most control
over performative
display

and behaving represented her social persona as "teacher." To be a teacher, she had consciously isolated certain qualities of her self. "Personality" and "social persona" are two ways of performing in a social context. Social persona draws on a higher degree of performance awareness than does personality. When Rosenthal played the "character" of the "charming hostess" in *Traps*, she drew on aspects of her social persona.

The category "self in play" was not part of Rosenthal's *Gaia* demonstration but it is applicable to certain activities of the workshop. For example, she asked us to "do an action with your hands. Make it larger, abstract the action from its original intent. Let it affect your spine. Let it affect your whole body until you move in space. Relate your action to the person next to you" (Rosenthal 1985c). Focusing attention on the task I lost self-consciousness and "flowed" with the action (see Csikszentmihalyi 1975). The "self in play" is a nonconscious self.

My model's next category, "character," was partially detectable during Rosenthal's *Gaia* demonstration. The protagonist, a bag-lady clown, is as Rosenthal said, a "kind of character." She is not a fully developed personality, but by wearing a clown mask and sleeping among a pile of garbage some elements of character and place are suggested. Here is where Rosenthal's specialty comes into play: within a single character two distinct personae – a clown and a bag lady – clash with each other. A third persona, represented by Rosenthal reciting in cabaret-style a sophisticated text on the subject of death, offsets the other two. Rosenthal dissociates three channels of expression – visual appearance, body language, and verbal text – using each to represent a different persona. Such an integration of diverse personae to a "kind of character" is very different from the psychologically and physically integrated characters of orthodox Western theatre.

This kind of fabrication leads to the final category within the realm of extra-daily techniques: the pure version of an "esthetic persona." Rosenthal's highly stylized version of the goddess Gaia serves as a good example. Rooted in one spot Rosenthal orates in a deep and roaring voice as Mother Earth about her power for creation and destruction. Throughout this speech she moves through a series of postures that resemble stylized animal configurations which are typical of Asian martial arts. Instead of performing a character in the orthodox sense, Rosenthal isolates, enlarges, and interweaves distinct qualities of her vocal and physical instrument personifying self-made metaphors to create esthetic personae, such as Gaia.

The "self in ritual" potentially exists in every sacred or secular ritual where participants may temporarily lose everyday self-awareness. This transcendence of the self can happen as a believer goes into trance during a Baptist church service or as a Greenwich Villager joyfully dances in New York's Halloween street parade. Rosenthal uses ritualistic actions – intended to engage the community of spectators – such as strewing beans in *Traps*, or having spectators light sparklers in *My Brazil*, or drumming at the conclusion of *Gaia, Mon Amour*. But there are differences between what Rosenthal does and "ordinary" ritual. Ritual is frequently automatic, built into certain kinds of social behavior. Rosenthal creates ritual in the esthetic realm. She is reflexively aware of the qualities and effects of her outer displays.

The last of my categories, "techniques of virtuosity," is the equivalent on the esthetic plane of the social "self in ritual." Both are psychophysical ways of transcending or transforming the self beyond a daily and even extra-daily context of communication. "Techniques of virtuosity" – as used, for example, by acrobats – employ consciously trained behavior, and an awareness of outer display. In these aspects they resemble the category of "esthetic persona." But in contrast to "esthetic persona" this kind of performance mode is primarily task-contained and not actively communicative. It goes beyond "esthetic persona" because the performer (e.g., an acrobat) psychophysically transforms her/himself to a degree that breaks with the network of daily and extra-daily forms of communication (see Barba 1986b: 139). This element does not occur in Rosenthal's performance art.

PERFORMING AS COMMUNICATION

In conclusion, let me suggest a modification of Schechner's scheme of performing as a "double negative" (1985). Figures 22.5 and 22.6 – two depictions of the same process – are informed by Barba's findings in the realm of performance technique and Goffman's analysis of the social and esthetic versions of the self.

Communication is not possible between a "pure me" (myself) and a "pure other" (self of another person). Communication is the fabrication of personae that make contact and interact with the other's multiple personae. Performing is a means to communication. Through personae a so-called individual can reveal a large or small part of the "me." I have indicated this graphically by the proximity or distance of the "persona" to the "me" end of the linear model (Figure 22.5). In the circular version of the model (Figure 22.6), the different personae of the self are shown imbedded in the "created self," which is the personality in life or the character on stage. A personality or character is a balanced bunch of personae located between

Not Performing	←	Performing Creating a Self		→		Not Performing
					not	
THE OTHER	not	social	personality	social	not	ME
the other self	me	persona	(social)	persona	me	myself
		aesthetic persona	character (aesthetic)	aesthetic persona		

Figure 22.5 A linear model of performing as communication.

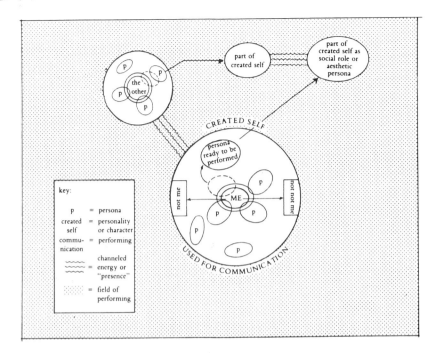

Figure 22.6 A circular model of performing as communication. (Plate graphic by Stuart McFeely.)

the "not me" and the "not not me" poles of the model; the "not me" and the "not not me" are in dynamic balance. Any particular social or esthetic persona can be very close to the "not me" or to the "not not me" pole, or anywhere in between. These multiple constructions of the self are the created personae of a person's daily life.

If this model is correct, then every small-scale interaction between human beings, that is, every act of interpersonal communication, is an act of performing. Only degree, intensity, and focus determine whether or not we speak of a private, intimate encounter, a social interaction, or an esthetic performance. Each culture develops and establishes various frameworks that are mutually recognized by interactants as regulating various communicative encounters. When I asked Rosenthal how she would explain her occupation to me if I were a person from a non-Western culture, she responded:

> I am an educator and an artist and my form is to put out works and to teach people to put out works that express concerns about themselves and the world and the universe in a way that is unorthodox, innovative, synthetic, and communicative.

> (Rosenthal 1985a)

23

TASK AND VISION

Willem Dafoe in LSD

Philip Auslander

I'm this particular guy who has to go through these particular paces. It's not so much that I'm putting forward my personality, but because of the various actions I have to do, I'm presenting my personality in how I field those actions. That is the acting in it. I'm a guy given a character, a performing persona, and I'm going through these little structures and how I field them is how I live in this piece.

(Willem Dafoe)

Task and vision, vision in the form of a task.

(John Ashbery, "Years of Indiscretion")

A discussion of Willem Dafoe is inevitably a discussion of the Wooster Group, the performance collective of which he is a member and which has been the most important formative influence on his approach to acting/ performing. Dafoe draws a distinction between these activities; his hesitation to make it categorical reflects the Group's multi-tracked, polysemic production style. The essential structural principle of its work is juxtaposition, often of extremely dissimilar elements (e.g., a reading of *Our Town* and a comedy routine in blackface in *Routes 1 & 9*). The performers refer to and practice a variety of performance modes and styles in each piece, ranging from realistic acting to task-based collage (*Point Judith*), from work on familiar texts to recreations of the Group's own processes and experiences. The Group's current (at time of writing) production, *LSD (... Just the High Points ...)*, is, amongst other things, a performance compendium which includes all of the interests just mentioned and restates images and concerns explored in previous pieces.

The baseline of the Group's work is a set of performance personae adopted by its members, roughly comparable to the "lines" in a Renaissance theatre troupe. These personae, while not fixed, recur from piece to piece and reflect to some extent the personalities and interactions of the collective's members.

These [pieces] are made specifically for us. In this configuration of people, we do tend to make characters, life characters and characters in the productions. If you want to get real blocky about it, Ron [Vawter] is tense, kind of officious; he's the guy who's the link to the structure, he stage-manages the thing, he pushes it along, he's got a hard edge. I serve the function of sometimes being the emotional thing. The man, *a* man.

Or, as Dafoe also puts it, Everyman.[1]

The interaction of these personae has provided the Group with a theme which, with variations, has been explored in a number of productions. In the first section of *Point Judith*, a one-act play, Vawter's character mocked Dafoe's (younger) man, calling him "Dingus," questioning his sexual prowess. In *Hula*, Vawter portrayed the leader of a seedy hula dance team trying to keep his second banana (Dafoe) in step and in line. Dafoe, in turn, seemed to be competing with him for the attention of the third dancer, acted (?)/danced (?) by Kate Valk. The second section of *LSD*, a reading of Arthur Miller's *The Crucible*, finds Vawter's Reverend Parris incoherently accusing Dafoe's John Proctor of witchcraft. Variations on the thematics of older man/younger man, boss/subordinate, oppressive conformity/good-natured anarchy are interlaced with undertones of sexual competition whenever the two performers work together.

The choice of Dafoe to represent emotional man is itself a (successfully) eccentric one. In films, he has played a series of punks, villains, down-and-outers. "[Film people] tend to see me as pretty tough, but they do on the street as well. The way people treat me in life is they treat me like I'm gonna slug 'em if, you know ..." Dafoe's stereotypically "tough" physiognomy plays against his emotional performance persona to create a blur: the actor who's perceived as tough on the street or in the context of film and its system of signs and icons is a leading man in Wooster Group performances because that is the function he fulfills in *that* context, relative to *those* other performers.

The Wooster Group's personae occupy an ambiguous territory, neither "non-matrixed" performing nor "characterization." This ambiguity was exemplified in *Hula* by the audience's uncertainty as to whether it was watching a group of New York avant-garde performers doing hula dances for reasons of their own or whether there was, in fact, a kind of scenario being played out. Dafoe smiled frequently and seemed genuinely to enjoy his dancing (by contrast with Vawter, whose main focus was on keeping the others in step). But who was smiling: Dafoe, enjoying the dance, or a dancer played by Dafoe, or both? There were characters, but so slightly delineated as to function almost as "subtext," but subtext for what? Dafoe observes that the characters were not formalized in any way; perhaps, as he suggests, what appeared in the performance to be a minimal, but nevertheless present, degree of characterization was simply "the baggage that comes along with having these particular people on stage" dancing together. The "characters" arose from the activity: the task and the specific performers engaged in it.

> When we make a theatre piece, we kind of accommodate what [the performers] are good at or how they read. They have functions, so it's not like we treat each other as actors and there has to be this transformation. We just put what Ron brings to a text and formalize it: it definitely comes from Ron as we know him, as he presents himself to the world and then, of course, when you formalize it and it becomes public in a performance, that ups the stakes a little bit. That's not to say Ron is just being himself, but you're taking those qualities that he has and you're kind of pumping them up and putting them in this structure.

The Wooster Group's process is self-referential and hermetic. Performances are structured around the performers and their personae, personae which are produced by the performers' confrontations with their material and with the act of performing. Dafoe: "I'm serving a structure I helped make and it helped make me in this public event."

The absence of transformation in Wooster Group performance, as compared with more traditional modes of acting, is important to Dafoe – he insists that the Group does not place the premium on believability demanded by realistic acting, with its implication that the actor is really experiencing the emotions he portrays. Referring to a section of *LSD* in which he places glycerin in his eyes to s(t)imulate tears (a motif of many Wooster pieces), Dafoe states,

> Once you show the audience you're putting it in, it takes the curse off of it. Then it takes away, "Oh, what a fabulous, virtuoso performer he is, oh, he's crying!" That's something I could do. But [using the drops] makes things vibrate a little more, because you get your cake and eat it, too. You see the picture of the crying man, you hear the text, you see the whole thing before you.

The Wooster Group would trade illusionism for a more profound ambiguity. The technical processes of acting are demystified, as by the glycerin, but the central issue of mediation, of what intervenes between performer and audience, is raised but left intentionally unanswered.

For Dafoe, performance is essentially a task, an activity: the persona he creates is the product of his own relation to the "paces" he puts himself through in the course of an evening. While unconscious of the audience, he is hyper-conscious of creating a public image. The multiple, divided consciousness produced by doing something with the knowledge that it is being observed, while simultaneously observing oneself doing it, yields a complex confrontation with self.

The more I perform, the more my relationship to the audience becomes totally abstract. Different performers, actors need different things. For example, Spalding [Gray] loves an audience. He really *feels* them out there. I don't. It's a totally internal thing. Even when [I] have a character, I'm always curious to see how I *read*, what people think I am, who I am, and then you lay the action on top of that so you're confronting yourself in these circumstances. It's open-ended. I'm not presenting anything; I'm feeling my way through. If you were acting something, if you were very conscious of acting a character, somewhere you would close it down, you'd present it. You'd finish it. In this stuff, you never know.

"Feeling his way through" the actions he has been assigned, the effects he knows he must produce, is the subject of Dafoe's performing. *LSD* is a layered production. In Part 1, the performers read from books; in Part 2, they "play" characters from *The Crucible*. Part 3 consists of a minutely accurate recreation of the Group's behavior while trying to rehearse Part 2 on acid. Even when playing a character, Dafoe perceives his internal process while performing only in terms of his consciousness of and relation to the performance context. He makes no distinction between being himself in the first part, playing John Proctor in the second and playing himself (stoned) rehearsing John Proctor in the third. All are manifestations of a single performing persona (Figure 23.1).

I never think about John Proctor. I do think about what the effect of a certain speech should be, or a certain section should be. I do respond to "here, you should relax a little bit more because you should have a lighter touch, he should be a nice guy here. Here, he can be pissed. Here, he's had it." And "he" is me because "John Proctor" means nothing to me. There's no real pretending, there's no transformation, John Proctor's no different than the guy reading the Bryan book [in Part I], he's no different than the guy in the third section who's saying, "Hey, come on, where the hell are we?" Just different action is required of him.

The complexity of his physical and vocal scores is liberating to Dafoe. Because his performance is not a matter of interpreting a role but of reenacting decisions based on the evolution of the Group's personae made in the construction of the piece, "it's just about being it and doing it." This leaves the mind free – instead of trying to fill the moment with emotions analogous to the character's (Stanislavsky), the performer is left to explore his own relationship to the task he is carrying out.

There are kinds of meditative moments in even the most active parts, of even *The Crucible*. There's a speech where I say, "Whore!"; I accuse Abigail. Sometimes my mind kind of wanders in that. There's a double thing happening. I'm saying the text, but I'm always wondering what my

Figure 23.1   Willem Dafoe in the Wooster Group's *LSD (... Just the High Points ...)*. (Photo by Nancy Campbell.)

relationship to the text is. Me, personally, not the character – 'cause I don't *know* about the character. If someone asked me about John Proctor the character, I wouldn't be able to tell him a thing.

The possibility of meditativeness leads to a kind of catharsis, defined entirely in terms of the performance structure.

The way I get off in the performances is when I hit those moments of real pleasure and real clarity and an understanding about myself in relationship to the structure; it is work, it is an exercise of me for two hours, behaving a certain way and it can become meditative.

The creation of persona from self results in a measure of self-understanding, although both process and product are bound by the idea of performance: persona as performing self/understanding of oneself as performer.

Film acting is the unavoidable point of reference for a definition of performance as the development of a persona. Dafoe has appeared in half a dozen commercial films as well as experimental ones. He sees his film persona (the tough guy) as basically similar to his Wooster Group persona (the vulnerable man), "the only difference being that I usually play something dark. In these films that I've done there's a real dark streak, there's a mean streak that I don't so much have [in Wooster Group pieces]." Dafoe draws parallels between the process of making a film and that of making a theatre piece. Typecasting, "the fact that they've cast in this role, is not unlike a certain kind of tailoring that we do at the [Performing] Garage." The technical requirements of film acting correspond to the score of a Wooster Group performance and provide Dafoe a similar opportunity for reflection on his relationship as a performer to an inclusive process.

> When you're doing a scene, you've gotta hit that little mark and if you don't hit the mark it spoils the shot. And, somewhere, I respond to that. Most people find that distracting, but that allows the frame for something to happen; it cuts down on my options and I'm a little more sure about what I want to do at any given point.

As in Group pieces, the imposition of a specific task creates a degree of freedom within the structure.

> You get no sense of having to produce anything. What you're thinking about in a funny way is your relationship, almost literally, to this whole big thing, the 20 guys around, the black box, you're dressed up in a suit or you're dressed up in leather. You get some taste of what they want you to come across with, but what energizes you is the *whole* situation.

It is this consciousness of the whole situation that Dafoe finds valuable in both his theatre and film work and which becomes the material of his performance. The issues he raises – persona, distance, audience perception of the performer, the performer's perception of himself – are always part of performance, but are usually sublimated, at least in conventional work, to emphases on character and psychology. Film has frequently played consciously with the ambiguities of persona, but often in a purely manipulative way, as when movies are tailored to the gossip surrounding their stars to create a low-grade illusion/reality frisson for their audience. The intent of Dafoe's work with the Wooster Group is to make these issues part of the performance's subject by acknowledging that the performers' personae are produced by the process as much as the process is produced by the performers. "Task and vision, vision in the form of a task;" the work's vision *is* the task as performed by a certain group of people, and the task is a vision of what the performance should be and what those people can do. Within this circular system, the performer's persona is at once his presentation of self to the audience and his image of himself performing. There is a certain frankness to the approach; the performer's image is generated by the activity of the moment, by what the audience sees him doing under the immediate circumstances. Task/vision, vision/task; "The perfection of a persona is a noble way to go."

24

DAVID WARRILOW: CREATING SYMBOL AND CYPHER

Laurie Lassiter

In the mid-1960s, David Warrilow was in Paris as an editor of the English language edition of the magazine, *Réalités*, a job he held for 11 years after graduating in French from Reading University, England. He met JoAnne Akalaitis in a theatre workshop, and she introduced him to Philip Glass, Ruth Maleczech and Lee Breuer, the people with whom he would later found the avant-garde theatre group, Mabou Mines.

> My meeting with those people who eventually formed Mabou Mines was radical to the change that took place in me. Meeting them made it almost inevitable. They shook me up so. Their way of looking at things and talking about things threw my whole structure of the universe into chaos.

He felt he had to reevaluate everything.

> The way that they were able to ask "Why not?" Why not the four of us work on Samuel Beckett's *Play* for four months in the evening when David is not at the office, and why not just leave it at that? We don't have to perform it; let's just do that. I hadn't come across that kind of thinking. It was new, vital and so compelling that even though it was scary, I decided to go with it. It was the beginning of a very long, difficult, joyful and extraordinary process that is still going on.

Warrilow had undergone no formal actor training and had only sporadically been involved in student theatre productions. He considers the work on *Play* his first serious acting. "We actually did do two performances," he says, "and I suppose I can date my serious pursuit of acting from that moment." The opportunity helped to provoke a crisis that was resolved through the choice of a new career. "In 1969, I realized that if I didn't do something about my life – with regard to whether I was an actor or not – I was going to be in deep trouble at some point." Although he found his job as an editor interesting and even exciting, Warrilow sensed that his commitment to it could never be complete. Unacknowledged aspects of himself claimed his attention. The possibility of taking himself seriously as an actor allowed him to leave "the middle class security" of his job for an uncertain but potentially fulfilling future.

> I had to decide whether I was going to say "yes" or "no" to this part of me which other people recognized with seeming ease, but I tended to treat as pastime, fun, escapism, whatever; this part of me which wanted to be on the stage and seemed to know how to be on the stage without training. So, with the encouragement of that same group of people, I gave up my job – I was about to be 36 – and took two suitcases and left Paris.

Carrying his passport, revised at the British embassy in Paris to read "actor" instead of "journalist" (a "symbolic but very real act"), Warrilow returned to his own country. Since he was English, London seemed the logical place for him to perform.

> It simply didn't work. Nobody took any interest in me whatsoever. Then came the suggestion, largely from Philip Glass and JoAnne Akalaitis, that we regroup in New York and start a theatre company of our own. There didn't seem to be a comfortable niche in the theatre as we saw it for what we were offering. So the idea was we'll just do what we want to do, which meant basically not doing straight plays – exploring, searching for something, one didn't exactly know what.

The group began work in New York on 1 January 1970. Warrilow was with Mabou Mines for nine years and performed in *Play*, *The Red Horse Animation*, *Music for Voices*, *The B-Beaver Animation*, *The Lost Ones*, *Cascando*, *Dressed Like an Egg* and *Southern Exposure*. He left the company in 1979.

As a freelancer, Warrilow has performed in a number of Samuel Beckett's plays, including *A Piece of Monologue*, specifically written for him, and *Ohio Impromptu*, *Catastrophe*, *What Where* and *That Time*. He has performed in Mary Overlie's dances, including *Window Pieces* and *Painter's Dream*. At the Guthrie Theatre, he has acted in *As You Like It*, directed by Liviu Ciulei; Andrei Serban's production of *The Marriage of Figaro*; *Heartbreak House*, directed by Christopher Markle; and *Hang On To Me* with director Peter Sellars. He recently performed in Sellar's *The Count of Monte Cristo* at the Kennedy Center. He has also been in numerous radio programs. His film credits include *Keep Busy* by Robert Frank and Rudy Wurlitzer, *Vestibule* by Ken Kobland, *Der Eintänzer* and *La Ferdinanda* by Rebecca Horn and the Joan Jonas video, *Double Lunar Dogs*. He played the role of the Old Man in Robert Wilson's *The Golden*

Windows, which opened at the Brooklyn Academy of Music in October 1985.

While he has performed in widely different forms – from the body of Mabou Mines' work to dance pieces to film to repertory theatre – Warrilow sees a great similarity among his roles in the sense that each one has been a learning experience in a step-by-step process. "A career, whatever that means, after all can only be one piece of work after another. One brick placed on top of another. The learning process itself never stops; the process of examination never stops."

At 50, Warrilow's main concern in his career is how to choose work. One of the criteria he has used is the quality of the writing. "I tried to make decisions about whether or not I thought that the language was deep enough, great enough ... I would stand off from the material: if it isn't as good as Shakespeare, Dante or the Bible, why should I bother?"

He now believes, however, that the writing is an unreliable guide. The roles of director and actor seem more important in determining the work's final impact.

> I found that an actor can bring something to language that is unfathomable, it's not knowable on a certain level of experience; it just appears. When it appears, it can illuminate words, phrases, sentences, paragraphs, chapters, scenes, in such a way that you almost don't know if it's great writing or perfectly ordinary writing.

When Warrilow agreed to work with Peter Sellars for the second time, he had not seen the script of *The Count of Monte Cristo*. After the first reading, he realized that the play would be quite different from the Dumas novel on which it was based.

> Peter Sellars had extracted material from the original novel. He added, in my case, quotations from the Bible. To some of the other characters he gave extracts or whole poems by Byron. Another dimension was added to Alexandre Dumas.

In production at the Kennedy Center, Warrilow found that the words were "immensely important" and that he had a "wonderfully written and constructed role, two roles in fact" – Old Dantes and the old priest, Faria. Old Dantes was set apart from the other characters and stage action by his appearance and movement quality, both of which served to intensify his presence.

> The way I looked, the way I moved, the way of not relating sometimes to what was going on on stage – sometimes it was about *not* speaking, often in a slightly prophetic landscape *vis-à-vis* the immediate action that was going on. Also the fact that I looked different from everybody else – I was

the only piece of anachronistic costuming, so I was set apart.

Given basic guidelines from Peter Sellars, Warrilow supplied the details of the characterization himself.

> He wanted to see some form of age, some evidence of starvation, alacrity of delivery and that the character would appear to certain eyes as a combination of simpleton–prophet. I would move, say words, find what my position on stage told me in relation to the other people and gradually find a place in myself that I knew how to go to fast and comfortably so that this character could appear.

Warrilow developed the role largely through the choice of physical traits that showed the character's inner experience. For example, Sellars wanted a slow-motion walk. Warrilow created a walk for Old Dantes in which his head is bowed slightly forward and his knees are bent enough so that he steps onto a flat foot rather than a normal heel-to-toe stride. He glides across the floor, his head and upper body remaining level. By drawing on his studies in *t'ai chi ch'uan* with Mabou Mines and by observing Tadashi Suzuki's company then performing *The Trojan Women* at the Kennedy Center, he made the walk stronger and more emphatic, while retaining stillness in the upper body. He then added a hand gesture.

> The character was, over a long period of time, dying of starvation. I knew that it would not be satisfying to me to place a hand over the stomach, which would be one's normal relationship to something like starvation . . . I then was drawn to think about the heart area because of the emotional nature of the relationship to the son, Edmond Dantes, who was to be in the scene with me. That, however, could look like a heart condition and be misleading. So I placed the hand just on the bottom of the rib cage on the left side and instead of laying it flat against the body as if to hold in pain, I let the hand open gently and slightly curved so that to me inside it felt like an acknowledgement of hurt, but a willingness to accept.

Later in the play, Warrilow changed his walk in order to portray the ghost of Old Dantes. He identified the essential character quality and placed it in his body.

> By the time I did the – let's call it the 80-foot walk – I was a ghost of that man, so I no longer needed this [the hand gesture]. That could go. I could stand upright because a spirit is upright. A spirit is perfect; it's the body that goes through these other . . . experiences. It was a slow walk, but a rather more normal one, so that it wasn't drawing attention to physicality, psychology, emotion or any of those things because it's about a spirit. A spirit moves more fluidly, just with infinitely more ease.

Once he had discovered the movement score, attention to his breathing helped to refine it.

> Possibly the most important thing to pay attention to is breathing. When I was not choreographing my breath properly, or if I was trying to push it and manipulate it in an uncomfortable way, something would start to go wrong. If the breathing was all right, everything else seemed to be all right. I didn't know how to do that slow-motion walk and do sporadic deep breathing. If I didn't breathe shallowly, my whole sense of balance went off.

In performing his other role, the old priest in the dungeon of the Château d'If, Warrilow relied on his breathing to regulate the effort necessary for a character of intense presence and magnified vocal expression. With long matted gray hair, a long black beard and a tattered robe, Faria resembled a Biblical prophet. A microphone amplified his speech and created reverberations. Warrilow sustained his voice's volume and power while coordinating his performance with another actor and the music. The first half was scored to Beethoven's string quartet Opus 95, and the second half intermittently to a string quartet by the Russian dissident, Schnittke. Warrilow constantly noticed the tempo, depth and audibility of his breathing. "What I found finally was that breathing was the one constant. Any performer, just like a woman giving birth, is well advised to pay particular attention to that human function and never to take it for granted."

Controlling his breathing enabled him to prepare for what was to come "in half a minute, in a minute, in three minutes." By focusing on his breath at a particular moment, he could easily regulate the speed or volume of his speech. In his 80-foot walk, he timed his movement so that he would arrive at the exact moment a certain line was spoken by an actor whose timing would change each night. By listening and focusing on his breathing, he was able to speed up or slow down imperceptibly.

> It's like driving a car and knowing you're going to need to turn off the highway at a certain point. You haven't reached that yet, but you know you are going to, you plan to; so something in your system is already dealing with that. You can't play the moment until it comes, but you can in some way anticipate it, it just doesn't need to show that that's what's going on. Quiet it down, or start to deepen the breathing, or have it be shallow, all that purposefully instead of accidentally.

A key process for Warrilow is the exchange between the structure of an acting score and the experience of flow. In *Ohio Impromptu*, which premiered at Ohio State University in 1981 and opened in New York at the Harold Clurman Theatre in 1984, director Alan Schneider urged an exact conformity to the stage directions in Beckett's text. Warrilow, who played the Reader, says:

> It is highly choreographed. I mean, choreographed to the point where the conventional actor, if I can call him that, would probably find it absolutely intolerable and insulting. I have an entirely different experience of it. To me, the greater the degree of accuracy of the parameters, the greater the freedom of action within.

In rehearsal, Schneider drilled the actor playing the Listener (Rand Mitchell) so that his hand on the table would be as close as possible to a photographic representation of Warrilow's hand on the other side of the table. Warrilow would place himself at the table so that his left hand rested parallel to the book before him in a position mirrored by the Listener. One finger of his right hand, which was shading his eyes, would touch the hairline of his white wig.

Though the score is precisely structured in space, Warrilow emphasizes that there is no such thing as sameness in any two performances. He examines a brief section of his performance in *Ohio Impromptu* as though under a magnifying glass, revealing the level of the unexpected always present in live performance:

> I'm now going to the book to take the page, which can be recalcitrant, and I have to deal with it, and it's going to come up, and that page doesn't know what "same" means, by the way. And it's going over, and then the page bends, slightly in the middle, and I let it down so that there is the minimum of stress and the maximum of soundlessness. Then I'm going to have to let go of the page. Now I'm going to put my hand down, back down on the table, in such a way that it's not going to be different from his hand. This is like a breath almost, this hand coming down. With the exhale, there's a settling that happens.

For Warrilow, performance structure and processual flow are two sides of the same coin. No matter how strictly choreographed a piece, a level of improvisation occurs.

> Improvisation only means that which is not foreseen, that which appears at the moment. Something is always appearing at the moment. The point is how much attention do you pay to it. I now pay great attention to what happens in the moment, and it's part of the flow of each performance. It is what brings to life the structure.

A central force in Warrilow's career has been his belief that human beings are "not immutable organisms;" rather, they can change their behavior and attitudes to be more comfortable and productive. This belief, underlying his ability to create a new career for himself as an actor at 36, has enabled him to move into different realms of performance and to cross genre lines. A clear example is his work with choreographer Mary Overlie.

> In the work I've done with Mary Overlie, she has invited me to improvise to a certain degree within a particular structure. Mary Overlie seems to me to be a very rich amalgam of commitment to structure and mental process and a deep investment in the inner and spontaneous process that is always present in performance.

At the same time that he was drawn to Overlie's work, he had reservations about performing in a dance because he didn't consider himself a "dancer." Through his participation, however, he realized that dance was not alien to his own experience.

> I looked at myself more carefully. I have always loved to dance. My mother taught me ballroom dancing when I was 14 and 15, and I used to go to formal dances with my parents in white tie and tails. All of which was a bit of a contrivance so that when my father was at the bar, my mother could have a partner – in me. I got to experience the pleasure of dancing. And I was good at it.

The obstacle that he assumed he would have to overcome was one of attitude. "I was making those demarcations and separations and erecting barriers between those various activities – my body didn't."

Through the acknowledgement of his skills and the acceptance of responsibility for them, the solution was found.

> Somewhere in me is the ability to visualize and then actualize line – line like painterly, sculptural, dancerly line, and shape. And to use the body as a way of creating symbol and cypher and of depicting energy in action and in space ... It was always there. The question was: would I accept it and use it or would I deny it? Every day that goes by I understand that there is something in me that has always been there ... that I haven't yet fully said yes to.

At one time, Warrilow also sensed a dividing line between his own experience and that of musicians. "I used to envy musicians. My attitude was: they have something I don't have. I love what they have. What a shame." During a performance, he broadened his definition of what a musician is in order to extend the category within which he was working.

> When I was performing *The Lost Ones* – I might have done the piece already a hundred times when this happened – an understanding came to me that I was a musician, if only because I used and modulated my voice.

This insight allowed him to approach the text from a different orientation.

> I therefore decided, privately, that I was going to perform that piece as if I

were playing a piano concerto. I was not going to, in any way, pay attention to the intellectual, academic literary *meaning* of the phrases. I decided to perform it as if it were all notes.

By enlarging his sense of himself as a performer to include "musician" as well as "actor," Warrilow deepened the experience of the play, both for himself and, apparently, for the audience.

What I discovered when I did that in *The Lost Ones* was that some other level of experience appeared both for me and for the audience. People seemed to receive it on a deeper level that they didn't quite know how to describe. The very fact that audiences who didn't speak English could be just as enthusiastic as those who did was and is very mysterious to me.

By performing the words as a musical score, Warrilow recognized how the actor may transmit something that is beyond his own understanding.

Things would appear to me from the text that I hadn't quite known were there. It's very difficult to describe. Sometimes when you are dealing intensely with the production and giving of a word or phrase which you know, you think you know by heart, you suddenly *hear* it for the first time. And you don't quite know what's happening. You say, but I thought I knew what this was. Well, then you know you don't know what it really is.

His discoveries caused him to reconsider what an actor's function is.

I am responsible for certain aspects of a performance, but there's a whole other level which is coming from outside of me. What I'm supposed to do is channel that, whatever it is. My image of it is that energy – light – is coming to the top of my head, which is where the "soul" is supposed to enter the body; and that I am to channel it. It is channeled this way … goes through the vocal, physical, breathing mechanism which is called David Warrilow and then it is given to whomever is waiting to receive it.

Warrilow's relationship to the audience has undergone a shift over a long period of years.

There was a time when my perception of the audience was "us" and "them." I was so full of anxiety and insecurity that I was not able to enter into the proper flow of the exchange, as I now perceive it can be and ideally must be … I therefore was for a long time in the position of investing a great deal of energy in defending what I was doing against supposed criticism – often because of the unusual nature of the material or style that I was involved in.

When he first performed *The Lost Ones*, directed by Lee Breuer in a Mabou Mines production, he had little time to think about what the response of the audience might be. The performance took place only three weeks after the

Figure 24.1 David Warrilow and William Raymond in *Dressed Like an Egg*. (Photo by Richard Landry.)

decision to do it as a staged reading. "That process was so rapid," he says, "and my evaluation of the material so fearful and inaccurate that my prediction was that it would be intolerable to an audience." In fact, audience reception of *The Lost Ones* was quite favorable, changing Warrilow's views.

> What I had to understand about the actor's relationship to the audience ... with a piece of work that one would consider dense and difficult and to some people dark was to what point members of an audience are willing to be challenged, the degree of courage that they bring to the theatre experience.

Focusing on refining his art frees Warrilow from trying to control audience response. His concern is self-mastery.

> If I as an actor invest myself to the best of my ability in the work I have chosen to present – if I give it my best energy – then there's a chance that the audience can trust what is going on on stage. If I hold back, if I sit in judgment on myself or the material or the audience, then there is less chance that the audience is going to be justified in trusting and therefore joining the experience. If the actor is willing to go through some kind of transmutation, then the audience can, too.

NOTES

1 GENERAL INTRODUCTION

1.   Given the fact that acting/performance is embedded in social processes,
     Margaret Drewal asserts that "neutrality is an impossibility," that is, "the
     point is that performers and scholars alike are engaged in re-presentation,
     indeed representation – not as mimesis (the visualization of some internal
     idea or feeling), but rather as transformational process (kinesis) – either to
     reinforce dominant or established discourses, even if unconsciously, or to
     contest, resist, and undermine them" (1991: 32).

2.   McConachie suggests that an appropriate unit of analysis in theatre history
     is the "theatrical formation," that is, "the mutual elaboration over time of
     historically-specific audience groups and theatre practitioners participating in
     certain shared patterns of action" (1989: 232). I would suggest that within
     any theatrical formation there are a number of specific "formations" each of
     which is focused on a shared pattern of action, that is, in contemporary Euro-
     American productions there are a design formation, acting/performance
     formation, directing formation, etc. Specific theatrical formations would each
     have their own sub-cultural dynamics, that is, the shared patterns and
     dynamics of a "collective" formation would be quite different from a
     hierarchically ordered top–down directorial formation, which in turn is quite
     different from the formation assumed in the traditional Kerala dance-drama
     kathakaḷi, the Japanese *nō* theatre, or annual community performances such
     as those in New Glarus, Wisconsin of Schiller's *Wilhelm Tell*.
         The specific network of relationships which is of concern here, the "acting/
     performance formation," is constituted in the mutual elaboration over time of
     an historically-specific group of practitioners participating in a shared pattern
     of action elaborated according to a specific paradigm of acting and drama-
     turgy.

3.   See Andrew Apter's "Open Letter to Theatre Educators" (1992) written on
     behalf of the Board of Governors in response to the content of scene work
     presented by college students at the Irene Ryan Award competition for
     outstanding work in acting. In the scene work presented, "Especially
     disturbing was the tendency to link sexuality with violence and the con-
     sequent objectification of the human body" (1992: 3). The open letter asserts
     that "the content of the presentations ... reflects an abrogation of the
     teacher's responsibility to encourage students to examine the implications of
     the scenes on which they are working. In this world of crisis, it is increasingly
     imperative that we teach as well as train" (1992: 3).
         On the theatre's resistance to non-traditional casting, see Newman
     (1989).

4.   These two sets of assumptions are (sub)culturally, contextually, and genre
     specific. From a practitioner's point of view "inside" a system of acting
     practice, these two sets of assumptions often remain at the periphery of
     consciousness (if at all) since when one becomes enculturated into a system
     of practice it often feels natural. On the other hand, practitioners may choose
     to challenge these assumptions and contextually-specific limits, violating

normative assumptions about the body-in-performance, thereby embarking on the creation of an alternative theory of acting.

5. On genres see McConachie (1989).

2 INTRODUCTION TO PART I

1. For overviews of critical theories and methodologies see Eagleton (1983) and Reinelt and Roach (1992). Easthope and McGowan (1992) includes an excellent selection of readings from primary sources and therefore serves as a good companion volume to Eagleton and Reinelt and Roach. For an excellent discussion that bridges the gaps between the dramatic text and performance through a consideration of the nature of action, see Alice Rayner's recent *To Act, To Do, To Perform* (1994). For earlier, quite reliable if standard histories of acting see, for example, Mullin (1975), Barnett (1977, 1978), and McArthur (1984).

2. The writings of Herbert Blau (1982a, 1982b, 1992) and Hollis Huston (1984, 1992) are meta-theoretical in a different way – they are philosophical meditations on various aspects of the phenomenon of performance practice, and/or the relationship between performance and thought.

3. I use acting in its broadest sense, based on its root meaning derived from the Latin *actum*, to mean "a thing done." The actor is "one who does things" (Partridge 1983: 5). I often use performer and performance interchangeably with actor and acting, recognizing that perform derives from the Latin "*per-*, thoroughly + *fournir, fornir*, to complete" (485). An actor/performer is a doer who brings things to completion.

    Some of my thinking about these issues was stimulated by discussions with anthropologist Peter Claus, at an international conference on performance in Calcutta, India, and with theatre scholar Mark Weinberg. An earlier version of part of this essay was published in 1989(b).

4. Although it would be a serious mistake to collapse ideology into language, an awareness of how an Althusserian notion of ideology saturates language (Turner 1990: 26) is important as we consider how to think and talk about the practice of acting. For further discussions of ideology see Hall (1982), Turner (1990: 197–225), Easthope and McGowan (1992: 41–66), and Eagleton (1991).

5. Although it may appear that I am assuming the subject as a stable identity, this is not so. I will later clarify.

6. For a specific re-reading of the scientific, objectivist, positivist language of Sonia Moore's interpretation of Stanislavsky in America, and a critique of its limitations, see Zarrilli (1989b).

7. Drew Leder has reminded us of how Cartesian dualism has shaped our view of the world as arrayed in an "hierarchical opposition" where "women have consistently been associated with the bodily sphere. They have been linked with nature, sexuality, and the passions, whereas men have been identified with the rational mind. This equation implicitly legitimizes structures of domination ... The same terms can serve to justify class and labor inequities. Lower-class workers are seen as just bodies who must be supervised by

management 'minds.' . . . Our relation to other cultures has been shaped by much the same logic. Societies more obviously tied to the body and the earth are labeled as primitive and viewed with suspicion. The superior nature of Western rationality, with its literate, mathematical, and scientific modes, is all but assumed" (1990: 154).

8. See, for example, Merleau-Ponty (1962, 1964, 1968), Levine (1985), Yuasa (1987), Nagatomo (1992a, 1992b). Sheets-Johnstone (1992), Scarry (1991), Turner and Bruner (1986), Jackson (1989), Lakoff and Johnson (1980), Lakoff (1987), Johnson (1987), and Butler (1990). This type of paradigm shift is an example of the general process of shifts discussed by Thomas Kuhn (1962), summarized by Joseph Roach: "Any paradigm has *anomalies* – facts which refuse to fit any theory. As a group of *practitioners* in any field continues its investigations, anomalies tend to proliferate. When such unsolved *puzzles* have multiplied to the point at which they subvert confidence in the paradigm, a *crisis* will develop. If, at this time, there appears to be a competing paradigm which will resolve the anomalies, accounting for more of the known facts, then the old paradigm will collapse and the new one will be adopted" (Roach 1985: 13). Although Kuhn's narrative of breach, crisis, and resolution by replacement is itself modernist and therefore problematic, from a post-modern perspective I would *not* expect there to be a "new" paradigm which will replace the old one, but rather a series of provisional alternatives (practices and narratives).

9. Radical resurrections of the body have permanently altered the role that the body and physicalization plays in training most American actors today. Movement-based approaches to acting (King 1971, 1981) are now common-place, and the three most recent books published on a textually-based Stanislavskian approach to character acting all pay particular attention to the role of the body and physical in acting. Both Richard Hornby (1992) and John Harrop (1992) reject (explicitly or implicitly) a Strasbergian-based version of an over-indulgent method approach to character acting, and replace it with their own revisions of a textually-based approach to acting building on the later Stanislavskian notion of physical action; both foreground the problem of dualism and attempt to bring the body fully into the process of creating a character by defining acting as a psychophysiological *gestalt* which requires the actor to become skilled through physical discipline and control; both use the active, physiologically-suggestive metaphor of the actor as "athlete;" and both clearly differentiate between the everyday experience of emotion and the similar, yet different texture of theatrical "emotions." Finally, David Cole, in his *Acting as Reading* (1992), calls our attention to the fact that there is a physical dimension to the act of reading itself which is "no less physical than acting itself" (1992: 29). Cole's main argument is that "*acting is the recovery of a 'lost' physical of reading*" (1992: 1; see also 50–136).

10. For excellent discussions of the dual problems of objectivity and subjectivity see Best (1986) and Lakoff and Johnson (1980).

11. For the seminal critique of Western projections onto "the Orient," see Said (1978).

12. For definitions and discussions of postmodernism see Lyotard (1979),

Schechner (1982), Hutcheon (1989), Jameson (1991), Birringer (1991), Reinelt and Roach (1992).

13. The relevance of the problem of the subject to the making of art is an essential part of contemporary feminist theory and criticism (Butler 1990).

14. If, as Philip Auslander defines it, deconstruction "is the perception of difference" (Chapter 5), the phenomenon of acting is perhaps one of the most obvious examples of the constant play of difference available to us, an example from which an alternative discourse and method might come. One promising approach would draw on Drew Leder's phenomenological account of the body (1990) which directly addresses deconstruction by focusing on the role of *absence* in constituting the experience of the body. For Leder the recent attention given to the body and to re-establishing a corporealized existence "can only be understood in relation to the modes of absence inherent in the body" (1990: 3), to the "disappearance of the body." The body can no longer be considered simply as a physical object. It must also be considered as the "lived body" or the "body-as-experiencer." Therefore, the body is simultaneously both "subject and an object available to external gaze" (Leder 1990: 6). The actor, performing in space and through time, perhaps best exemplifies the body's simultaneous deployment as both the object of third-person gaze and the "lived body" of first-person awareness. When concentrated in a particular moment (of acting), one's body seems to "disappear:" one is so totally focused in the moment that the body is "absent" at the very moment when spectators might experience it as most "present." Following Peggy Phelan's provocative study of the problem of "the real and representation" (1993), I would prefer to mark this sign of presence with the possibility of its absence, as (im)material (ir)reality, leaving open to negotiation in the performative moment the particular configuration of the relationship between the actor and the (ir)real.

15. Although speaking of the gendered body, Judith Butler's critique of essentialist concepts of "self" and "identity" is applicable to a discourse of the actor's "presence:"

> the epistemological paradigm that presumes the priority of the doer to the deed establishes a global and globalizing subject who disavows its own locality as well as the conditions for local intervention ... Ontology is, thus, not a foundation, but a normative injunction that operates insidiously by installing itself into political discourse as its necessary ground.
>
> (Butler 1990: 148)

This is precisely the question that Auslander addresses at length in Chapter 5.

16. Natalie Crohn Schmitt, in her 1990 discussion of the relationship between twentieth century views of science and acting/performance, illuminates the antipathy between the positivist science admired by Stanislavsky and the Heisenbergian indeterminacy practiced by John Cage and other happenings artists. Crohn also puts Viola Spolin and Joseph Chaikin/the Open Theatre in the Heisenbergian camp. In positivist Stanislavskian acting everything has a reason and is determined; in Heisenbergian performance everything is open to chance.

17. Foregrounding these "shifting perspectives" *in performance* is characteristic not only of many postmodern performances but also of folk performances which allow the playing of multiple voices – especially in opposition to hegemonic monologism.

3 THE ACTOR'S PRESENCE: THREE PHENOMENAL MODES

1. For a thorough examination of Rousseau's complaint against the theatre, see Jacques Derrida (1980) 'From/Of the Supplement to the Source: The Theory of Writing', *Of Grammatology*, trans. Gayatri Spivak, Baltimore: Johns Hopkins University Press, pp. 269–316.

2. All quotations are from Peter Handke (1969) *Offending the Audience* in *Kaspar and Other Plays*, trans. Michael Roloff, New York: Farrar, Straus and Giroux.

3. Kenneth Burke (1953) *Counter-Statement*, Los Altos, Calif: Hermes Publications. The Burke statement reads: "The hypertrophy of the psychology of information is accompanied by the corresponding atrophy of the psychology of form."

5 "JUST BE YOUR SELF": LOGOCENTRISM AND DIFFERENCE IN PERFORMANCE THEORY

1. For a primary discussion of logocentrism see Derrida (1976) *Of Grammatology*, trans. Gayatri Spivak, Baltimore: Johns Hopkins University Press, pp. 30 ff.

2. See, for example, Jacques Derrida (1982) 'Differance' in *Margins of Philosophy*, trans. Alan Bass, Chicago: University of Chicago Press, pp. 9 ff); Derrida (1981a) 'Semiology and Grammatology' in *Positions*, trans. Alan Bass, Chicago: University of Chicago Press, pp. 17–36; Derrida (1976) *Of Grammatology*, trans. Gayatri Spivak, Baltimore: Johns Hopkins University Press, pp. 30 ff.

3. In an excellent article on the question of deconstruction in the theatre, Gerald Rabkin indicates that the director is the primary "deconstructor" of the theatrical text. This stand assumes that we can read the director's concept back through the production elements, including the actor's performances. If we take Derrida's notion of *differance* seriously, such a perception is impossible: the play of difference which makes up the discourse of theatrical elements will inevitably mediate between the director's concept and what the audience sees (Rabkin 1983: 55 ff).

   Derrida's own version of conventional theatre seems to me somewhat naive. He writes that "The stage is theological for as long as its structure, following the entirety of tradition, comports with the following elements: an author–creator who, absent and from afar, is armed with a text and keeps watch over, assembles, regulates the time or the meaning of the representation, letting this latter *represent* him as concerns what is called the content of his thoughts, his intentions, his ideas." This author–creator "enslaves" actors, directors, etc. (1978: 235). As I will try to show here, the theatre remains theological so long as it is logocentric and the *logos* of performance need not take the form of a playwright's or creator's text.

4. See, for example, Keir Elam (1980) *The Semiotics of Theatre and Drama*, London: Methuen, pp. 85–7; and Wilfred Passow (1981) 'The Analysis of Theatrical Performance,' trans. R. Strauss, *Poetics Today* 2, 3: 244–6.

5. Wiles' suggestion that Stanislavsky's use of a fictional voice to present his ideas makes his system seem more "organic" than it is suggests an interesting avenue for further discussion.

6. Derrida's dismissal of Brecht is unjustifiably and surprisingly abrupt: "Aliena-tion only consecrates ... the nonparticipation of spectators (and even of directors and actors in the creative act)" (1978: 244).

7. I have been quoting from *Towards a Poor Theater*, published in 1968. Although Grotowski turned his back on performance in 1970 and focused his attention on experiential, paratheatrical events, his work is still founded on self-revelation and still confronts the issues raised in that book. For a comparison of Grotowski's earlier and later work and further discussion of the therapeutic nature of both, see my essay 'Holy Theatre and Catharsis', *Theatre Research International* (1984) 9, 1: 16–29.

8. An example of performance criticism which takes the latter approach is Sylvere Lotringer's excellent essay on Mabou Mines, 'Shaggy Codes', *Drama Review* (1978) 22, 3: 87–94.

6 INTRODUCTION TO PART II

1. The most extensive study of the culturally and historically variable assump-tions about the body and definitions of science which inform Western acting is that by Roach (1985) *The Player's Passion: Studies in the Science of Acting*.

2. Feminist theory has also been extremely important in encouraging reconsi-derations of the body, as well as discourses and representations of the body. See in particular Butler (1990) and Forte (1992).

3. On Meyerhold see Braun (1969).

4. About this encounter see Zarrilli (1986) and especially Brandon's (1989) more complete history.

5. For well informed scholarly accounts on a few major genres of Asian performance and their acting techniques, reference may be made to the following sources on selected genres: on the training and performance of the *kabuki* actor see Brandon *et al.* (1978) and Dunn and Torigoe (1969). On the training and acting of *nō* and *kyōgen* actors, and for translations of Zeami's treatises on acting see Berberich (1984, 1989), Bethe and Brazell (1978, 1982–3, 1990), Brazell (1988), Nearman (1978, 1980, 1981, 1982–3, 1984a, 1984b), Ortolani (1972, 1983, 1984), Raz (1983), Rimer and Yamazaki (1984).

On the training and performance of the *kathakali* actor see Namboodiri (1983) and Zarrilli (1984a, 1987, 1990). For a translation of the *Nāṭyaśāstra* see Ghosh (1961, 1967), and for one commentary see Kale (1974). For a general introduction to Indian genres of performance and acting in the traditional and modern Indian theatres see Richmond *et al.* (1990). For a study of acting in the devotional drama tradition see Haberman (1988).

On the training and acting of the traditional Beijing opera performer see Mackerras (1975), Scott (1957, 1983), and Wichmann (1991).

Note that this selection is somewhat arbitrary and is intended to give the reader a place to begin an exploration of acting techniques in selected Asian genres of performance. For a more complete bibliography see the sections on Asian performance in Fleshman (1986).

6. For a wide variety of arguments and perspectives on various aspects of intercultural performance and problems of translation across cultures see Fischer-Lichte *et al.* (1990), Marranca and Dasgupta (1991), and Scolnicov and Holland (1989). On the controversies surrounding Peter Brook's production and film, *The Mahabharata*, see Dasgupta in Marranca and Dasgupta (1991), Carlson and Pavis in Fischer-Lichte *et al.* (1990), Hiltebeitel (1992), and the complete volume edited by Williams (1991).

7. See also Eugenio Barba's (1972, 1990) reflections on the vision of performance provided him by the *kathakaḷi* actor.

8. The positive prospect of intercultural exploration which informs Barba's *Dictionary* is also a potential problem. Although as a "dictionary" the text appears "open," in its collage-like eclecticism which follows no master narrative and in the interculturalism displayed in its images, examples, and techniques, the text is ultimately one which closes in on itself through Barba's two frame narratives, through the subtitled (single) discourse of the "secret art of the performer" (which concludes as Barba reads a single image which sums up "all the recurring principles which are the basis of the actor's and dancer's pre-expressivity" – the Salome in St Mark's Basilica, Venice [1991: 268]) and through the lack of a bibliography which might lead the actor/reader not simply through a cycle of readings and re-readings of images and texts within the Text but also *outward* to resources which might further define differences. Even though Barba is clear that his task is not that of cultural anthropologists or anthropologists of performance, given the depth of his knowledge of these fields it would have been helpful to point his readers to sources through which they might understand how such "secrets" of performer's arts may, or may not, be considered secrets in some of the cultures of origin.

In the final sentence of his opening manifesto, Barba concludes, "This is a question of understanding not technique but the *secrets of technique*, which one must possess before one can go beyond technique." I would agree with Barba that, for those actors seeking to work on virtuosic extra-daily techniques, it is an important part of a process to discover a means of (using Barba's own term) "dilating" oneself in order to go "beyond technique;" however, to call the relationship to one's technique through which one must pass in order to go beyond the surface of that technique "secret," is to continue to propagate and project a mystifying discourse onto the phenomenon of "the beyond."

For further discussion of some of the problems and promises of Barba's intercultural ISTA projects, see Zarrilli (1988).

9. For a discussion of the problems with the (R)eal, see Phelan (1993).

10. For a collection of essays on the use of Asian martial arts in American actor training see Zarrilli (1993).

11. Etienne Decroux said, "Underneath the stew pot, there's the flame. That's why it boils. That's why the lid lifts off. There must be something underneath. Whatever one says or does, there's something underneath and that something is work. And work is not agitated movement. It is discipline" (1978a: 23).

12. For one extensive discussion of the breath in Indian psychophysiology as interpreted through Ayurveda and yoga, see Zarrilli (1989a).

13. For a further discussion of the issues raised by Bloch and her colleagues, see Bloch and Santibañez-H (1972), Santibañez-H and Bloch (1986), Bloch (1993), and especially the interdisciplinary set of commentaries from a variety of scientists, scholars, and theatre practitioners on the essay included in this volume (Bloch 1988). Bloch (1988) is also an excellent source of further reading on scientific studies of emotional expression and the biological bases of performance.

     Along different but somewhat related lines, one of Eugenio Barba's collaborators, Jean-Marie Pradier (1990) has been working toward developing a "Biological Theory of the Body in Performance." He hypothesizes "that the performing arts, particularly dance and mime, have a sensory–motor stimulation function for the audience" and argues for considering the body in performance in not only its cultural but also its biological context (1990: 93).

14. Bloch and her collaborators go beyond Ekman's more limited attention to expression in the face by establishing that "it is the performance of the respiratory–posture–facial pattern of an emotion that evokes the corresponding subjective activation or feeling in the performer as well as in the observer" (Chapter 15).

15. The training which Bloch and her associates have developed is not dissimilar in intent to the systems of training which Delsarte and Meyerhold developed which were to be a systematic means through which emotional expression might be actualized as the actor worked from the outside inward. According to a Jamesian theory of emotions, physical changes in posture etc. automatically trigger an emotional response.

7 MEYERHOLD'S BIOMECHANICS

1.   The author would like to thank Stella Hamershlag, Daniel Gerould, Bernard Koten, Aimée Su, and M. S. Ivanova for their invaluable assistance.

9 ACTOR TRAINING IN THE NEUTRAL MASK

1.   This and subsequent quotations of Lecoq are taken from notes of an interview by Sears Eldredge, trans. Fay Lacoq, in Eldredge, "Masks: Their Use and Effectiveness in Actor Training Programs," Diss. Michigan State University, 1975.

10 EASTERN AND WESTERN INFLUENCES ON PERFORMER TRAINING AT EUGENIO BARBA'S ODIN TEATRET

1. As mentioned above, Barba was Grotowski's assistant prior to forming the Odin Teatret. In *Towards a Poor Theatre* he records the training exercises developed by Grotowski and his actors during this period, among which is a series of composition exercises similar to those used by the Odin (Grotowski 1968: 142–5).

2. For Barba's own detailed analysis of these and other principles, see the chapters "Theatre Anthropology: First Hypothesis" and "Theatre Anthropology" in Barba (1986a).

11 BALI AND GROTOWSKI

1. In Balinese theatre, in addition to physical positions and their execution (*wiraga*), such as agem, there are two other elements that complete the effectiveness of acting work onstage. These are: *wirasa*, the feeling of what is being performed; and *wirama*, the musicality of the acting. For the purposes of this article, discussion of these two elements is not necessary.

2. Ed. note: for a full discussion of the "three brain" concept–reptilian, old mammalian, and new mammalian – and the relation to trance and other kinds of performance, see Turner (1983, reprinted in Turner 1986). Possibly Grotowski was aware of Turner's writing on this subject.

13 MY BODIES: THE PERFORMER IN WEST JAVA

1. Some may question my ability to analyze this system without letting preconceptions from my own background and training color the study. To an extent these factors will intervene. If they did not exist, I would not be trying to articulate these ideas for the readers of this essay. My argument, however, is that the system reprograms the body/mind of the student without attention to the personality that the trainee brings to it. Though my reprogramming may be more extensive and is augmented by exposure to dance systems of a wider area of the Pacific Rim, I feel that my body is still open to the meanings of the practice in itself. Indeed, practice is the only way to get beyond the simple introductions that are found in books and the fragmented, albeit tantalizing information about meanings that come from performers. Because principles of *ilmu gaib* (secret mystical knowledge) and *kabatinan* (spiritual practice) are involved with most traditional performance, the conversations that surround verbalizations about it are charged. If a teacher teaches wrongly, it can cause dispersal of his or her own store of spiritual power, or even worse, sickness or bad luck. If the teacher speaks and students have not already intuited through doing the ideas that the teacher articulates, they cannot understand what is being taught. Most performers say their teachers gave them little direct explanation of mantras or movements. Explanations are considered dilutions of the real thing – the doing. I invite performers to test my hypotheses by exploring the performance practices of West Java – while

acknowledging that other performers would not necessarily concur with all of my interpretations.

2. Two major cultural groups exist and continue to influence each other's arts in West Java. The highland areas are comprised of Sundanese speakers who, starting two hundred years ago, borrowed many things from the north coastal area where Javanese speakers predominate. The major borrowings have been from the region of the old kingdom of Cirebon, where the arts remain distinct from those of the better-known Central Javanese kingdoms of Solo and Yogyakarta. The generalizations I make about stylization and distancing apply to the performances of both the Sundanese and Cirebon areas.

3. The importance of the solo dancer/puppeteer role is probably related to the shamanlike power needed for exorcistic performances, called *ruwatan* (see Foley 1984). To do these rituals a performer must have spiritual power which is thought to be acquired with difficulty, and, once acquired, best kept at some distance from the spiritual power of another lest the other create a kind of spiritual static, interfering with the first's power/performance. Such circumstances may have contributed to the preference for solo performers.

4. This is true of the mask and puppet theatre of West Java, but in theatre by humans (*wayang orang*) and dance dramas (*sendratari*), specialization is evident in performance practice – not in the training – which requires all performers to master the full cycle of characters. Human theatre has grown up in West Java during the current century.

5. I will use the example and borrow related material from the *wayang golek cepak*, the 200-year-old Sundanese puppet theatre which derives from the Cirebon region where masks and puppetry are closely interrelated and are traditionally the purview of a single artist. The same mask/puppet/character types are common to virtually all theatre forms of the Sundanese, Javanese, and Madurese language areas, implying that the progression of four or five character types was basic to all of these ethnic groups. Indeed, a related grouping of four prime characters exists in other Southeast Asian areas, including Bali, Java, Malaysia, Thailand and Cambodia.

6. The topeng is today danced either during the day or at night. Most performers specialize only in mask performance. Some dalang, such as those of Losari, still do puppet or masked dance drama performances in addition to mask dance performances. The oral tradition indicates that this was more common in the past.

7. Kalijaga and other Islamic mystics may indeed have reordered the traditional arts of the Hindu–Javanese heritage in this period, but the roots of these practices are probably part of the archaic heritage of the Malayo–Polynesians that inhabited the archipelago even earlier. Though the structure that we see today may have been set when Kalijaga lived, the dance has changed since his time. For example, the dancer today wears a neck ornament distinctly like a European tie and one of the characters wears a starched collar, remarkably like one appropriate to a European shirt of the early part of this century.

8. There is no term that dancers in Indonesia use to refer to this concept. I reiterate that those who learn this system learn by rote and, hence, would not necessarily analyze the body usage verbally, as I do here.

9. The mask dancer of topeng does not speak since the mask is held to the face by biting a piece of leather attached to the inside of the mask. My comments on voice, therefore, are drawn from the practice of the rod puppet theatre. In masked performances, the clown performer or a musician of the *gamelan* speaks for the character using a voice which replicates the puppet theatre's vocal conventions.

10. As is customary in Indonesia, the opposite is sometimes true, too. The Pamindo character is sometimes said to be male – in Losari this mask is used for Panji and in some places it is called Samba, after a son of Kresna. However, most performers think of Pamindo as female; it is significant that females in dance plays and puppet presentations correspond in movement and appearance to the Panji or Pamindo character types.

11. Reverence for the hornbill and the frigate bird, as old religious figures in various areas of the Pacific including Micronesia, and the tendency to enact the movements of this bird in dance may be related (see Holt 1967: 106; Xavier 1976: 45–7).

12. Also known as Rawana, Dasamuka is the king of Alengka. Pancasona is a power acquired by Dasamuka which let him live again each time he touched the earth.

13. This character, who uses fully visible energy, is presented most routinely for Western audiences. The explosions of emotion that we have come to expect in performance, the wide use of the space, jumps, and the high physical center found in ballet are closer to Klana than to any of the other characters.

14. Puppet plays such as *Arjuna's Meditation* may corroborate the importance of the upper spine area in the dance of Klana. Nirwatakawaka, whose type (puppet mask) is identical to Klana, has a secret power located at the back of his throat which allows him to live forever. It seems possible to me that the narratives of such plays, when reaffirmed by the practice of dance, may be referring to characteristics of the human neural system.

15. Shelly Errington (1990) notes that terms such as 'natural' mask are actually deep cultural choices. In Indonesia, what a Westerner might call "natural" (deeply felt, emotionally fraught, a pouring forth of sound or energy), fits better into the category of "demonic" or "ogrely" and is therefore considered by Indonesians most unnatural.

16. The *sintren*, a village trance dancer of the Cirebon region, is said to be possessed by a goddess (*bidadari*) who descends from the heavens. Her dance exhibits an energy use which is analogous to the refined aspects of topeng (see Foley 1985).

17. It seems likely that the snake association is related to the use of reptiles in Micronesian dances where iguana or lizard dances stand in marked contrast to frigate bird movements. The contrast seems analogous to the bird–snake dichotomy and may be an adaptation of the same thinking to the changing ecology of the Pacific Islands.

18. Even if it seems that the varied sexual responses of the two genders present some analogy – the relaxed, floating Pamindo (female) and excited, driving Klana (male) – indigenous commentary denies this analysis. Indeed, each

character is ideologically linked with the opposite of what this sexual interpretation would indicate. The red Klana mask, while always representing a male in stories and puppet plays, is said to indicate the females menses, and the white mask of the refined character, closer to females in stories and puppet plays, is associated with semen.

19. I think it likely that topeng masks are related to Japanese *no* which also has a range of masks from god to demon. Possibly much of the imagery traveled with Hindu–Buddhism to the archipelago. Zarrilli's (1989a) discussion of the rising vital power in Indian martial arts and the kundalini yoga's awakening of the serpent power to seek liberation, a state beyond death, illness and worldly care, also seems related. I suspect however that the imagery (bird/serpent, world tree) and the basics of the typology of character preceded Indian influence in this area and was merely reconfirmed and reinterpreted by it. Thus it may stem from common thinking about the body that predated the Hindu impact in Indonesia beginning about the first century, and was merely elaborated during the Hindu–Javanese period before being reformulated by Sufi thinkers in the sixteenth century. It has been reworked by many generations of dalang since.

20. For recent discussions of ideas of power in Southeast Asia see Errington (1990); Keeler (1987); and Zurbuchen (1987: 46–7).

14 "ON THE EDGE OF A BREATH, LOOKING"

1. The final version of this essay has been inspired, in part, by some of Herbert Blau's writings, especially *Take Up the Bodies* (1982a: 86) from which the title is taken.

2. Such undisciplined energy is not peculiar to American actors. Zeami compares the undisciplined but vibrant energy of the young actor to that of the tree squirrel – exciting but unfocused and uncontrolled (Nearman 1980). There seem to be no cultural barriers to such indiscipline.

3. Scott published widely on the theatres of China and Japan, and is especially noted for his understanding of traditional Chinese acting (1955, 1957, 1967, 1969, 1975, 1983). Unfortunately, his visionary practical work of training and directing actors is little known except to his students. Scott himself had learned *t'ai chi ch'uan* as a personal discipline and as a means of understanding the "basic working principles" of the Chinese actor's stage technique.

4. In contemporary Euro–American theatre, at least four primary paradigms of acting/performance are currently operative, each of which assumes a different relationship between the performer and what is performed: (1) playing a character in which it is assumed that the actor must craft, shape, and embody an identifiable role, "mask" or *dramatis persona* played in a particular style and according to a set of conventions (melodrama, realism, etc.); (2) an Artaudian/Grotowskian type of acting in which the actor/performer does not attempt to construct a character as a separate *dramatis persona*, but rather plays each moment in a psychophysiological score without the intercession of character, and/or improvises each moment (Spolin 1963); (3) a Brechtian-

based acting in which the actor displays the character by being an observer to his or her own actions while in the act of performing them; and (4) a performance in which the performer repeats a sequence of actions which does not constitute a character.

There is, of course, free play between and among these paradigms. John Rouse's description of the Wooster Group's performance of *LSD (. . . Just the High Points . . .)*, is a case in point as he differentiates between the psychologically realistic style of acting required of a "normative" production of Miller's *The Crucible* in which each actor plays a character, and the type of acting in which the Wooster Group's actors engaged: "Lines were delivered at a frantic pace, sometimes at high volume. During Miller's scenes of hallucination and hysteria some performers displayed a highly theatricalized mania, some crawled under the table. But the acting made no attempt at psychological realism. The characters were displayed, not embodied" (1992: 150).

Joseph Chaikin sought to erase stereotypical characterization as an unnecessary intermediary between the actor and the immediacy of the performative moment. He announced that "The study of character is the study of 'I' in relation to the forces that join us, [that is] . . . The notion of characterization as understood in our American theater is archaic and belongs with the whole hung-up attitude about the 'other.' Characterization formerly has been simply a set of mannerisms which disguise the actor and lend atmosphere" (1972: 11, 17).

5. My representation of this experience as taking place between cultures is not ideologically unproblematic. My own search for "useful" techniques that first took me to India, and which led to a "transformation," to a certain degree follows the now classic pattern of the Westerner traveling to the East for "enlightenment" – a pattern which I have critiqued elsewhere. The difference, if there is one, lies in my reflexive attention to the problems and ideology of the encounter. Also, I firmly believe that a similar experience and result to those described here might just as well have occurred for me had I gone to France and studied Corporeal Mime in 1976–7 instead of going to India.

As Vasudha Dalmia-Lüderitz points out, this narrative could be critiqued as yet another "attempt to come to terms with the urban, post-industrial . . . search for the Asiatic within, whereby the difference, often consisting of all that has been marginalized in one's own culture, is projected onto the other, often preempting thereby any real effort to understand and represent with any degree of responsibility the cultural reference thus invoked" (1992: 9–10). to temper this sobering criticism, I refer the reader to my other attempts responsibly to understand and represent what are the primary cultural referents of this study, that is, *kalarippayattu* and *kathakali* of Kerala (see in particular Zarrilli 1984a, 1989a, 1992).

6. I returned for more advanced training under Govindankutty Nair in 1980, 1983, 1985, 1988, 1989, and 1993. In 1989 I also studied with C. Mohammed Sherif and Sreejayan Gurukkal at the Kerala Kalarippayattu Academy, Kannur. In 1989 I also began training in yoga with Chandran Gurukkal of Azhicode, Kannur District, and in 1993 I continued yoga training with Dhayanidhi in Thiruvananthapuram.

7. I remind the reader that *kathakali* actors are as prone to undiscipline as are

Americans and *nō* actors. I witnessed a performance of three *kathakaḷi* plays on 19 February 1993, in celebration of Śivaratri at the Śiva temple near Wadakancherry, Kerala, South India. In the first play of the night, *Nala Caritam* (First Day's Play), one of the most renowned of today's master actors, Kalamandalam Gopi Asan, was performing the title role of Nala opposite his somewhat junior counterpart, my former teacher M.P. Sankaran Namboodiri – an actor just beginning to reach his performative potential – in the role of Hamsa. While Namboodiri gave a rich, complex, full performance of his role, Gopi was criticized by connoisseurs in attendance for his overacting in the opening scenes of the play, that is, an illustration of his occasional "undisciplined" if sometimes brilliant powers of interpretation and expression. In the second play of the night, senior actor Padmanabhan Gopi Asan played the title role of the demon-king Narakasura in *Narakasura Vadham*, and, like Namboodiri's performance, exhibited that supremely *kathakaḷi*-esque "total" engagement and control of the entire bodymind in filling out each dramatic moment and image in the text – performances in which the text is corporeally inscribed in the actor's body. The third and final story of the night was a performance of *Kiratam* featuring junior teachers and actors. From my critical perspective, the performance of *Kiratam* was a disaster. In contrast to the performance of Namboodiri and Asan, the younger actors were, to use the same terms I might use for bad acting in the United States, never "in the moment," that is, they were "anticipating" the next beat of their score. They were "overacting" and "playing to the gallery." For example, the actors playing Arjuna and Śiva in disguise as a hunter, two epic characters who most represent and embody the disciplining self-control of the yogic strain of Indian philosophy, cosmology, and embodied practice, were totally out of control, going so far in their frenzied battle with one another as to pick up and use the wooden stools onstage as "weapons" with which to attack one another!

8. Although certainly characteristic of American male sports, this willful, aggressive, assertive approach to one's body-in-training is not restricted to Americans. Many Malayali males undergoing training suffer the same problems I have recounted here, with the same results – unnecessary tension.

9. Scott had the foresight to insist, even in a University setting where classes usually meet only two or three times per week, that this psychophysiological training regime *had to be repeated daily* if it were to be of potential benefit to students.

10. Students participating in the training program include undergraduate and M.F.A. graduate students of acting, as well as students of dance, performance art, and/or performance theory with a commitment to exploring theory in practice. Naturally, both graduate and undergraduate acting students are simultaneously enrolled in other studio classes in acting, movement, and/or voice. I wish to acknowledge the extremely important role that these complementary disciplines play in helping to realize the vision of training articulated here under the capable guidance and with the active support of my colleagues Patricia Boyette, Karen Ryker, and John Staniunas.

11. For *kaḷarippayaṭṭu* practitioners the lower abdominal/pelvic region is known as the "root of the navel" (*nabhi mula*) – the place to and from which the

breath travels. For a full discussion of the indigenous concepts, see Zarrilli (1989a).

12. Although the seven phases Schechner identifies are based on a contemporary Western experimental model of theatre and therefore could be considered problematic if assumed as a universal progression for all performances, it is a useful place to begin this discussion of training toward (workshops, rehearsals, warm-ups) performance for the American actor.

13. Japanese philosopher Yasuo Yuasa explains how non-Western philosophical systems and their related disciplines of practice have long recognized that "the mind–body issue is not simply a theoretical speculation but it is originally a practical, lived experience (*taiken*), involving the mustering of one's whole mind and body. The theoretical is only a reflection of this lived experience" (1987: 18). Yuasa argues that, except for the phenomenological movement, the Western philosophical tradition has always asked, " 'What *is* the relationship between the mind–body?' " In contrast, Eastern body–mind theories begin by asking, " 'How does the relationship between the mind and body *come to be* (through cultivation)?' or 'What does it *become*?" (1987: 18). For an additional discussion of the importance of understanding performance itself as a process, see Drewal (1991).

14. In this selective presentation of Artaud's vision of the actor, I have abstracted his incisive description of the psychophysiological basis of the actor's art from his very problematic metaphysical speculations. Unfortunately, Artaud wedded the physiological with the mystical and cosmological.

15. There is a striking similarity between Bloch's description of her techniques and results (Chapter 15) and those of *kathakaḷi*.

15 EFFECTOR PATTERNS OF BASIC EMOTIONS

1. The experiments described here and the development of the training method were done between 1971 and 1973 in Santiago, Chile, where the authors (S.B. and G.S.H.) worked at the Department of Physiology of the Medical School and at the Department of Psychology (Universidad de Chile). Pedro Orthous (deceased in 1974) was Régisseur and Professor of Dramatic Art at the Drama Department of the Universidad de Chile. Without his participation in this research, the first applications of the reported method to theatre performance would not have been possible.

We are greatly indebted to Elena Berger for conducting the yoga and relaxation exercises and to Horacio Muñoz-Orellana, a Chilean régisseur resident in Denmark, for many enriching discussions and for the development of new theatrical exercises in his current work with this method. And last but not least is our grateful recognition of the many actors and students from different countries who were open to our ideas and who were willing to participate in the experiments.

A partial report of this work was given at the International Colloque on "Théâtre et sciences de la vie" in Paris, France, 4–6 June 1984.

16 INTRODUCTION TO PART III

1. Of the numerous recent books published on techniques for training actors which do not focus on the method, I will only mention two: those of Balk (1985) and Gronbeck-Tedesco (1992).

2. On the historical Stanislavsky see his own books (1948, 1958, 1963), as well as Benedetti (1982), Houghton (1936), Gordon (1987), and Mitter (1992). For re-readings of Stanislavsky which historicize and contextualize his ideas see Rayner (1985), Schmitt (1986, 1990), Hobgood (1991), and Carnicke (1993). On Michael Chekhov see the most recent edition of his seminal text on acting with Mel Gordon's useful introduction (1991).

   On Strasberg and various versions of American method acting see Hethmon (1965), Moore (1960, 1965, 1979), Kazan *et al.* (1984), and Munk (1966). See also the two special issues of the *Drama Review* (Fall, Winter, 1964) on Stanislavsky and Stanislavsky's legacy in America. For rereadings of American method acting see Carnicke's (1984) and (1993) critiques of the problems with translations of Stanislavsky's texts on the basis of which many ideas of American method acting were formulated. Benedetti's new translation of Stanislavsky (Stanislavsky 1993), Jenkins and Ogden-Malouf (1985), Zarrilli (1989b) and McConachie (1993).

3. On Brecht and acting see also McDowell (1976), Hernadi (1976), and Esslin (1990).

4. On Fo see also Mitchell (1984) and Fo (1987, 1992). For other more general studies of comedy, clowning, and politics see Jenkins (1988) and Schechner (1985).

5. For the most recent information on Boal see Boal (1990, 1992), the special *TDR* issue on Boal (1990: 34, 3), and Schutzman and Cohen-Cruz (1994). Boal's model of the actor as enabler has also been usefully developed and employed in British style theatre-in-education and British style educational drama. On theatre-in-education see Jackson (1980, 1993), O'Toole (1976), Redington (1983), and Vine (1993).

6. From their interviews with numerous feminist theatre workers, Jenkins and Ogden-Malouf found few who worked "with realistic material in a strictly iconic fashion, because the performer in realism is unable to transcend gender boundaries" (1985: 66). They also reported Betty Bernhard's observation

   > that socialization in American culture creates male actors who must work through layers of defenses in order to gain access to their emotional resources (thus the great popularity of Method-oriented approaches) and female actors who must overcome scores of self-effacing habits in order to gain presence and claim focus on the stage (for which little acting pedagogy exists).
   >
   > (Jenkins and Ogden-Malouf 1985: 68)

7. For other important contributions to feminist considerations of acting see Brunner's (1980) interview with Sklar, Zeig (1985), Blair (1985), and Forte (1992).

8. For further reading on acting Beckett see Kalb (1989).

17 BRECHT AND THE CONTRADICTORY ACTOR

1. For a recent example of this absolutizing tendency, see Timothy J. Wiles' discussion of Brecht in his *The Theater Event: Modern Theories of Performance*, Chicago: University of Chicago Press, 1980. The tendency towards generalized comparisons with Stanislavsky mars one of the most recent contributions to the discussion of Brecht and the actor, Margaret Eddershaw's otherwise frequently interesting examination, "Acting Methods: Brecht and Stanislavski," in *Brecht in Perspective*, Graham Bartram and Anthony Waine (eds), New York, Longman, 1982: pp. 128–44.

2. Brecht, in a discussion with students and professors at the Universität Greifswald, 1954, "Über die Arbeit am Berliner Ensemble," in Werner Hecht (ed.) *Brecht im Gespräch, Diskussionen, Dialogue, Interviews*, edition suhrkamp 771, Frankfurt/Main, Suhrkamp, 1975, p. 123. All translations in the essay are the author's.

3. Today, over thirty-five years after Brecht's death, such invaluable discussion based on rehearsal observation is virtually impossible to come by. However, a monograph now being prepared by John Fuegi for Cambridge University Press's Directors in Perspective series promises to provide us with further detailed accounts of Brecht's work with his actors. Fuegi has had access to Brecht's co-workers, to tape recordings and notes of rehearsals, and to his own vast knowledge and experience of Brecht's theatre.

4. On the other hand, concentration on Brecht's work with actors at the Ensemble precludes consideration of such aspects of his work as the interrelationship of theory and practice during the late 1920s when Brecht was evolving his theory of the *Lehrstücke*, the Learning Plays.

5. Given the fairly widespread misconception represented by Eddershaw's statement that Brecht founded the Berliner Ensemble "primarily to facilitate the perfect staging of Brecht's own plays" (137), it should be stressed that Brecht and his actors developed their interest in interpretational techniques for the full range of the world's dramatic literature, from Sophocles' *Antigone* to Synge's *Playboy of the Western World*. Of the Ensemble's fifteen most important productions during Brecht's lifetime, only four were plays by Brecht.

6. "Anmerkungen zur Aufführung 1949"; reprinted in *Materialien zu Brechts Mutter Courage und ihre Kinder*, ed. Werner Hecht, edition suhrkamp 50, 10th edn 1976, Frankfurt/Main: Suhrkamp, 1964. I have altered the format of this list which is printed in paragraph form, the individual sentences being separated by ellipsis points.

7. Roland Barthes provides an excellent discussion of the dialectical development of beats in the first scene of *Mother Courage*, using photographic illustrations, in his "Seven Photo Models of Mother Courage," trans. Hella Freud Bernays, *Drama Review*, 1967, 12, 1: pp. 44–55.

8. Palitzsch in an interview with Artur Joseph for his *Theater unter vier Augen: Gespräche mit Prominenten*, Köln, Kiepenheuer und Witsch, 1969, p. 178.

9. For further discussion on Brecht's use of "quoted" gestures throughout a production, see Walter Benjamin's *Versuche über Brecht*, edition suhrkamp

172, 2nd edn, Frankfurt/Main, Suhrkamp, pp. 26–7.

10. Käthe Rülicke-Weiler points this out in *Die Dramaturgie Brechts: Theater als Mittel der Veränderung*, 2nd edn, Berlin, Henschel, 1968, p. 206.

11. Brecht, as reported by Hans Joachim Bunge, 'Über eine Neuinszenierung der Dreigroschenoper: Ein Gespräch zwischen Brecht und Giorgio Strehler am 15.10.1955 über die bevorstehende Mailänder Inszenierung,' in Siegfried Unseld (ed.) *Bertolt Brecht Dreigroschenbuch: Texte, Materialien, Dokumente*, Frankfurt/Main, Suhrkamp, 1960, p. 134.

12. See Brecht's description, "Anmerkungen zur Aufführung 1949," *Materialien*, p. 76.

13. The *Gesammelte Werke* misprints "Stadium" (stage) for "Studium" (study).

14. Käthe Rülicke-Weiler in *Sinn und Form*, 2nd Special Brecht Issue, 1956, as quoted by Albrecht Schöne, "Bertolt Brecht: Theatertheorie und dramatische Dichtung," in Theo Buck (ed.) *Zu Bertolt Brecht: Parabel und episches Theater*, LGW Interpretation 41, Stuttgart, Klett-Cota, 1979, p. 39.

15. This labeling of Brecht's second and third phases is Peter Palitzsch's, as quoted by Hans Daiber, *Deutsches Theater seit 1945*, Stuttgart, Reklam, 1976, p. 218.

16. See Herbert Blau, 'The Popular, the Absurd and the *Entente Cordiale*,' *Tulane Drama Review*, 5, 3 (1961): 121.

17. Brecht's productions are, of course, famous for rehearsal periods lasting six months or longer. As Peter Palitzsch has pointed out in a personal interview (3 March 1979), however, Brecht's early productions at the Ensemble were often worked up relatively quickly; the *Hofmeister* had only about nine weeks of rehearsal, for example. Brecht began to indulge in long rehearsal periods during his last years, when he was both very ill and intent on developing his young directors and actors. The issue is not whether a Brechtian approach needs six months of rehearsals, but that it needs as long as necessary to proceed effectively through Brecht's three phases.

18 DARIO FO: THE ROAR OF THE CLOWN

1. This work with Dario Fo was supported by a Sheldon Fellowship from Harvard University.

19 FORUM THEATRE

1. Now [1991] I have been involved in several hundred such performances, in dozens of countries; most recently, the Theatre of the Oppressed Encounter at Massy in Paris (March–April 1991) brought together more than twenty Theatre of the Oppressed groups, practicing the method in seventeen countries.

2. For Newspaper Theatre, see Augusto Boal (1985) *The Theatre of the Oppressed.*

3. Since writing this in 1978, I have done a number of experiments of this nature

in many countries. I have even directed Bertolt Brecht's *The Jewish Wife* and played it in a Forum session in Paris in 1984. Similarly, Sophocles' *Antigone* has been done as a piece of Forum Theatre in Lausanne, Switzerland.

20 AN EPIC SYSTEM

1. It should be noted that I have consciously chosen not to capitalize the word "method" when referring to "method acting" simply because I believe it has already been capitalized for far too long.

2. I acknowledge a debt to Lauren Love's "Approaches to Feminist Perform- ance," in which she discusses "a kind of hybrid Brechtian method technique" (1989: 12), as my first exposure to the concept in writing.

3. See Love (1989: 7–14) for an insightful analysis of Hagen's essentialism and reinscription of white, male, upper class ideology.

4. Cole and Chinoy go so far as to claim that "nonillusory" epic acting is "marked by declamation" (1970 [1949]: 260).

21 RESISTING THE "ORGANIC:" A FEMINIST ACTOR'S APPROACH

1. *Much* of my training focused on method acting technique, not all. I attribute my "anti-organic" impulses to my work as an apprentice at Milwaukee's Theatre X, and to the Asian theatre discipline which lured me to the University of Wisconsin–Madison's graduate program (Chapter 14). The productions at Theatre X were decidedly non-realistic, and the training in the Asian theatre program focused on external-to-internal approaches to acting. Through that rigorous physical regimen, which involved the conscious intellectual/ emotional "filling up" of codified forms, I became aware of my body as it is presented to produce meaning to an audience. I am convinced that in the absence of such training and its adjunct philosophies as well as a healthy dose of materialist feminist theory in my "academic" graduate courses, I would not have reconsidered the organic approach.

2. In my experience theatre practitioners, regardless of their approaches, understand that, though they may muster every bit of their coercive creative might, no two members of an audience will understand their message in the same way, and certainly not in the way they intended. Feminists have also begun to theorize in the areas of semiotics and reception which should help theatre practitioners to broaden their scope when shaping their work.

23 TASK AND VISION

1. All quotations in this essay are from an interview with Willem Dafoe.

BIBLIOGRAPHY AND REFERENCES CITED

Aaron, Stephen (1986) *Stage Fright: Its Role in Acting*, Chicago: University of Chicago Press.

Adler, Stella (1988) *The Technique of Acting*, New York: Bantam.

Agnew, Jean-Christophe (1986) *Worlds Apart: The Market and the Theater in Anglo–American Thought, 1550–1750*, Cambridge: Cambridge University Press.

Anderson, Benedict (1972) 'The Idea of Power in Java', in Claire Holt, Benedict Anderson and James Siegel (eds) *Culture and Politics in Indonesia*, Ithaca: Cornell University Press, 1–69.

Appadurai, Arjun and Breckenridge, Carol (1988) 'Why Public Culture', *Public Culture* 1, 1: 5–9.

Appelman, Dudley (1967) *The Science of Vocal Pedagogy: Theory and Application*, Bloomington: Indiana University Press.

Apple, Jackie (1983) 'Performance: The State of the Art', *Cal Arts* 9,2: 12–13.

Apter, Andrew (1992) 'An Open Letter to Theatre Educators', *Association for Theatre in Higher Education (ATHE) News* 6, 3: 3.

Archer, William and Lowe, Robert (eds) (n.d.) *Hazlitt on Theatre*, New York: Hill and Wang.

Arjo, Irawati Durban (1988) Personal communication, 12 May.

―― (1989) 'Female Dance in West Java', *Asian Theatre Journal* 6, 2:168–179.

Artaud, Antonin (1958) *The Theater and Its Double*, trans. Mary Caroline Richards, New York: Grove Press.

―― (1964) *Le théâtre et son double*, Paris: Editions Gallimard.

Ashby, Clifford (1963) *Realistic Acting and the Advent of The Group in America, 1889–1922*, unpublished dissertation, Stanford University.

Aston, Elaine and Savona, George (1991) *Theatre as Sign-System: A Semiotics of Text and Performance*, London: Routledge.

Auslander, Philip (1984) 'Holy Theatre and Catharsis', *Theatre Research International* 9, 1: 16–29.

―― (1986) ' "Just Be Your Self," Logocentrism and Difference in Performance Theory,' *Art & Cinema* 1: 10–12.

Babcock, Barbara (1980) 'Reflexivity: Definitions and Discriminations', *Semiotica* 30, 1/2: 1–14.

Balk, H. Wesley (1985) *Performing Power: A New Approach for the Singer–Actor*, Minneapolis: University of Minnesota Press.

Barba, Eugenio (1972) 'Words or Presence', *Drama Review* 16,1: 47–54.

―― (1979) *The Floating Islands*, Holstebro, Denmark: Odin Teatret.

—— (1982) 'The Way of Opposites', *Canadian Theatre Review* 35, Summer: 12–37.

—— (1985a) *The Dilated Body*, Rome: Zeami Libri.

—— (1985b) Interview with author, Nordisk Teaterlaboratorium, Holstebro, Denmark, 5 September.

—— (1986a) *Beyond the Floating Islands*, New York: Performing Arts Journal Publications.

—— (1986b) 'Theatre Anthropology', in *Beyond the Floating Islands*, New York: Performing Arts Journal Publications, 135–156.

—— (1986c) 'The Female Role as Represented on Stage in Various Cultures', Program for the International School of Anthropology in Holstebro, Denmark.

—— (1990) 'Eurasian Theatre', in Erika Fischer-Lichte, Josephine Riley and Michael Gissenwehrer (eds) *The Dramatic Touch of Difference*, Tubingen: Gunter Narr Verlag, 31–6.

Barba, Eugenio and Savarese, Nicola (1985) *Anatomie de l'acteur*, Cazilhac, France: Bouffonneries Contrastes, Zeami Libri, International School of Theatre Anthropology.

—— (1991) *A Dictionary of Theatre Anthropology: The Secret Art of the Performer*, London: Routledge.

Barba, Eugenio, Barker, Clive and Pradier, Jean (1985) 'Theatre Anthropology in Action', *Theatre International* 1: 11–25.

Barish, Jonas (1981) *The Anti-Theatrical Prejudice*, Berkeley: California University Press.

Barnett, Dene (1977) 'The Performance Practice of Acting: The Eighteenth Century, Part I: Ensemble Acting', *Theatre Research International*, 157–86.

—— (1978) 'The Performance Practice of Acting: The Eighteenth Century, Part II: The Hands', *Theatre Research International*, 1–19; 'Part III: The Arms', 79–93.

Barrault, Jean-Louis (1975) *Comme je le pense*, Paris: Editions Gallimard.

Barthes, Roland (1967) 'Seven Photo Models of Mother Courage', trans. Hella Freud Bernays, *Drama Review* 12, 1: 44–55.

—— (1972) *Critical Essays*, trans. Richard Howard, Evanston, Ill: Northwestern University Press.

—— (1977) *Image/Music/Text*, trans. Stephen Heath, New York: Hill & Wang.

Barton, Robert (1981) 'Strutting and Fretting: Shakespeare and the Novice Actor', *Theatre Journal* 33, 2: 231–45.

Bates, Brian (1957) *The Way of the Actor*, Boston: Shambala.

Beck, Julian and Malina, Judith (1970) 'Messages', in Toby Cole and Helen Krich Chinoy (eds) *Actors on Acting*, New York: Crown Publishers, 654–63.

Beckerman, Bernard (1990) *Theatrical Presentation: Performer, Audience and Act*, New York: Routledge.

Belo, Jane (1960) *Trance in Bali*, New York: Columbia University Press.

Belsey, Catherine (1980) *Critical Practice*, London: Methuen.

Benedetti, Jean (1982) *Stanislavski: An Introduction*, New York: Theater Arts Books.

Benedetti, Robert L. (1973) 'What We Need to Learn from the Asian Actor', *Educational Theatre Journal* 25: 463–8.

―――― (1976a) *The Actor at Work*, Englewood Cliffs, NJ: Prentice-Hall.

―――― (1976b) *Seeming, Being and Becoming: Acting in Our Century*, New York: Drama Book Specialists (Publishers).

Benjamin, Walter (1967) *Versuche über Brecht*, edition suhrkamp 172, 2nd edn, Frankfurt/Main: Suhrkamp.

Bentley, Eric (1953) *In Search of Theatre*, New York: Knopf. ('The Purism of Etienne Decroux', 184–95.)

Berberich, Junko Sakaba (1984) 'Some Observations on Movement in *Nō*', *Asian Theatre Journal* 1, 2: 207–16.

―――― (1989) 'The Idea of Rapture as an Approach to Kyogen', *Asian Theatre Journal* 6, 1: 31–46.

Berlau, Ruth, Brecht, Bertolt, *et al.* (1952) *Theaterarbeit: 6 Aufführungen des Berliner Ensembles*, Dresden: VVV Dresdener Verlag.

Best, David (1986) 'Meaning in Artistic Movement: The Objective and the Subjective', in Bob Fleshman (ed.) *Theatrical Movement: A Bibliographical Anthology*, Metuchen, NJ: Scarecrow Press, 3–28.

Bethe, Monica and Brazell, Karen (1978) *Nō as Performance: An Analysis of the Kuse Scene of Yamamba*, East Asia Papers 16, Ithaca: Cornell University China–Japan Program.

―――― (1982–3) *Dance in the Nō Theater*, East Asia Papers 24, 3 volumes, Ithaca: Cornell University China–Japan Program.

―――― (1990) 'The practice of *nō* theatre', in Richard Schechner and Willa Appel (eds) *By Means of Performance*, Cambridge: Cambridge University Press, 167–93.

Birdwhistell, Ray L. (1970) *Kinesics and Context: Essays on Body Motion Communication*, Philadelphia: University of Pennsylvania Press.

―――― (n.d.) *Expressions of Emotions in Man*, Philadelphia: University of Pennsylvania Press.

Birringer, Johannes (1991) *Theatre, Theory, Postmodernism*, Bloomington: Indiana University Press.

Blacking, John (1985) 'Movement, dance, music and the Venda girls' initiation cycle', in P. Spencer (ed.) *Society and the Dance*, Cambridge: Cambridge University Press, 64–91.

―――― (1977) *The Anthropology of the Body*, London: Academic Press.

Blair, Rhonda (1985) 'Shakespeare and the Feminist Actor', *Women and Performance* 2, 2: 18–26.

Blau, Herbert (1961) 'The Popular, the Absurd and the *Entente Cordiale*', *Tulane Drama Review* 5, 3: 119–51.

—— (1976) 'Seeming, Seeming: The Disappearing Act', *Drama Review*: 20, 4: 7–24.

—— (1982a) *Take Up The Bodies: Theatre at the Vanishing Point*, Urbana: University of Illinois Press.

—— (1982b) 'Universals of Performance; or Amortizing Play', *SubStance* 37/38: 140–61.

—— (1991) 'The Surpassing Body', *Drama Review* 35, 2:74–98.

—— (1992) *To All Appearances: Ideology and Performance*, London: Routledge.

Bloch, Susana (1988) 'Commentaries on "Effector patterns of basic emotions" by S. Bloch, P. Orthous and G. Santibañez-H', *Journal of Social and Biological Structures* 11: 201–11.

—— (1993) 'Alba Emoting: A Psychophysiological Technique to Help Actors Create Real Emotions', *Theatre Topics* 3, 2: 121–38.

Bloch, Susana and Santibañez-H, Guy (1972) 'Training of "emotional effection" in humans: Significance of its feedback on subjectivity', in S. Bloch and R. Aneiro-Ribe (eds) *Simposio Latinoamericano de Psicobiologia del Aprendizaje*, Santiago: Publicaciones de la Facultad de Medicina, Universidad de Chile, 170–84.

Bloch, Susana, Orthous, Pedro and Santibañez-H, Guy (1972) *Orbita* 9, 8–20.

Boal, Augusto (1985 [1979]) *Theatre of the Oppressed*, New York: Theatre Communications Group.

—— (1990) 'The Cop in the Head: Three Hypotheses', *Drama Review* 34, 3: 35–42.

—— (1992) *Games for Actors and Non-Actors*, trans. Adrian Jackson, London: Routledge.

Bolton, Gavin (1984) *Drama as Education*, New York: Longman.

Bourdieu, Pierre (1977) *Outline of a Theory of Practice*, Cambridge: Cambridge University Press.

Brandon, James R. (1978) 'Training at the Waseda Little Theatre: the Suzuki Method,' *Drama Review* 22, 4: 29–42.

—— (1989) 'A New World: Asian Theatre in the West Today,' *TDR*, 33, 2: 25–50.

—— (1990) 'Contemporary Japanese Theatre: Interculturalism and Intraculturalism,' in Erika Fischer-Lichte, Josephine Riley and Michael Gissenwehrer (eds) *The Dramatic Touch of Difference*, Tübingen: Gunter Narr Verlag, 89–97.

Brandon, James R., Palm, William P. and Shively, Donald H. (1978) *Studies in*

Kabuki, Honolulu: University of Hawaii Press.

Braun, Edward (1969) *Meyerhold on Theatre*, New York: Hill and Wang.

Brazell, Karen (ed.) (1988) *Twelve Plays of the Noh and Kyogen Theatres*, New York: Cornell Univ. East Asian Papers.

Brecht, Bertolt (1964a) 'Alienation Effects in Chinese Acting,' in *Brecht on Theatre*, ed. and trans. John Willett, N.Y.: Hill & Wang, 91–99.

—— (1964b) *Brecht on Theater*, John Willett (ed.), New York: Hill & Wang.

—— (1966) 'Notes on Stanislavski', trans. Carl Muller, in Erica Munk (ed.) *Stanislavski and America*, Greenwich, CT: Fawcett, 124–36.

—— (1967a) *Gesammelte Werke in 20 Banden*, Werner Hecht (ed.), Frankfurt/Main: Suhrkamp.

—— (1967b) *Schriften zum Theater*, Frankfurt-am-Main: Suhrkamp.

—— (1975) 'Über die Arbeit am Berliner Ensemble', in Werner Hecht (ed.) *Brecht im Gespräch, Diskussionen, Dialogue, Interviews*, edition suhrkamp 771, Frankfurt/Main: Suhrkamp.

Brecht, Stefan (1988) *The Bread and Puppet Theatre, Vols One and Two*, London: Routledge.

Brook, Peter (1968) *The Empty Space*, London: Penguin Books.

Brown, E. (1969) *Meyerhold on Theatre*, London: Methuen.

Brown, Richard P. (1972) *Actor Training I* New York: Drama Book Specialists (Publishers).

Bruner, Edward M. (1986) 'Ethnography as Narrative', in Victor W. Turner and Edward M. Bruner (eds) *The Anthropology of Experience*, Urbana: University of Illinois Press, 139–58.

Brunner, Cornelia (1980) 'Roberta Sklar: Toward Creating a Women's Theatre, an interview', *Drama Review* 24, 2: 23–40.

Bunge, Hans Joachim (1960) 'Über eine Neuinszenierung der Dreigroschenoper: Ein Gespräch zwischen Brecht und Giorgio Strehler am 15.10.1955 über die bevorstehende Mailänder Inszenierung', in Siegfried Unseld (ed.) *Bertolt Brecht Dreigroschenbuch: Texte, Materialien, Dokumente*, Frankfurt/Main: Suhrkamp.

Burke, Kenneth (1953) *Counter-Statement*, Los Altos, Calif: Hermes Publications.

Burns, Edward (1990) *Character, Acting, and Being on the Pre-Modern Stage*, New York: St Martin's Press.

Butler, Judith (1990) *Gender Trouble: Feminism and the Subversion of Identity*, London: Routledge.

Carnicke, Sharon (1984) '*An Actor Prepares/Rabota aktera nad soboi, Chast'l*: A Comparison of the English with the Russian Stanislavsky', *Theatre Journal* 36, 4: 481–94.

—— (1993) 'Stanislavski Uncensored and Unabridged,' *TDR* 37, 1: 22–37.

Carreri, Roberta (1985) Interview, Nordisk Teaterlaboratorium, Holstebro, Denmark, 26 August.

Case, Sue-Ellen (1988) *Feminism and Theatre*, New York: Methuen.

—— (ed.) (1990) *Performing Feminisms: Feminist Critical Theory and Theatre*, Baltimore: Johns Hopkins University Press.

Casey, Edward (1976) *Imagining: A Phenomenological Study*, Bloomington: Indiana University Press.

Chaikin, Joseph (1980 [1972]) *The Presence of the Actor*, New York: Atheneum.

Chekhov, Michael (1985) *Lessons for the Professional Actor*, Deidre Hurst du Prey (ed.), New York: Performing Arts Journal Publications.

—— (1991) *On the Technique of Acting*, New York: Harper.

Chin, Daryl (1991) 'Interculturalism, Postmodernism, Pluralism', in Bonnie Marranca and Gautam Dasgupta (eds) *Interculturalism and Performance*, New York: Performing Arts Journal Publications, 83–95.

Christensen, Anna (1983) 'Rachel Rosenthal's Performance Work', Unpublished manuscript.

Christoffersen, Erik Exe (1993) *The Actor's Way*, London: Routledge.

Cieslak, Ryszard (1991) 'Running to Touch the Horizon', Interview by Marzena Torzecka, trans. Susan Bassnett, *New Theatre Quarterly* 7, 27:261–3.

Clay, Jack (1972) 'Self-Use in Actor Training', *Drama Review* 16,1: 16–22.

Clifford, James (ed.) (1986) *Writing Culture*, Berkeley: University of California Press.

Clurman, Harold (1975) *The Fervent Years*, New York: Harcourt, Brace, Jovanovich.

Coger, Leslie Irene (1966) 'Stanislavsky Changes His Mind', in Erika Munk (ed.) *Stanislavski and America*, Greenwich, CT: Fawcett, 60–5.

Cohen, Robert (1978) *Acting Power*, Mountain View, CA: Mayfield.

—— (1984) 'Research and Development Report', Unpublished manuscript, University of California–Irvine.

Cole, David (1992) *Acting As Reading: The Place of the Reading Process in the Actor's Work*, Ann Arbor: University of Michigan Press.

Cole, Toby and Chinoy, Helen Krich (eds) (1970 [1949]) *Actors on Acting*, New York: Crown Publishers.

Copeau, Jacques (1970) 'Notes on the Actor', trans. Harold J. Salemson, in Toby Cole and Helen Krich Chinoy (eds) *Actors on Acting*, New York: Crown Publishers, 216–25.

Csikszentmihalyi, Mihaly (1975) *Beyond Boredom and Anxiety*, San Francisco: Jossey-Bass.

Culler, Jonathan (1982) *After Structuralism*, Ithaca: Cornell University Press.

Curjel, Hans (1967) 'Brechts *Antigone*-Inszenierung in Chur 1948', in Werner

Hecht (ed.) *Die Antigone des Sophokles: Materialen zur Antigone*, edition suhrkamp 135, Frankfurt/Main: Suhrkamp, 137–8.

Daiber, Hans (1976) *Deutsches Theater seit 1945*, Stuttgart: Reklam.

Dalmia-Lüderitz, Vasudha (1992) 'Encountering the Other, Accosting the Self', *Journal of Arts and Ideas*, 19–43.

Darwin, Charles (1965 [1872]) *Expression of Emotions in Man and Animals*, Chicago: University of Chicago Press.

Davis, Tracy C. (1991) *Actresses as Working Women: Their Social Identity in Victorian Culture*, London: Routledge.

de Certeau, Michel (1984) *The Practice of Everyday Life*, Berkeley: University of California Press.

Decroux, Etienne (1963) *Paroles sur le Mime*, Paris: Gallimard.

—— (1978a) 'The Origin of Corporeal Mime', *Mime Journal* 7/8:8–28.

—— (1978b) 'The Marionette', *Mime Journal* 7/8: 41–8.

—— (1978c) 'Hugo and Baudelaire', *Mime Journal* 7/8:49–58.

Delaumosne, L'Abbé *et al.* (1893) *Delsarte System of Oratory*, New York: Edgar S. Werner.

Delza, Sophia (1972) '*T'ai Chi Ch'uan*: The Integrated Exercise', *Drama Review* 16, 1: 28–33.

Derrida, Jacques (1976), (Second edn 1980), *Of Grammatology*, trans. (and preface) Gayatri Spivak, Baltimore: Johns Hopkins University Press.

—— (1978) *Writing and Difference*, trans. Alan Bass, Chicago: University of Chicago Press.

—— (1980) (first edn 1976) *Of Grammatology*, trans. (and preface) Gayatri Spivak, Baltimore: Johns Hopkins University Press.

—— (1981a) *Positions*, trans. Alan Bass, Chicago: University of Chicago Press.

—— (1981b) *Dissemination*, trans. Barbara Johnson, Chicago: University of Chicago Press.

—— (1982) *Margins of Philosophy*, trans. Alan Bass, Chicago: University of Chicago Press.

Diamond, Elin (1985) 'Refusing the Romanticism of Identity: Narrative Interventions in Churchill, Benmussa, Duras', *Theatre Journal* 37, 3: 273–86.

—— (1988) 'Brechtian Theory/Feminist Theory: Toward a Gestic Feminist Criticism', *Drama Review* 32, 1: 82–94.

Diderot, Denis (1970) 'The Paradox of Acting', in Toby Cole and Helen Krich Chinoy (eds) *Actors on Acting*, New York: Crown Publishers, 162–70.

Diderot, Denis and Archer, William (1957) *The Paradox of Acting* and *Masks or Faces*, New York: Hill & Wang.

Dietchman, Sherry (1990) Unpublished performance journal.

Dietrich, John and Duckwall, Ralph (1983) *Play Direction*, 2nd edn, Englewood Cliffs, NJ: Prentice-Hall.

Dolan, Jill (1988) *The Feminist Spectator as Critic*, Ann Arbor: University of Michigan Press.

—— (1990) '"Lesbian" Subjectivity in Realism', in Sue-Ellen Case (ed.) *Performing Feminisms: Feminist Critical Theory and Theatre*, Baltimore: Johns Hopkins University Press, 40–53.

Drewal, Margaret (1991) 'The State of Research on Performance in Africa', *African Studies Review* 34, 3: 1–64.

Dunn, Charles J. and Torigoe, Bunzo (trans. and eds) (1969) *The Actor's Analects*, New York: Columbia University Press.

Dychtwald, Ken (1977) *Bodymind*, Los Angeles: Jeremy P. Tarcher.

Eagleton, Terry (1976) *Marxism and Literary Criticism*, Berkeley: University of California Press.

—— (1983) *Literary Theory: an Introduction*, Minneapolis: University of Minnesota Press.

—— (1991) *Ideology: An Introduction*, London: Verso.

Easthope, Anthony and McGowan, Kate (eds) (1992) *A Critical and Cultural Theory Reader*, Milton Keynes, Bucks: Open University Press.

Eddershaw, Margaret (1982) 'Acting Methods: Brecht and Stanislavski', in Graham Bartram and Anthony Waine (eds) *Brecht in Perspective*, New York: Longman, 128–44.

Edwards, Barry (1981) 'Theatre Anthropology: An Approach to Biomechanics', *Momentum* 6, 1 (Spring): 23–5.

Ehrenzweig, Anton (1967) *The Hidden Order of Art*, Berkeley: University of California Press.

Ekman, Paul (1984) 'Expression and the Nature of Emotion', in Klaus R. Scherer and Paul Ekman (eds) *Approaches to Emotion*, Hillsdale, NJ: Lawrence Erlbaum Associates Publishers, 319–43.

Ekman, P., Levenson, R. W. and Friesen, W. V. (1983) 'Autonomic Nervous System Activity Distinguishes Among Emotions', *Science* 221: 1208–10.

Elam, Keir (1980) *The Semiotics of Theatre and Drama*, London: Methuen.

Eldredge, Sears (1975) 'Masks: Their Use and Effectiveness in Actor Training Programs', Ph.D. Diss., Michigan State University.

Ellman, Richard (1988) *Oscar Wilde*, New York: Vintage Books.

Errington, Shelley (1983) 'The Place of Regalia in Luwu', in Lorraine Gesick (ed.) *Centers, Symbols and Hierarchies*, New Haven: Yale University Southeast Asia Studies, 194–241.

—— (1990) 'Power and Difference: A Theoretical Overview', in Jane Atkinson and Shelley Errington (eds) *Power and Difference: Gender in Island Southeast Asia*, Palo Alto: Stanford University Press, 1–58.

Esslin, Martin (1976) *Artaud*, London: John Calder.

—— (1990) 'Some Reflections on Brecht and Acting', in Pia Kleber and Colin Visser (eds) *Re-Interpreting Brecht*, Cambridge: Cambridge University Press, 135–46.

Farrimond, William (1981) 'Actor Education: An Interdisciplinary Approach – Analysis of the Training and Performance Principles Applied by Eugenio Barba and the Actors of Odin Teatret in 1981', Masters Thesis, University of Copenhagen.

Fast, Julian (1971) *Body Language*, New York: Pocket Books.

Feldenkrais, Moshe (1966) 'Image, Movement, and Actor: Restoration of Potential', *Drama Review* 10, 3: 112–26.

Feldshuh, David (1976) 'Zen and the Actor', *Drama Review* 20, 1: 79–89.

Feral, Josette (1989a) 'Mnouchkine's Workshop at the Soleil', *Drama Review* 33, 4: 77–87.

—— (1989b) 'Building Up the Muscle: An Interview with Ariane Mnouchkine' *Drama Review* 33, 4: 88–97.

Fischer-Lichte, Erika (1989) 'Theatre and the Civilizing Process: An Approach to the History of Acting', in Bruce McConachie and Tom Postlewait (eds) *Interpreting the Theatrical Past: Essays in the Historiography of Performance*, Iowa City: University of Iowa Press, 19–36.

—— (1992) *The Semiotics of Theater*, Bloomington: Indiana University Press.

Fischer-Lichte, Erika, Riley, Josephine and Gissenwehrer, Michael (eds) (1990) *The Dramatic Touch of Difference: Theatre, Own and Foreign*, Tübingen: Gunter Narr Verlag.

Fleshman, Bob (ed.) (1986) *Theatrical Movement: A Bibliographical Anthology*, Metuchen, NJ: Scarecrow Press.

Fo, Dario (1987) *The Tricks of the Trade*, London: Routledge.

—— (1992) *Plays: One*, London: Methuen.

Foley, Kathy (1984) 'Dalangs and Dukun, Spirits and Men', *Asian Theatre Journal* 1, 1: 52–75.

—— (1985) 'The Dancer and the Danced: Trance and Theatrical Performance in West Java', *Asian Theatre Journal* 2, 1: 24–40.

—— (1987) 'Unmasking Topeng: Cosmology, Cosmogony and Change in the Mask Dance of West Java', Paper presented at the Graduate Dance Ethnology Conference, University of California at Los Angeles.

Foreman, Richard (1976) '"Ontological–Hysterical" Manifesto I', in Kate Davy (ed.) *Richard Foreman: Plays and Manifestos*, New York: New York University Press, 67–79.

—— (1981) 'How Truth . . . Leaps (Stumbles) Across Stage', *Performing Arts Journal* 5, 2: 91–7.

Forte, Jeanie (1985) 'Rachel Rosenthal: Feminism and Performance Art', *Women and Performance* 2, 2: 27–37.

—— (1992) 'Focus on the Body: Pain, Praxis, and Pleasure in Feminist Performance', in Janelle Reinelt and Joseph Roach (eds) *Critical Theory and Performance*, Ann Arbor: University of Michigan Press, 248–62.

Foucault, Michel (1972) *Power/Knowledge*, New York: Pantheon.

—— (1979) *Discipline and Punish*, New York: Vintage Books.

—— (1988) 'Technologies of the Self', in *Technologies of the Self*, Luther H. Martin *et al.* (eds) Amherst: University of Massachusetts Press, 16–49.

—— (1990 [1978]) *The History of Sexuality, Vol. I*, New York: Vintage Books.

Freire, Paulo (1972) *Pedagogy of the Oppressed*, London: Penguin.

Freytag, Gustav (1908) *Technique of the Drama*, 4th edn, Chicago: Scott, Foresman.

Gadamer, Hans-Georg (1975) *Truth and Method*, trans. G. Barden and J. Cumming, New York: Crossroad.

Ghosh, Manomohan (trans. and ed.) (1961) *The Nāṭyaśāstra*, Vol. 2, Calcutta: Asiatic Society.

—— (1967) *The Nāṭyaśāstra*, Vol. 1, 2nd rev. edn, Calcutta: Manisha Granthalaya.

Gillette, William (1970) 'The Illusion of the First Time in Acting', in Toby Cole and Helen Krich Chinoy (eds) *Actors on Acting*, New York: Crown Publishers, 564–7.

Goffman, Erving (1974) *Frame Analysis*, New York: Harper & Row.

Goldberg, RoseLee (1979) *Performance: Live Art 1909 to the Present*, New York: Harry N. Abrams.

Gordon, Mel (1987) *The Stanislavsky Technique*, New York: Applause Books.

—— (1991) 'Introduction', in Michael Chekhov *On the Technique of Acting*, New York: Harper, ix–xxxiv.

Gordon, Mel and Lassiter, Laurie (1984) 'Acting Experiments in The Group', *Drama Review* 28, 4: 6–12.

Grady, Sharon (1992) 'A Postmodern Challenge: Universal Truths Need Not Apply', *Theater* 23, 2: 15–20.

Gray, Paul (1966) 'From Russia to America: A Critical Chronology', in Erika Munk (ed.) *Stanislavski and America*, Greenwich, CT: Fawcett.

Greene, Naomi (1970) *Antonin Artaud: Poet Without Words*, New York: Simon & Schuster.

Gronbeck-Tedesco, John L. (1992) *Acting Through Exercises: A Synthesis of Classical and Contemporary Approaches*, Mountain View, CA: Mayfield.

Grotowski, Jerzy (1967) 'Towards a Poor Theatre', *Drama Review* 11, 3: 60–5.

—— (1968) *Towards a Poor Theater*, New York: Simon & Schuster.

—— (1969) *Towards a Poor Theater*, London: Methuen.

Haberman, David L. (1988) *Acting as a Way of Salvation*, New York: Oxford.

Hagen, Uta (1973) *Respect for Acting*, New York: Macmillan.

Hall, Stuart (1982) 'The Rediscovery of Ideology: Return of the Repressed in Media Studies', in M. Gurevitch, *et al.* (eds) *Culture, Society, and the Media*, London: Methuen, 56–90.

Handke, Peter (1969) *Offending the Audience* in *Kaspar and Other Plays*, trans. Michael Roloff, New York: Farrar, Straus and Giroux.

Harrop, John (1992) *Acting*, London: Routledge.

Hebdige, Dick (1982) 'Posing . . . Threats, Striking . . . Poses: Youth, Surveillance, and Display', *SubStance*, 37/38: 68–88.

Hecht, Werner (ed.) (1964) *Materialien zu Brechts Mutter Courage und ihre Kinder*, edition suhrkamp 50, 10th edn 1976, Frankfurt/Main: Suhrkamp.

—— (1967) *Gesammelte Werke in 20 Bänden*, Frankfurt/Main: Suhrkamp.

—— (1972) *Sieben Studien über Brecht*, edition suhrkamp 570, Frankfurt/Main: Suhrkamp.

—— (1975) *Brecht im Gespräch, Diskussionen, Dialogue, Interviews*, edition suhrkamp 771, Frankfurt/Main: Suhrkamp.

Henderson, Mary C. (1986) *Theater in America*, New York: Abrams.

Hernadi, Paul (1976) 'The Actor's Face as the Author's Mask: On the Paradox of Brechtian Acting', *Yearbook of Comparative Criticism*, Vol. 7: *Literary Criticism and Psychology*, University Park: Pennsylvania State University Press, 125–36.

Hethmon, Robert H. (ed.) (1965) *Strasberg at the Actors Studio: Tape-Recorded Sessions*, New York: Viking Press.

Hiltebeitel, Alf (1992) 'Transmitting Mahabharatas: Another Look at Peter Brook', *Drama Review* 36, 3: 131–59.

Hirsch, Foster (1984) *A Method to Their Madness: The History of the Actors Studio*, New York: W. W. Norton.

Hobgood, Burnet M. (1991) 'Stanislavski's Preface to *An Actor Prepares* and the Persona of Tortsov', *Theatre Journal* 43, 2, 219–28; 'Stanislavski's Preface to *An Actor Prepares*', *Theatre Journal* 43, 2, 229–32.

Hofstadter, Douglas R. (1980) *Gödel, Escher, Bach: An Eternal Golden Braid*, New York: Vintage Books.

Holt, Claire (1967) *Art in Indonesia: Continuity and Change*, Ithaca: Cornell University Press.

Hornby, Richard (1992) *The End of Acting: A Radical View*, New York: Applause Books.

Houghton, Norris (1936) *Moscow Rehearsals: The Golden Age of the Soviet Theatre*, New York: Grove Press.

Houghton, Norris (1936) *Moscow Rehearsals: An Account of Methods of Production in the Soviet Theatre*, New York: Harcourt, Brace and Co.

Huston, Hollis (1984) 'The Gest of Breath', *Theatre Journal* 36, 2: 199–211.

—— (1992) *The Actor's Instrument: Body, Theory, Stage*, Ann Arbor: University of Michigan Press.

Hutcheon, Linda (1989) *The Politics of Postmodernism*, London: Routledge.

Innes, Christopher (1993) *Avant-Garde Theatre 1892–1992*, London: Routledge.

Jackson, Michael (1989) *Paths Toward a Clearing: Radical Empiricism and Ethnographic Inquiry*, Bloomington: Indiana University Press.

Jackson, Tony (1980) *Learning Through Theatre: Essays and Casebooks on Theatre in Education*, Manchester: Manchester University Press.

—— (ed.) (1993) *Learning Through Theatre: New Perspectives on Theatre in Education, International Edition*, 2nd rev. edn, London: Routledge.

Jacob, Stanley W., Francone, Clarence Ashworth and Lossow, Walter (1982) *Structure and Function in Man*, Philadelphia: W. B. Saunders.

Jacobson, Edmund (1924) 'The Technic of Progressive Relaxation', *Journal of Nervous Mental Disorders* 60, 6: 568–78.

Jameson, Fredric (1991) *Postmodernism or the Logic of Late Capitalism*, Durham, NC: Duke University Press.

Jenkins, Linda Walsh and Ogden-Malouf, Susan (1985) 'The (Female) Actor Prepares', *Theater* 17:1, 66–9.

Jenkins, Ron (1988) *Acrobats of the Soul*, New York: Theatre Communications Group.

Johnson, Mark (1987) *The Body in the Mind: the Bodily Basis of Meaning, Imagination and Reason*, Chicago: University of Chicago Press.

Johnson, Richard (1986) 'What is Cultural Studies Anyway?', *Social Text* 16: 38–80.

Joseph, B. (1951) *Elizabethan Acting*, London: Oxford University Press.

Kakutani, Michiko (1984) 'When Great Actors Put Their Stamp on a Role', *New York Times*, 20 May: sec. 2, page 1.

Kalb, Jonathan (1989) *Beckett in Performance*, Cambridge: Cambridge University Press.

Kale, Pramod (1974) *The Theatric Universe*, Bombay: Popular Prakashan.

Kaplan, E. Ann (1983) *Women and Film: Both Sides of the Camera*, London: Methuen.

Kaplan, Harold M. (1960) *Anatomy and Physiology of Speech*, New York: McGraw-Hill.

Kazan, Elia, Bromberg, J. E. and Strasberg, Lee (1984) 'Outline for an Elementary Course in Acting (1935)', *Drama Review* 28, 4: 34–7.

Keeler, Ward (1987) *Javanese Shadow Plays, Javanese Selves*, Princeton, NJ: Princeton University Press.

Kerenyi, C. (1963) *Prometheus: Archetypal Image of Human Existence*, New York: Bollingen Foundation; distributed by Pantheon Books.

Kierkegaard, Soren (1959) *Either/Or*, trans. Walter Lowrie, Garden City, New York: Doubleday.

King, Nancy (1971) *Theatre Movement: The Actor and His Space*, New York: Drama Book Specialists (Publishers).

—— (1981) *A Movement Approach to Acting*, Englewood Cliffs, NJ: Prentice-Hall.

Kirby, E. T. (1972) 'The Delsarte Method: 3 Frontiers of Actor Training', *Drama Review*, 16, 1: 55–69.

Kirby, Michael (1965) 'The New Theatre', *Drama Review* 10, 2: 23–43.

Kondo, Dorrine K. (1990) *Crafting Selves*, Chicago: University of Chicago Press.

Kott, Jan (1992) 'Grotowski, or The Limit', in *The Memory of the Body: Essays on Theatre and Death*, Evanston, Ill: Northwestern University Press.

Kristeva, Julia (1969) *Semiotik: Recherches pour un semanalyse*, Paris: Editions du Seuil.

—— (1982) 'Psychoanalysis and the Polis', in Toril Moi (ed.) *The Kristeva Reader*, New York: Columbia University Press, 301–20.

Kuhn, Thomas S. (1962) *The Structure of the Scientific Revolutions*, Chicago: University of Chicago Press.

Kumiega, Jennifer (1985) *The Theater of Grotowski*, New York: Methuen.

Lakoff, George (1987) *Women, Fire, and Dangerous Things: What Categories Reveal about the Mind*, Chicago: University of Chicago Press.

Lakoff, George and Johnson, Mark (1980) *Metaphors We Live By*, Chicago: University of Chicago Press.

Langer, Susanne K. (1953) *Feeling and Form*, New York: Charles Scribner's Sons.

—— (1967) *Mind: An Essay on Human Feeling, Vol. 1*, Baltimore: Johns Hopkins University Press.

Laughlin, Karen (1990) 'Brechtian theory and American feminist theatre', in *Re-Interpreting Brecht*, Cambridge: University of Cambridge, 147–60.

Leabhart, Thomas (1975) 'Etienne Decroux on Masks', *Mime Journal* 2: 54–62.

Leder, Drew (1990) *The Absent Body*, Chicago: University of Chicago Press.

Lessac, Arthur (1967) *The Use and Training of the Human Voice*, New York: Drama Book Specialists (Publishers).

Levin, Harry (1950) 'Notes on Convention', *Perspectives of Criticism*, Cambridge, Mass: Harvard University Press.

Levine, Donald Nathan (1985) *The Flight From Ambiguity*, Chicago: University of Chicago Press.

Lewis, Robert (1958) *Method – Or Madness?*, New York: Samuel French.

Linklater, Kristin (1976) *Freeing the Natural Voice*, New York: Drama Book Specialists (Publishers).

Lotringer, Sylvere (1978) 'Shaggy Codes', *Drama Review* 22, 3: 87–94.

Love, Lauren (1989) 'Approaches to Feminist Performance', Unpublished MFA thesis, University of Wisconsin–Madison, Department of Theatre and Drama.

Lukács, Georg (1974) *Soul and Form*, trans. Anna Bostock, Cambridge, Mass: Massachusetts Institute of Technology Press.

Lust, Annette (1974) 'Etienne Decroux: Father of Modern Mime', *Mime Journal* 1: 14–25.

Lyotard, Jean-Francois (1977) 'The Unconscious as mise-en-scène', in Michel Benamou and Charles Caramello (eds) *Performance in Postmodern Culture*, Madison: Coda Press, 87–98.

—— (1979) *The Postmodern Condition*, Minneapolis: University of Minnesota Press.

McArthur, Benjamin (1984) *Actors and American Culture, 1888–1920*, Philadelphia: Temple University Press.

McConachie, Bruce A. (1985) 'Towards a Postpositivist Theatre History', *Theatre Journal* 37, 4: 465–86.

—— (1989) 'Reading Context Into Performance: Theatrical Formations and Social History', *Journal of Dramatic Theory and Criticism*, 3, 2: 229–37.

—— (1993) 'Metaphors We Act By: Kinesthetics, Cognitive Psychology, and Historical Structures', *Journal of Dramatic Theory and Criticism* 7, 2: 25–45.

McDowell, Stuart (1976) 'Actors on Brecht', *Drama Review* 20, 3: 101–16.

McGaw, Charles (1965) *Acting is Believing: A Basic Method*, 2nd edn, New York: Holt, Rinehart & Winston.

—— (1980) *Acting is Believing: A Basic Method*, 4th edn, New York: Holt, Rinehart & Winston.

McGrath, John (1981) *A Good Night Out: Popular Theatre: Audience, Class, and Form*, London: Eyre Methuen.

Mackerras, Colin (1975) *The Chinese Theatre in Modern Times from 1840 to the Present Day*, Amherst: University of Massachusetts Press.

Magarshack, David (trans.) (1961) *Stanislavsky on the Art of the Stage*, New York: Hill & Wang.

Maisel, Edward (ed.) (1969) *The Resurrection of the Body: The Writings of F. Matthias Alexander*, New York: Dell.

Marowitz, Charles (1961) *Stanislavsky and the Method*, New York: Citadel.

Marranca, Bonnie and Dasgupta, Gautam (eds) (1991) *Interculturalism and*

Performance, New York: Performing Arts Journal Publications.

Martin, Carol (1993) 'Anna Deveare Smith: The Word Becomes You' (Interview), *Drama Review* 37, 4: 45–62.

Mathews, Brander (1958) *Papers on Acting*, New York: Hill & Wang.

Matley, Bruce (1980) 'West Germany's Systematic Approach to Actor Training', *Theatre Journal* 32, 3: 329–36.

Mauss, Marcel (1967) *The Gift: Forms and Functions of Exchange in Archaic Societies*, trans. Ian Cunnison, E. E. Evans-Pritchard (ed.) New York: Norton. Originally published in 1925.

—— (1973) 'Techniques of the body', *Economy and Society* 2, 1: 70–88.

Meisner, Sanford and Longwell, Dennis (1987) *Sanford Meisner on Acting*, New York: Vintage Books, Random House.

Mekler, Eva (1988) *The New Generation of Acting Teachers*, New York: Penguin Books.

Merleau-Ponty, Maurice (1962) *Phenomenology of Perception*, London: Routledge & Kegan Paul.

—— (1964) *The Primacy of Perception*, Evanston, Ill: Northwestern University Press.

—— (1968) *The Visible and the Invisible*, Evanston, Ill: Northwestern University Press.

Meyerhold, Vsevolod (1922) *The Actor of the Future of Biomechanics*, Ermitazh, 6, Moscow.

Miller, Perry (1956) *Errand into the Wilderness*, Cambridge, Mass: Harvard University Press.

Mitchell, Tony (1984) *Dario Fo: People's Court Jester*, London: Methuen.

Mitter, Schomit (1992) *Systems of Rehearsal: Stanislavski, Brecht, Grotowski, and Brook*, London: Routledge.

Moore, Sonia (1960) *The Stanislavski Method*, New York: Viking.

—— (1965) *The Stanislavski System*, New York: Viking.

—— (1979 [1968]) *Training an Actor: The Stanislavski System in Class*, New York: Penguin Books.

Mullin, Donald C. (1975) 'Methods and Manners of Traditional Acting', *Educational Theatre Journal* 27, 1: 5–22.

Munk, Erika (ed.) (1966) *Stanislavski and America*, Greenwich, CT: Fawcett.

Nagatomo, Shigenori (1992a) 'An Eastern Concept of the Body: Yuasa's Body-Scheme', in Maxine Sheets-Johnstone (ed.) *Giving the Body Its Due*, Albany: State University of New York Press, 48–68.

—— (1992b) *Attunement Through the Body*, Albany: State University of New York Press.

Nagler, A.M. (1952) *Sources of Theatrical History*, New York: Theatre Annual.

Namboodiri, M. P. Sankaran (1983) 'Bhava as expressed through the presentational technique of kathakaḷi', in *Dance as Cultural Heritage*, Vol. I, *Dance Research Annual*, 14: 194–210.

Nearman, Mark (1978) 'Zeami's *Kyui*, A Pedagogical Guide for Teachers of Acting', *Monumenta Nipponica* 33, 3: 299–332.

—— (1980) '*Kyakuraika* Zeami's Final Legacy for the Master Actor', *Monumenta Nipponica* 35, 2: 153–98.

—— (1981) 'Zeami on the Goals of the Professional Actor', in Judith Mitoma Susilo (ed.) *Japanese Tradition: Search and Research*, Los Angeles: UCLA Asian Performing Arts Summer Institute, 43–51.

—— (1982–3) '*Kakyo* Zeami's Fundamental Principles of Acting', *Monumenta Nipponica* 1982, 37, 3: 333–74; 37, 4: 459–96; 38, 1: 49–70.

—— (1984a) 'Feeling in Relation to Acting: An Outline of Zeami's Views', *Asian Theatre Journal* 1, 1: 40–51.

—— (1984b) 'Behind the Mask of Noh', *Mime Journal* 4: 20–64.

Newman, Harry (1989) 'Holding Back: The Theatre's Resistance to Non-Traditional Casting', *Drama Review* 33, 3: 22–36.

Nietzsche, Friedrich (1967) *The Birth of Tragedy*, trans. Walter Kaufman, 1st Vintage edn, New York: Vintage Books.

Norris, Christopher (1987) *Derrida*, London: Fontana.

Oida, Yoshi (with Lorna Marshall) (1992) *An Actor Adrift*, London: Methuen.

Ortolani, Benito (1972) 'Zeami's Aesthetics of the Noh and Audience Participation', *Educational Theatre Journal* 24, 2: 109–17.

—— (1983) 'Spirituality for the Dancer–Actor in Zeami's and Zenchiku's Writings on the No', in Betty True Jones (ed.) *Dance as a Cultural Heritage*, vol. 1, New York: Congress on Research in Dance, 147–58.

—— (1984) 'Shamanism in the Origins of No Theatre', *Asian Theatre Journal* 1, 2: 166–90.

Osiński, Zbigniew (1986) *Grotowski and His Laboratory*, trans. and abridged by L. Vallee and Robert Findlay, New York: Performing Arts Journal Publications.

O'Toole, John (1976) *Theatre in Education*, London: Hodder & Stoughton.

Panskepp, J. (1982) 'Toward a General Psychological Theory of Emotions', *Behavioral and Brain Sciences* 5: 407–67.

Partridge, Eric (1983) *Origins: A Short Etymological Dictionary of Modern English*, New York: Greenwich House.

Pasolli, Robert (1972) *A Book on the Open Theatre*, New York: Avon.

Passow, Wilfred (1981) 'The Analysis of Theatrical Performance', trans. R. Strauss, *Poetics Today* 2, 3: 237–54.

Patraka, Vivian M. (1989) 'Lillian Hellman's *Watch on the Rhine*: Realism, Gender, and Historical Crisis', *Modern Drama* 32–1 (March): 128–45.

Pavis, Patrice (1982) *Languages of the Stage*, New York: Performing Arts Journal Publications.

Pezin, Patrick (ed.) (1982) 'Improvisation: Anthropologie Théâtrale', *Bouffonneries* 4: 1–124.

Phelan, Peggy (1993) *Unmarked: The Politics of Performance*, London: Routledge.

Pick, T. Pickering and Howden, Robert (eds) (1977) *Gray's Anatomy*, New York: Bounty Books, 352–4.

Pigeaud, G. Th. (1938) *Javaanse Volksvertoningen*, Batavia: Volkslectuur.

Pisk, Litz (1975) *The Actor and His Body*, New York: Theatre Arts Books.

Poggi, Jack (1973) 'The Stanislavsky System in Russia', *Drama Review* 17, 1: 124–33.

Pradier, Jean-Marie (1990) 'Towards a Biological Theory of the Body in Performance', *New Theatre Quarterly* 6, 2: 86–98.

Quambar, Akhtar (1974) *Yeats and the Noh*, New York: Weatherhill.

Quinn, Michael (1990) 'Celebrity and the Semiotics of Acting', *New Theatre Quarterly* 6, 2: 154–61.

Rabkin, Gerald (1983) 'The Play of Misreading: Text/Theatre/Deconstruction,' *Performing Arts Journal* 19: 44–60.

Rafferty, Ellen (ed.) (1989) *Putu Wijaya in Performance: a Script and Study of Indonesian Theatre*, Madison: University of Wisconsin–Madison Center for Southeast Asian Studies.

Rayner, Alice (1985) 'Soul in the System: on Meaning and Mystique in Stanislavski and A. C. Bradley', *New Theatre Quarterly* 4, 338–45.

—— (1994) *To Act, To Do, To Perform*, Ann Arbor: University of Michigan Press.

Raz, Jacob (1983) *Audience and Actors: A Study of Their Interaction in the Japanese Traditional Theatre*, Leiden: E. J. Brill.

Redington, Christine (1983) *Can Theatre Teach?*, London: Pergamon.

Reinelt, Janelle (1990) 'Rethinking Brecht: Deconstruction, Feminism, and the Politics of Form', *Brecht Yearbook*, 15: 99–110.

Reinelt, Janelle G. and Roach, Joseph R. (eds) (1992) *Critical Theory and Performance*, Ann Arbor: University of Michigan Press.

Richards, Jeffrey (1991) *Theater Enough: American Culture and the Metaphor of the World Stage*, Durham: Duke University Press.

Richmond, Farley, Swann, Darius and Zarrilli, Philip (1990) *Indian Theatre: Traditions of Performance*, Honolulu: University of Hawaii Press.

Rimer, J. Thomas and Yamazaki, Masakazu (1984) *On the Art of the Nō Drama: The Major Treatises of Zeami*, Princeton, NJ: Princeton University Press.

Roach, Joseph R. (1980) 'G. H. Lewes and Performance Theory: Towards a "Science of Acting" ', *Theatre Journal* 32, 3: 312–28.

—— (1985) *The Player's Passion: Studies in the Science of Acting*, Newark: University of Delaware Press [1993 Edn University of Michigan Press].

—— (1989) 'Power's Body: The Inscription of Morality as Style', in Thomas Postlewait and Bruce A. McConachie (eds) *Interpreting the Theatrical Past*, Iowa City: University of Iowa Press, 99–118.

Rogers-Aguiniga, Pamela (1986) 'Topeng Cirebon: The Masked Dance of West Java as Performed in the Village of Slangit', Master's thesis, University of California at Los Angeles.

Rolfe, Bari (1972) 'The Mime of Jacques Lecoq', *Drama Review* 16, 1: 34–8.

Rosenthal, Rachel (1979) 'The Death Show', *High Performance* 2, 1: 44–5.

—— (1980) 'Bonsoir, Dr Schon!', *High Performance* 2, 3–4: 90–1.

—— (1981) *Soldier of Fortune*, Unpublished script.

—— (1984a) Telephone conversation with author, 31 January.

—— (1984b) Telephone conversation with author, 8 October.

—— (1985a) Interview with author, New York, 8 June.

—— (1985b) Interview with author, Los Angeles, 5 July.

—— (1985c) Workshop, New York University, 21 May–7 June.

Rotimi (Ife), Ola (1990) 'Much Ado About Brecht', in Erika Fischer-Lichte, Josephine Riley and Michael Gissenwehrer (eds) *The Dramatic Touch of Difference*, Tübingen: Gunter Narr Verlag, 253–61.

Rouse, John (1992) 'Textuality and Authority in Theatre and Drama: Some Contemporary Possibilities', in Janelle G. Reinelt and Joseph R. Roach (eds) *Critical Theory and Performance*, Ann Arbor: University of Michigan Press, 146–58.

Rubin, Lucille S. (ed.) (1980) *Movement for the Actor*, New York: Drama Book Specialists (Publishers).

Rülicke-Weiler, Käthe (1968) *Die Dramaturgie Brechts: Theater als Mittel der Veränderung*, 2nd edn, Berlin (East): Henschel.

Ryle, Gilbert (1949) *The Concept of Mind*, Chicago: University of Chicago Press.

Said, Edward W. (1978) *Orientalism*, New York: Pantheon.

Saint-Denis, Michel (1969) *Theatre: Rediscovery of Style*, New York: Theatre Arts Books.

—— (1982) *Training for the Theatre*, New York: Theatre Arts Books.

Santibañez-H, Guy (1976) 'Subjective–gnostic, specific and inspecific aspects of emotion and motivation: Emoting reflexes', in *Brain and Behaviour Research*, vol. 6: 191–209.

Santibañez-H, Guy and Bloch, Susana (1986) 'A Qualitative Analysis of Emotional

Effector Patterns and Their Feedback', *Pavlovian Journal of Biological Science* 21, 3: 108–16.

Sartre, Jean-Paul (1976) *Sartre on Theater*, trans. Frank Jellinek, New York: Pantheon Books.

Saussure, Ferdinand de (1966) *Course in General Linguistics*, trans. Wade Baskin, New York: McGraw-Hill Paperbacks.

Savran, David (1988) *Breaking the Rules: The Wooster Group*, New York: Theatre Communications Group.

Sayler, Oliver (1925) *Inside the Moscow Art Theatre*, Boston: Little, Brown.

Scarry, Elaine (1991) *The Body in Pain*, Oxford: Oxford University Press.

Schechner, Richard (1966) 'Introduction: Exit Thirties, Enter Sixties', in Erika Munk (ed.) *Stanislavski and America*, Greenwich, CT: Fawcett.

—— (1973) *Environmental Theatre*, New York: Hawthorn.

—— (1976) 'From Ritual to Theatre and Back', in Richard Schechner and Mady Schuman (eds) *Ritual, Play, and Performance: Readings in the Social Sciences/Theatre*, New York: Seabury Press, 196–222.

—— (1977) *Essays on Performance Theory 1970–1976*, New York: Drama Book Specialists (Publishers).

—— (1982) *The End of Humanism*, New York: Performing Arts Journal Publications.

—— (1985) *Between Theater and Anthropology*, Philadelphia: University of Pennsylvania Press.

—— (1993a) 'Ron Vawter: For the Record' (Interview), *Drama Review* 37, 3: 17–41.

—— (1993b) 'Anna Deavere-Smith: Acting as Incorporation', *Drama Review* 37, 4: 63–4.

Schechter, Joel (1985) *Durov's Pig: Clowns, Politics and Theatre*, New York: Theatre Communications Group.

Scherer, K. R., Summerfield, A. B. and Wallbott, H. G. (1983) 'Cross-National Research on Antecedents and Components of Emotion: a Progress Report', *Social Science Information* 22: 355–88.

Schmitt, Natalie Crohn (1981) 'Theatre and Children's Pretend Play', *Theatre Journal* 33, 2: 213–30.

—— (1986) 'Stanislavski, Creativity, and the Unconscious', *New Theatre Quarterly* 2, 8: 345–51.

—— (1990) *Actors and Onlookers: Theater and Twentieth-Century Scientific Views of Nature*, Evanston, Ill: Northwestern University Press.

Schöne, Albrecht (1979) 'Bertolt Brecht: Theatertheorie und dramatische Dichtung', in Theo Buck (ed.) *Zu Bertolt Brecht: Parabel und episches Theater*, LGW Interpretation 41, Stuttgart: Klett–Cota.

Schrag, Calvin O. (1969) *Experience and Being*, Evanston, Ill: Northwestern University Press.

Schutzman, Mady and Cohen-Cruz, Jan (eds) (1994) *Playing Boal: Theatre: Therapy, Activism*, London: Routledge.

Scolnicov, Hanna and Holland, Peter, (eds) (1989) *The Play Out of Context: Transferring Plays from Culture to Culture*, Cambridge: Cambridge University Press.

Scott, A. C. (1955) *The Kabuki Theatre of Japan*, New York: Collier Books.

—— (1957) *The Classical Theatre of China*, London: George Allen & Unwin.

—— (1967) *Traditional Chinese Plays, Vol. I*, Madison: University of Wisconsin Press.

—— (1969) *Traditional Chinese Plays, Vol. II*, Madison: University of Wisconsin Press.

—— (1975a) 'Reflections on the Aesthetic Background of the Performing Arts of East Asia', *Asian Music* 6, 1–2: 207–16.

—— (1975b) *Traditional Chinese Plays, Vol. III*, Madison: University of Wisconsin Press.

—— (1983) 'The Performance of Classical Theater', in Colin Mackerras (ed.) *Chinese Theater From Its Origins to the Present Day*, Honolulu: University of Hawaii Press, 118–44.

—— (1993) 'Underneath the Stew Pot, There's the Flame . . . *T'ai Chi Ch'uan* and the Asian/Experimental Theatre Program', in Phillip Zarrilli (ed.) *Asian Martial Arts in Actor Training*, Madison: Center for South Asia, University of Wisconsin–Madison, 48–61.

Serban, Andrei (1976) 'The Life in a Sound', *Drama Review* 20, 4: 25–6.

Sergeant, E. S. (1917) 'A New French Theatre', *New Republic* 10: 350–2.

Seyler, Athene (1990) *The Craft of Comedy*, London: Routledge.

Shaner, David Edward (1985) *The Bodymind Experience in Japanese Buddhism*, Albany: State University of New York Press.

Sheets-Johnstone, Maxine (ed.) (1992) *Giving the Body Its Due*, Albany: State University of New York Press.

Shaw, George Bernard (1931) *Our Theatres in the Nineties*, in *Collected Works*, Ayot St Lawrence edn, New York: W. H. Wise.

Shawn, Ted (1963) *Every Little Movement*, New York: Dance Horizons.

Shickel, Richard (1985) *Intimate Strangers: The Culture of Celebrity*, New York: Doubleday.

Shklovsky, Victor (1965) 'Art as Technique', *Russian Formalist Criticism: Four Essays*, trans. Lee T. Lemon and Marion J. Reis, Lincoln, Nebraska: University of Nebraska Press.

Sklar, Deidre (1985) 'Etienne Decroux's Promethean Mime', *Drama Review*, 29, 4: 64–75.

Smith, Wendy (1990) *Real Life Drama: The Group Theatre and America, 1931–1940*, New York: Knopf.

Snow, Stephen (1986) 'Intercultural Performance: The Balinese–American Model', *Asian Theatre Journal* 3, 2: 204–32.

Sontag, Susan (ed.) (1976) *Antonin Artaud: Selected Writings*, New York: Farrar, Strauss & Giroux.

Spivak, Gayatri (1976) (second edn 1980), 'Preface' (and trans.) in Jacques Derrida *Of Grammatology*, Baltimore: Johns Hopkins University Press.

Spolin, Viola (1963) *Improvisation for the Theater*, Evanston, Ill: Northwestern University Press.

Stanislavski, Constantin (1922 [1955]) in Toby Cole (ed.) *Acting, Handbook of the Stanislavski Method*, New York: Crown Publishers.

—— (1936) *An Actor Prepares*, trans. Elizabeth Reynolds Hapgood, New York: Theatre Arts Books.

—— (1948) *My Life in Art*, New York: Theatre Arts Books.

—— (1958) *Stanislavski's Legacy*, New York: Theatre Arts Books.

—— (1961) *Stanislavsky on the Art of the Stage*, trans. David Magarshack, New York: Hill & Wang.

—— (1963) *An Actor's Handbook*, New York: Theatre Arts Books.

—— (1968) *Building a Character*, Elizabeth Reynolds Hapgood (ed.), London: Eyre Methuen (originally published 1949, New York: Theatre Arts Books).

—— (1993) 'From *The Actor: Work on Oneself*', trans. Jean Benedetti, *Drama Review* 37, 1: 38–42.

States, Bert O. (1985) *Great Reckonings in Little Rooms: On the Phenomenology of Theater*, Berkeley: University of California Press.

Stebbens, Genevieve (1977) *Delsarte System of Expression*, New York: Dance Horizons.

Storey, Robert F. (1978) *Pierrot: A Critical History of a Mask*, Princeton: Princeton University Press.

Strasberg, Lee (1941) 'Acting and the Training of the Actor', in John Gassner (ed.) *Producing the Play*, New York: Dryden Press, 128–62.

—— (1987) *A Dream of Passion: The Development of the Method*, Evangeline Morphos (ed.) Boston: Little, Brown.

Strehler, Giorgio (1977) *Für ein menschlicheres Theater*, trans. and ed. Sinah Kessler, Berlin (East): Henschel.

Suanda, Endo (1983) 'Topeng Cirebon: In its Social Context', Master's thesis, Department of Music, Wesleyan University, Greenwich, Connecticut.

Sukarya, Ukan (1977) Personal communication, 7 September.

Suzuki, Tadashi (1986) *The Way of Acting*, New York: Theatre Communications Group.

—— (1991) 'Culture is the Body', in Bonnie Marranca and Gautam Dasgupta (eds) *Interculturalism and Performance*, New York: Performing Arts Journal Publications, 241–8.

Symons, Arthur (1927) *Eleanora Duse*, New York: Duffield.

Taviani, Ferdinando (1992) 'In Memory of Ryszard Cieslak', *New Theatre Quarterly* 8, 31: 249–60.

Todd, Mabel (1968) *The Thinking Body*, Brooklyn: Dance Horizons.

Torzecka, Marzena (1992) 'Running to Touch the Horizon: Ryszard Cieslak interviewed by Marzena Torzecka', *New Theatre Quarterly* 8, 31: 261–3.

Turner, Graeme (1990) *British Cultural Studies: An Introduction*, Boston: Unwin Hyman.

Turner, Victor (1974) *Dramas, Fields and Metaphors: Symbolic Action in Human Society*, Ithaca: Cornell University Press.

—— (1982) *From Ritual to Theatre: The Human Seriousness of Play*, New York: Performing Arts Journal Publications.

—— (1983) 'Body, Brain, and Culture', *Zygon* 18, 3: 221–46.

—— (1986) *The Anthropology of Performance*, New York: Performing Arts Journal Publications.

Turner, Victor W. and Bruner, Edward M. (eds) (1986) *The Anthropology of Experience*, Urbana: University of Illinois Press.

Vanden Heuvel, Michael (1991) *Performing Drama/Dramatizing Performance*, Ann Arbor: University of Michigan Press.

van Erven, Eugene (1988) *Radical People's Theatre*, Bloomington: Indiana University Press.

Veltrusky, Jiri (1978) 'Contribution to the Semiotics of Acting', in Ladislav Matejka (ed.) *Sound, Sign and Meaning: quinquagenary of the Prague Linguistic Circle*, Ann Arbor: Dept. of Slavic Languages and Literatures, University of Michigan, 553–606.

Vine, Chris (1993) 'Theatre in Education and Theatre of the Oppressed', in Tony Jackson (ed.) *Learning Through Theatre*, London: Routledge, 109–27.

Vineberg, Steve (1991) *Method Actors: Three Generations of an American Acting Style*, New York: Schimer Books, Macmillan Press.

Wagner, Roy (1981) *The Invention of Culture*, Chicago: University of Chicago Press.

Watson, Ian (1993) *Towards a Third Theatre: Eugenio Barba and the Odin Teatret*, London: Routledge.

Weber, Carl (1967) 'Brecht as Director', *Drama Review* 11, 1: 102–3.

Weedon, Chris (ed.) (1987) *Feminist Practice and Poststructuralist Theory*, New York: Basil Blackwell.

Wekwerth, Manfred (1975) *Schriften: Arbeit mit Brecht*, Berlin (East): Henschel.

—— (1980) 'Brecht Theater in Gegenwart' (Stockholm Seminar 1978), in

Wolfgang Fritz Haug, Klaus Pierwo and Karen Ruoff (eds) *Aktualisierung Brechts*, Argument Sonderband 50, Berlin: Argument–Verlag.

Wethal, Torgeir (1985) Interview with Ian Watson, Nordisk Teaterlaboratorium, Holstebro, Denmark, 2 September.

Wichmann, Elizabeth (1991) *Listening to Theatre: The Aural Dimension of Beijing Opera*, Honolulu: University of Hawaii Press.

Wilde, Oscar (1979) *The Importance of Being Earnest* in *Penguin Plays*, New York: Penguin Books.

Wiles, Timothy J. (1980) *The Theater Event: Modern Theories of Performance*, Chicago: University of Chicago Press.

Willett, John (ed. and trans.) (1964) *Brecht on Theatre*, New York: Hill & Wang.

Williams, David (ed.) (1991) *Peter Brook and the Mahabharata: Critical Perspectives*, London: Routledge.

Williams, Rolf S. (1988) 'An Actor's Process: Michael Frayn's "Noises Off" and C. P. Taylor's "Good"', Unpublished MFA thesis, University of Wisconsin–Madison, Department of Theatre and Drama.

Wilshire, Bruce (1982) *Role Playing and Identity: The Limits of Theatre as Metaphor*, Bloomington: Indiana University Press.

Wilson, Garff B. (1966) *A History of American Acting*, Bloomington: Indiana University Press.

Worthen, William B. (1984) *The Idea of the Actor: Drama and the Ethics of Performance*, Princeton: Princeton University Press.

Xavier, Sister Mary (1976) 'Dancing and Singing in the Gilbert Islands', *Mana Review* 1, 2: 43–9.

Yuasa, Yasuo (1987) *The Body: Toward an Eastern Mind–Body Theory*, Albany: State University of New York Press.

Zarrilli, Phillip B. (1984a) *The Kathakaḷi Complex: Actor, Performance, Structure*, New Delhi: Abhinav.

—— (1984b) ' "Doing the Exercise": The In-body Transmission of Performance Knowledge in a Traditional Martial Art', *Asian Theatre Journal* 1, 2: 191–206.

—— (1986) 'Asian Martial Arts and Performance', in Bob Fleshman (ed.) *Theatrical Movement: A Bibliographical Anthology*, Metuchen, NJ: Scarecrow Press, 453–65.

—— (1987) 'Where the Hand [Is] . . .', *Asian Theatre Journal* 4, 2: 205–14.

—— (1988) 'For Whom Is the "Invisible" Not Visible?: Reflections on Representation in the Work of Eugenio Barba', *Drama Review* 32, 1: 95–106.

—— (1989a) 'Three Bodies of Practice in a Traditional South Indian Martial Art', *Social Sciences and Medicine* 28, 12: 1289–1310.

—— (1989b) 'Thinking and Talking About Acting: Re-Reading Sonia Moore's *Training an Actor*', *Journal of Dramatic Theory and Criticism* 3, 2: 1–15.

—— (1990) 'What does it mean to "become the character?" ', in Richard

Schechner and Willa Appel (eds) *By Means of Performance: Intercultural Studies of Theatre and Ritual*, Cambridge: Cambridge University Press, 131–48.

—— (1992) 'To Heal and/or to Harm: The Vital Spots (Marmmam/Varmam) in Two South Indian Martial Traditions. Part I: Focus on Kerala's Kalarippayattu'; 'Part II: Focus on the Tamil Art, Varma Ati', *Journal of Asian Martial Arts* 1, 1: 36–67; 1, 2: 1–15.

—— (ed.) (1993) *Asian Martial Arts in Actor Training*, Madison: Center for South Asia, University of Wisconsin–Madison.

—— (1994) Review of '*Actors and Onlookers, The Actor's Instrument, The End of the Acting, Acting*', *Drama Review*, 38, 1: 177–82.

Zeami, Motokiyo (1984) *On the Art of the Nō Drama: The Major Treatises of Zeami*, trans. and introduction by J. Thomas Rimer and Yamasaki Masakazu, Princeton: Princeton University Press.

Zeig, Sande (1985) 'The Actor as Activator: Deconstructing Gender Through Gesture', *Women and Performance* 2, 2: 12–17.

Zimmermann, Francis (1983) 'Remarks on the conception of the body in Ayurvedic medicine', in Beatrice Pfleiderer and G. D. Sontheimer (eds) *South Asian Digest of Regional Writing, Vol. 8 (1979): Sources of Illness and Healing in South Asian Regional Literatures*, Heidelberg, 10–26.

Zorn, John W. (1968) *The Essential Delsarte*, Metuchen, NJ: Scarecrow Press.

Zurbuchen, Mary (1987) *The Language of Balinese Shadow Theatre*, Princeton: Princeton University Press.

BIBLIOGRAPHICAL NOTE:

Actors speaking on acting

TDR has published a number of special issues devoted to acting which include either interviews with actors and/or essays based on interviews with actors which include extensive quotations from actors about their process.

1. *TDR* 20, 3, 1976 includes interviews with and/or essays on: Joanne Akalaitis, Joseph Chaikin, Joan MacIntosh, Meredith Monk, Sue Sheehy, Priscilla Smith, and Kate Manheim.

2. *TDR* 23, 1, 1979 includes interviews with and/or essays on Spalding Gray and Winston Tong, among others.

3. *TDR* 25, 3, 1981 includes interviews with and/or essays on Joseph Chaikin and Elizabeth LeCompte, among others.

4. *TDR* 29, 4, 1985 includes interviews with and/or essays on Marina Confalone, Roger Rees, Bert Andre, Moo-Sung Chun, among others.

5. See also the following individual interviews in *TDR* by Richard Schechner: 'Talking with Kate Manheim: Unpeeling a Few Layers', 1987: 31, 4: 136–42. 'Kazuo Ohno Doesn't Commute', 1986: 30, 2: 163–9.

INDEX

Note: Numbers in italics refer to illustrations.